Workers and Workplaces in Revolutionary China

Edited by
Stephen Andors

ROUTLEDGE REVIVALS
Routledge
Taylor & Francis Group

First published in 1974
by M.E. Sharpe Inc.

This edition first published in 2016 by Routledge
2 Park Square, Milton Park, Abingdon, Oxon, OX14 4RN
and by Routledge
711 Third Avenue, New York, NY 10017

Routledge is an imprint of the Taylor & Francis Group, an informa business

Publisher's Note

The publisher has gone to great lengths to ensure the quality of this reprint but points out that some imperfections in the original copies may be apparent.

Disclaimer

The publisher has made every effort to trace copyright holders and welcomes correspondence from those they have been unable to contact.

A Library of Congress record exists under LC control number: 76053710

ISBN 13: 978-1-138-19197-6 (hbk)
ISBN 13: 978-1-315-64017-4 (ebk)
ISBN 13: 978-1-138-19199-0 (pbk)

EDITED WITH AN
INTRODUCTION BY
STEPHEN ANDORS

Workers and Workplaces in Revolutionary China

M. E. SHARPE, INC.
White Plains, New York

901 North Broadway, White Plains, New York 10603

Library of Congress Catalog Card Number: 76-53710
International Standard Book Number: 0-87332-094-8

Printed in the United States of America

Contents

Preface

This volume is an attempt to let the revolutionary vision that has been so much a part of the politics of Chinese industrial development speak for itself through books and documents published and widely read in China. The nature of politics in the post-Mao Tsetung era is still impossible to discern, but it is certain that this vision will continue to play a crucial role in shaping the patterns of conflict even as it did before Mao's death. Whether it will in the future become an increasing part of the reality of life in China's industrial system as it has so clearly done in the past is a question that will only be answered by the results of the conflict that continues to be part of the politics of industrial development.

I would like to thank Douglas Merwin of M. E. Sharpe, Inc., for his help in conceiving of the idea for this book and for his encouragement while it was in preparation. Professor Sidney Greenblatt of Drew University was the first to bring the materials on the pre-1949 Shanghai Docks and Nanyang Brothers Tobacco Company to the attention of Western scholars through his efforts as editor of Chinese Sociology and Anthropology.

Stephen Andors

Columbia University
October 20, 1976

Introduction

Stephen Andors

In the winter of 1973-74, some of the workers on one of the loading docks in a district of Shanghai harbor put up a big-character poster, or "ta-tzu-pao." They urged their fellow workers to "be the masters of the wharf" and not "the slaves of tonnage." They went on to argue that the use of bonuses and money incentives related to the absolute levels of tonnage they handled ultimately led to inefficiency, mitigated against worker involvement in planning and technical innovation, and generated wasteful competition between work squads. The editors of Jen-min jih-pao (People's Daily) noted that the issues raised were of fundamental political significance in socialist society.

In the winter of 1948, a worker on the Shanghai docks named Little Number Four Son Hsia froze to death during a snowstorm because he could find no sheltered place to sleep. His fellow workers fortunate enough to find room huddled in the foul smelling, freezing public toilets along the sprawling treaty port's shoreline, while many others were forced to sleep in semi-sheltered areas out-of-doors.

These are only two of the many similar images which emerge so starkly from the materials presented in the pages that follow. They illustrate not only the enormous material improvements which have characterized China's industrial and economic transformation, but also the nature of the political vision which has informed the daily life of the Chinese working class. This book begins and ends with descriptions of the Shanghai docks, and presents key documents which illuminate both the unique characteristics and the universal interest of China's industrialization effort.

The early stages of industrialization and technical transformation of the economy and society were not auspicious, as the first section in this book clearly reveals. It is the complete translation of a book published in Shanghai in the spring of 1966 at a time when the rumblings of the forces that were soon to be unleashed during the Cultural Revolution were shaking the foundations of established power within many factories. The book was designed to be part of an effort to make the Chinese masses more aware of their own history and was used to stimulate discussion in many industrial enterprises.

Life and work on the preliberation Shanghai docks, according to the book, were shaped from the beginning by a powerful imperialism whose internal rivalries did little to diminish the strength with which it confronted the people at the basic levels of Chinese society. With vivid imagery, and no pretense at presenting a "balanced" evaluation of what was, to the Chinese workers on the docks, a rapacious and greedy system, the book traces the impact of imperialism on Chinese society.

China's urban and suburban economy and its class structure were profoundly influenced by the imperial presence. Local agricultural lands and peasant villages rapidly disappeared before the expanding construction of deep-water port facilities. A group of Chinese compradors grew up to serve as links between China and foreign traders. A complex hierarchy of Chinese labor contractors, gang bosses, and foremen grew rich and relatively powerful recruiting, managing, and greedily exploiting Chinese workers for the even richer and more powerful foreigners who owned almost all the dock facilities of any size or consequence. The Chinese entrepreneurial bourgeoisie was weak, and its ability to accumulate and invest capital in strategic sectors for growth and development of the overall economy was sharply constrained by the context within which it found itself. But cruelty, poverty, and exploitation did not disappear even if the nationality of owners and entrepreneurs changed.

The problems faced by the dock workers were rooted in the institutions and relationships which were the basis of daily life and labor organization. They were not the result of the evil designs of immoral individuals or the nefarious doings only of Western imperialists, though examples of both were certainly not unknown.

Working conditions were incredibly harsh, and were only made more so by foul and freezing weather in winter and scorching heat in summer. There was little or no mechanization, and backbreaking physical effort was required to lift the heavy loads out of the holds of ships. Human life was cheaper than machinery, and this calculus was reflected in daily work routines and living conditions. Adequate food, clothing and shelter were never assured. Workers lived and slept in public toilets and patched and repatched their old clothes until the quilted rags weighed many times more than a new garment. Discipline was enforced crudely and viciously. Beatings, torture, and murder were not uncommon. Gangsters, thugs, hitmen, secret societies, clan organizations, and the general scramble for work in a labor surplus economy served to split and frighten workers, making collective opposition difficult. The outstanding features of working class life on the docks of treaty-port Shanghai were backbreaking manual labor, extreme hardship, and cruel exploitation.

The main demands put forth by revolutionary organizations, therefore, were for basic economic and material security and for technical innovation and mechanization to transform working conditions. The immediate postliberation period addressed these problems, and it brought to an end many of the most inhuman and dangerous conditions under which the dockworkers lived. The overall economic structure and division of labor on the waterfront were rationalized, and the pace of technical innovation and mechanization was stepped up considerably. The most onerous and backbreaking aspects of loading and unloading work were reduced or eliminated altogether by relatively simple technical reforms.

The locus of political power at least at the top levels of harbor administration and dock organization also began to shift noticeably away from the foreigners, Chinese owners, and compradors and toward Communist Party and trade union officials. Nevertheless, gang bosses and labor contractors on the basic levels clung to power for years. More important in the long run, though, was the fact that compared with workers, the technicians, administrators, and former owners retained a good deal of authority in day-to-day production relations. The Communist Party was, at this time, far less concerned with political problems which revolved around the relationships between workers and managers than it was with matters which revolved around exercising broader political power and social control over the docks and Chinese society.

If conditions on the Shanghai docks were brutal and harsh, conditions in other areas of China's relatively small industrial sector were not much better, though urban industry seemed to offer a better chance of survival than the abysmal poverty and insecurity of the rural hinterlands. To illustrate the situation, portions of a much longer and more detailed study of China's pre-1949 cigarette and tobacco industry follow in the next section. Along with textiles and matches, the cigarette and tobacco industry was among the most active areas for Chinese, as opposed to foreign, capital. These excerpts are from the study of the Nanyang (South Seas) Brothers Tobacco Company first published in 1958 as part of a campaign called the "Four Histories movement." Actually, this movement had begun even before 1949 and had continued through the 1950s. (1)

Focusing on (1) villages, (2) families, (3) factories, and (4) mines, historical surveys like this study of a major Chinese capitalist enterprise served to help revolutionary organizers understand the specific problems that they were likely to face in an effort at political mobilization. They were also important in providing cadres with technical information and detail about production so vital in getting the economy back on its feet and establishing a firm base of support in urban centers for what had largely been a rural-based revolutionary movement. (2)

The picture of daily life that emerges from the Nanyang Tobacco Company study is one of severe economic exploitation and unhealthy working conditions. The absence of a direct foreign presence in the company, as compared with the direct and active intervention of imperialist power on the docks, made it easier for Chinese workers to organize and bargain with the Chinese capitalists, who did not enjoy the support of a powerful state apparatus. Even so, the limited bargaining and negotiating that did take place was marked by enormous difficulty and met serious repression.

Most of the workers in the tobacco-processing and cigarette-making factories of this large company were females, and they were active leaders in the labor movement which blossomed in the 1920s before the "White Terror" of 1927 weakened and almost destroyed the urban revolutionary forces that had been growing. Even at times of considerable strength, the pre-1949 urban labor movement remained divided. Small but significant differentials in wages exacerbated competition within the working class. Male workers consistently enjoyed relatively greater pay for the same or roughly similar work and clerical workers and supervisory personnel received higher wages than ordinary workers, skilled and unskilled. Poverty and grave insecurity only aggravated these divisions, making it relatively easy for management to buy off certain workers, often turning them into active informants and anti-union leaders. Reprisals took the form of docking workers' pay or summary firings, and once dismissed it was not easy for a worker to find another job because "troublemakers" were usually blacklisted.

The pace of work was hectic, and the piece wage payment system was a constant and hated threat forcing a high level of physical effort out of workers just to get enough money to survive from day to day. Female workers suffered more than male workers under this system since they were all unskilled laborers and hence all on piece wages, while skilled male workers could receive monthly wages. Female workers, therefore, could not afford even the time to take off from their work positions to eat lunch. Forced to eat while working, many consumed large quantities of tobacco particles that got stuck to their food, and as a result, became quite ill.

Both male and female workers finally succeeded in organizing and rebelling against these conditions, and the details of the "Great Strike in Shanghai in 1924" as it unfolded in the plants of the Nanyang Brothers Tobacco Company are told in another brief excerpt from this long book. There are fascinating accounts of management's unscrupulous and often violent efforts to repress the strike and to buy off its leaders, and many examples of almost funny, but ineffectual, distortions of the grievances and issues as they were presented in the newspapers of the time. Workers were first of all angry about arbitrary dismissals of those who had been active in the struggle for better working conditions. They wanted better wages, and were unhappy over rules of discipline and the attitudes and behavior of technicians or administrators, many of whom had been educated in the West or in Western schools in China.

As on the Shanghai Docks, most of the more outrageous signs of exploitation and misery were frontally attacked in the immediate aftermath of liberation in 1949. As economic reconstruction got underway, working and living conditions improved fairly rapidly, and social welfare and insurance programs provided most workers with far more health care and material security than they had ever had before. Only minor changes in the technical and organizational aspects of work were able to eliminate the more dangerous and unhealthy abuses of the old factories.

The period of reconstruction that began in 1949 also witnessed growing Soviet aid and advice to the badly shattered and still small industrial sector. From 1949 to 1953, the Soviet Union began a large scale program of industrial cooperation with China, pledging itself to the building of important heavy industrial enterprises and providing technical and administrative advice on how to run them. Yet the Soviet impact, as crucial as it was to be in rebuilding and expanding China's heavy industrial sector, was limited by cultural, historical, technical, and not least of all, political constraints. (3)

From 1953 to about 1956, the Chinese nevertheless attempted

to transplant the Soviet systems of industrial planning and factory management, though the effort was never carried out with inordinate enthusiasm. The centralized planning apparatus, working through control and supervisory departments within factories, and the technocratic-bureaucratic implications of the Soviet style "one-man management" seemed to reinforce the inequality and bureaucratization endemic in pre-1949 Chinese society and industry. Moreover, these factors combined with the emergence of crucial problems of economic development and administration, triggering a search for alternatives to the Soviet model. (4)

In many ways the Soviet system utilized the same kinds of incentives, the same division of labor, and the same criteria for defining and evaluating the performance of individuals and of industrial enterprises as those prevalent in the industrialized capitalist countries. Soviet planning was, of course, far more centralized and comprehensive than in even the largest Western or Japanese corporations, and there was no private ownership of factories, mines, or dockyards to form the basis for vast discrepancies in wealth. Yet, within factories in the West, Japan, and the USSR, workers and managerial staff (both administrative and technical) were clearly divided according to the mental-manual labor functions, and within society there was a similar though not identical system of income, educational, and general social inequality which was linked closely to the needs generated by the system of production.

Beginning with the anti-rightist campaign and rectification campaigns of 1957, and in more obvious fashion with the emergence of the Great Leap Forward in 1958, the Chinese made a decisive and revolutionary break with this pattern of industrialization and management. The two documents which begin the third section of this book come from the spring of 1958, at the beginning of what was later to prove to be a major national experiment in new forms of industrial organization. They are, therefore, of major significance in the history of post-1949 China. In a practical and measured way, they describe the specific characteristics and problems of the new approach to management, and illustrate the boldness of the Leap's break with Soviet and Western industrialization patterns.

Wang Hao-feng's speech summing up the experiences of five innovative industrial enterprises in Heilungkiang Province, and later the Jen-min jih-pao editorial comment on these experiences, indicate a good deal of excitement coupled with not a little uncertainty about future developments. In stressing the emergence of "two participations," direct worker participation in management and cadre participation in production, these experiments aimed to go far beyond a representative and indirect form of distributing power to workers in factories through workers' congresses. In fact they aimed at nothing less than ultimate elimination of the gap between mental and manual labor, between workers and managers. Rules and regulations which defined individual jobs and the structure of authority and responsibility were to be revised to reflect this commitment. The concept was bold indeed, and to emphasize its unprecedented nature, the watchword was caution and careful experimentation, at least in the spring of 1958.

The system of factory management described in these two documents quickly became known as the "two participations and one reform" system, and over the next two years it spread to enterprises all over the country. During the Leap, enthusiasm and euphoria generated in the course of transforming management often obliterated the cautious but deliberately revolutionary experimentation that was supposed to mark these efforts.

The years between the Great Leap Forward and the Cultural Revolution, therefore, were filled with disagreement and contradiction about how to evaluate the unprecedented experiments that had grown out of the Leap Forward. (5) Apparently many people, especially those involved with problems of macroeconomic coordination, wanted to return to the bureaucratic-technocratic Soviet-type planning system, while others wished to perfect methods that had just begun to evolve during the Leap. By 1966 it had, however, become clear to almost everyone involved in these very serious arguments that the Great Leap Forward experiments in participatory and democratic factory management were inseparably linked to the much wider problem of planning and coordination within the industrial sector of the economy, and through this were ultimately connected to China's whole strategy of economic development and technical transformation.

It is in this context that the Tach'ing model, discussed in detail in the essay by Hsü Chin-ch'iang, represents a systematic attempt to reconcile the political implications of the Great Leap experiments in factory management to a compatible but much more comprehensive vision of planning and industrialization. This long essay, which first appeared in the theoretical economic journal Ching-chi yen-chiu (Economic Research) in April 1966, contains fascinating detail on worker participation in management, on the role of incentive systems in facilitating this, and on how cadres reconcile their participation in production with coordinative functions necessary for overall decision-making.

The changes in micro-management are, moreover, directly linked to changes in society as a whole. The essay discusses how the relationship between work and residence influences people's personal values, daily routines, and family life; how planning is affected by the relationship between units of economic and political authority; and how new patterns of industrial and agricultural, urban and rural development affect the whole atmosphere of social life. Not only does this essay raise fascinating issues about the future shape of industrialization in China, but it puts Western and Soviet development in a new perspective as well. (6)

Tach'ing was, however, in many ways unique. A new industrial project, in a previously nonindustrial area of China, involved in a high priority, nationally assisted effort of petroleum development, Tach'ing was free of many of the constraints that were operative in other development projects which did not enjoy such national attention. Nor did it have the problems of already urbanized, industrialized areas. Tach'ing, therefore, was not the only "model" of revolutionary industrial management and development to grow out of the debates and divisiveness which followed in the wake of the controversial and pathbreaking Great Leap. During the Cultural Revolution another model, the Anshan Iron and Steel Works, also emerged.

Anshan first openly emerged as a revolutionary model of industrial management during a Cultural Revolution mass campaign launched to study and criticize the "Seventy Articles for Industry," a program developed in 1961-62 in answer to the economic crisis of the post-Leap period and in direct opposition to the thrust of Leap experiments. "The Constitution of the Anshan Iron and Steel Works" was counterposed to the Seventy Articles — it too had been propagated at about the time of the immediate post-Leap crisis, reportedly by Mao Tse-tung in 1961. The Anshan Constitution was a positive summation of the principles that had been embodied in Leap experiments in participatory management.

In the course of the campaign in which the Seventy Articles were pitted against the Anshan Constitution, the former was criticized especially for insisting that in technologically sophisticated, large-scale, modern industry, experts had to wield power over workers. The basis for this power, argued those who supported the Seventy Articles, lay in two things. One was the need to calculate "scientific" quotas and norms and to supervise workers to see that these were in fact met. Piece wages and bonuses would be the positive incentives for maximum effort. Moreover, these scientifically calculated quotas and norms would serve as the basis for statistical data to be fed into the planning hierarchy where they were to become the raw input into the further calculation of mandatory targets to be sent down to the enterprise for future output. These principles were precisely those which characterized the Soviet system. The fact that Anshan was chosen as a model alternative only underlined the seriousness with which the Chinese had experienced, analyzed, criticized, and consciously rejected this kind of management and the planning implications it carried.

Anshan was one of the oldest, largest, most modern, and technically sophisticated industrial complexes in China. Located in a highly industrialized and urbanized part of Liaoning Province,

Anshan had been occupied by the Japanese and used by them during World War II. It had been badly shattered by years of war, and in 1949 it became one of the most important and intensive sites of the Soviet aid effort in China. Soviet aid was often established on the basis of the "sister plant" system, whereby a plant in the USSR would establish close relationships with a similar "sister" enterprise in China and then supply not only technical and mechanical equipment, but administrative and managerial advice as well. It seems that Anshan's sister plant in the USSR was the giant Magnitogorsk Iron and Steel complex.

There can be little doubt that the attempt to build Anshan in Magnitogorsk's image had a direct impact on the technical and human relationships within Anshan, and also on the control mechanisms which fit Anshan into the larger economy. The essay by Hung Hang-hsiang, written on the tenth anniversary of the Anshan Constitution's promulgation, must, therefore, be read in this context. It portrays the principles of management developed first during the Great Leap Forward, the two participations, one reform (of rules and regulations), and triple combination (of workers, technicians, and administrators working together to deal with all aspects of management and production) as a "great pioneering act in the history of the international proletarian movement." Particularly noted is the theoretical and practical importance of this approach to industrial management in solving crucial problems of social transformation between nonsocialist and socialist society, and while this does not mean the automatic attainment of communist ideals, it does guarantee a powerful weapon in the struggle to reach them. By clear implication, the Chinese argue, this problem of how to deal with the realities of modern industrial organization in a manner consistent with socialist political principles is something the Soviets have not even come close to solving.

In addition to stressing the importance of the Anshan Constitution in contributing to a crucial theoretical and practical area of Marxism, Hung's essay is also very explicit on the central problem of the role of technical and engineering personnel and of scientific knowledge in influencing the social structure of socialist society. Rather than oppose political revolution for the sake of development of science and technology, both, the essay argues, must proceed simultaneously. Political revolution means that scientific and technical knowledge must become the property of the workers, that its distribution is a fundamental political question because only with it in possession can rational decisions be made in actual production. To confine the distribution of this knowledge to only a relatively few experts means ultimately to put power in their hands, especially in a socialist society where private property is no longer the basis of political and social power. There can be no doubt from this essay that this commitment is to represent a strategic as well as operational guide, and it is from this principle that methods of planning and management must evolve through a process of trial and error.

It is also clear that the realities of inequality and differences in family and educational background, as well as in individual capability and personality, have not escaped the Chinese. That is why the essay sees the implementation of this principle of socialist politics as a process. Yet, while the essay admits that production, which must be based on existing inequalities, and revolution, which must be aimed at potential equality and community, might conflict at certain times on certain problems, such conflict is to be solved by giving priority to the revolutionary commitment. Workers must be provided the opportunity to participate, learn, and improve their skills and knowledge. Thus, while production can temporarily depart from a theoretical maximum, it can never be ignored; nor can it be an excuse to ignore basic political principle.

The resolution of actual problems in accordance with these principles of the Anshan Constitution gives Chinese politics and planning at the grass roots its unique shape, fascination, flexibility, complexity, and energy. The Communist Party, because its members are supposedly most aware of the issues and alternatives, must be at the center of this planning and political conflict. Thus does Hung Hang-hsiang explain the meaning of the Anshan Constitution and the very general implications it has in shaping the power structure and goals of industrial enterprises.

An investigation report concerning the small parts section of the diesel engine workshop of the Peking General Internal Combustion Engine Works, the subject of the next document, provides a much more detailed description of what goes on within factories. This essay was written in 1971 when extensive reforms and organizational changes were being implemented in factories all over the country in response to criticism resulting from the Cultural Revolution. In this plant, post-Cultural Revolution changes saw workers on work squads gain more influence in making plans for the work sections, the administrative level above the squad. Planned targets communicated to the sections from higher levels of authority still formed the basis of all discussion in the squads, and revisions in the plans were clearly to be marginal. Nevertheless, the fact that everyone knew how the activities of the individual and small group fit into the larger picture had a positive impact on morale and efficiency. Changes in the original plans, while quantitatively not great, could be qualitatively significant in making daily work and coordination proceed more smoothly and efficiently. In arranging operational procedures and taking more authority to arrange inter-work squad cooperation, workers gained significantly more control over the daily work routine and did have some impact on the nature of input-output norms in the production process.

As workers took a greater part in discussing and revising plans, and in influencing quotas and norms, there was a major change in the incentive system. Most crucial was the fact that the formulation of quotas and norms, the basis of all plans at higher levels, once made the province of direct and indirect worker participation, were also separated from the distribution of bonuses and other monetary incentives. A change of this kind in the incentive system also meant a change in the intensity and quantity of higher-level supervision over workers. The discussion of this matter is particularly illuminating in this investigation report, and the vital ramifications it has on production quality, efficiency, cooperation, and morale are all brought out. Similar kinds of issues are discussed in relation to changes in rules governing the division of labor, especially those dealing with job definitions. Once their output was separated from bonuses and monetary incentives, workers were clearly anxious to broaden the scope of work within which their skills and knowledge could be utilized, and this had a positive impact on production. As workers learned to broaden their skills, they were able to facilitate participation in higher-level management and planning for other workers, and morale improved in the enterprise as work tasks were more evenly and equitably distributed. Technical innovation procedures also underwent significant change once the division of labor among squads and individuals became more flexible and once the incentive system changed.

Investigation reports like this one frequently appear in the Chinese press, and they are very useful in showing all the many interrelationships between technical and human factors in enterprise management. Unfortunately, not all of these reports are as detailed and enlightening as this one.

A more general comparative perspective on what the Chinese see as the major differences between socialist and both capitalist and revisionist management is the subject of the fourth section. This is a complete translation of another book, On the Management of Socialist Enterprises, which originally was published in China in 1974, at a time when conflict over many of the changes of the Cultural Revolution was intensifying in many sectors of Chinese society, including industrial enterprises. The book seems to be the result of close collaboration between a group of people based at Futan University in Shanghai, a group of cadres or workers from some Shanghai factories, and a group of people from vaguely identified "concerned departments," presumably within Shanghai's municipal government. It seems probable that the authors of these essays formed a more or less close knit unit with the university as the key link. All the authors from factories represent those using relatively sophisticated technology, and the authors from concerned departments seem to represent planning and accounting. These factories and departments would logically, as a result of reforms in technical and general education in the Cultural Revolution, have established some kind of link with local universities. Futan could easily have been the focus of this integration. All but one of the essays were originally published in Shanghai's Chieh-fang jih-pao (Liberation Daily), which implies that the municipal governmental or Party authorities approved of them. The essay by Kung Hsiao-wen, who is also editor of the book, first appeared in Hsüeh-hsi yü p'i-p'an (Study and Criticism), a journal edited at Futan and published in Shanghai. At least one essay is by a member of Futan's department of political economy. (7)

Many of the themes in the essays in this book are similar to the basic propositions developed in Hung Hang-hsiang's essay on the Anshan Constitution. But here, the issues are related more directly to broader theoretical problems of Marxist political economy. Kung Hsiao-wen, in the introductory essay, emphasizes what many Westerners seem to miss in Marx, but something absolutely central to his thinking: the idea that capitalism begins with a fundamentally different view of the worker than does socialism. While Kung doesn't discuss the concept of alienation, or even use the term, and while he does not go into all the philosophical implications of the labor theory of value, he does insist that workers in a capitalist or revisionist factory are (and must be) defined as "hired laborers" rather than as human beings, the masters of their own creations and history. Because the essence of the "hired laborer's" experience is giving up one's life in exchange for money, money and externally imposed restrictions are respectively the carrot and the stick of management systems in those plants. But in a socialist factory, it must be a matter of political principle to treat workers as "masters" and to reinforce this image by really giving workers power, responsibility, and control consistent with the technical realities of production and the educational level of the work force. Discipline must flow from dedication to the goals of creating greater collective well being and a classless society, as well as from rules and regulations formed after discussion and consultation with workers. Kung's essay indicates that there is little theoretical disagreement on these principles, but that there is not an inconsiderable amount of practical controversy about how to implement them. Especially important is the relationship between current production goals and current worker capabilities, as well as the difficulty of evaluating the difference between rules and regulations which reflect technical and production requirements and those which reflect the political desire to keep workers subordinate to an elite group of privileged specialists.

In one way or another, this is the central theme of the book On the Management of Socialist Enterprises. Pointing not only to the question of ownership of the means of production and to changes in technological development as influencing management, Chiang Yang-nan notes in the next essay that it is unequivocally the general class structure of society that gives management its character. The class relations of the society will be reflected in the production relations among people in industrial enterprises, but at the same time, these same production relations can have a direct impact on the wider class structure. Since the relationships between workers and managers is the central focus of these relationships, it follows that socialist enterprises must embody different power relations between these two groups than do capitalist enterprises.

In the next essay, I Miao-chang argues that relationships between workers and administrative-technical personnel can become similar to class conflict under certain conditions, especially if managers begin to use their positions to seek privileges, ignore participation in labor, and are arrogant and arbitrary. Both I Miao-chang and Chiang Yang-nan argue that there is a need for management to coordinate production, but both recognize that rules and regulations designed to do so are not only a technical matter but a political matter. Not only do they regulate the care and maintenance of machinery, outline production sequences which flow from the technology being used, and outline safety and quality procedures; they also distribute power and define tasks so that groups and individuals receive different benefits in terms of the work they have to do and the control they have over their time.

The next essay, by Yang Ying-hsün, argues a crucial point: while productivity is the sole criteria by which the rationality of rules and regulations is judged in a capitalist (or revisionist) enterprise, the criteria for rationality in a socialist enterprise must be whether or not a rule or regulation redistributes power to workers in such a way that the worker-manager relationship is an increasingly egalitarian one. Production is not to be ignored, but neither can it take precedence over this principle. In practice, this means that workers must be consulted in depth before any rule or regulation is put into effect, and that cadres must take part in labor even while they must be able to explain and justify the controls and supervision that they wish to exercise over the production process. Moreover, as workers gain more experience and knowledge, and as technological conditions permit, rules and regulations must be allowed to change accordingly and increasingly in the direction of worker-manager symbiosis. The essay by Hung Lai-chi discusses this process of change in more detail.

In reality, of course, rules and regulations which redistribute power to workers and simultaneously regulate production with maximum efficiency are not immediately nor unanimously agreed upon. What seems rational and necessary to an older, conservative worker may seem like political suppression to a younger and more militant one who has less experience in the realities of production; what seems proper to an unskilled, inexperienced worker may seem to be the epitome of unnecessary control and supervision to a skilled and intelligent one. One factory may, because of its location or the nature of the work force, require much stricter and more centralized authority than another turning out the same or similar products. There is no doubt that workers in the same factory may be very unequal in their capacity or willingness to operate autonomously, and can have sharp disagreements about the degree of external discipline and supervision that is required under given historical and technical conditions. All of these problems are discussed quite openly in Wu Yüeh-hua's essay, with a very interesting answer to consider.

Even when power is redistributed to workers, it is obvious that in reality some workers will have more power and responsibility than others under the new rules and regulations. Ts'ao Pao-mei recognizes this dilemma in the next essay, and argues that the "ta-tzu pao," or "big-character poster," is a vitally important mechanism of participation for workers who do not have direct responsibilities for management. His argument to institutionalize the big-character poster does not in itself seem a terribly revolutionary idea, however, unless it is combined with the far more basic notion of changing rules and regulations on a periodic basis.

The essay by Tan Hsi shifts the focus of the book to the question of the role of profit and price in socialist planning. Arguing that profit and need do not always coincide, that the market value of an item (which is reflected in the price determined by scarcity and previous development of the national economy) does not necessarily coincide with the use value it has in overall rational, proportionate, and humane economic development, Tan Hsi concludes that profit must be subordinated to both plans and to the needs of others in determining the choices of those who control the investment funds and production decisions of the enterprise. Economic accounting, i.e., the calculation of costs based on prices and productivity to give an overall profit picture of the enterprise, can and should be useful in finding inefficiencies and sources of waste and is therefore a signal to enterprise workers and managers as well as planners about where to improve their performance. But its role must not be extended to determining what to produce or where to produce it.

The last two essays in On the Management of Socialist Enterprises focus on the administrative structure of industrial enterprises and on the relationship between structure and participation. Kung Ching argues that it is necessary to be flexible and nondogmatic about the formal organizational structure of a factory, but he is clearly not ready to suggest alternatives to the basic division of factory administration into three levels of the factory, workshop, and basic-level work groups. The author is, however, more willing to challenge the role of various supervisory departments and functional sections which are less directly related to the technical requirements of production than the workshops and work groups. These supervisory departments and functional departments can be the subject of very careful organizational experimentation. The essay by Fu P'ei-tzu discusses the way in which revolutionary committees in factories, as new elements in the post-Cultural Revolution administrative structure, facilitate worker participation at the very top levels of management.

The theoretical generalizations about socialist management are not always implemented in the rush of events and the pressures for production that characterize China's attempt to escape from poverty and technical backwardness. The essays in Kung Hsiao-wen's book recognize this, but with few exceptions really point to methods, directions, and principles much more than to concrete tactics and pictures of practical application. Yet, these general methods and principles are part of reality, interacting with it and often shaping the way in which questions are posed, even which problems are perceived in daily work. There is perhaps no clearer evidence of this than the Shanghai dock workers' big-character poster "Be the Masters of the Wharf, Not the Slaves of Tonnage."

Even after all the very important changes in management and living conditions that had occurred since 1949, work on the Shanghai docks and in her shipyards was still very hard. The last two documents in this collection illustrate this. The big-character poster of the dockworkers was obviously triggered by the sheer intensity of physical effort required to load and unload the big freighters. It seems that the leadership cadres of the 5th loading and unloading district often talked about worker control over the pace and intensity of work and about "relying on the masses," but in practice they did not really think that this would allow them to get the maximum effort from the workers so that they could make reports of very high levels of tonnage loaded and unloaded to their superiors. Instead of taking the time to make workers aware of the importance of their tasks to the economic development of the nation and the city, and relying on this consciousness to stimulate effort, and instead of allowing workers to prepare their own work schedules and loading and unloading strategies, the dock leaders appealed to the obvious desire of workers to get finished with a terribly hard job. They also used pressures and money incentives and praised those individuals and groups who handled the most tonnage regardless of how this effected the work of subsequent shifts or who had decided on the methods to be used.

Given the commitment of the dock leadership only to maximizing production, they had to push workers to a limit in productivity that, in the short run, would not have been attained if workers had decided on these matters themselves based simply on their love for the kind of work involved. As the big-character poster reveals, however, this was only part of the situation. Workers' interests, it seems, lay not in unloading the absolute maximum of tonnage, getting the job over with, taking a shower, resting, and returning the next day to repeat the same backbreaking routine over and over again (the slaves of tonnage), but in deciding for themselves how to load or unload, promoting further technical innovation and mechanization, and rationalizing and equalizing tasks between different shifts and locations of work. While in the short run this may have meant slightly less productivity, in the medium and certainly the long run, it would have meant even greater commitment to the job, more mechanization, and hence greater productivity.

Though the work remains hard on the docks of Shanghai, the grievances reflected in this big-character poster are at an entirely different level than what freezing workers forced to sleep in public toilets might have demanded back in 1948-49. The last document in this collection illustrates that even in the short run workers' interests might not necessarily contradict maximum productivity. Especially where workers' skills are great, where there is a conscious commitment to goals which transcend immediate self-gratification, and where there is a feeling of solidarity and perceived justice, greater workers' control can mean greater output and more attention to efficiency. The participation of cadres in labor, especially where the labor is very hard, often provides precisely this kind of organizational climate (8) and is a major part of the incentive systems in Chinese Industry.

The unique and difficult path that China's industrialization has taken, highlighted by the books and documents in this collection, has special relevance for developing economies. The way in which the major problems and universal dilemmas of development in the contemporary world were confronted is worth serious attention and study. For example, technical and engineering talent has been harnessed to the development process without at the same time forming a relatively privileged group of urban-based bureaucrats whose consumption habits, life styles, salaries, and places of residence facilitate the activities of multinational corporations but simultaneously create obstacles to the accumulation process so necessary for investment and growth in productive capacity.

The organizational and political context of development in China has allowed for the tapping of the accumulated energy and wisdom of workers whose skills and experience were so vital to early capitalist development in Europe and the United States, but whose potential contributions to industrialization seem so easily ignored by technocratic-bureaucratic approaches to planning and organization. China's overall industrialization strategy has emphasized a planned and proportionate geographic and regional development that would have been impossible by relying on investment decisions governed simply by profit criteria based on the marketplace. It has emphasized and creatively built institutional support to balance the crucial relationship between industry and agriculture; and in general it has, by shaping the class structure of contemporary Chinese society, not only fostered a good deal of equality within the country but also limited the distorting social and economic impact that so often results from policies of those groups which seek integration with the structure of power and the values which dominate the world market.

All of these aspects of industrialization in China are related, for without the ability to assimilate and effectively utilize in development the scarce technical and engineering knowledge of the educated, and to supplement this group with the revolutionary role of the Chinese working class, China's ability to conduct business in the world market on terms compatible with her long-term balanced development and independence would have been seriously compromised if not destroyed. In a very real sense, the transformation of the Shanghai docks, illustrated by the materials that begin and end this book, represents the problems that the Chinese faced in common with many other countries, and they also illustrate some of the results obtained so far.

Yet, the Chinese approach to industrial management is of relevance not only to countries facing the prospects of economic modernization, industrialization, and technological transformation. In their handling of the division of power and responsibility within factories, in their insight into the relationship between planning in the economy and management within the enterprise, and in their vision of how a developed agro-industrial society should embody certain concepts of human community, the Chinese have broached problems that are increasingly the focus of debate and anxiety in the already industrialized nations. (9) Though these problems are perhaps differently perceived in China than they are in richer and economically more developed nations, Chinese thinking on these matters and Chinese experiences that touch on them, even by accident, should not on political, ideological, or ethnocentric grounds be ignored.

Notes

1) See Shih Ch'eng-chih, "A Tentative Discussion of the 'Four Histories' and the 'Cultural Revolution'," translated in Chinese Sociology and Anthropology, V:3 (Spring 1973). The original Chinese version of this article appeared in Ming-pao yüeh-k'an (Ming Pao Monthly — Hong Kong), No. 75 (March and April 1972).

2) Ibid.

3) For details, see Stephen Andors, Socialist Civilization and Revolutionary Industrialization: China 1949 to the Present

(New York: Pantheon, 1977), Chapter 3. Also, Bill Brugger, Democracy and Organization in the Chinese Industrial Enterprise (New York: Cambridge University Press, 1976).

4) Andors, Socialist Civilization, Chapter 3.

5) Stephen Andors, "Factory Management and Political Ambiguity: 1961-1963," The China Quarterly, No. 59 (July-September 1974). Also Andors, Socialist Civilization, chapters 5 and 6.

6) Ibid., chapters 7 and 8.

7) It is interesting to speculate on the relative role of universities, factories, and government departments in providing opportunities for publication in important newspapers, magazines, or books. Given the importance of the media in providing recognition to models, a recognition that is central to the system of incentives in society, but also in conveying political messages, it would seem that access to the media is both a prime goal and a prime arena for conflict. Of course, groups formed as a result of links generated by education and economic interchange need not mean anything more substantive in terms of disagreements than a paradoxical but quite real competition for public recognition of the group's contribution to an egalitarian, cooperative socialism. This would make group conflict in China quite important, but yet quite different from superficially the same competition in other societies.

8) The concept of organizational climate is discussed in George A. Litwin and Robert A. Stringer, Motivation and Organizational Climate (Cambridge, Mass.: Harvard University Graduate School of Business, Division of Research, 1968).

9) See Andors, Socialist Civilization, for a fuller treatment of Chinese thinking and experience in regard to these themes.

I Changes at the Shanghai Harbor Docks

by Ch'en Kang

Ch'en Kang, Shang-hai ma-t'ou ti pien-chien [Changes at the Shanghai Harbor Docks]. Shanghai: Jen-min ch'u-pan-she, 1966. This complete translation is taken, with minor editorial revisions, from Chinese Sociology and Anthropology, V:3 (Spring 1973) and VII:2 (Winter 1974-75). Translated by Jay Mathews.

Contents

Preface

Before liberation, Shanghai was an important base for imperialist military, political, economic, and cultural aggression against China. The docks of old Shanghai harbor were a bridgehead for imperialist aggression directed against Shanghai and then spreading out across all of China. They were a foothold for imperialism to oppress and exploit the blood and sweat of the people of Shanghai and the whole nation.

After the Opium War, the imperialists used cannon to open up the port of Shanghai and built here many new-style docks. They used these docks to carry out economic aggression to dump great quantities of poisonous goods and surplus materials into China; at the same time, they took much of China's precious natural resources and wealth in gold and silver home to their own countries, thus deepening China's own poverty and backwardness. The imperialists also used the Shanghai docks to carry out military aggression. The Shanghai docks often served as a springboard for invasion in the armed aggression the imperialists launched against China or in their armed interference in Chinese internal affairs. The imperialists also used the Shanghai harbor docks in service of all their other aggressive activities.

The imperialists' appropriation of the old Shanghai harbor docks went on for nearly one hundred years. They did all sorts of bad things here; in collaboration and collusion with the reactionary Chinese authorities, they used their running dogs, the compradors and feudal bosses, to place the dock workers under terribly brutal reactionary control. These man-eating wolves brought back to the docks the savagery of the Middle Ages. Basically, they did not treat the dock workers as human beings. In their eyes, the dock workers were merely two-legged beasts of burden.

During the long years and months before the liberation, the dock workers were oppressed to the lowest rungs of the old society. They suffered especially severe oppression and exploitation at the hands of imperialism, feudalism, and bureaucratic capitalism. Whether it was a freezing cold December or a scorching sun was in the sky, no matter if their shoulders were loaded until their skin was bleeding, no matter if their legs ran until the pain was unendurable, no matter if their loads were so heavy they appeared to be broken at the waist, they still had to carry heavy loads on muddy or gravel roads, struggle with the dangerous "over-the-mountain leap" and "corkscrew leap," and expend their own blood and sweat so that Chinese and foreign capitalists could produce higher profits.

The Shanghai dock workers labored like animals from year to year and month to month so that Chinese and foreign capitalists could build up tremendous wealth, but they themselves were not well fed or well clothed. For them, "bamboo pressed their shoulders, sticks struck their chests, and small change filled their pockets." They were unable to rent rooms and could only sleep in the street out in the open, "with the blue sky as a roof and their backbones as mattresses," or crowd into dark, smelly tent cities. They ate breakfast but no dinner; they usually ate bean refuse and vegetable skins to satisfy their hunger. What they wore were "old caps shredded like blossoming flowers on their heads, clothes patched together like the Eight Trigrams on their bodies, ruined shoes held together with golden threads of rope on their feet." They covered themselves with torn waste cotton and torn sacks full of holes. It was hard to raise a family, much less provide for oneself, and it was often the case that "the robust man cannot provide for a family of three; his wife gathers vegetable skins and his child picks up odds and ends." To sum up, their lives were inhuman.

Under the cruel heel of the imperialist and Chinese capitalists, a strong and robust young dock worker invariably had lost his ability to work by middle age and was kicked out the door by the imperialists and Chinese capitalists.

The Shanghai dock workers were the first generation of China's working class. Under the leadership of the Chinese Communist Party, they had a glorious history of revolutionary struggle. They launched countless heroic struggles against the cruel oppression of the Chinese and foreign capitalists. With the instructions and inspiration of the Party, in the practice of struggle, they gradually realized that if working people were to achieve liberation, they had to do it by way of armed struggle. Because of this, in the War of Resistance against Japan and the War of Liberation, many dock workers hurried from their villages to join the ranks of their own class in the New Fourth Army and the later People's Liberation Army.

After the liberation of Shanghai, the working class seized power, the dock workers acted as leaders in the state apparatus and in business enterprises, and the docks returned to the arms of the people. Under the leadership of the Party, they banished the imperialists, suppressed the counterrevolutionaries and local despots, and, with a growing spirit of initiative, carried out dock construction. After as little as ten years or so of effort, they have brought about an incredible transformation in the Shanghai docks; the dock ownership system has changed, longshoremen's work is basically mechanized, the spirit and appearance of the dock workers has changed greatly, and their creativity and activism in production has thoroughly developed. Production has increased steadily, good men are doing good deeds, progressive collectivization has occurred, and "five-good" workers and staff are appearing in large numbers. The safety and health of dock workers has been ensured, and their material and cultural lives have shown remarkable improvement.

The Shanghai docks under the imperialist control of the past were completely at the service of imperialists, and domestic reactionaries and exploiting classes, and were hell for the dock workers. After the liberation, under the farsighted leadership of the great Chinese Communist Party, the docks have completely changed their appearance. The changes in the Shanghai docks vividly and forcefully prove the superiority of the socialist system. Our objective in putting together this pamphlet is to let the reader consider the appearance of the Shanghai docks under two kinds of social system, and show the reader the different positions and experiences of dock workers in the new and old societies.

We hope this pamphlet can help old workers remember the bitterness of the old days and think of the sweetness of today, and help workers of the latter generation understand the kinds of pain and oppression suffered by the old workers in their day. We must not forget the past; we must not forget the terrible straits in which our hundreds of thousands of dock worker brothers in the world still remain; we must not forget the two-thirds of the world's population that remains unliberated. Instead, we will devote ourselves even more to the Chinese Communist Party, to Chairman Mao, and to the socialist system. With our bodies on the docks, our thoughts on the nation, and our eyes on the world, we raise high the red flag of Mao Tsetung Thought over the people's docks, carry forward the revolution to the end, make even greater achievements in production, and make even greater contributions to building a socialist motherland and aiding the world revolution.

In the process of writing this pamphlet, we regretted that there was no data that can more completely sum up the heroic struggle of the old Shanghai dock workers, for it is not possible to present completely the heroic history of the Shanghai dock workers in the last one hundred years. As for the other defects and mistakes in this pamphlet that have also been difficult to avoid, we hope the readers will point them out and correct them.

May 1966

1

The Docks of Old Shanghai Harbor Were a Springboard for Imperialist Aggression

I. A Product of the Invasion of Guns and Steamships

The evolution of the old Shanghai harbor docks was closely related to imperialist aggression. Long before the Opium War in 1840, Shanghai was already an important area for domestic commerce. Many native boats that plied the rivers and seacoasts were constantly anchored in the harbor. On both banks of the Whangpoo River at that time there were already several old-style docks and warehouses that the native boats used. When the Opium War broke out, the English aggressor army invaded the Yangtze River valley, occupied Shanghai, and committed many terrible crimes. They went up the river as far as Nanking and forced the Ch'ing government to sign the unequal "Treaty of Nanking." Because of this, Shanghai was coerced into opening as a trading post for foreign commerce in 1843. The foreign capitalist aggressors began to establish in Shanghai a base for aggression.

The first foreign ships to arrive in Shanghai were mostly private opium-carrying Western-style sailing vessels — opium clipper ships. These ships were carrying harmful opium, which was unloaded onto opium barges outside Woosung and pulled by transfer boats into the harbor. Therefore the foreign aggressors built at that time at Wai-t'an a few small-scale

"Chiu Shang-hai kang ti ma-t'ou shih ti-kuo-chu-i ch'in-lüeh ti t'iao-pan."

transshipment docks to be used for opium smuggling. Around 1860, when foreign ships invaded our navigable rivers and seacoasts, shipping in Shanghai harbor speedily developed. At this time the foreign aggressors further forcibly occupied native soil along both shores of the Whangpoo and built a great many ship docks and warehouses to serve their aggressive activities.

The first major concentration of steamship docks and warehouses that the foreign aggressors built was north of the Woosung River (commonly called the Soochow River) on the Kangk'ou shore and Whangpoo River zones; later it gradually expanded to the Pootung, Yangshupoo, and other areas. They went up the banks of the Whangpoo River for about ten miles, so that the docks and warehouses of every imperialist nation were spread far and wide. By the eve of the War of Resistance against Japan, 71 percent of the total length of the Shanghai docks and 79.2 percent of the entire warehouse area were owned by imperialist nations. Moreover, the docks and warehouses held by the imperialists were all along the deep water shoreline, so advantageous to shipping, where giant ocean liners could anchor, conditions which were extremely beneficial for conveying cargo. Because of this, the docks and warehouses along the harbor were almost completely monopolized by the imperialist countries.

Among these imperialist countries, England, the United States, and Japan occupied the principal positions. The dock and warehouse enterprises at that time were closely connected to the steamship companies. England, the United States, Japan, and other imperialist countries usurped the Chinese shipping industry for themselves. They each established shipping companies in China that used Shanghai harbor as a principal base. Because of this, Shanghai harbor became the center of the imperialist shipping industry in our country. These foreign businesses and shipping companies all had their own docks. For example, the T'aiku, Lanyen, and other docks of the English T'aiku Company; the Kung Ho Hsiang, Shuent'ai, and other docks of the Yiho Company; the Dollar docks of the

American President Steamship Lines; and the Huishan, SanLing, and other docks of Japan's Japan Sea Postal Service; the Osaka docks of the Osaka Commercial Society — these and the companies of Germany, France, and other nations all had their own docks. These docks were all arranged on the important plots of ground along both banks of the Whangpoo River. At that time, there was a popular ballad: "From east to west of the Whangpoo, Great Britain, the Flower Flag (indicates the American imperialists), France, and the little Japanese devils go all the way to Yangshupoo without the slightest retreat." These lyrics amply illustrate the situation under which every imperialist power of the day had parceled out the Shanghai docks.

Among the few docks owned by Chinese capitalists, aside from the bureaucratic capitalist China Merchant Steamship Company's eastern warehouse opposite Shanghai and the Chin Li Yuan and a few other docks, those operated by private capitalists included only the China Dock Company and the Tatong, Tata, Chushao, Hungsheng, and a few other docks. These docks were very small in scale, their locations were very inconvenient, they could not handle large ships, and basically they did not play a very important role. After the victory in the War of Resistance against Japan, the Kuomintang reactionaries nonetheless "appropriated" several docks held by the Japanese aggressors, and the importance of bureaucratic capitalist possessions increased. Yet the English and American imperialists still held their monopolistic positions, from which they continued to control the dock and warehouse enterprises in Shanghai harbor.

Before the liberation, through nearly one hundred years of capitalist monopolization of the Shanghai harbor docks, these docks were used to carry out a multitude of evil activities. Great amounts of foreign produce passed along the docks to the shore, to be dumped on the entire country; at the same time, great quantities of wealth also passed along the docks, were loaded onto foreign ships, and were taken back to the imperialist lair, deepening the poverty and hardship of the Chinese people. The imperialist nations also used the Shanghai harbor docks as a tool for their armed aggression and interference in domestic affairs. When the imperialists incited wars of aggression, the armies of aggression brought by warships usually landed in China via the Shanghai docks to slaughter the Chinese people. Besides this, the imperialists often brought in large amounts of ammunition through the Shanghai docks to supply reactionaries, who used it to suppress popular resistance. They even transported reactionary troops and helped the reactionaries fight the civil war. There was not one bit of this kind of aggressor activity that was not carried out through the docks. Thus, before the liberation, the Shanghai docks were a springboard for imperialist aggression.

II. An Open Road to Dumping and Plunder

After Shanghai was opened up, the first thing the foreign capitalist aggressors dumped in Shanghai was opium, which poisoned the people. This opium was first brought by a special kind of opium smuggling clipper ship, but later, steamships were also used to transport it in great amounts. According to rough statistics, in the 30 years after Shanghai opened in 1843, the total amount of opium brought into Shanghai by the foreign capitalist aggressors was more than one million cases, which was at that time about 55 percent of the 1.8 million total cases of opium brought into the whole city. Opium brought into Shanghai harbor, outside of that sold there, was mostly distributed throughout the country by means of various waterways. It poisoned the broad masses of the people. The foreign opium peddlers, with this filthy and disgusting "commerce," used harmful poison to acquire great wealth. Take the one million cases of opium brought into Shanghai harbor in these 30 years alone: its estimated worth must have approached the surprising figure of 500 million taels (1/16 catty) of silver. This wealth of course was the silk and tea and other produce and the great amount of silver that had to be bought with the blood and sweat of the laboring people, the devoted production of the broad masses of laboring people. In this way, through Shanghai harbor, the wealth was transferred from the docks to the steamships of the foreign aggressors, fastened down, and taken away.

From the middle of the nineteenth century to the early part of the twentieth century, opium was Shanghai harbor's principal foreign import. Besides this, there was also a rapid increase in the dumping of all kinds of industrial products. These imported foreign industrial products consisted almost entirely of various kinds of consumer and luxury goods, with the greatest portion, in value, taken up by luxury goods specially supplied for the enjoyment of the exploiting class. The dumping of these foreign goods forced the collapse of China's traditional handicraft industry and caused a large group of laborers to lose their livelihood and suffer additional poverty. For example, the importation of foreign textiles [yang-pu] and foreign yarn [yang-sha] destroyed the handcrafted textile industry that had existed in the Shanghai suburbs. This created a great deal of unemployment among the people. The more foreign goods that piled up at the Shanghai harbor docks, the more poverty stricken the lives of urban laborers and the deeper their bitterness.

Before the liberation, Shanghai was the imperialists' largest base for economic aggression in China. Foreign commerce in Shanghai harbor comprised more than one-half of all foreign commerce in China. Because of the dumping of imperialist goods, this commerce of aggression each year produced a huge excess of imports into China, so that in 1933 the amount of the unfavorable excess of imports in Shanghai reached more than 420 million yuan in silver. This great wealth was brought on the docks and loaded on foreign steamships and shipped to the lair of the imperialists.

There is simply no way to estimate the amount of wealth the imperialists plundered and took back through Shanghai to their countries. They not only exported many goods, such as raw silk, tea leaves, cotton, wood oil, hog bristles, ore, and various other products, but also plundered a great deal of gold and silver and turned the Shanghai docks into the country's most important port for the export of gold and silver. For instance, in 1932 our nation's total exports were more than 59 million customs house gold units (equal to more than 23 million American dollars), all of which was shipped from Shanghai to America. In 1933 the total exports were more than 35 million customs house gold units (equivalent to more than 14 million American dollars), which also was all shipped from Shanghai to the two imperialist nations of America and England. In 1934, through the influence of the American imperialist "silver policy," great amounts of Chinese silver were exported — the total value of silver shipped out that year was more than 267 million yuan, of which more than 230 million yuan was exported from Shanghai. Because of this, Shanghai at that time became entirely a tool for the imperialists to absorb the blood and sweat of our nation's laboring people, and the docks provided a convenient means of transport for the imperialists' plundering activities.

After the victory in the War of Resistance against Japan, American imperialism became much stronger and used Shanghai harbor to carry out its ruthless dumping and plundering. Docks and warehouses, both large and small, along the Whangpoo River were filled with American imperialist "surplus goods," "relief goods," and all kinds of smuggled products. In 1946, declared American imports reached more than 300 million American dollars, but in addition, there were still "duty-free" and smuggled goods valued at many times that amount. From luxury cars, silk stockings, rouge and lipstick, and rough paper to powdered milk, flour and incense spoiled by damp and mildew, copper and iron scrap, and other kinds of trash and rubbish — like a tidal wave they flowed over the docks, bubbled up onto the land, flooded the markets, and overflowed to the point where they destroyed the already weakened original people's industries. As a result more than one-third of the industrial workers in this city lost their jobs. This is the disaster not too long past that the people of Shanghai still remember today.

Before the liberation, during the last hundred and more years in which Shanghai harbor occupied its humiliating semi-colonial position, the docks were used by the imperialists as a clear field to dump products and plunder China's wealth. The blood and sweat of the laboring people, like the waters of the Whangpoo River, flowed away under the docks.

III. A Shortcut to Military Invasion and Armed Intervention

The docks in the past not only provided the imperialists an advantage for economic aggression but also were used by them as a shortcut to military invasion and armed intervention. After Shanghai was opened, the Whangpoo River was usually filled with foreign warships, and every imperialist nation had special naval docks in Shanghai harbor. Whenever the Chinese people began a struggle to resist imperialism, large groups of foreign aggressor troops would disembark from the docks and suppress the uprising with arms. In early 1874 the Shanghai people opposed the expansion of the "foreign concessions" and the razing of private homes, and they carried out a large-scale struggle; at that point, French and American marines disembarked at Wai-t'an and shot and killed people. As another example, the Shanghai small cart (wheelbarrow) workmen went on strike to oppose an increased tax by the "concessions" administration. Bold and active, they carried out a heroic struggle with the mounted policemen of the foreign "concessions" and utterly defeated them. At that point, the foreign warships anchored in the middle of the Whangpoo River fired their guns to intimidate those on shore, and foreign marines marched ashore and carried out a coordinated campaign of suppression. After that, every time a mass anti-imperialist movement began, the aggressors always used this method of suppression. Foreign marines were always disembarking from the foreign-held docks to slaughter the Chinese people. At the beginning of 1927, as the great revolutionary tide was approaching Shanghai, the imperialists went into a panic and the imperialist nations, led by England and America, frantically shifted a large group of ships and troops. More than 20,000 foreign aggressor troops gathered in Shanghai at that time, and the number of foreign warships in the Whangpoo River exceeded 125.

Twice when the Japanese imperialists fomented war in Shanghai, the "January 28" and "August 13" incidents, they relied on docks on the banks of the "concessions" for transport of a large body of troops with weapons and ammunition, so that they could land and make war. In the "January 28" incident of 1932, the Japanese imperialists brought in an aggressor army of 100,000 and a large body of airplanes and artillery as a massive threat to the Chinese army and people resisting Japan. In the "August 13" incident of 1937, the scale of this kind of military movement was increased.

After the Japanese aggressors surrendered in September 1945, the American imperialist Seventh Fleet immediately entered the Whangpoo River. Shanghai harbor filled with large and small American warships. Several large-style docks were forcefully expropriated by the American aggressor army. They anchored their warships and unloaded weapons and all sorts of military goods, and piled high the warehouses along the river with weapons and ammunition designed to slaughter the Chinese people. American flags flew all over Wai-t'an and the area was filled with American soldiers; it had become completely an American "occupied territory."

Besides direct military action, the imperialists still also habitually interfered in Chinese internal affairs, supported reactionary authorities, and used the docks at the harbor entrance to bring in ammunition and transfer troops for the reactionaries. Early in 1860, at the time of the Taiping revolutionary struggle, the foreign aggressors supplied large amounts of ammunition without a letup to the reactionary Ch'ing army through Shanghai harbor and helped the Ch'ing government suppress the Taiping revolution. According to incomplete statistics, from 1859 to the beginning of 1864, the amount of ammunition supplied by foreign enterprises in Shanghai to the Ch'ing army through customs was 3,800 pieces of Western artillery of all kinds, 42,600 rifles, 15,500 artillery shells, 163 million rifle rounds, 1 million pounds of gunpowder, 23,600 piculs [1 picul = 133.33 pounds] of saltpeter. Besides this, there were also many direct transactions that did not go through customs but were quite substantial. This ammunition was all unloaded on the Whangpoo docks and transported to every corner of the country so that the reactionary Ch'ing army could slaughter the people.

In the winter of 1861, as the Taiping army's attack force neared Shanghai, the Ch'ing army stationed in Shanghai was exhausted and panic-stricken. All the English ships in league with the English imperialists were shifted to the Yangtze and brought the 8,000 troops of the reactionary boss Tseng Kuo-fan and his henchman Li Hung-chang from Anching to Shanghai and landed them as guards to strengthen the reactionary force.

Afterward, Shanghai became for a long period the headquarters of the conspiracy of reactionaries and imperialists, and Shanghai harbor became the greatest transfer point for the imperialists' supplying of ammunition to the reactionaries. The unestimated amount of ammunition that was routed through Shanghai harbor docks caused grievous adversity for the Chinese people. From the Ch'ing government to the northern warlords to the Kuomintang reactionaries — they all acquired a great deal of foreign ammunition through the port of Shanghai, which served as the capital for their pursuance of civil war. Especially after the Japanese surrender, the American imperialists and the Kuomintang reactionaries, in order to seize the fruits of victory, collaborated together; using Shanghai harbor as a central base, they employed the American warships and boats exclusively to convey large amounts of troops and weapons quickly to the civil war battle fronts so the Chiang bandits could attack the liberated areas. Moreover, the American imperialists ceaselessly brought great amounts of ammunition from overseas to supply the Chiang bandits who were slaughtering the Chinese people. It is difficult to calculate the volume of reactionary troops and ammunition transported via the Shanghai docks in the four years of the War of Liberation. By the end of 1948, the Kuomintang reactionaries were already faced with a disintegrating situation. The American imperialists were trying in vain to help the Chiang bandits carry out their last-ditch struggle through a new "Aid to China Bill," which provided for the use of Shanghai harbor as the main entry point for American ammunition to help Chiang, and even directed that the American navy dispatch five warships of more than 5,000 tons each to rush in weapons and cartridges. According to materials disclosed by the American imperialists themselves, in just one part of November of that year, the value of the weapons and cartridges given to the Chiang bandits with no strings attached by the American military command in Shanghai reached 66.4 million American dollars. This is proof of the American and Chiang reactionaries' use of the Shanghai docks to acquire ammunition to slaughter Chinese people.

Before the liberation, the Shanghai docks under the control of the imperialists and reactionaries were mainly used to carry out these kinds of criminal activities, which severely jeopardized the interests of the Chinese people. At that time, the docks seemed to be chains which bound the Whangpoo River, which restrained the pulse of the economy and gripped the throat of the Chinese people.

2

The Docks of Old Shanghai Harbor Were an Instrument of Class Exploitation

I. The Bloodsucking Foreign Bosses

The imperialists seized the Shanghai docks not only to accommodate all the aggressive economic and military activities they carried out, but at the same time to use the docks for direct exploitation. For many years they reaped huge profits from the dock and warehouse industry.

The dock and warehouse industry before the liberation was a "black door" leading to great treasure. The income of the principal businesses on the docks at that time consisted of the loading and unloading labor charges, warehouse rents, mooring charges, and various other warehousing charges.

The loading and unloading labor charges constituted the most basic and important income of all, making up more than 70 to 80 percent of the income of all the businesses combined. On the one hand, the imperialists (foreign bosses), Chinese capitalists, compradors, labor contractors, and other members of the exploiting classes carried out exploitation that sucked the lifeblood of the Chinese people and took by far the greatest percentage of the labor charges. On the other hand, in conjunction with the loading and unloading of merchandise, they created many different kinds of charges, took all they could in fees, and made use of every opportunity to take more. They

---

"Chiu Shang-hai kang ti ma-t'ou shih chieh-chi po-hsüeh ti kung-chü."

took these extra expenses and, through the vendors, charged them to the consumer, thus directly and indirectly exploiting the broad masses of working people and seizing heaps of blood-stained riches.

In the semicolonial period of Shanghai harbor, the greatest oppressors in Shanghai were the foreign bosses who sucked the blood of the Chinese people.

When the imperialists first built the docks, they ruthlessly plundered what belonged to the Chinese people. To meet the needs of constructing the docks, they seized public land on both banks of the Whangpoo River and occupied the water routes. They ignored our nation's sovereignty and created a tragedy whereby peasants lost their homes and were left destitute. It is difficult to dig out examples of this practice from earlier periods, but this sort of thing continued to happen even after the turn of the century. In 1917 the American imperialist Robert Dollar, when he built the Dollar docks at Pai-lien-ching on the eastern bank, ordered that Kao Ta-nien, Ku Sheng-fa, and other local ruffians and loafers forcibly purchase river-front land. Using every kind of pretext, they reduced the land's value and destroyed many farming peasants who had no way to protect themselves or their families. At the same time, they outrageously and unreasonably closed off public roads and closed down the Chiang family ferry, one of the eight large ferries on the Whangpoo, in order to extend the limits of the Dollar docks. They even went so far as to fill in one of the five sides of Pai-lien-ching harbor to provide a base for the Dollar docks. Pai-lien-ching harbor was an important traffic route for the three hsien of Shanghai, Ch'uan-sha, and Nan-hui. It was usually used by many boats, but after the imperialists forcibly filled it in, the water currents became much more treacherous. It created a bottleneck blocking traffic, seriously affecting the safety of navigation for small Chinese boats, increasing the dangers and difficulties to Chinese sailors, and producing unending incidents of boat crashes and sinkings. In 1932, when the English imperialist Kung Ho Hsiang Dock Company expanded the Chi-chang warehouse and docks on the eastern bank, they also used local bullies to take the people's property by force. When one peasant named Liu resolutely refused to sell, Grant [Ke-lan-t'e], the head of the Kung Ho Hsiang Dock Company, resorted to a malicious scheme. He built the docks so that the Liu land was completely surrounded by the walls of the dock enclosure. Then he instructed the dock guards to harass the Liu family in a hundred different ways and make it difficult for them to leave their property. He also dumped piles of coal cinders on the fringe of the Liu land, so that after it rained a few times, Liu's once fine fields became one large pond. In this way he drove the peasant named Liu to suicide and then went ahead and occupied the land.

The dishonest profits the foreign bosses made in the operation of the dock industry were readily noticeable. After all, the fact that they sucked the blood and sweat of the Chinese people in untold quantities was not something one could call a secret. It was something outsiders could not help but notice. But from the bits and pieces of evidence gathered, we can also see the inner workings of the system by which they carried out this ruthless exploitation. The warehouse rents and mooring fees that the dock companies collected from their customers all went to the companies themselves. Beyond this, they took by far the greatest portion of the labor charge for unloading and loading goods — usually more than 70 or 80 percent of that charge. For instance, in 35 years of operation of the English Kung Ho Hsiang docks, from 1906 to 1940, the foreign bosses swallowed up on the average 76.62 percent of the loading and unloading labor charges each year. What is more, their percentage regularly increased from year to year, so that if the 35-year period in Shanghai just mentioned were divided up, the percentage increased from 66.03 percent in 1906 to 72.77 percent in 1937, then to 83.47 percent in 1940 and to 85.62 percent in 1941. This was really an incredible rate of exploitation! But this example actually fails to illustrate sufficiently the exploitative system of the foreign bosses. Besides what they received in labor charges, the dock companies still had income from warehouse rents and mooring fees, which all went to the foreign bosses alone.

With labor charges for so many different kinds of goods, the depth of this exploitation was shocking. For instance, as noted in the account books of the Japanese commercial Whangpoo docks, the charge stipulated by the dock company for unloading barrels of tobacco leaves was 3.70 yuan per bucket*, of which the foreign bosses took 3.32 yuan. The remaining 0.38 yuan was given to the compradors and labor contractors, and after they deducted their share, the rest was given to the workers. Or, to take another example, the labor charge for cast iron was 2.02 yuan per ton. The foreign bosses took 1.52 yuan, and the rest, 0.50 yuan, went to the compradors and labor contractors. For sundries the labor charge was 0.14 yuan per item, of which the foreign bosses gave the compradors only .028 yuan. With the labor charge being reduced bit by bit to a pitiable amount, with layer by layer of deductions by the compradors and labor contractors, practically nothing trickled down into the hands of the workers.

The English, American, Japanese, and all the other imperialist docks in the main used these same proportions for dividing receipts. It is not surprising that the foreign bosses wanted the major share of these innumerable profits and treasure. From an inspection of the figures in the account books of the Kung Ho Hsiang Dock Company, from 1906 to 1927 the annual profit of the company climbed to about 700,000 taels of silver. From 1931 to 1940 the average annual profit of the Kung Ho Hsiang Dock Company reached more than 1.36 million yuan. The foreign bosses of the Kung Ho Hsiang occupied the docks for 78 years. One can see upon reflection how much of the blood and sweat of the Chinese people were exploited during that long period of time.

To take another example, the American commercial Dollar docks, although on a smaller scale than the Kung Ho Hsiang docks, still employed a means of exploitation no less severe than that at Kung Ho Hsiang. During the War in the Pacific, the Dollar docks were occupied by the Japanese army. But

*One t'ung (square wooden bucket) is said to hold six pints. — Tr.

after the Japanese aggressors surrendered, despite the fact that there had been unbearable destruction, the Dollar docks resumed operation without basically increasing their investment at all. All they had were two rickety cranes and a few typewriters. They relied completely on the blood and sweat of the oppressed workers and made a windfall, collecting in a short six-month period from November 1945 to May 1946 a net profit of more than one billion yuan in bogus Nationalist currency. At the foreign exchange rate at that time, this was the equivalent of about 447,000 American dollars. At that time, when a commercial ship docked and unloaded 2,000 tons of goods, the income of the Dollar docks would be 5,000 American dollars. If a "tramp steamer"* came at some irregular, unscheduled time and there were enough goods to unload, then the income per ship might reach 10,000 American dollars. By far the greatest portion of that was clear profit for the dock company. Exploitation was extraordinarily severe. Jefferson [Chieh-po-sheng], the head of the Dollar firm in 1948, said that in the two years 1946 and 1947 the Dollar docks earned 2.5 million American dollars. This enormous treasure was, of course, entirely drawn from exploitation of the Chinese people.

The foreign bosses ruthlessly raked in their profits and, through diversion of the workers' labor charges, desperately scraped and sucked the workers' blood and sweat. On the other hand, they also manipulated the loading and unloading prices, arbitrarily raising the rates and creating several erratic trends that directly and indirectly influenced the Chinese economy and the lives of the laboring people. The Kung Ho Hsiang docks, through their power to utilize and monopolize goods, controlled rates on the Shanghai docks. Whenever there was a lot of unloading and loading to do, they went ahead and forced prices upward. When there was little business, they forced prices down below the competition and squeezed other companies out of business. After the victory in the War of Resistance

*Yeh-chi ch'uan, literally "wild rooster boat." — Tr.

against Japan there was a great deal of movement of military supplies and high-quality goods into Shanghai harbor, and the business at the docks was abnormally "prosperous." As soon as the Kung Ho Hsiang bosses saw the opportunity for speculation, they united with the two foreign companies, Dollar and T'aiku, and along with the bureaucratic capitalist Commerce Bureau and the national capitalist China Dock Company, organized a bloc for monopolizing dock rates. In fact, changes in prices were completely dictated by the foreign bosses, with Grant, the head of the Kung Ho Hsiang, holding arbitrary power. With a telephone call he would notify each company to raise its prices, and all the prices would go up. Sometimes a telephone call in the morning doubled prices and another telephone call in the afternoon doubled them again. As a result of this extravagant overpricing, sometimes just the labor charge for loading and unloading came to more than half the price of the goods themselves.

Besides this, it also should be noted that these imperialist capital docks were all a part of the imperialist monopoly of capital in China, just as the Kung Ho Hsiang Dock Company was an enterprise of the English Shang Yi Ho business house network. The relationship of the Dollar docks and the American President Lines Company was also extremely close. Because of the special advantages supplied by the Shanghai docks, each of the docks' capitalist cliques received extra benefits from each other. The impact of this single factor became increasingly difficult to calculate.

II. Compradors Acting as the Tigers' Paws

In semicolonial, semifeudal old China, the exploitative activities of imperialists usually depended on the help of compradors. Compradors were the agents of the foreign bosses, the loyal lackeys of capitalism who gave their all to serve the foreigners. In a thousand and one ways they squeezed the blood and sweat of their own country's working people and offered it to the foreign bosses, taking small profits out of it for themselves, licking up scraps underneath the foreigner's bowl and getting fat.

The dock compradors' exploitation of the dock workers was extremely severe, and they had a great many ways to carry out that exploitation. Their main sources of income were warehousing contracts, loading contracts, and other means of extortion.

Foreign commercial dock warehouses usually engaged compradors to manage the buildings. The foreign bosses paid the compradors a fixed customary amount. From this, the comprador hired the staff and workers to manage the warehouse and paid their salaries, and thus exploitation went on. Underneath the comprador was usually the comprador's cashier's office, which employed a second- or third-class comprador acting as the comprador's assistant to coordinate the work and manage the accounts. In addition, he had foremen, apprentices, and other hired workers who managed the actual jobs. Except for the second- and third-class compradors, who had comparatively high salaries, the wages of the average workers were meager. By far the greatest portion of the money contracted for the warehouse was gobbled up by the comprador. For example, before the War of Resistance Against Japan, when the Kung Ho Hsiang dock comprador Kan Han-chü managed warehouses for the English foreign bosses, his monthly salary for one three-story warehouse was 294 yuan. In fact, Kan Han-chü employed only three staff workers and an apprentice to manage all the business of the one warehouse, and gave each worker an equal wage of 10 yuan, or 40 yuan in all, leaving a net 254 yuan in exploitative profits. Accordingly, a comprador rarely controlled only one warehouse. A small operation was at least a few warehouses; a large operation was more than ten warehouses. Each month the compradors must have exploited huge sums simply from managing warehouses.

In addition to this, the compradors on the docks generally all worked simultaneously as chief labor contractors. They utilized their advantageous positions as compradors either by directly handling the loading and unloading work on the docks held by the foreign bosses, by parceling it out to others, or by setting up their own labor accounting offices, finding a few second-class labor contractors and waiting for the profits to come pouring in. For instance, the Whangpoo dock comprador Ch'i Yung-ch'ing, the Huishan dock comprador Huang Chi-t'ang, the Huashun dock comprador Huang Ch'ing-hua, and others all combined their positions as compradors with jobs as chief labor contractors and administered a double dose of exploitation.

As mentioned above, the exploitation of the workers' labor charges by the foreign bosses was very severe, and more than 70 to 80 percent of the dock companies' income from labor charges was eaten up by the foreigners. The percentage of labor fees given to the comprador amounted to no more than 20 to 30 percent, and of this remnant the comprador necessarily pocketed more than 60 percent. For example, when the tobacco barrels mentioned earlier were unloaded, two workmen rolled each barrel and the dock company received from the merchant 3.70 yuan in labor charges for each barrel. The foreign bosses pocketed 3.32 yuan, or nearly 90 percent of it, and the remaining 0.38 yuan was given to the comprador, who squeezed out 60.53 percent of it, pocketing .23 yuan, and gave the remaining 0.15 yuan to the labor contractor. The labor contractor pocketed 0.07 yuan for each barrel, and the two workmen each got only 0.04 yuan. For another example, the labor charge for cast iron was 2.02 yuan a ton, of which the foreign bosses held onto 1.52 yuan, and gave 0.50 yuan to the comprador. The comprador took 60 percent of that, pocketing 0.30 yuan, and of the remaining 0.20 yuan, the labor contractor took 0.14 yuan. Only 0.06 yuan found its way to the workers' hands.

The severe degree of exploitation can be seen from the distribution of labor charges for standard goods. The difference in the income of workers and exploiters that can be clearly seen from the distribution of labor charges for large shipments of goods even more clearly reveals the severity of the exploitation on the docks. For example, in late July of 1937, the steamship Hsin Ning-t'ing-k'ao-t'uo-hao anchored at the

Whangpoo docks. It carried 9,270 tons of steel, which, altogether, took 12 days to unload, with 275 men working each day, a total of 3,300 man-days. The dock company received a labor charge of 21,428.22 yuan, plus the nonscheduled arrival fee, anchoring fee, and other fees, which made a total of 22,726.56 yuan received. The Tungyang Company bosses kept 16,693.81 yuan and gave the comprador 6,032.75 yuan. The comprador kept 2,712.75, plus extra subsidies of 0.20 yuan per ton, giving himself 40 percent, for a total income of 3,454.40 yuan. The remaining labor charge of 3,320 yuan still had to be divided among the large and small labor contractors. Sixty percent of the labor subsidies came back to them, and the total that finally trickled down to the workers was only 1,911.00 yuan. Spreading that over 3,300 man-days, each worker each day received no more than 0.58 yuan. This amount not only could not begin to compare with the more than 16,690 yuan taken in by the Tungyang bosses, but was as nothing when measured against the more than 3,450 yuan kept by one comprador. Also, with their shares several thousand times as large as the workers' shares, the compradors still had other forms of exploitative income.

The so-called labor subsidy was not limited to a single kind of extra income for the comprador. The comprador took advantage of his close contact with foreigners and, acting in his second special capacity as a large chief labor contractor, usually in the name of nonexistent workers, he extorted money from the owners by every fraudulent rule available, adding minor expenses, subsidies, etc. In reality the extra income all became spoils shared by the comprador and chief labor contractor, and the workers did not get a cent of it. For example, of the subsidies charged at the Whangpoo docks, the comprador Ch'i Yung-ch'ing took four-tenths, the large and small labor contractors divided up three-tenths, and the remaining three-tenths was divided into 30 shares, 12 going to the comprador's dependents (first and second wives, etc.), two to the small comprador (the comprador's son), two to the second-class comprador, one to the third-class comprador, and the other 13 taken by workers in the company's accounts office and coolie accounts office, and by the assistants and runners. But summing it all up, the comprador still got more than half of the labor charge.

Besides pocketing the labor charge, subsidies, and salaries of staff employees, there were other sources of comprador exploitation, such as storage costs, management of goods costs, night work costs, night work meal subsidies, baggage costs, boat tickets charges, and so on. Moreover, there was also skulduggery in the warehouses, thievery and fraudulent selling, heavy loads going into the warehouse and light loads coming out, 1,000 items coming into the warehouse but only 800 items being reported, and so on, layer upon layer without end. Kung Ho Hsiang dock comprador Kan Chih-hsien (the son of Kan Han-chü) each day provided food for his employees to eat on the docks, but it was never necessary to spend money to buy rice and coal. It was all taken from what companies had stored in the warehouse and the comprador had canceled off the records.

It is not surprising that from this severe and profound exploitation, compradors all piled up substantial fortunes and led shameless lives of debauchery day and night without letup.

III. The Profit-Grabbing Chinese Capitalists

Before the liberation, most of the docks and warehouses at Shanghai harbor were held by the imperialists, and the Chinese bureaucratic capitalists held only a small portion of them. The docks of the bureaucratic capitalists — for example, the Chin Li Yuan docks of the Commerce Bureau, and so on — never failed to call in foreigners to serve as managers. The management was carried out under the comprador system, and the enterprise was completely dependent on foreign capital. Those managers severely exploited and oppressed the workers and ruthlessly ransacked the people's wealth on behalf of the four great families.*

As for the dock and warehouse industry of the private

*The Chiang, Soong, Kung, and Ch'eng families. — Tr.

capitalists, they had only 15 percent of the total length of all docks in the harbor, and only 12 percent of the total area of all warehouses. Moreover, they were positioned inconveniently, where the water was not deep enough. Their equipment was primitive. They were very small. Their operation was decentralized and haphazard. Generally they were all attached to a privately operated steamship company, and everything supplied was for the use of the company's steamships. At that time the only comparatively good-sized independent private dock enterprise was the China Dock Company on the Whangpoo, which at the beginning was called the Yi T'ai Hsing Dock Company. It was established in 1918, and its business gradually expanded until, in 1927, it was reorganized as the China Dock Company and encompassed the Tung family ferry's north and south warehouses, the White Lotus River and Chou Society ferries, and several other docks. Under the monopolistic control of the foreign aggressors, the congenitally weak privately operated docks basically could not compete with the imperialist docks and could only do what leftover business the foreign bosses disdained. For example, consider the loading and unloading of coal. The foreign bosses were afraid that it would dirty their docks and have a bad effect on their business in other goods. They were not very willing to handle it, so they turned it over to the Chinese commercial docks. Also, the steamships that some private Chinese companies sailed along the rivers and seacoasts were not large, and they all anchored at docks with which their companies were associated. They provided the principal business of the private capitalist docks.

In spite of this, the capitalists of the private dock industry never passed up a single opportunity for exploitation. Although the amount of income they exploited did not approach what the foreigners were making off with, the methods and degree of their exploitation were no less severe than those of the foreign bosses.

The capitalists of the Yi T'ai Hsing Dock Company originally peddled coal for the K'ai Luan mining agency run by the English imperialists. During World War I they chartered foreign steamships to transport the coal and earned a tidy profit. The more coal business they did, the larger they grew. They opened many mines and enterprises and became big capitalists exploiting the workers. The amount of coal they transported each year usually reached 2 million tons. They had to have special docks and warehouses for the coal ships to anchor and for the storing and unloading of coal, so they organized the Yi T'ai Hsing Dock Company and supplied their own coal management services and increased their coal sale profits, at the same time increasing their exploitation of the dock workers. One small investment brought in a great deal. Their profit-making abacus was handled with great skill.

Since the Yi T'ai Hsing docks were established by the capitalists for their own convenience in transporting coal, the coal warehouse fee and other fees were of course not the main sources of the management's income. Instead, the loading and unloading labor charges increased to become the principal source of the capitalists' exploitation. From 1922 to 1925, the Yi T'ai Hsing south warehouse dock had a total income of 1,628,068.35 yuan, while the income from the labor charge was 1,080,099.82 yuan, or 66.3 percent of the total income. The net income the dock company received from the labor charge was 588,929.05 yuan, 54.5 percent of the income from the labor charge. The total income of the Yi T'ai Hsing north warehouse dock in the years 1920 to 1927 was 1,235,895.76 yuan, while the income from the labor charge was 1,014,170.81 yuan, 82.1 percent of the total income. The net income of the dock company from the labor charge was 642,468 yuan, 63.3 percent of the labor charge income. From these examples, it can be seen that the dock workers' labor charge was the most important exploitative income device available to the dock capitalists.

Through this severe exploitation, the Yi T'ai Hsing Company's Tung family ferry north and south warehouses, at their two separate locations, piled up profits each year. The profits accumulated by the two docks together in 1922 totaled 68,269.53 yuan; the 1925 profits were 88,765.60 yuan, and in

1927 they increased to 299,340.00 yuan. From 1922 to 1930 the total profits of the two docks reached 1,257,402.59 yuan. The capitalists reaped a huge fortune from managing the docks. If this did not come from exploiting the bodies of the workers, where could it have come from?

The capitalists thought of every possible means of making money. Because at that time the imperialists' power in Shanghai harbor was very great and the "Foreign Warehouse Bill" had gone into effect, to carry out their terrible business Chinese capitalists had to find a foreign "boat manager" (the representative of a steamship company). Therefore, although the Yi T'ai Hsing Dock Company drew completely on Chinese capital, it had to find ways to hang up a foreign flag and use money to find an English commercial operative to act as a representative. Moreover, the company had to hire a foreigner at a high price to act as "dock demon" (the dock manager, commonly called the "dock demon" by the workers). In addition, it asked the Whangpoo's chief mobsters Chang Ah-liu and Chia Fu-t'ien to serve as dock "advisors." By these means, in league with imperialism and the evil power of feudalism, the Chinese capitalists oppressed the workers and even cleared the way for their own exploitation by the foreigners.

The Yi T'ai Hsing docks as a rule flew a foreign flag, had a foreigner's name on their signboard, and frantically entrusted themselves to the "protection" of imperialism. Yet when suddenly the situation was transformed and the high tide of revolution against imperialism surged upward, they turned their ships to steer with the wind, took down the foreign flag, and put up the Chinese flag and signs identifying themselves as Chinese capitalists. This sort of vulgar, opportunistic behavior was nothing more than a way to create business and scheme for more profits. For instance, in the May 30 movement of 1925, the Shanghai workers went on a general strike, and all the workmen on the foreign commercial docks absolutely refused to load or unload goods for the imperialists. As soon as the capitalists of the Yi T'ai Hsing Company saw that the situation was not favorable for them, they urgently notified the dock's foreign management to change to the Chinese flag. They immediately sent two flags, asking the foreign management to see personally that they were raised immediately so as to avoid being hurt by the strike. But at the same time, they also took advantage of the opportunity presented by the tie-up of the foreign commercial docks (because the strike had stopped all loading and unloading) and secretly dispatched foreigners to do business with the foreign commercial ship companies and persuade the foreign ships to anchor at Yi T'ai Hsing docks. The capitalists thought only of their own profit schemes. They did not care in the least what effect those schemes had on the anti-imperialist movement. Even when the English, Japanese, and American imperialists madly slaughtered Chinese people, the capitalists went so far as to lose all semblance of conscience and secretly supplied coal to every imperialist factory. They permitted the Japanese coal ship Tien Wan to anchor at the docks and gathered together a large group of reactionary police and troops to force the workers into unloading the goods. From this perspective it can be seen that the capitalists only sought advantages that made their own schemes possible. They basically did not care about the national interest and were content to oblige the imperialists.

The Yi T'ai Hsing docks' main business was the storage of coal, and here the capitalists had a way of falsifying accounts, of deceiving their customers and increasing their own profits. When the coal entered the warehouse, according to rules for deducting what was destroyed or wasted, it was generally figured that 98 percent was left, so that 1,000 tons of coal was only figured as 980 tons, and the extra 20 tons became extra income for the dock company. Moreover, the coal was stored outdoors, and when it rained or snowed it was easy for the coal to absorb water and increase its weight, so that 1,000 tons could become 1,050 tons. By the time the client picked up the goods noted in the warehouse voucher, each 1,000 tons had become only 980 tons, and these dock capitalists had pocketed 70 tons of coal. Of course, the client that picked up the coal could not suffer too much of a loss, for in the end he passed the cost of the added expense on to the consumer, and those who suffered were, as usual, the great masses of working people.

The Yi T'ai Hsing Dock Company made money. It expanded in size and was reorganized as the China Dock Company. In 1927 when the reorganization occurred, its total capital was 300,000 yuan, but by 1934 it had swiftly increased to 3 million yuan. Following the expansion of the scope of the dock operations, the capitalists greatly increased their exploitation of the dock workers.

In the period of the War of Resistance against Japan, the China Dock Company docks were occupied by the Japanese aggressors and suffered a great deal of destruction. After the victory in the War of Resistance against Japan, the Kuomintang reactionaries rushed to bring in American imperialist "surplus goods." Ships in Shanghai harbor brought in these tainted goods in "abundance," and the dock and warehouse industry indulged in a great deal of profiteering. After the capitalists of the China Dock Company docks recaptured their docks, they basically did not add to their investment, but recovered the remaining broken down equipment and resumed operations. At that time the docks were completely covered with American goods and business was truly booming. With the docks in operation day and night, night crews usually had to be added, but the capitalists used the addition of night duty as an excuse to increase the labor charge to their customers. A half-night's work added 50 percent to the bill, and a whole night's work doubled the bill. The labor charge the capitalists were peeling off was already quite high, and by doubling the amount, their exploitative income increased greatly. At this time the China Dock Company, in collaboration with the Kung Ho Hsiang, T'aiku, Dollar, and other dock companies of the foreign capitalists and the docks of the bureaucratic capitalist Commerce Bureau, with the Kung Ho Hsiang Dock Company in command, organized a small monopolistic clique to control the dock charges and raise prices at will. These increased dock charges were of course in the end just added to the price of goods and were borne by the poor, suffering laboring people. The China

Dock Company and the Commerce Bureau, in order to strengthen exploitation, were content to act as slaves for the imperialists. They stuck to the tails of the foreign bosses and were at their beck and call. They fanned the flame of imperialism and together with the imperialists seized the wealth of their country's laboring people.

Through their many exploitative activities, the China Dock Company received a tremendous windfall in the two or three years following the victory in the War of Resistance Against Japan. According to the accounts, the amounts of the net profits they received during these years were as follows:

1945	Bogus KMT currency	3,481,925.79 yuan
1946	Bogus KMT currency	536,316,512.24 yuan
1947	Bogus KMT currency	2,644,868,494.88 yuan
1948	Bogus gold certificates	359,147.11 yuan

Although there was runaway inflation at that time and currency had swollen at an alarming rate, it was the laboring people who suffered. The capitalists really could not lose. From the very beginning the capitalists of the China Dock Company took whatever money they made and immediately put it in foreign exchange, converting it into American dollars. On the eve of the liberation, the China Dock Company had accumulated a total of more than 500,000 American dollars. Besides that, within these few years they had erected six warehouses, a pine dock, and two dormitories. They still had in addition some open-air warehouses and so on. Taken together, the company's assets had to be worth 500,000 or 600,000 American dollars. Together with their glittering gold stocks, their assets totaled about one million American dollars. That is to say, starting in the autumn of 1945, when the China Dock Company resumed operations, within two to three years the company had exploited one million American dollars. This was terribly devastating exploitation!

IV. The Man-Eating Labor Contractors

The foreign bosses, compradors, and Chinese capitalists on the docks exploited the workers very severely, but they were also quite crafty in avoiding direct employer-employee relationships with the workers. Instead, they used labor contractors to control and manage the workers. The labor contractors relied on support from imperialism, the reactionary political authority of the day, and the evil power of feudalism to monopolize the loading and unloading work on the docks, supervise the workers, and ruthlessly exploit them.

The exploitation carried out by the labor contractor extended through several levels of his organization. Under the chief labor contractor there usually were "accountants" and "assistants." They were the labor contractor's helpers and assisted him in the work of coordinating and supervising the loading work and managing the accounts of income and expenses. Underneath the "assistant" were also several "dock runners." They were little helpers of the labor contractor who usually patrolled the docks. These men were all lackeys of the labor contractor and depended on him for their lives. In addition to these, underneath the chief labor contractor were also many second-class labor contractors, who divided the loading work on the docks among themselves into many small sections. Each held sway over one job and split the take with the chief labor contractor. At that time the loading work on the docks under this feudal leadership system was split into many kinds of jobs, such as bearing poles, shoulder carrying, storage loading, transfer to ship's hold, transfer to warehouse, transfer to transshipment boat, and so on. There were many different names, designations galore, but actually none of this came about because of the needs of the workers but was the result of the labor contractors' division of the work. For example, imports and exports at the T'aiku docks had to change hands seven times, going through workers six times. Underneath the chief labor contractor of the Commerce Bureau's Chin Li Yuan dock, work was divided into pole bearing, shoulder carrying, northern and southern Pacific region exports, Yangtze exports, fresh goods newly arrived, and several other categories. Each had a second-class labor contractor, and one contractor could not encroach upon another. Underneath the second-class labor contractor there sometimes was also a third-class contractor, and occasionally a group of little headmen following directly behind who were called "little foremen." The little foremen were responsible for mustering the workers and handling the loading work. The second-class contractors notified the small foremen to assemble the workers to do the work. The greatest portion of dock work was organized under this system, but each dock was not completely the same. There were many people on one level at one place, and few people at that level at another, all determined by the condition of the loading and unloading work and the feudal leadership relationships at the dock.

The labor contractor's exploitation of the workers was both covert and overt and appeared in many different forms, but its principal form was the accounts breakdown. The chief labor contractor first and foremost pocketed by far the largest part of the labor fee received from dock company executives. The remainder went down through the overlapping layers of second- and third-class contractors, each taking a cut, so that only the last bits went to the workers. Actually, that only left the little pieces no one else wanted. For example, after the chief labor contractor of the Commerce Bureau's Chin Li Yuan docks, Pao Ch'ao-yün, received the labor fee for loading and unloading, he first set aside two-tenths for the "expenses" incurred by the labor contractor in maintaining social contacts through entertaining. Then he took 40 to 50 percent of the remaining eight-tenths for himself. This was already more than half, and the remainder still had to go to the pockets of the second- and third-class contractors. For example, the chief contractor of the China Dock Company, depending on the kind of goods involved, took 40 to 80 percent of the labor fee. The labor contractor of the Tata docks, besides the 60 to 70 percent he openly appropriated, also took an additional 10 percent for the "welfare fund." Actually, this "welfare fund" was just another word for exploitation. The workers basically did not have any "welfare."

There was no rule as to the amount the second-class contractors received. It depended basically on the different conditions on each dock and the types of goods; but the exploitation by the second-class contractors was still extremely severe. For instance, the second-class contractor Shao Hui-t'ing took from four-tenths to more than six-tenths of the labor charge. The second-class contractor Hsu Chin-sheng in one day grabbed the equivalent of the shares of 32 men. One second-class contractor, under the unloading labor contractor Lai Ming-hsing, took charge of one hatchway, received 17 yuan, and gave his workmen only 2.50 yuan, peeling off 85 percent for himself. In addition to this, the small labor contractor and small foremen also had to take a cut. The amount of their cut was not fixed, and the small foremen wanted at least a double share. When the money finally filtered down to the workers, it could virtually be divided no further.

Even when the workmen divided up this minuscule remaining portion of the labor charge, the labor contractor still had to participate. For instance, the Kung Ho Hsiang dock labor contractor Sung Yu-shu had to be figured into the accounts breakdown as receiving $3\frac{1}{2}$ shares (one for himself, one for his wife, one for his son, and even one-half of a share for the dog the family kept). At that time 18 crews gathered in the warehouse each day, and he got $3\frac{1}{2}$ shares for each crew, or 63 shares a day. The T'aiku Dock Company labor contractor Chou Tuan-jui followed the same practice. His wives, children, servants, hatchetmen, cats, and dogs all had to receive their proper shares. Chang Chih-fa, another Kung Ho Hsiang labor contractor, charged the water and electric bills run up by his own family to the company and thus took the money from the workers. Other labor contractors universally ate up these extra, blank shares. When there obviously were only 10 men working, they insisted that the shares be divided as if there were 12 men. Fifteen men working had to be figured as 20 men. The excess shares became income for the labor contractor.

The accounts breakdown was an overt form of exploitation. There also were hidden forms of exploitation. When a labor contractor did his bookkeeping, he often concealed the true tonnage or value of a shipment. If there clearly were 1,000 tons, he would insist there were only 800. If he received a labor charge of 1,000 yuan, he would tell the workers it was only 700 yuan. With a stroke of his brush, he could jumble the accounts so that no one could figure out what was going on. The workmen knew very well something was wrong, but they could not ask questions, because the minute anyone began to ask questions, the labor contractor would fire an angry look at him and say: "Your sainted mother! Certainly your uncle can deduct things from your pay. And if I do deduct, what are you going to do about it?" Or he would pat his pistol and say, "Do you know what this is?" If a workman protested, at the very least he would not be able to get a work permit next time and would not be able to work. At the most he would suffer terrible persecution.

Sometimes the labor contractor simply did not give the workmen any money at all but forced them into working for nothing. Wu Ch'i-yu, the small labor contractor at the Commerce Bureau's third dock, required his workers to do "volunteer labor" for him every year at spring festival time. They put in a day's work for free. They were not given a cent, and he called this compensation for his losses in paying out so much for social functions in that season. Even at other times they often had to perform this "voluntary labor."

Besides the stipulated labor charge, the labor contractor still could charge the merchant a subsidy or expenses. There were a great many names for these illegal extra fees. For loading vehicles there was a vehicle-loading fee, for transshipment there was a transshipment fee, for rainy days there was a rainy day fee, for rush loading there was a rush-loading fee. When goods were left on the docks overnight, there was an insurance fee and an overnight fee. There were also extra fees for hot days, cold days, and so on. The amount of income from subsidies, expenses, and the like was very great, and it all came back to be divided up by the large and small labor contractors. The workers could not get their hands on any of it.

Although this was the case, the labor contractors still were unwilling to give the workers their meager portion of the labor charge right away. They would wait several days, dragging it out, before settling accounts. Workers basically lived from day to day, and they could not wait. Moreover, with the galloping inflation that existed before the liberation, the little money the workers earned became worthless in the space of the several days they waited before they received it, and they could not buy anything with it. Meanwhile, the labor contractors were using the labor charges they had delayed paying to the workers. They were making a great deal of money by hoarding, speculation, and exploitation. On the other hand, with the worker's family waiting for rice for the family pot, he had no choice but to take out loans from the labor contractor at exorbitant interest rates. And this was only one form of exploitation by the labor contractors. For instance, the Sheng Chi Company's field supervisor Lin Hsing-sheng lent workers money, each day adding 40 percent interest. If the money was not paid back in three days, the borrower was scolded and beaten.

Besides this, the labor contractors would also unexpectedly give the workers "small anticipatory gifts" to extort from them "offerings of gratitude." Each and every New Year's festival and "wedding, funeral, feast, or celebration" in the labor contractor's family meant that the workers all had to send gifts. This was exploitation in disguise, which occurred several times a month. There were many names for these "small anticipatory gifts" — a birthday for the living, a birthday for the dead, an infant's first three days, an infant's first month, a son's marriage, a daughter's wedding — all requiring the workers to give money. If they had no money, then they had to borrow some in order to send a gift. One labor contractor decided to have two "birthdays" in one year. The first part of the year had passed and he wanted another one for the last part of the year. The "great fortieth birthday" was also stretched out over three years by some. The first year, the year before, was the "preparatory celebration"; the second year was the "proper birthday"; and the third year was the "birthday by Western calendar reckoning." On the Soochow River there was even a labor contractor who, every time a daughter was born to him, forced the workers to pay a "dowry fee."

In any case, this way of stacking the deck and taking a high percentage of the profits from the workers was only one more means by which the labor contractors exploited the workers. Those workers who were not willing to pay, who would not "show their deference," did not get any work the next time. The workers were forced to expend their blood, sweat, and money until there was nothing left.

This severe exploitation squeezed out the workers' blood and sweat. The labor contractors truly "ate men without even spitting out the bones." They all became wealthy men as their family fortunes accumulated. Before the War of Resistance against Japan, in the second decade of the Republic [1921-1931], two labor contractors of the K'ai Lan docks, Chang Hsi-hua and Wei Ch'eng-chi, already were millionaires with fortunes of one to two million yuan. The Dollar docks labor contractor Chia Po-hsing, in the space of the 18 months from the beginning of 1946 to the end of June 1947, outside of all of the money he received from the docks themselves, exploited the workers to net the equivalent of more than 2.8 million catties of rice. That averaged out to 5,200 catties of rice a day, which would be enough to feed one man for 14 years. In two or three years he built ten transshipment boats and two three-story Western-style buildings. The chief labor contractor of the Commerce Bureau's sixteenth storage dock, Pao Ch'ao-yün, from the time he took over at the dock opened three coal-ball factories and built three three-story buildings.

The tremendous assets of the imperialists, the compradors, the Chinese capitalists, the labor contractors, and the other exploiting classes were all built on the blood, sweat, pain, and agony of the broad masses of dock workers. Let us look now at the way the dock workers in those years worked and lived.

3

"Coolie" – Two-Legged Beast of Burden

I. Backbreaking Work

Before the liberation, the dock workers were pushed down to the very lowest rung of society. The foreign bosses, compradors, Chinese capitalists, and labor contractors exploited the workers' bodies to gain tremendous riches. Moreover, the workers were never treated like men and were always addressed with every kind of profanity. The imperialists called the workers "coolies." These exploiters often said, "You can't find a three-legged frog, but there are lots of two-legged asses." They treated the dock workers like two-legged beasts of burden. The real truth is that in the course of a day the dock workers worked longer and harder than beasts of burden.

The loading work on the docks at that time completely depended on the physical labor of the dock workers. The foreign bosses and the Chinese capitalists, in order to seize maximum profits, went all out in utilizing inexpensive human labor and were not willing to use machinery. Although at that time there were one or two cranes on the Kung Ho Hsiang and Dollar docks, they were only used for making advertisements and putting on

"'K'u-li' – liang-tiao t'ui ti niu-ma."

displays and were actually rarely operated. If the owner of the goods requested that machinery be used in the loading or unloading, the charges skyrocketed. So customers did not ask that machinery be used, and no matter how heavy the goods, they were all moved by dock workers.

Under the management of the feudal monopoly system, work on the docks was divided into categories such as pole bearing, shoulder carrying, vehicle loading, coal loading, storage loading, and so on, but no matter what kind of work, it always involved using the arms and shoulders to move things around. The two main categories of work were shoulder carrying and pole bearing.

Shoulder-carrying workers had no working tools whatsoever other than ragged shoulder pads. They had to rely completely on their two shoulders to carry goods, and the goods they carried were mostly bags of rice, sugar, or beans, with each bag weighing somewhere between two and three hundred *chin* [catties]. In addition, they carried incredibly heavy bundles of cowhide, straw mats, or medicines weighing between five and six hundred *chin* each.

The pole bearers used poles and ropes to carry goods. Usually there were two men to one pole. For especially heavy loads, at times they needed several poles, sometimes more than ten at a time. The goods they carried included bags of cotton, boxes of calico, bundles of cowhide, barrels of caustic soda, rolls of paper, cast iron, steel pieces, and other boxed goods. The loads weighed at least four or five hundred *chin*, and there were some weighing more than a thousand *chin*.

The dock workers carried these heavy burdens, with several hundred *chin* of goods bearing down on their bodies, not just one hour, or two hours, but more than ten hours in succession. They went back and forth between the docks and the warehouses, each day running more than ten miles without complaint. Actually, beasts of burden did not do as much work as that. It drained the workers' blood and sweat.

The roads on which the dock workers ran more than ten miles a day bearing heavy burdens were not at all level. The roads at the docks at that time were not soft mud roads but were made of crushed rock, laid out unevenly with high and low spots. After three steps there would be a pit, after five steps a ditch. When it rained, there were puddles everywhere. Falling and slipping, it would have been hard to walk steadily there in any case; think how much harder it would be to do it bearing several hundred chin of goods. The workmen wore straw sandals on their bare feet as they walked on the crushed rock, which was like walking on sharp knives. With the heavy weight pressing down on their shoulders, the bottoms of their feet ached so much that they could hardly stand it. A pair of straw sandals did not last half a day before they disintegrated. On cold winter days, the straw sandals froze solid and the workers' feet froze until they were purple, cracked, and bleeding. As soon as their feet scraped against the crushed rock or pieces of frozen mud, fresh blood poured from their frozen feet, so that each step left a bloody imprint and by afternoon the blood and flesh were stuck to the straw sandals and they could not take them off.

Even if the roads had been flat and not considered difficult, carrying loads upstairs would still have been difficult. A great many of the warehouses on the docks had more than one story. A warehouse like the Hsiang-lung-mao had three stories, so the workers carrying several hundred chin of goods from the docks to the warehouse had to take more than 500 steps and then, having entered the warehouse, had to climb up 82 steps to the third floor. At the very least they made ten trips a day and at most more than a hundred trips a day. After a worker was finished, his feet felt like steel filings; they were so hard and heavy he could not lift them. But the workers, forced by the need to make a living, absolutely had to give their all; they bent over and climbed the stairs step by step. As if it was not difficult enough to climb the stairs, they also had to creep along gangplanks. The dock bosses, in order to conserve storage space, demanded that goods be piled high, filling each room until it could hold no more. For this purpose a few seven- or eight-inch-wide gangplanks were set up and the workers were told to carry the goods across them. The workers crossed one by one; they were not allowed to go together, and if their steps slowed the least bit, the foreman's whip or cane would strike them. If they were not careful, the next time it would happen again.

It went on like this from dawn to dusk. After the workers finished work, they staggered away exhausted. Their legs were so tired they just would not move. Their skin was scraped off their shoulders so that blood poured over them. Their waists felt like they were broken; they could not even bend over. If they wanted to sit down and rest, they had to lean against a wall and, using their two arms to support them, roll onto the ground. They sleepily fell and could not rise again. The only way to eat was lying face down. The next morning they would get up, but only if they first turned over and, face down on the floor, used their hands to push themselves up slowly, struggling to get up and go to work again.

Workers new to pole bearing always found that the poles bore down so hard that they squeezed out pus and blood. The workers had no money for doctors, and all they could do was apply bean curd skins to their shoulders, wrap them in pieces of cotton, or strip open the wound so the pus and blood could flow freely. The men all just kept going despite the pain. Some men who had been bearing poles for some time found that their shoulders toughened under the grinding weight of the poles. They would grow soft hairs one or two inches long. The heavy burdens also changed the men's psychological makeup.

Described above were the conditions on the docks. If a man worked in the ship's hold as a stevedore [lun-chuang], this also meant suffering. The stevedores lifted the goods in the hold, and no matter whether the bundles weighed several hundred chin or the boxes of machinery weighed several thousand chin, they had to be moved around by workers using long suspension poles. Some small boats had no suspension poles, and the work was even more difficult. The ships' holds were stuffy and dark; there was no equipment to let air circulate. On extremely hot summer days when the metal hull of the boat was made boiling hot by the heat of the sun, the temperature rose above forty degrees centigrade and sweat poured down endlessly into the workers' mouths. Moreover, there was no set length of time for the work of the stevedores. They had to unload all the goods from the hold before they could rest. Sometimes they had to work continuously for several days and nights. And if they had a fixed time to unload and load a boat that was on a schedule, they had to work at a greatly accelerated pace. Once they had finished, they could not stay and rest but had to hurry frantically on to work elsewhere.

The dock workers carried on this terribly hard labor even on the cold days after the winter solstice when they worked with nothing on their backs and on days when they became so exhausted that their bodies were covered with sweat and they were so thirsty they could not stand it. But they had to keep working, so they could not drink even a single mouthful. On the docks the only time they were supplied with tea was during the period each year from the day of the Dragon-boat Festival [the fifth day of the fifth lunar month] to the Mid-Autumn Festival [the fifteenth day of the eighth lunar month]. But they were given only two pots of tea into which they had to pour several pots of their own water or just plain river water. The purpose of using cold water was, first, because the labor contractor wanted to save money and, second, because he was afraid that if the workers had hot water to drink they would lounge around and waste time. If the workers drank several mouthfuls of this cold water and then slowed down in the slightest, the labor contractor would snatch away the bamboo tube the worker was drinking from and throw it into the Whangpoo River. As for washing, there was not much of it to speak of. After the workers finished work, they could wring the sweat out of all their clothes, and then the only thing they could do was either wash them a bit in the Wangpoo River or run them under the filthy water being discharged from the undersides of the steamships.

The workers not only labored under these awful conditions, but they had not the slightest assurance of their personal safety. The Chinese and foreign capitalists and labor contractors paid attention only to their own profit margins. They did not think the lives of the workers were worth a cent, to the point that they forced the workers to do every kind of dangerous job. That usually resulted in deaths or serious injuries. For instance, in 1940 an Italian ship carrying a poisonous material in the form of a yellow powder anchored at the Kung Ho Hsiang Docks. Because the material was poisonous, preventative measures had to be taken. The boat company accordingly gave the boss of the Fu An Transfer Company, which was handling the unloading, an extra subsidy. Once the boss of the Fu An Company received this extra payment he said: "What preventative measures can we take? Whoever spills the poison is dead!" Then he told the foremen to call the workers to work, with none of them knowing the true story. Not long after they started, a large chunk of poison broke off and fell to the ground. As a result, thirty-four workers were poisoned, and one died. After this incident, the injured workers' families asked the labor contractor for money for medical treatment or funerals. The labor contractor said truculently, "If you're looking for money, you can expect to get as much from debtors in T'i-lan-ch'iao (a local prison) as from me." Before the liberation, on the old Pai-tu Dock a similar incident occurred. Three workers were poisoned and died. To take another example from before the liberation, on the Wai-tan Dock an incident once occurred as men were transporting nitric acid, one container per trip. Yuan Sung-lin, the labor contractor who was nicknamed "The Third Bandit," ran up, took one look, and scolded them maliciously: "Who told you just one container at a time? You SOBs, give me two at a time and make it snappy!" There was nothing the workers could do but start carrying two bottles at a time. One old worker named Tung started out with another worker, but because the goods were too heavy and the hold of the ship was very high, all at once Tung slipped and was covered with nitric acid. He shook with agonizing pain from head to foot. Terrified, he leaped into the river, but at that time a strong tide was running. Once having fallen into the river, he could not get out. It was the next day before they found his body.

In another instance, a foreign ship carrying barrels of tobacco leaves docked at the Kung Ho Hsiang Docks in 1945. Before they began to unload the ship, the workers discovered that the chains and hooks on the unloading poles were broken and could not be used. They pointed out to the labor contractor, Shen Chang-fa, that the boat masters had to change the hooks before they could work. Shen Chang-fa said with an angry look: "If you want a livelihood, get busy for me! If you're scared, you don't have to work!" He thus forced them to start working. As was to be expected, the first time they tried to pick up four barrels with a hook, the pole trembled, the chains broke, and the tobacco barrels fell back into the hold and crushed a worker named Shen to death. Afterward, when the worker's relatives asked Shen Chang-fa for money to pay for his burial, Shen Chang-fa responded: "I wasn't responsible for him when he was living. Why should I care for him once he's dead?"

There are an inexhaustible number of examples like this. Before the liberation it was a common occurrence for workers to be crushed to death or to fall to their deaths. Even if they were lucky enough to survive, they usually were crippled. If they did not break a hand or a leg, they would begin to spit blood or suffer a hernia or some other illness. Yet even if one's body was shuddering with sickness, he was still forced to work. One old worker named Hsü once was among twenty-four men using twelve poles to lift a large steel beam that weighed more than two tons on the Lung-hua-jih-hui Harbor Docks. They had not carried it more than a few steps when old Hsü felt a sudden, intense pain and saw golden stars bursting before his eyes in great profusion. He had strained himself too much and had suffered a hernia. He was afraid of causing an accident so he did not dare drop his load. While he desperately held up his end, he said to the labor contractor: "I've got a hernia. I can't carry this. Please let me stop!" The labor contractor stared at him and chided him: "You SOB, what is all this jabbering? It won't kill you. You can't stop. Keep going!" Old Hsü staggered a few steps until he could bear it no longer. He again asked the labor contractor for a rest. The labor contractor said: "If you want to rest, you can, but of course you'll have to pay the wages of these twenty-three men." Hsü was at a loss when he heard this. All he could do was grit his teeth and carry on. When he was finally able to drop his burden, he fell to the ground unconscious.

Cruel labor contractors, when they went to the extent of using workers who were sick from overwork, intensified their exploitation that much more. For instance, there was once an old worker named P'an who had worked more than half a day on the Kung Ho Hsiang Docks when he suddenly vomited blood. He said to the labor contractor, Chang Chih-fa: "I vomited blood, I can't work." Chang Chih-fa replied, "If you don't work, then you don't need to be paid." It was already afternoon, and he had worked more than half a day for nothing. He did not get a penny. He went home and nursed his injuries for six months. He could not go to the docks, and his family went through all sorts of hardship and difficulty.

Under the cruel blows of this kind of overwork, most of the dock workers lost their ability to work very early in life. By the time most were middle-aged they could not work at all. On the Whangpoo Docks there used to be an able bag carrier named Hung Ta. When he was young he could carry two rice bags weighing two hundred or more chin each, or ten bags of wheat flour. But when he reached forty years of age, he could not even carry one bag of rice. He was driven away from the docks by the labor contractor. One cold December night he froze to death beside a toilet on Darien Road.

II. The "Over-the-Mountain Leap" and the "Corkscrew Leap"

In dock loading and unloading before the liberation, there were always gangplanks. Particularly the workers who carried coal had to have gangplanks to do their work. Unloading coal from the steamships and piling it on "coal mountains" both required suspending very long gangplanks. Sometimes between two "coal mountains" it was also necessary to suspend a gangplank. This was called the "over-the-mountain leap." The gangplank for the "over-the-mountain leap" was more than two feet wide and ten to twenty feet above the ground, supported underneath by high stools. Each gangplank was thirty or forty feet long, and usually six or seven of them were connected together, which was called a "six-stage leap" or a "seven-stage leap." Some even had as many as ten stages. Some of the narrow gangplanks for transferring coal were only seven or eight inches wide and were even more dangerous. Two coal-loading workers manning one pole would carry a coal basket weighing more than two hundred chin. All day long they ran back and forth on these narrow, steep, high gangplanks which shook with every step. Every day they had to carry at least two or three hundred baskets. Furthermore, they had to work very fast because if they were slow the labor contractor would withhold their wages. If the contractor suspected a coal carrier was too slow, he did not want him.

As if the narrow, long, high "over-the-mountain leaps" were not already dangerous enough, the planks supported a long line of workers hurrying along carrying coal baskets. This naturally caused the gangplanks to shake and shudder. Furthermore, the workers could not clearly see where they were stepping — but there is no need to go into any more detail about that situation. Two men, one in front and one in back, lifted the coal basket, but they had to walk sideways and shout a cadence or they could not coordinate their movements. If a worker was the least bit careless, he would fall off the gangplank and more than two hundred chin of coal would crash down on him. If his head was not cracked open, he would at least suffer a broken back or leg. Therefore, the workers always said, "You cross the third leap, it shakes, your foot steps into thin air, and your life is over."

When there was wind, rain, or snow or when men worked

during the night, the "over-the-mountain leaps" were especially dangerous. The wind often blew hard on the Whangpoo River, and the gangplanks suspended from the sides of the ships shook even more terribly. Moreover, after the coal ships had been unloaded and their holds emptied, the ships rose up out of the water. If there was also a flood tide, the sides of the boat might rise more than twenty feet above the dock and make the gangplanks even steeper. When it rained or snowed, the gangplanks were wet and slippery. On very cold days, the ropes on the coal baskets froze so they were hard and stiff. Ice formed on the gangplanks so that it was even harder to take the smallest step. During night work, lamps lit the gloom, but visibility was not good, and the danger was even greater. Anyway, no matter what the weather, the coal-loading workers all had to risk their lives on the gangplanks, and accordingly, work accidents involving death and injury occurred regularly. Innumerable workers were killed or crippled underneath the gangplanks. The workers all referred to the "over-the-mountain leap" as "Hell's Bridge" [<u>Nai-ho-ch'iao</u> — a bridge in purgatory which all departed spirits are forced to cross]. They said: "Hell's Bridge, Oh! Hell's Bridge. You run with your coal basket along the bridge. Cross the bridge, and you get a few cakes. Fail, and you lose your life."

In addition, there was the "corkscrew leap," another exhausting job. The "corkscrew leap" was used to discharge cargo from a ship's hold. This occurred occasionally in the handling of a small ship's goods when the ship had no loading poles and had to rely solely on manpower to unload the hold. Workers carried the load out in baskets, one basket at a time. To carry the goods up from the bottom level, they had to lay down gangplanks for the men to walk on. But, because the ship's hold was small, the gangplanks had to curve, bit by bit, as they descended into the hold. They looked like a corkscrew spiraling down to the bottom of the hold. Thus, it was called the "corkscrew leap." Because the ship's hold was small, the gangplanks that were used were also small, only about a foot or so wide and six or seven feet long. When they were built, they were suspended in space from the mouth of the hold. The top end of the first gangplank was placed at the mouth of the hold and secured with rope. Then it slanted down. The bottom end was placed on top of a crosspiece that was also secured to the mouth of the hold with rope. Underneath that another gangplank was laid, and in this way, piece by piece, the planks descended to the bottom of the hold, all suspended in space and secured by ropes. The hold of the average small boat was ten or twenty feet deep, so six or seven gangplanks had to be attached together. Following the wall of the hold, the gangplanks descended about $1\frac{1}{2}$ revolutions before they reached the bottom. Workers wound their way up and down these gangplanks carrying goods.

On these short, narrow, steep, winding gangplanks, workers carried goods, basket by basket, with a few hundred chin per basket. To make matters even worse, there were men walking back down with their empty baskets on the same gangplanks that men were walking up, and they constantly had to give way to each other. On some particularly small boats, the "corkscrew leaps" were so crowded that two men carrying a basket together had to duck their heads and bend at their waists, with one hand supporting the carrying pole and one hand holding the basket rope, winding their way up step by step. With the slightest mishap, they could lose their footing and fall to the bottom of the hold, being killed or at least injured. In the period of the War of Resistance, there was a worker named Chou Kuang-yü who was carrying goods on the "corkscrew leap" when his basket rope snagged on a gangplank. His body was pulled off balance, and he and his goods fell to the bottom of the hold. He was killed instantly. Because the "corkscrew leap" was suspended in space, had no supports underneath it, and relied completely on the ropes securing it from above and because there were men with heavy loads walking on the gangplanks, moving constantly, it was easy for the ropes to slip off so the gangplanks collapsed. This could mean a serious accident causing workers to be crushed or to fall to their deaths. Therefore, the workers said, "The corkscrew leap is deadly for workers."

The workers on the "corkscrew leap" all had to be especially powerful and robust; but no matter how strong they were, after more than ten hours a day carrying goods on these gangplanks, they were exhausted. Such difficult days of overwork made the workers especially susceptible to injuries like hernias or swelling of the scrotum. The work of transferring coal on the "corkscrew leap" was especially exhausting and made workers susceptible to illness and injury, and therefore the workers were fearful anytime they saw the "corkscrew leap." But they could not stop working.

Sometimes even the "corkscrew leap" was not adequate, and a many-leveled "scaffolding" had to be fashioned from pieces of wood. The workers stood on the "scaffolding" and, using their hands and shoulders, lifted the goods onto their heads. Level by level, they lifted the goods to the deck of the ship. One worker would crouch down and take the goods from the shoulders and head of the worker below him. Then he would slowly stand up and use his shoulders to push the goods onto his head. But each pair of shoulders could only raise the load a meter. It usually took three or four lifts to get the goods from the bottom of the hold up to the ship's deck, or sometimes even six or seven lifts. Among the goods being raised were bags of rice and sugar weighing two to three hundred chin each and bundles of cotton weighing four to five hundred chin each. One crew had to raise at least sixty to seventy bags, sometimes even more than a hundred bags. After lifting, one's waist could not unbend, and one's legs could not bend. This kind of inhuman labor led to workers being considered "living machines" that needed no oiling.

III. Mean Wages

How much did the dock workers earn for leading these burdensome lives? "Bamboo pressed their shoulders, sticks struck their chests, but only small change filled their pockets" — this was the dock workers' authentic description of their own situation.

At that time, there was not a single worker permanently

employed at the docks. Whenever a certain number of workers was needed, that number was rounded up. Each day workers carrying shoulder pads, poles, and ropes would run here and there on their own looking for work. They found it only on a day-to-day basis. The exploiters gave these itinerant workers an insulting title — "tramp labor."

The itinerant dock workers not only could not find work every day, but usually could only find work fifteen or sixteen days a month. The remaining half of the time there was no work and thus no income. Therefore, the dock workers of that era were frequently in a state of semiunemployment. They had to worry every day about whether they could find work. In order to find work, whether it was in freezing December or in the full summer heat of July, whether snowflakes were flying or lightning mixed with thunder, they had to get up before daybreak, their stomachs empty, and wait hours at the dock gate for the labor contractor to call their name and fill out a work ticket. If a worker was in a position to get a work ticket, then he was all right for this one day at least. But if he could not get a work ticket, then he had to run elsewhere, and sometimes he would run to several docks in succession without getting a work ticket. On such days all he could do was tighten his belt and go hungry. When few boats arrived at the docks or when there were successive days of rainy weather, then it was a common occurrence for days to go by without being able to get a work ticket. In this situation entire families suffered terrible famines.

Even for the lucky ones who got work tickets, a day's work could not be guaranteed. If a new worker arrived at the dock for the first time, the labor contractor required an "examination" in which he checked to see if the worker could perform in accordance with the objectives of the exploiters. In this so-called "examination," conducted at a moment when the worker was not really prepared, the labor contractor would tell several of his henchmen to lift up a heavy bag and drop it from high up onto the worker's body. If he managed to remain standing, he could stay and earn a living. But if he was smashed to the ground, then the labor contractor sent him away.

Sometimes the labor contractor could use the "examination" to exploit workers into working for no pay. He would tell the workers to work for two or three hours and that afterward he would select the "qualified" workers and take their names down for work tickets. Moreover, during this "examination" period, often the heaviest work was done. For instance, he would tell the workers to carry several hundred chin of Tsingtao salted fish. Sometimes workers who were somewhat weak physically, looking for work desperately, would work for two or three hours until they were exhausted and could work no longer. Then the labor contractor would not issue them a work ticket. They would not receive a penny, and the several hours' work would be in vain.

Even when a worker got a work ticket and worked a whole day, he still could not count on being paid. During the working periods, thoroughly wicked labor contractors would endlessly call the roll of workers to change their work tickets. Each time the ticket was changed, the old work ticket became useless and could not serve as a certificate for receipt of wages. There was no definite time for changing work tickets. On a single day it could happen four, five, or six times. At the time of the change, if the worker was at the urinal or simply failed to hear and did not change his work ticket, after work he could receive no wages. Moreover, each time the tickets were changed, some workers would be lost from the list, and as a result the labor contractor would disclaim the need to pay their wages.

Finally, after all this suffering, when a worker counted on his work ticket bringing him wages, the labor contractor had a hundred delays and schemes to keep from paying. For instance, when worker Lu Ch'ang-ken carried loads on a hot summer day with no shirt on, he had no place to put his work ticket, and all he could do was stick it in the waist of his trousers. But he did not foresee that the ticket would become soaked with sweat and so messed up that when he went to receive his wages, the labor contractor would say his work ticket was counterfeit and would refuse to pay his day's wages.

With these multiple hardships piling up each day, how much

money could anyone actually earn? The very mention of it is detestable, but the wages that the workers received were only the barest, pitiable remnants of what was left after the capitalists, compradors, and labor contractors had peeled off their shares. The wage system on the docks at that time was very confusing — in some cases it was based on a daily accounts breakdown, in some cases on piecework. It was very difficult to get any fixed calculations. Overall, before the War of Resistance against Japan when the value of currency was still relatively stable, an especially strong dock worker could earn about two hundred pieces of copper a day, or the equivalent of about six or seven ten-cent pieces. A worker of average strength could only earn about a hundred copper pieces, the equivalent of four or five ten-cent pieces. As for those workers without much strength, it was very hard to say. They did odds and ends, sometimes earning a few dozen copper pieces, sometimes less than a dozen. Furthermore, at that time the dock workers did not have work every day. In one month they might have worked at most ten days or so, each month earning at most only thirteen or fourteen yuan and as little as less than ten yuan. Out of this they still had to deduct expenses for such things as gifts for the labor contractors. It was very hard to maintain a family on what remained in light of the cost of goods at that time, and as a result their wages "didn't support the old and didn't support the young. They only supported one middle-aged person who didn't eat his fill." The sons and daughters of dock workers at that time had to go out and seek a livelihood at a very early age. Some went on the docks to become child laborers. Life for the child laborers on the docks was not easy, but their income was extremely low. For instance, dragging along a bundle of palm leaf fans which weighed somewhat under a hundred chin only fetched them a couple of copper pieces. Dragging a hundred bundles only brought them twenty copper pieces. Another example is rolling oil barrels. Rolling one barrel of oil brought two or three copper pieces. In one day, they could only roll twenty copper pieces worth at most, which was only enough to buy a few large biscuits. Speaking of rolling barrels of oil, it was a truly difficult task. The barrels of oil weighed several hundred chin, and the paths on the docks were not very level. They went up and down, up and down, with pits and ditches. Rolling the barrels took a great deal of energy. On a summer day, the oil barrels were heated by the sun until they were like flatirons and burned the hands. On a winter day, ice formed on the outside of the oil barrel so that when hands pushed it, skin stuck to the sides of the barrel. Some children went to the docks to sift coal. They sifted for more than ten hours a day, but they only earned about ten copper pieces, which at that time was only equal to one ten-cent piece at most.

At the time of the War of Resistance Against Japan, the situation was even worse. The price of goods was rapidly rising, and the little money that the workers received was of even less use. Before 1940 a dock worker could get one, two, or three dollars [k'uai-ch'ien] for a day's work, but real wages at that time had already declined greatly and were not worth even a few prewar ten-cent pieces. In the aftermath of the War of Resistance, work on the docks became more and more scarce, while the price of goods became more and more expensive. There was no way to calculate the value of one's wages. The most one could accumulate in a day was enough for one or two chin of things like cornmeal, cracked wheat, beans, and mixed dry goods, all moldy and rotten. After the victory in the War of Resistance, the price of goods climbed indescribably. Sometimes the labor contractors simply did not distribute wages. When accounts were figured up, they bought some cigarettes and fruit candy with the money and gave each worker a few cigarettes or a few pieces of fruit candy, and that was considered their wages. The workers who received this could neither laugh nor cry. They did not know how they could feed their families.

The exploiters on the docks exploited the workers with such cruelty, yet they still said: "The workers can't have any more provisions. Once they eat their fill they're not willing to work." These blood-sucking demons, according to this man-eating principle, used hunger to compel the workers to barter their lives away.

IV. A Sad Life

Under the heavy exploitation of the foreign bosses and the Chinese capitalists, compradors, and labor contractors, the result of the dock workers' expenditure of blood and sweat was only the tiniest, pitiable wages. Basically they could not even maintain the very lowest standard of living nor make any living to speak of. Therefore, the dock workers of that era often said, "You carry the packages to the shore, but if you don't eat bean refuse and vegetable skins, then you have to beg for food."

Bean refuse and vegetable skins were the dock workers' usual foods. Besides these, there were also moldy, worm-ridden cornmeal and bran which were boiled with the vegetable skins they picked up and turned into one awful mess. They had two meals of that each day. Sometimes they could buy some cracked wheat or else sweep up the wheat dropped on the floor of the docks, bring it back, and boil it into a gruel. That was considered the very best eating. When there was no work, they stopped cooking and cut down on their meals. They often did not take down the cooking pot for several days. As the days lengthened, the only thing to do was go into the streets and beg for food. The worker Hsü Yü-ts'ai had once been injured while working. He had to lie at home and could make no living at all. The only thing that could be done was to have his mother go out each day and beg for food. Usually she begged as late as midnight before she had something she could bring home with her. Sometimes the begging brought in nothing, and all they could do was suffer with their hunger. Situations like this were very common among dock workers.

Dock workers all worked and ate on a day-to-day basis. They had breakfast but no dinner and at least half the time had no provisions for their families at all. Early each day they would get up and go to the docks with empty stomachs. They would wait to receive a work ticket, and only then could they go to the vendor at the entrance to the docks and buy a large biscuit on credit. Once they ate it, they had enough energy to work. If they did not get a work ticket, they had no hope of getting work on that day, and the vendor was not willing to give them credit.

Under these circumstances, it was hard enough for a worker to make enough to supply just his needs alone. Workers with families found life that much more difficult. As a result, "the robust man cannot provide for a family of three; his wife gathers vegetable skins, and his son picks up odds and ends." Once there was an old worker named Wang who worked on the docks before the liberation. His wife worked at the Ta Feng textile factory. Even so, they could not support their two small children and had to give them away.

Both hungry and cold, the dock workers could neither satisfy their hunger nor have enough clothes to cover themselves. All year they wore "old caps shredded like blossoming flowers on their heads, clothes patched together like the Eight Trigrams on their bodies, and ruined shoes held together by golden threads of rope on their feet." The so-called "Eight Trigrams garments" consisted of several ragged pieces of cloth stitched together. No matter if it was winter or summer, a dock worker had only this one ragged set of clothes to wear. One old worker wore a single pair of pants for more than twenty years. If a hole appeared in one patch, he would sew another patch on it, but a hole would appear in that patch, until who knows how many layers of cloth there were. From being patched up too much, that one pair of pants weighed 4½ chin. Another old worker wore a tattered lined jacket for twenty-eight years. There was also an old worker who, at age nineteen (in 1927), spent more than two hundred coppers in a used clothing store to buy a used cotton jacket and wore it straight through to the liberation, twenty-three years in all. In those days, there were not many dock workers who had cotton-lined clothes to wear in the winter. Generally, two pairs of unlined pants were worn through the winter, but if one had tattered hemp bags to wrap around himself, he was considered well off. Sometimes when a worker was so frozen he could not stand it, his only recourse was to take rice straw and wrap it around the legs of his pants in order to fend off the cold. The whole year workers went barefooted. Usually they had to keep their pair of straw sandals, which they bought for a few copper pieces, in their waistband until they had some work to do. The sandals were valued just as if they were really treasures like the "golden-threaded shoes." When the straw sandals wore out, the workers could not take them off and throw them away but had to go out and find straw twine to patch them up so they could be worn again. Thus, the workers at that time, when they had nothing else to do, sat down and repaired their sandals.

Clothing and sandals were never sufficient, but bedding was not even worth mentioning. Most dock workers generally had no cotton bedding. In winter, if they did not cover themselves with sacks full of holes, all they had was their own "Eight Trigrams coats." And those who had cotton quilting had little more than a pile of refuse cotton full of holes. It did not cover a man. It could not ward off the cold or protect him from the wind. For instance, in the family of a worker named Hsü there were seven children and adults, all sharing one rotten bit of refuse cotton as a quilt. If someone was covered, someone else was cold. If it was warm here, it was cold over there. Or, for another example, the rotten cotton quilt of a worker named Wang was used for more than thirty years because he could never afford to get another.

The problem of housing was even more difficult. In old Shanghai, land went for astronomical prices, and although there was plenty of housing, there was no place for a dock worker. Many workers had to sleep in the streets out in the open "with the blue sky as a roof and their backbones as mattresses." At that time, the Chin-ling [Nanking] East Road near Shihliupoo was a place where many dock workers roosted at night. For seven or eight years before the liberation, one worker named Liu slept on the sidewalk of the Chin-ling East Road. Immediately after the liberation, he was finally able to move into a house for the first time. Above the sidewalks on both sides of the Chin-ling East Road there were stables which warded off the wind and rain, so it became a good spot for workers to sleep outdoors. If one went there early and found a place to lie along the foot of the stable wall, one could minimize the effects of the wind and rain as well as the booted feet of the foreign police. But if one arrived late, all that could be done was to sleep along the side of the road and not only be blown by the wind and soaked by the rain but also be kicked by the big boots of the foreign police. If there was a typhoon and flood, the road would be filled with deep water, and no one could sleep but had to stand in the water and wait for daybreak.

When winter came, it was even harder to sleep on the road. All the workers could do was crowd into public toilets and spend the night there, avoiding the wind and snow. At that time, the public toilets near the docks were completely filled with dock workers each winter. For instance, the worker Liu Chih-k'ang lived in the toilet outside the Pai-tu Bridge for four whole years, from age twelve to age sixteen. But the number of public toilets before the liberation was very limited — how many dock workers could they accommodate? The only thing most workers could do was hold fast to their places along the side of the road. Each time cold air came south, many men froze to death. Hsia Hsiao-szu-tzu [Little Number Four Son Hsia], who worked on the Kung Ho Hsiang Docks for forty years, froze to death in 1948 at the entrance to Yung-ting Road during a great snowstorm.

Some workers with families built grass huts along uncultivated parts of the riverbank and called these "home." Before the liberation, the Pootung and Yangshupoo banks were lined with these ramshackle homes, and many of them were dock workers' residences. In these shanty districts, there were garbage piles, swamps, foul-smelling ditches, and scattered graves everywhere. Disease was rampant. The environment was extremely bad. The grass huts in which the dock workers lived could withstand neither sun nor rain. They were simply unfit for habitation, looking like low, short "dragons rolling in the earth." Some of these "rolling dragons" did not even have doors. A shoulder cloth was attached to the head of the "rolling dragon," and they called that a door. The worker Hsü Yü-ts'ai used reeds to build a little hut in the shape of a scholar's hat right outside the brick wall of a dock toilet. His family lived there. In the summer it was foul smelling and oppressive, and in winter one's whole body froze stiff. Sometimes ice formed on the floor, and they could not sleep. All the family could do was huddle together and try to warm the air around them.

Some workers spent money to rent lodgings, but the situation there was evidently no better than in the straw shacks. For instance, the worker Ch'en Chin-hua lived with seven other men. Eight men in all had to squeeze into only one little loft. If one of them went to the toilet in the middle of the night, he returned to find there was not even a place to put his foot. The worker Li Lin-ken lived with eight members of his family in one loft.

A small labor contractor would often recruit some particularly strong workers to live in his own house and would use them as key workers whom he controlled; that is, they would serve as his basic capital in carrying out jobs for the large labor contractors. Each time a dock had to have workers to load and unload, the large labor contractors would order men from the small labor contractor, and the small labor contractor would have the workers who lived in his house go out and work. No matter if it was clear or rainy, cold or sunny, no matter if there was a typhoon or snowstorm, once the small labor contractor gave the word, the workers had to go to the docks and risk their lives. The wages they received were even smaller than those of the other men. The workers who lived in the small labor contractor's house had to pay for their board, and this was just one more form of exploitation. For instance, before the War of Resistance, workers who lived with their labor contractor had to pay fifty copper pieces a day for their board, for which the labor contractor supplied a few meager and foul-smelling salted vegetables. Each day's ration was worth at the most about twenty pieces of copper. Besides this, the labor contractor also took a percentage of the winnings in regular gambling sessions. He forced the workers to gamble. If someone refused to gamble, he was driven out the door and told he could no longer live there. As a result, everyone always lost — the only one who won was the labor contractor.

The workers allowed to live with the small labor contractor

were those with some strength, those who could do the work. When a worker became old and lost his strength and could no longer be a useful object for exploitation, he was pushed out the door without the slightest bit of sympathy. For example, two brothers, workers Li Ta and Li Erh, lived in a small labor contractor's home from the time they were young men. But they became old and could not do the work. On a cold December day, the two old men, both sick, were thrown out the door by the small labor contractor.

Before the liberation, dock workers did the work of beasts, but the lives they led were not like those of beasts. The workers' lives were worse — they suffered far more injuries, and there was also naturally a great deal of disease. At that time the dock workers' general occupational diseases included: stomach illnesses, hernia, serious expansion of veins in the lower limbs, asthma, bronchitis, high blood pressure, tuberculosis, swelling of the joints, and so on. Moreover, a worker often suffered from several diseases at the same time. At that time, when a worker got sick, he had no money for medical treatment. "The doors of the hospitals are only partly open. Those who are sick but have no money — do not enter" — this was of course often heard. As a result of the oppression of those both sick and poor, the death rate was very high.

The death rate among the sons and daughters of the dock workers was even higher. If one had two children, one of them would not live. Some workers had seven or eight children, and only one or two survived. Sometimes not a single one survived. As for the dock workers' children that lived, as soon as they could understand anything, they had to strive to support themselves. Naturally there was no point in talking about their learning to read or write. They and their parents were alike in that the great majority of them were illiterate.

The life of the dock worker before the liberation was tragic. All human rights were taken from him, and from generation to generation he suffered endless agony.

4

Maniacal Blood Debts — Class Persecution

I. Demons and Serpents on the Docks

The Shanghai Harbor docks were a black hell before the liberation. The dock workers were not only the victims of severe exploitation, but they also suffered maniacal persecution. The class enemy, in order to maintain this dog-eat-dog system of exploitation, crushed any worker resistance and carried on an extraordinarily cruel and vindictive, bloody system of control. These enemies built up a blood debt to the dock workers of old Shanghai which accumulated steadily. On the docks at that time, the local bullies had formed gangs. They usurped authority and acted against the law. It was a dark and gloomy world. This evil domination was, of course, inseparable from the class exploitation and class oppression of the old society.

In colonial and semicolonial old Shanghai, the greatest exploiter on the docks was imperialism. Imperialism headed all the evil forces in old Shanghai. All the evil men and events on the docks at that time had something to do with imperialism. Therefore, imperialism was the chief enemy of the dock workers of old Shanghai and was the chief offender oppressing and persecuting the dock workers.

Old Shanghai was an important base for imperialist aggression against China. There the imperialists had set up a whole choking structure for colonial domination, including police stations. They posted marines and plotted to use military power to protect the aggressors' interests. Since the docks were tools for the imperialists to carry out aggression, they were of course

"Hsüeh chi — feng-mang ti chieh-chi po-hai."

subject to the imperialists' armed "protection." Actually, at that time whenever anti-imperialist activity took place in any part of Shanghai or when the dock workers went on strike to oppose exploitation and oppression, the bosses of the foreign commercial docks immediately called for imperialist warships to come in and anchor off a nearby riverbank. They rattled their sabers and made faces to intimidate and suppress the people and dock workers of Shanghai. In addition, the foreign police immediately went to the docks and arrested, beat, and slaughtered workers at will.

During the period when the Japanese aggressors occupied Shanghai, the Japanese soldiers stationed at each dock were even more likely to murder workers arbitrarily. They committed innumerable terrifying, cruel, and vindictive acts. After the victory in the War of Resistance against Japan, the American imperialists took the place of the Japanese imperialists. On the Dollar, Kung Ho Hsiang, and other docks, the extensive American military police and the American shore patrol supervised and persecuted the dock workers.

The imperialists also used their loyal lackeys, the compradors, to strengthen their cruel and vindictive domination of the dock workers. Those compradors who concurrently acted as chief labor contractors were even more nakedly vicious and savagely oppressed the dock workers.

Besides these, there was a group of stooges retained by the imperialists as night watchmen and guards. These loyal hired ruffians acted tyrannously on the docks, oppressing and mistreating the workers at will.

Sometimes imperialists at the foreign commercial docks took a direct hand in persecuting the workers. For example, before the War of Resistance, the American President Line's ticket department chief McCarthy [Mai-chia-se] lived in a Western-style house on the riverfront of the Dollar Docks while recovering from an illness. He was bored, so he went to the entrance to the docks and conducted a search of the workers, forcing the men to take off their clothing and stand in a line so he could make the search. This stirred up the workers' resistance.

The imperialists and the Chinese reactionaries always conspired and worked together. The reactionary police department habitually carried out the foreigners' orders and happily served as lackeys of imperialism. They served the foreign bosses so faithfully that the minute they received a telephone call from the foreign bosses they would dispatch a large group of policemen to suppress and arrest workers.

As has been said above, in old Shanghai the docks operated by the imperialists were not the only ones under direct control of foreign bosses. The docks operated by the Chinese capitalists often also used the power of imperialism to oppress the workers. They unpityingly spared no expense to hire foreigners to serve as dock managers, and they asked a foreign business house to act as their agent. The bureaucratic capitalist China Merchants Steamship Company once had an American dock boss named Kagen [K'ai-ken] who was especially vicious toward the workers on the docks. When he walked along the road, if people were not careful to stay out of his way, he would viciously kick them out of his way without a word. The workers hated him with every bone in their bodies.

The imperialists, compradors, and Chinese capitalists all endorsed the feudal leadership system. In this system, the labor contractors directly carried out the bloody domination of the dock workers. For instance, a labor contractor for the Dollar Docks, Chia Sheng-fa, was originally a local hoodlum. When the Dollar Docks began to be built, he worked as an agent for the American imperialists. He helped the foreign bosses residing in that area to carry out intimidation, oppression, utilization, and exploitation, and to steal outright a great slice of territory. In this way, he curried favor with the American chiefs and became the principal labor contractor for the Dollar Docks, establishing "Chia Fu-chi's Shoulder Carriers Accounts Office." He rode the workers' backs, being lenient and severe in turn. His son, Chia Po-hsing, later inherited the chief labor contractor job and carried on as a loyal lackey of the American imperialists. Chia Po-hsing once took a trip to America with the comprador of the Dollar Steamship Company and studied

American-style "culture." Afterward he treated his workers with twice as much brutality and viciousness and labored for the American chiefs even more slavishly.

To take another example, the two Ch'en brothers, who were chief labor contractors for the Fu An Transfer Company, were completely dependent on English imperialism. In league with the manager of the Yi Ho Yang Company's shipping department, they grabbed loading and unloading jobs on the Kung Ho Hsiang Docks and other docks and accumulated an enormous pile of blood-soaked riches. The labor contractor for the Japanese commercial Ta-fan Docks, Li Jung-luan, depended on the power of Japanese imperialism. He toadied to the Japanese commercial Ta-fan Company manager, Ku-ch'i ts'u-lang, and grabbed the transfer jobs on the Ta-fan Docks.

A great many labor contractors also served as hatchetmen for the imperialist colonial rulers. For example, the labor contractor for a dock in the Shihliupoo area, Chu Te-piao, served before the War of Resistance as an "informer" for the "French Concession" police. During the period of the Japanese puppet government, he also served as an intelligence agent for the high command of the Japanese Army's military police. The Ta-ta Docks labor contractor Ch'in Shu-ming, while the Japanese aggressors occupied Shanghai, served as an intelligence organization leader, detective, and antismuggling chief. Other feudal bosses also abused their power and oppressed the dock workers in league with the imperialist powers.

Next, the labor contractors used the evil power of hoodlum gang organizations to persecute the workers. The docks of old Shanghai Harbor had a well-known gangster underworld. Lording it over all the docks were a few truculent, cruel gang chiefs. Through the feudal clique system, labor contractors were allied with a group of rogues, relying on the powerful gangster chiefs and using these "godfathers" as their patrons. Some of the labor contractors, such as Huang Chin-jung, Tu Ming-sheng, Chang Hsiao-lin and others, were apprentices to the gangster bosses. At the same time, they themselves expanded their power, hauling in many "disciples" to serve as their own henchmen.

For instance, a chief labor contractor in the Soochow River area, an evil bully named Hsia Chin-shan and nicknamed "commander in chief of the labor contractors," was a famous gangster leader who had a large group of henchmen working for him.

These criminals relied on the evil power of the gangs. They habitually did evil things and abused the workers. In league with people above and below them, they held a tight grip on the docks, each maintaining their despotism in one area and forming several "feudal kingdoms." On the eve of the liberation, the 266 Shanghai Harbor docks were controlled by various major and minor gangster chiefs — "a tiger on top of each mountain" — each having his own turf. On their own turf, the bosses were local emperors. Furthermore, by the tradition of the times, some sons succeeded their fathers, and some disciples succeeded their mentors. Sometimes both would accumulate disciples and engage in armed conflict to seize the turf. These bosses, on every level, major or minor, blatantly "opened the temple to receive their disciples." They broadened their personal power and protected their exploitative positions. Generally people like second and third class labor contractors and foremen served as the apprentices and underapprentices of the great bosses. They even coerced some of the workers to participate in the gang and attempted to use the gang organization's so-called "law of the gang" and "law of the family" to suppress any resistance by the workers. At the same time, they extorted gifts on the pretext of "paying respects to the master" — fulfilling the ordinary obligations to a superior. This raised the exploitation of the workers to a new level. In addition to this, the feudal bosses on the docks tried as hard as they could to develop all sorts of hoodlum bands and expand their own power. The docks at that time were full of all sorts of strange-sounding and terribly ugly names, such as the "Thirty-six-man Party," the "Twenty-eight-man Party," the "Five Tigers and One Leopard," the "Nine Dragons," the "Thirteen Guardians," the "Eight Big Demons and the Eight Little Ghosts," the "Southern Despot," the "Northern Despot," the "Thin Knife Gang," and so on. All operated on the docks.

The gangster bosses usually used feudal superstitions to control the workers. For instance, the chief investigator for the Kung Ho Hsiang Docks, Yü Shou-huan, set up a "Good Fortune Chapel," a "Good Luck Chapel," a "Common Origin Chapel," and other superstitious organizations in the Pootung area. On the pretext of bringing in more disciples, he collected more than a hundred henchmen. For another example, the boss of the Tata Docks Baggage Company called the baggage workers from the docks together at Pootung for a mass service in a temple on the twenty-fourth day of every twelfth lunar month. This was called "drinking to their unity." According to the usual rites for divining the future, the boss, as chief of the group, asked how their solidarity would fare in the coming year. This gave him an opportunity to talk rubbish like "families have a head; temples have a priest," using the occasion as a pretext to mislead the workers and solidify his own feudal control.

On the other hand, the feudal bosses also used provincial attitudes to subjugate the workers. Several home-area fraternal organizations had been founded which honored one's native place. Whether it was the Hupei Society, the Ningpo Society, the Yen-ch'eng Society, the T'ung-chou Society, or whatever, each area had a society, and antagonism grew among them. This resulted in the phenomenon of division among the workers, even to the point of instigating the workers to fight with one another. This was even more convenient for the bosses' manipulative control. This local-area solidarity was the backdrop for the power of the feudal gangs. The heads of the local-area factions were also gang leaders. Thus, the feudal gangs were a principal mainstay of reactionary control on the docks of the old society. They were an important tool for the exploiter classes' class oppression of the dock workers.

In addition, the labor contractors were intimately associated with the power of the reactionary spies. For example, the Dollar Docks labor contractor we have spoken of previously, Chia Po-hsing, was not only a labor contractor and an imperialist lackey but also held a string of official titles in the reactionary government. He began participating in Kuomintang reactionary organizations in 1936. He served as a member of the Kuomintang Shanghai "Dock Regulation Committee." In 1941 during the period of the Japanese imperialist war of aggression against China, he collaborated with the Japanese military police officer Ku-k'ou shao-tso, the traitor Ch'en Ya-fu, and others to organize the "Shanghai Dock Labor Mutual Aid Society" and served as its general manager. Afterward, he also served as head of the service department in the Social Bureau of Wang Ching-wei's puppet government. After the Japanese surrender, Chia Po-hsing collaborated with one other labor contractor and with Wang I-te, the Kuomintang district secretary, to organize a Kuomintang party branch in Pootung's Pai-lien-ching area. In 1946 he took a hand in organizing a volunteer marine patrol, appointing himself its overseer. In 1947 he served as the principal committee member of the "Dock Workers Welfare Committee" of the Kuomintang Social Bureau office. He concurrently served as an administrative officer of the Kuomintang Shanghai bureau's fifty-eighth section which was responsible for the docks. He also campaigned for the "National Representative Assembly." You can see that Chia Po-hsing did not only use his status as a labor contractor and imperialist lackey to oppress and abuse the dock workers. He was also an official for the Kuomintang reactionaries.

After the victory in the War of Resistance, the Kuomintang Shanghai Customs House took over the Japanese imperialists' Whangpoo Docks and assumed the exploitative position of the Asian foreign bosses. At the same time, they abolished the comprador system and contracted out the job of dispensing the dock loading and unloading work to a "marketing company." The people behind this "marketing company" included high officials of the Kuomintang Shanghai Customs House and the great gangster chief (the boss of the T'ien-shan Theatre) Ku Chu-hsuan. Together they inherited the positions of the compradors and chief labor contractors of the days when the Japanese imperialists occupied the docks. They continued to oppress and exploit the dock workers.

The Kuomintang reactionary spy organization's relationship with the bosses on the docks was extremely close. Many of the bosses, major and minor, were also spies. For instance, the southside despot, bandit, and labor contractor Ch'in Shu-ming at the beginning catered to the French imperialists and worked behind the scenes in collaboration with the inspector of the "French Concession" police. After that he transferred his allegiance to the intelligence director for the Japanese aggressors. After the Japanese aggressors surrendered, he transferred his allegiance to the justice director of the Kuomintang police department, Chou Kuang-hui, taking this man as his "godfather" and becoming a "high official in the transition of power." Moreover, he participated in the Chiang bandits' spy organization and was an investigator for the Central Control Bureau. He was nicknamed "the old man of the three dynasties," and he habitually followed his whims on the docks, being alternatively lenient and harsh and abusing the workers. His offenses mounted to heaven. For another example take T'ien Yung-fu, the labor contractor who served as an interpreter for the Japanese military police during the occupation by the Japanese aggressors. After the Japanese aggressors surrendered, he went over to the side of the Chiang bandit spies and served as intelligence director for the Seventh Battalion of the Kuomintang Sung-hu vigilante command. The boss of the Pootung Kung Ho Hsiang Docks, Ch'en Sheng-t'ang, worked as an investigator for the Chiang bandits' Central Control Bureau. He served under the command of Lu Ching-shih, the chief of spies, and worked as chief of the spy organization's "work protection division." He was a sinister, evil man and was nicknamed "marshal of the vultures." A Pootung labor contractor named Ch'iu An-t'ai was originally a pirate but afterward became an official and served as head of the commando organization of the Wang Ching-wei puppet government spy organization's "Number Seventy-six" intelligence unit. After the surrender of the Japanese aggressors, he went over to the side of the Chiang bandit clique and worked with the security bureau of the spy organization. He served as chief of the marine investigations battalion, as chief of the work protection group, and also as investigator for the Sung-hu vigilante command and a member of the Kuomintang district office executive committee.

On the docks at that time, in addition to central control, military control, and other parts of the professional spy system, there were also the so-called "work protection group," "renovation society," and other reactionary organizations, not to mention the Kuomintang itself and the San-ch'ing t'uan. The great majority of the major and minor labor contractors and their henchmen and lackeys participated in these organizations. For instance, the chief labor contractor for the China Merchants Steamship Company Docks in the Shihliupoo area, Pao Ch'ao-yun, participated in the Kuomintang, the "Hsing-Chung hsieh-hui" [Prosperous China Society], the "Hsieh-i she" [Heroes Society], the "Ch'un-i she" [Purity Society], and the "Hu-kung tui" [Work Protection Society]. The "dock runners" under his control, all comparatively young, joined the "Hu-kung tui," and Pao Ch'ao-yun's nephew headed the organization, with his second-grade labor contractor's son as second in command.

These bandit despots, working in collaboration with reactionary spies, used each other to expand the fires of their tyranny. As ferocious as tigers on the docks, they abused the workers. Sometimes, the spy apparatus also used this group of despots on the docks to suppress the revolutionary movements of that day. For instance, in March 1947 Ch'in Shu-ming gained control of the Kuomintang Sung-hu vigilante command. He gathered a large group of hoodlums who rushed into T'ung-chi University in the middle of the night and beat and arrested the patriotic students. In 1948 T'ien Yung-fu, leading more than forty of his henchmen, destroyed the student movement at Chiao-t'ung University. Another labor contractor, Chu Te-piao, hired some hatchetmen for the reactionaries — at a price of one peck of rice per man — and sent them to Chiao-t'ung University where they beat up patriotic students.

Before the liberation, the docks were infested with these demons and serpents who, in collaboration with each other, bore down on the workers and for a long time carried out ferocious class persecution. The dock workers' hatred of them was as deep as the sea and as heavy as a mountain.

II. A Deep, Bloody Hatred That Can Never Be Forgotten

It was the usual thing in old Shanghai for the dock workers to be scolded and beaten. At that time, the most common forms of persecution were beatings with fists, feet, or whips. Although the foreign bosses and capitalists hid behind the scenes and very few of them personally lifted a hand, there was not a single labor contractor, guard, or whoever was acting as their henchman who had not, under their orders, beaten up workers. For instance, Chang Chih-fa, the labor contractor of the Kung Ho Hsiang Docks on the Poohsi bank, ordinarily carried a bamboo switch on the docks. He would not let the workers rest, and if he saw the work slowing down, he would strike out with the switch. In order to give the workers unusually cruel beatings, he would usually wear extremely heavy gold rings on his hands. When he struck a worker in the face, the whole side of his head would be bloodied. Chu Te-piao, the labor contractor for the docks in the Shihliupoo area, usually carried a pistol on the docks and wielded a cowhide whip. He supervised the workers on the job and unnecessarily struck them with his fist. He used to say he punched with 200-pound fists. After he had punched a worker, he would viciously inquire, "How do you like that taste of my 200-pound fists?" Sometimes he would beat a worker's buttocks to a pulp and then apply salt to the wound, increasing the pain. It was an act of incomparable cruelty.

Under these conditions, dock workers were injured or killed in beatings innumerable times. For instance, a worker named Li on the Dollar Docks was kicked in the stomach by the labor contractor Chia Po-hsing because he picked up a couple of handfuls of rice that had fallen on the ground. He fell to the ground and could not move. He was carried home, but three days later he died. Or, for another example, a dock worker for the Tata Docks, Chi Shun-yung, pulled a hand truck on the docks.

One summer night in 1948, he took some goods to Chiang-wan for a younger brother of the labor contractor Chu Te-piao. By the time he made the delivery it was the middle of the night, already eleven o'clock, and Chi Shun-yung asked the labor contractor for a little money for dinner. Chu Te-piao's brother berated him in a loud voice and gave him a terrible beating. His whole face was bleeding, and he fell to the ground. A worker who had come with him put him on his wagon and pulled him back home. But Chi Shun-yung had suffered brain damage. From that time on he was a simpleton.

The hatred and abuse of the class enemy did not stop at striking workers with just fists and feet. There were other kinds of weapons. Besides the usual collection of whips and sticks, inside some whips were strips of lead and wrapped around some sticks were pieces of iron. When they struck someone, it was not a case of severed tendons or broken bones, but of serious internal injuries. Sometimes they even split open a worker's head and face using huge clubs, hand hooks, steel rods, and iron bars. Beating a worker to death was simply not a noteworthy occurrence. For instance, the Whangpoo Docks labor contractor P'eng K'un once said: "The boss has money for wages. There are able-bodied men in the jails. If we beat a worker to death, so what?" Wu Ta-t'ou, the chief of the guards for the China Merchants Steamship Company Docks, called over five henchmen when he wanted to beat up a worker. Four men held the worker's arms and legs, one man held the worker's head, and Wu himself, using a heavy, thick bamboo stick, smashed the man several times, quickly beating him to death. Then he tossed the body on the road. He personally beat several workers to death in this way.

These despots often hung workers up and beat them. Sometimes they would snap workers into manacles on an iron railing and then beat them to a pulp. Sometimes they would use rope to hang a worker from a tree or a utility pole by his two thumbs. They then flogged him continuously for several hours and let him hang there for a day. For instance, the Chung-Hua-nan Warehouse had a worker named Little Number Five [Hsiao wu-tzu] from Yangchow. Because the man picked up some coal scraps and was seen by the capitalist henchman in charge of the night watches, he was bound with his hands behind his back, hung from his hands at the gate to the dock, and beaten with a stick. After the beating, he could not work for two months and had to rely completely on others for sustenance. There was also a worker called Yang-tzu who was hung up and beaten at the Chung-Hua-nan Warehouse until his buttocks were bruised and swollen. His pants were so stuck to him that he could not take them off. He had to cut them off with a knife.

After a worker was beaten, he was usually thrown into a cell. Before the liberation, nearly every dock had a special little cell for keeping workers. For instance, the American Commercial Dollar Docks, besides having one public jail, also had a secret dungeon. The public jail was for prisoners arrested by the Kuomintang police and was called the police room. (This building is now a worker's bathhouse.) The other, secret, jail was located in the basement of an office building and served as a private dungeon on the docks. Innumerable workers were locked up in these two jails. After they were locked up, they had to pay a "fine" before they could go free. Workers without money would ask the labor contractor to pay the fine for them. In any case, the labor contractor could take the amount out of their wages, so there was no fear that the workers would not pay up. After being beaten, some workers were locked up for one, two, or three days. They were given no food or drink and were both cold and hungry. After a worker went free, he had to go right back to work. One worker named Ting Lao-i fainted from hunger after being locked up. His fine was paid for him, and he was set free, but he could not rest. He had to dash back immediately to the docks to work so he could earn some money to buy something to eat. Ignoring his hunger, he lifted the iron poles. Who knows how many men with empty stomachs, their legs weak and unable to hold themselves up, actually fell into the Whangpoo River and drowned.

There were several private dungeons on the Kung Ho Hsiang Docks: a small room in a building at the entrance of the Shang-chin Road Docks and a room at the east end of some sailors' quarters were both formerly dungeons where the American military police beat workers to force confessions out of them. There were also a place where the dock guards locked up and beat workers and a room where the labor contractors beat confessions out of them. After a worker had been locked in a cell, he was hung up and beaten and then locked with manacles to the bars on the cell window. After the victory in the War of Resistance, the Kung Ho Hsiang Docks also used bunkers filled with foul-smelling water which had been left behind by the Japanese aggressors as watery cells in which to lock up workers. At the T'aiku Docks underneath the Number Six Warehouse, there was also a watery dungeon. No matter whether the weather was cold or hot, the rowdies would tie workers down in foul water higher than their waists and then pour freezing water over them. The China Merchants Steamship Company Docks in the area of Shihliupoo also had several dungeons. They were called special rooms and were equipped with ropes and instruments of torture used to hang up and beat workers.

Sometimes, after a worker was locked up in one of the small disciplinary cells on the docks, he was sent to the reactionary government's prison to be locked up. There he suffered even worse persecution. For instance, during the period of rule by the enemy and its puppet government, a henchman of the Dollar Docks chief of watchmen, Cheng Liang-ts'ai, stole a client's large bundle of cotton and blamed it on three workers. He had them taken to the T'i-lan-ch'iao prison to be locked up for a long time. At that point, two of the men found a way to pay 100 yuan each and have themselves set free. The third worker had a wife and four children, all of whom depended on him, but he had no way to pay such a sum. He could not go free and as a result finally died in jail.

The imperialists treated the dock workers extremely cruelly, but during the period when the Japanese fascist aggressors occupied Shanghai, the slaughter suffered by the dock workers was even more severe than usual. After some workers were beaten but had not yet expired, they were dropped into the river by the barbaric Japanese soldiers and drowned. On the Ch'iu River Docks used by the Japanese army, a worker named Hung went to the toilet and was singled out for loafing on the job. They tied him to a piling underneath the dock. When the tide came in, he was not set free but drowned, kicking and screaming. Pootung's T'ung-t'ai Warehouse had a worker named Little T'ai-chou. Because he had tuberculosis, the Japanese aggressors finally took him to the middle of the river on a steam launch and threw him into the water. On the Hui-shan Docks, there once was a worker who was so fatigued that he could not move. The Japanese aggressors tied stones to his body and threw him into the Whangpoo River. The horribly evil Japanese aggressors thought up every possible way to torture workers. During the cruelest winter, they would tie a rope around a worker's waist and push him into the Whangpoo River. They would let the freezing river water soak him for several minutes, drag him back on shore, beat him with sticks, push him back into the water, and so on ten times or more until the torture brought on his death. In boiling hot summer weather, with the blazing sun hanging in the sky, the iron poles on the docks became burning hot. The Japanese aggressors would push workers onto the sun-heated iron poles to burn their skin. When the burned human skin fell off, it was just as if it had been scalded with boiling water. The Hsin-k'ai River area had a worker named La-wu-san-tzu who was arrested one summer by the Japanese aggressors. They peeled off his clothes and threw them on the ground. Then they pushed him onto the iron poles to burn. After his skin had burned, they pulled him up and flung him down again. They repeated this several times, so that his wounds were extraordinarily severe and he could not return to work for a long time. Sometimes the Japanese aggressors used mint leaves or opium to burn the workers' skin directly, so that several workers even today have the scars of those burns. On the Whangpoo Docks there is a worker named Ko who was hung up by Japanese soldiers and burned senseless with mint leaves many times.

In addition to this, there were several workers who were

stabbed to death by the bayonets of the Japanese aggressors, bitten to death by their mad dogs, or even buried alive. During the period of the Japanese occupation, on the I-t'ai-hsing-nan Warehouse Docks alone, the number of workers stabbed to death by bayonets reached more than 110. At the Lung-mao Warehouse there was a limestone pit. The Japanese army often threw workers into the pit and let them blister to death in the limestone paste. The Chung-Hua-nan Warehouse had a small group of carriers, perhaps 72 workers in all. During the period of the occupation more than 10 of them were buried alive.

In the period of the War of Resistance against Japan, the Japanese aggressors captured large groups of workers on the docks and sent them to the Northeast, Chekiang, or elsewhere as "laborers." Of the men who were seized, the vast majority were so badly treated that they died. Only a very small number of men was able to return. At that time, the labor contractors usually received money from the Japanese army. Under the guise of "enlisting laborers," these contractors tricked the workers for the benefit of the Japanese army. The workers did not know the exact details, so when the labor contractors asked for men to work, quite a few were fooled into accepting. After the workers were assembled, they were forcibly captured by the Japanese army. For instance, Chang Ch'ang-ken, an underling of labor contractor T'ien Yung-fu, at one point in 1939 tricked more than a hundred workers and turned them over to the Japanese army. They were sent to Chekiang, Ningpo, Hsiao-shan, and elsewhere to work, and in the end only about forty of them returned home.

After the victory in the War of Resistance, the American gangsters abused the workers on the docks at will with the same brutal violence used by the Japanese devils. One worker named Cheng, while at the entrance to the Hui-shan Docks, was struck in the eye and blinded for no reason by an American soldier. Old Yang, the boat loader, was once working on a boat when an American carelessly walked by and bumped into the chain hanging from Old Yang's loading pole, getting grease stains on his clothes. He took his anger out on Old Yang and had the watchmen on the dock beat him senseless. Then the American had him locked up in a small dungeon where he was tortured. There was also a worker named Hsü who, before the War of Resistance, had his two hands tied behind his back and was pushed into the Whangpoo River by Japanese soldiers. Fortunately, he was rescued by another worker. However, after the victory over the Japanese, he was arrested and locked up by the American military police who beat him until he fainted and died.

In the period of the War of Resistance, the dock workers were often seized by the Japanese army to be "laborers." After the victory in the War of Resistance, the Kuomintang reactionaries likewise used the pretext of "enlisting laborers" to trick large groups of workers for the American imperialists. They were sent to Ch'ung-sheng Island to handle the transshipment of the American army's "surplus goods." The workers who were tricked into this were locked in iron chains on the island and made to suffer the insults and harsh treatment of the American soldiers. Very few of them lived to return home.

To sum up, the persecution and destruction suffered by the dock workers before the liberation can be cited, but can never be described in full. The bloody facts forced the dock workers to realize that the imperialists and reactionaries were their deadly enemies and the only thing to do was to struggle resolutely against them.

III. The Resistance and Struggle of the Dock Workers

Where there is oppression, there is struggle. During the long period before the liberation when the Shanghai dock workers were under the bloody control of the imperialists and the class enemy inside the country, they were exploited and persecuted. They found it intolerable and carried out ceaseless and determined resistance and struggle against the imperialists and the domestic class enemy. Some of these struggles were locally conducted by only a small number of workers who directly opposed persecution and exploitation by the foreign bosses, compradors, Chinese capitalists, and labor contractors. In other instances, these struggles were carried on by the entire body of harbor workers in accordance with the revolutionary situation at that time. For instance, early in 1905 during the Shanghai people's patriotic anti-American movement, the dock workers of Shanghai Harbor plunged into this anti-American struggle and completely stopped the loading and unloading of American goods. Another example came after the explosion of the "May Fourth" Incident in 1919 when the Shanghai workers actively expanded and developed a vigorous and vital labor strike movement. At that point the boat workers left the boats and went ashore, and the dock workers stopped all loading and unloading. This forced the imperialist steamships to stop sailing completely. A large group of them lay anchored in the harbor and could not budge.

After the Chinese Communist Party was founded in 1921, it led the workers into a revolutionary struggle. It devoted all its efforts to organizing a workers' movement. At this time, the Party began work among the dock workers. It strengthened their leadership by dispatching several comrades to take charge of organizing a revolutionary movement among the dock workers. On the Whangpoo Docks, these comrades opened up a night school to teach worker culture and spread the message of the revolution. At the same time, they treated the workers' illnesses, asking them about their various ailments. This was the first time in history that the dock workers had received solicitude, instruction, and friendship. From that time on they had leaders. They saw a brilliant future before them and foresaw the direction of the struggle.

In 1925, the "May 30" Incident occurred. The English, Japanese, and American imperialists massacred Chinese workers and students and incited the wrath of the broad masses, who started a great wave of patriotic struggle. The Shanghai workers were on the very forefront of the struggle. They resolutely opposed the imperialists and carried out a general strike. More than twenty thousand dock workers throughout the harbor actively plunged into this struggle, joining demonstrations, supporting strikes, walking off the docks, and refusing to load or unload goods for any foreign steamer. They persisted for a long time and profoundly attacked imperialism. Many of the foreign steamers anchored in the harbor could not move. Their goods could not be unloaded, and the harbor could not be opened. The two English companies, Yiho and T'aiku, and the Japanese Jihching Company had more than sixty boats tied up. Although the foreign bosses on the docks tried every possible method of inducement and intimidation, they could not shake the dock workers' determination to struggle. For instance, at the Japanese commercial Huishan Docks was the Japanese steamship, "T'ai Ch'ien," carrying 2,400 tons of cotton yarn. The dock workers refused to unload it, so the imperialists used bribes, promising each man 3 yuan in wages; but the workers replied: "It is useless to talk about 3 yuan. If you gave each of us 300 yuan we still wouldn't go to work." To take another example, the Japanese commercial Whangpoo Docks at that time had fifty or sixty workers who had begun to strike. These Asiatic foreign bosses directed the labor contractor Yang Te-piao to order the lackeys under his control to close the iron gates on all four sides of the docks. Then he was to call in seventy or eighty henchmen to beat up several workers in an attempt to use violence to intimidate the workers into going back to work. But the workers not only did not submit, they resolutely left the docks. The scheme of the imperialists and their labor contractors could not be carried out. There was also the foreign boss of the English commercial Lanyents'ung Docks and his comprador, Yang Wei-pin, who went so far as to coerce workers to go back to work during the general strike. This led a large group of workers to rush onto the Lanyents'ung Docks to support the workers there in their refusal to go to work. After a struggle, the strike carried on as before.

While this was going on, the Chinese capitalists in the dock business were thinking only of their personal profits and actually pitilessly sold out their own people. In the midst of a great, surging people's anti-imperialist movement, they were growing increasingly intimate with the imperialists. They loaded and unloaded the struck foreign ships and destroyed the dock workers' strike. For instance, at the China Docks during the movement, they secretly loaded and unloaded coal ships numerous times to supply coal covertly to various imperialist enterprises. These docks also permitted the Japanese steamship "T'ien" to tie up there and, in collaboration with the reactionary police and the Feng-hsi warlord, forced the workers to unload the coal that the "T'ien" carried. These actions were repeatedly restrained by the masses of workers and forced the capitalists to notify the Japanese ships to anchor somewhere else.

The strike of the dock workers began in the latter part of May and persisted until the middle of August. It repeatedly laid waste to the sabotage of the imperialists and other reactionary powers and energetically supported the anti-imperialist struggle of all Shanghai's people. But the Shanghai Chamber of Commerce, representing the big bourgeoisie, intentionally held up the striking workers' relief funds, forcing tens of thousands of the dock workers to fall into difficult economic circumstances. Dock workers never knew where their next meal was coming from anyway. This just made their lives more unbearably difficult. But even at this point in the strike, they turned down the enemy's bribes and endured tremendous hardships. They made a great contribution to the revolutionary movement. The bourgeoisie, by selling out the movement through compromise, increased the suffering of the dock workers. But they still struggled resolutely until finally, by the decision of the General Transport Labor Council, all they could do was end the strike.

After the Northern Expedition began, the Shanghai workers carried out armed uprisings on three occasions. Some dock workers participated in each of the uprisings. Under the leadership of the Party, they actively made preparations for the uprisings. According to the Party's directions, they secretly transported rifles, axes, hand grenades, and other weapons to Pootung and hid them there. They covertly studied how to use them and prepared for the battle. As soon as each uprising began, they all immediately plunged into the battle and exhibited the revolutionary spirit of fearless sacrifice and heroic tenacity.

The third armed uprising which began on March 21, 1927, was carried out at various locations. Dock workers, cigarette factory workers, textile factory workers, and iron factory workers participated in the Pootung uprising — more than 110 of them. First of all they attacked Pootung's Number Three Police Station and the neighboring police sub-stations at Lu-chia-tsui, Hsin-san-ching, and Lao-san-ching. They grabbed a bunch of rifles, armed themselves, and thus increased their fighting ranks. Then, at Yang-chia-tu, they intercepted the reactionary warlord troops that were trying to board ships and escape. At this point, the English battleships on the west side even began firing their guns to support the reactionary troops and to try to intimidate the workers. But the workers remained calm and finally disarmed more than 10 reactionary warlord officers that were boarding two wooden rowboats in an attempt to escape. The officers were forced to surrender. At the same time, the dock workers inspection units at Kao-ch'ang Temple and South Station in the Lu-nan area and others in the vicinity of Lu-tung and Kang-k'ou acted in concert with the factory workers inspection unit and joined the battle. They attacked the enemy's police stations and sent men to relieve those fighting in the Cha-pei area. By coordinating with each other to wage a battle in the whole city, they seized a victory.

After the "April 12" counterrevolutionary coup d'état, a white terror swept the whole country, but the revolutionary fire was not extinguished — it could not be extinguished. The Shanghai dock workers, under the leadership of the Party and with the workers of the whole city, resolutely continued the difficult underground struggle.

In 1931 when the Japanese imperialists instigated the "September 18" Incident and forcibly occupied our country's northeast provinces, the Shanghai dock workers gave free reign to their elevated spirit of patriotism and carried out a great anti-Japanese strike. More than thirty-five thousand people participated in the strike. In 1932 when Shanghai exploded into the War of Resistance against Japan with the "January 28" Incident, the dock workers even more resolutely refused to unload Japanese imperialist munitions. At one point when a huge shipment of ammunition for the Japanese aggressor army arrived at the Huishan Docks, they could not find workers to unload it. Through Chang Chia-te, the labor contractor at the San-ching Warehouse, they lured some workers over to the Hui-shan Docks. But when the workers saw that it was a job unloading munitions, they would not do it. The labor contractor first tried giving each worker one yuan in liquor money. He promised each man ten yuan in wages after the unloading was finished, but the workers, even though they were clearly starving to death, still would not do it. Afterward the Japanese aggressor army also beat and imprisoned workers, adding to the intimidation, but the workers still refused to load and unload. Instead, they dispersed.

In 1937 after the War of Resistance against Japan had broken out everywhere, the Kuomintang armies in the lower reaches of the Yangtze dispersed and scattered over a thousand miles, giving up a large portion of national territory. The Japanese aggressor army occupied Shanghai, taking over all of Shanghai Harbor so that the difficulties of the dock workers became even more severe. But still, one way or another, they carried out all kinds of anti-Japanese activity. Although the workers' lives got worse and worse, in order to drag out the enemy's boat-loading time, they would often take work tickets but not go to work. For instance, one time two large ships — the "Feng-t'ien" and the "Tientsin" — tied up at the Whangpoo Docks. Very early in the morning the workers received their work tickets, but just before the work was to begin they dispersed in all directions. Thus there was no way to unload the two ships — they could not move. Sometimes the workers who ran the cranes would intentionally lose the steam in the engines so that the cranes could not move and the goods could not be unloaded. When workers were pressed into loading and unloading goods for the enemy, they would break the machinery, producing a loss for the enemy. Sometimes they would intentionally smash the boxes or use hand hooks to tear open packages. Or they might just throw goods into the Whangpoo River.

During the war, the dock workers regularly aided the underground agents of the New Fourth Army and transported a great many important goods to the liberated areas to support the War of Resistance. When the workers moved goods for the Japanese aggressor army, they would intentionally slow down the work or, ignoring the dangers, smash the goods.

After the victory in the War of Resistance against Japan, the Chiang bandits, with the support of the American imperialists, began a counterrevolutionary civil war against the people. The price of goods climbed daily, and the workers' lives became much more difficult. The dock workers, under the direction of the Party, carried out a whole series of strikes. For instance, the workers of Pootung's Tatong Docks, under the leadership of the underground Party branch, established a labor union and demanded increases in pay from the chief labor contractor, Chia Po-hsing. When the labor contractor did not respond, the workers went on strike. Everyone sat on the docks and did not lift a hand. When two large ships tied up at the docks, there was no one to unload them, and they could not move. The foreign bosses and the labor contractor became terribly agitated and tried to coerce the workers into starting work. The workers said, "We can't eat, so we can't work." The foreign bosses and the labor contractor, in collaboration with the Kuomintang reactionaries, brought in more than thirty armed police from the Yang-ssu station and set up two machine guns to intimidate the workers. There were originally forty or fifty armed guards at the docks, so now altogether there were seventy or eighty thugs, baring their fangs and encircling the docks. The workers, under the correct leadership of the Party, took no notice of this pompous but empty show of force. They merely said, "If you want us to work, raise our pay." After a day's confrontation, there was nothing the reactionaries could do. They could not delay the unloading of the two ships any longer, so they responded to the workers' demands and raised their pay 60 percent. The strike was victorious.

In addition, the Ch'iu-chiang, T'aiku, Kung Ho Hsiang, and other docks all had strikes. Even though imperialists and domestic reactionaries of all kinds came in to disrupt and intimidate the workers, they could not be suppressed. The labor contractor of the Tung-chia-tu Docks, Ts'ai Hsüeh-k'o, called to them contemptuously: "What strike? This is the New Fourth Army — arrest them!" But the workers paid no attention to this, and the strike continued on unabated.

The Shanghai dock workers, in the long period of putting the idea of struggle into practice and with the education of the Party, gradually came to understand that if the laboring people were to achieve their liberation, they had to go the way of armed struggle and overthrow reactionary control before they could gain the final victory. Because of this, in the War of Resistance against Japan and in the War of Liberation, quite a few dock workers hurried to the countryside to join the ranks of their own class — the New Fourth Army and, later, the Chinese People's Liberation Army.

On the eve of the liberation, the defeated armies of the Chiang bandits were jammed into Shanghai Harbor, for the Whangpoo River offered their only avenue of escape. Yet they not only wanted to use the harbor to save their lives, they also wanted to use it to take great loads of goods with them and then, at the very last, to block it up. At this time, under the direction of the Party, the dock workers began their "antiplunder, antidestruction" struggle. They organized inspection units and security units to protect the people's property and prevent the destruction. At the same time, they used the tactic of work slowdowns to delay the loading of the goods. The more anxious the enemy became, the less effort the workers made. When the bandit army beat people, they stopped work altogether and went on strike. There was nothing the reactionaries could do about this — all they could do was leave behind most of the goods and just try, helter skelter, to save themselves. For instance, on the Ch'iu River docks, a great deal of military equipment and weapons was left behind, and at the Kung Ho Hsiang and Dollar docks a large collection of disassembled aviation equipment — part of the American imperialists' aid to Chiang — was left behind.

The dock workers of Shanghai Harbor went through a long period in the oppressive grip of imperialism, feudalism, and bureaucratic capitalism. They were exploited and persecuted, but they carried on a long struggle and finally, in accordance with the development of the revolution throughout the country, they realized their hopes and won liberation.

5

The Docks Return to the Embrace of the People

I. Triumph over Adversity, Shatter the Blockade

In the spring of 1949 the War of Liberation was winning victory after victory. The Chiang bandits were disintegrating, fleeing helter skelter. On May 27 the Chinese People's Liberation Army liberated all of Shanghai. From then on, the dock workers of Shanghai harbor, along with all the laboring people of the city, were able to clear away the mists and see the sun. They stood up straight and began brand-new lives. However, in the first period of the liberation, the workers still encountered many difficulties that were fairly serious. To begin with, as those altogether vicious reactionaries fled, they had committed innumerable evil acts and had carried out terrible destruction throughout Shanghai harbor's entrance and docks. For instance, quite a few boats had been stolen, and many docks had been burned or knocked down. Next, as the War of Liberation continued through the south, the enemy, who was entrenched on the islands up and down the coast, still had not been completely subdued. Mines were strung out outside the mouth of the Yangtze River, and the American-Chiang planes still carried out repeated harassment bombings of Shanghai. They recklessly tried to block the harbor and hinder the restoration of communications and transport. Accordingly, to a certain degree this affected the effort to normalize transport to the harbor and the loading and unloading work. In addition to this, after so many years under the heel of the Japanese and American imperialists and the Kuomintang reactionaries, the whole country's fundamental

"Ma-t'ou hui-tao jen-min ti huai-pao."

nature had been greatly injured, and the economy was decrepit. In the first days of the liberation, production could not be immediately restored in all phases. Because of this, commerce in Shanghai harbor could not avoid suffering some bad effects. There was comparatively little loading and unloading work in the harbor. This set of circumstances forced the dock workers, who had just been liberated from a hard and bitter situation in the old society, to contend with great problems in their new lives.

However, under Chairman Mao's wise direction that "where there is difficulty, there is hope, and where there is hope, there is a way" and under the correct leadership of the Party and the people's government, the dock workers of the entire harbor united as if they were one. They struggled courageously and soon conquered their difficulties. They smashed the enemy's blockade and bombing strategy, persisted in the unloading and loading work, gave support to transport work, accelerated production, and won a great victory.

Not long after the liberation, unions were established on the docks, and many grassroots cell and branch organizations continued to be set up. The workers, with the education of the Party and the unions, continuously raised their consciousness, and their revolutionary enthusiasm rose to a new high. At the same time, the Party and the people's government became a good deal more concerned with all phases of the dock workers' lives. They organized the workers for mutual aid production. They mobilized some of the workers to return to their villages and participate in agricultural production. They also adopted such methods as giving work instead of direct relief and distributing relief grain in order to help the dock workers overcome their temporary difficulties. The dock workers, blessed with the friendship and solicitude of the Party, greatly increased their awareness and reciprocated the Party's kindness with real action.

At this time, Shanghai's most needed goods were coal and grain. The two items had to be supplied to all the city's factories and inhabitants each day. With the support of the entire nation, the coal and grain were soon flowing in from the Yangtze and its tributaries. The dock workers duly organized the unloading. They worked day and night. They labored unselfishly, and their efficiency greatly increased. The quality of the unloading work increased steadily. They coordinated the transport of goods and guaranteed that the entire city would be supplied with coal and grain in good time. They thus won the first battle after the liberation.

At this time, the American-Chiang bandit bombings and destruction were madly continuing, and the docks along both banks of the Whangpoo River became important targets for the enemy bombs. The docks at Pootung, Yang-ching Harbor, Hsin-hua, Chang-chia-peng, Poohsi Kao-yang Road, Shihliupoo, and other areas were all bombed. But the courageous dock workers were undaunted by the enemy's violence. On the contrary, the bombing created a great feeling of indignation and led the dock workers to respond resolutely to the shameless abuse of the enemy's airplanes. They ignored the dangers of the enemy air raids and continued to carry out their loading and unloading work. On the docks they began to set up an air defense system, using the coal piles as bunkers. They established fire and rescue brigades. They organized worker inspection units that helped the Liberation Army patrol stand watch and prevent further destruction by bandit saboteurs. During the enemy air raids, they employed every possible means to make sure that their loading and unloading work continued and that supplies for the needs of the military and the people were guaranteed.

In this struggle against blockades and bombing, dock workers everywhere shared high spirits and firm determination. Their courage increased a hundredfold, and there was also a manyfold increase in the rate of the unloading and loading work. For instance, the Hung-sheng Docks unloaded the "Chiang-shun-lun," which carried more than ten thousand bags of provisions, in only twelve hours, twice as fast as usual. Unloading more than two thousand tons of coal on a coal ship moored at Lao-pai-tu took one gang of workers only an hour, reducing the boat's usual anchorage time by six hours. Although March 1950 was the period of the most blatant air raid activity by the enemy, the amount of material brought into Shanghai then, compared to June 1949 just after the liberation, was 3.6 times as much. This brave struggle of the boat workers and dock workers had much to do with this. The American-Chiang conspiracy to bomb recklessly and blockade the harbor was completely smashed.

The dock workers not only struggled bravely on the docks, persisting in the loading and unloading, but they also nurtured a spirit of ruling their own country and stood ready to aid the other areas being bombed. For instance, in the "February 6" bombing of 1950, several harbor docks were bombed, and the Yangshupoo Power Plant located on the Whangpoo River was also bombed. More than five hundred dock workers immediately rushed to the power plant and aided the rescue efforts. The power plant's coal transmission machinery was damaged by the bombing, and this hindered the supplying of coal to the plant's furnace. The dock workers who were there for the rescue work immediately took special action and organized a pole-bearing crew to take coal up to a fourth-story platform. In good time, they supplied the power plant's furnace with the fuel it needed. They refused to eat or rest. While carrying the coal, they chewed large biscuits. By joining with their brother workers at the power plant, they soon restored electric power to the entire city.

During the year following the liberation, the dock workers passed a rigorous endurance test and revealed a high level of class consciousness. They made achievements in their loading and unloading work and established merit in the struggle against the enemy. At the same time, they received the unlimited care and consideration of the Party and the people's government and overcame the temporary difficulties of the early months of the liberation.

In May of 1950, the Chusan Islands were completely liberated. The Harbor Department in cooperation with the People's Navy cleaned the mines out of the mouth of the Yangtze River and cleared away all obstructions to navigation. This was of great benefit to the speedy restoration of marine commerce and led production in the harbor to develop steadily. In October 1950 the people's government also established the Shanghai Area Harbor Affairs Administrative Office in order to unify the administrative work at the harbor docks. Gradually the administration of the docks adopted regularized procedures. At the same time, under the direction of the Party's "Develop Production, Let the Economy Flourish" policy, production everywhere in the country was quickly restored, and the movement of commerce through Shanghai Harbor speedily increased. This accompanied a corresponding development of the loading and unloading work on the docks.

II. Struggle against Local Despots, Wipe out the Mass of Demons

In order for production to move forward on the docks, all the obstacles inherited from the old society still had to be removed. In particular, the feudal bosses, who for so long had cheated the workers and done all kinds of evil in collaboration with the imperialists and reactionaries, had to be cleaned out first of all. When the liberation took place, for a while nothing was done about the bosses and local despots who had originally held sway on the docks. For a short period of time, they remained at large and continued to exploit the workers. For instance, the T'aiku Docks labor contractor, Kuo Wei-shan, during the first period of the liberation was still embezzling about half of the workers' wages. In 1950 while taking responsibility for the loading and unloading of the "Chi-nan-lun," he extorted more than 1,100 yuan (old jen-min-pi) from three days' wages of three hundred workers. Ko Ch'un-fang and Ch'ien Jen-chieh, labor contractors for the Kuan-ch'iao-min-nan Docks, were still extorting more than 30 percent of the workers' wages. Some labor contractors even said to the workers, "You workers who are changing the social order cannot put yourselves above the labor contractor." They were blatantly ferocious. In addition to this, the American and Chiang reactionaries were not reconciled to being ousted from the Chinese mainland. Before their frantic escape, on the one hand they carried out mad destruction of the facilities in Shanghai Harbor, and on the other hand they arranged for large numbers of spies to infiltrate the country. Since the docks under the old society were the places where the reactionaries' power was the most ferocious, the docks made the most convenient hiding places for them. On the docks, large numbers of runaway landlords, disbanded troops, and bandit spies were hidden. In collaboration with the bosses and local despots who were there already, they made vain attempts to lay the groundwork for brash moves. They plotted further destruction.

This group of counterrevolutionaries hated the Communist Party and the laboring people with every bone in their bodies. Together with the American imperialists and the Chiang bandits they tried in vain to make a comeback and bring about the restoration of the black control that existed before the liberation. They wanted to ride anew on the backs of the workers, abuse their power tyrannically, and run roughshod over the people. At the beginning of the liberation, the managerial system they used on the docks temporarily still had not been formally changed. They not only continued to handle the loading and unloading work and engaged in extortion, but in many places they also carried out counterrevolutionary, destructive activities. They spread rumors and sowed seeds of discord in the relations between the workers and the Party, saying such things as "Chiang Kai-shek will come to Shanghai for the Mid-Autumn Festival." They pressured workers not to join labor unions. For instance, T'aiku Docks labor contractor Hsü Shih-lien said to workers who joined labor unions, "When the Kuomintang returns they'll cut off your heads." Some bosses even cried out, "Anyone who goes off with the labor union cadres will get a taste of my knife." Some counterrevolutionary elements even joined the union organizations and tried to take them over in order to carry out their destructive designs. For instance, the spy Yang Jun-sheng seized the position of chairman of the Whangpoo Dock Workers Union. Yü Hang dock boss and local despot Ch'in Shu-ming actually passed himself off as a liaison officer of the Shanghai

General Labor Union and plotted to manipulate the unions. Such men did not let the workers participate in political activities. They made havoc of the meetings the workers held. They kept the workers from participating in demonstrations, and they did not permit them to sing revolutionary songs. Feng Yang-lin, a boss on the T'aiku Docks, even instigated disturbances, had his henchmen beat up union cadres, and halted loading and unloading work on the docks for more than a day at a time. From June 1949 to November 1950 these counterrevolutionary elements provoked both large and small destructive incidents, more than four thousand of which have been recorded. Furthermore, they besieged unions and transport companies on more than eight occasions. During the "February 6" bombing of Shanghai by the Chiang bandits and when the American imperialists incited the war of aggression against Korea, this group of counterrevolutionaries and robbers became even more ferocious. For instance, T'ien Yung-fu, the labor contractor for the China Merchants Steamship Company's Number Three Dock, exacted a five-yuan "registration fee" from each worker and said, "The Kuomintang will have to return before we can give you any work to do." Some of these bosses also collected and made a list of names of military representatives and activists in preparation for a "settling of accounts" when the Chiang bandits returned.

The broad masses of dock workers could no longer endure the crimes of this group of bosses, despots, and counterrevolutionaries. They continually demanded that the unions and the people's government suppress and punish these reactionary bandits who were intent on harming the people and destroying the revolution. In order to completely uproot the feudal system of control on the docks, to consolidate the fruits of the revolutionary victory, to strike at counterrevolutionary powers, and to preserve the dock workers' livelihood and order and peace in society, the Party and the people's government actively supported the dock workers' demands. In March 1950 the Government Administrative Council of the Central People's Government promulgated its "Decision to Abolish the Feudal System of Control in All Areas of the Transport Industry." Beginning in the latter half of 1950, part of Shanghai Harbor's docks began a struggle against local despots under the leadership of the Party. In the spring of 1951, the struggle against local despots on the docks was united with the movement to suppress counterrevolutionaries and was developed everywhere. On a large scale, it purged the bosses, local despots, and all the counterrevolutionaries who had been entrenched for so long on the docks.

After the struggle against the local despots began, the hopes which the dock workers had nurtured for so many years were realized. The hatred they had nursed for generations approached a time of reckoning. They jubilantly ran around telling each other the good news, expressing their gratitude for the actions of the Party, actively accusing the local despots, bosses and counterrevolutionaries of their crimes, joyfully participating in the public trials, and supporting the people's government in its arrests and trials of these bandits. For instance, more than two hundred workers at the Pootung Kung Ho Hsiang Docks, after they heard the news that the public security office had arrested Ch'en Sheng-t'ang, the spy, despot, and boss of those docks, leapt with joy and said, "A thousand-chin load has been taken off our heads."

The dock workers, who had suffered the cruel persecution of the feudal bosses for such a long time, immediately demanded public trials for the bosses guilty of these most heinous crimes. They demanded to confront these bandits and charge them with their acts of wickedness. They demanded to pour out before the masses the bitter water accumulated in their hearts over so many years. Subsequently, the whole harbor waterfront was divided into four areas in which general accusation meetings were held. Altogether more than 15,700 people participated in this kind of severe class struggle. Several old workers told the meetings of the grievous history of exploitation, persecution, and humiliation which they had personally suffered under the local despot bosses. For example, a worker named Li made this charge against Whangpoo spy boss P'eng K'un: "In 1948, when I was a luggage carrier, P'eng K'un's father, son, and several others rode hard on me and beat me about the head until my blood flowed and I blacked out. I suffered severe head injuries and could not work, causing great harm to my family of seven who had no means of support." A brother of worker Chin A-mao accused P'u-tung local despot boss Kuo Ping-hsuan of repeatedly kicking and then beating his little brother, Chin A-mao, to death with three carrying poles. At the meeting, one worker's wife retold with great pain and tears how Kuo Ping-hsuan locked her husband, Chu Ta-hai, in a cell and beat him to death. He frightened her father so much that he died. Kuo also appropriated everything left in their home, so that their two children starved to death. This family of five suffered so much that only she remained alive. Then Kuo Ping-hsuan seized the worker's wife herself. These awful crimes made the whole crowd gnash their teeth in anger.

The Kung Ho Hsiang Docks general boss, Chang Chih-fa, was also brought before the mass tribunal. A worker named Yü accused Chang Chih-fa of taking his wife and mother and beating his father to death on the road. His mother was so ill-treated that she perished. Another local despot boss, Ho Cheng-sung, not only committed bloody crimes before the liberation, but after the liberation he secretly hurried to Chusan Island, which at that time was still occupied by the American-Chiang clique, and made contact with the bandit spies. After he returned, he spread rumors and put up reactionary posters. The crimes of these counterrevolutionaries were all soon exposed by the masses.

After the public tribunals, the feelings of the workers intensified tremendously, and in great numbers they demanded to accuse the bosses of their crimes. Some workers were not ready to speak up when they came to the tribunals, but when they got home they could no longer hold their tempers, so they beat their breasts and stamped their feet in anger. They would pour out to their neighbors the injuries they had suffered in their own lives. Afterward, accusation meetings were held on every dock — fifty-two in all — and dock workers universally participated in the accusations. Some workers even participated five or six times, and the total number of those participating reached more than thirty-seven thousand people. At the meetings, the workers poured out their bitter waters and recounted the wickedness of the old society, raising their class consciousness. As one man, they demanded that the people's government sternly punish the principal evil elements and avenge the class hatred which had festered for generations.

The struggle against local despots and bosses was victorious, and those local despots and bosses who had committed heinous crimes were appropriately punished. Thus the roots of feudal oppression that had existed for so many years were pulled up and tossed away, and a whole new climate unfolded on the docks. The broad masses of dock workers found their minds were put at ease. They deeply appreciated the fact that without the Communist Party there would have been no new China and no transformation in the lives of the dock workers. They brought their warm feelings following the transformation with them to their work posts. They used real deeds to repay the Party's kindnesses, and thus the efficiency of transport work on the docks increased remarkably.

III. Increase Awareness, Reform Production

The struggle against local despots and bosses achieved a great victory. The local despots and bosses were overthrown, and the feudal system of control on the docks was thus eliminated. The dock workers, from a political standpoint, genuinely turned over a new leaf. But the control of the docks by the evil feudal powers of the old society had had a long history. The feudal bosses, in addition to using bloody terrorist violence to suppress the workers' resistance, also habitually used divide-and-rule tactics, deceit, superstition, and other methods to poison the workers' minds. Therefore, after the struggle against local despots and bosses, although the feudal system of control had been wiped out, the influence of feudal thinking still remained, and the factionalism among workers belonging to different hometown societies had still not disappeared. Some workers still could not draw a clear line in their minds between themselves and the class enemy. A few workers even held onto their superstitions and thought the exploitation and oppression suffered by laboring people before the liberation was the result of "tricks of fate" and the like. Such incorrect thoughts and feeble viewpoints also all had to be rectified. In addition, among the ranks of the dock workers were hidden some undiscovered counterrevolutionaries, landlords, and local despots who also had to be exposed and punished. If these problems were not suitably solved in good time, then the results of the victory of the workers' political struggle could not be guaranteed, and the activism of the dock workers in taking charge of their own affairs could not be brought into full play. At the same time, this would necessarily affect the progressively higher rate of loading and unloading on the docks and hinder the development of production. Because of this, after the victory in the struggle against the local despots and bosses, in the winter of 1952 the Party led all the harbor workers in developing a "Democratic Reform" Educational Movement. They demanded progressive pacification of the remnants of feudal thought and purification of the dock workers' ranks. They wanted to heighten consciousness, draw the line between themselves and the enemy, and strengthen solidarity.

The "Democratic Reform" Educational Movement began with remembering the bitterness of the old society. Dock workers in the old society suffered the most profound exploitation and the cruelest oppression. By drawing together these memories of deep pain and grief, they incited incomparable class hatred among the broad masses of workers. They repeatedly spit out the bitter waters of their past and recounted the crimes of the old society. Some workers in small group meetings cried out the tragic experiences of their own past and then went home to tell them to their wives and children. This stimulated the family's painful memories so that they recalled for each other the pain and bitterness existing before the liberation.

By remembering and pouring out their grievances, the broad

masses of dock workers increased their hatred of the old society and their love of the new society even more. They spat out bitter waters, dug out bitter roots, and more and more realized that the man-eating system of the old society was the source of the dock workers' difficulties. They clearly saw the class enemy's use of factionalism, trickery, and other poisonous tools of criminal control. They raised their consciousness and drew a clear line between themselves and the enemy. Some workers who in the past had been intimidated and tricked by the bosses and had joined the feudal gangs now saw the light. Many workers who in the past had fallen for the labor contractors' skill at sowing dissension, inciting evil, and playing one group against another now all realized that the feudal gangs and hometown clubs were measures the class enemy took to poison and control the workers. Thus, they eliminated factionalism and strengthened solidarity. For instance, among the workers were two brothers named Weng. Before the liberation, they worked on two different docks, were under the general direction of two different bosses, and thus separately participated in two different associations. Under the manipulations of their bosses, the two men fought over jobs for their respective gangs. The elder brother hit his younger brother on the head with a hook; the younger brother smashed his older brother's leg. Thereafter the two brothers became enemies. They were completely estranged and did not speak to each other for more than twenty years. When they met on the street, they would exchange angry glances. It was not until this time of pouring out grievances that they realized how terribly harmed they had been by the old society and how they had been tricked by the class enemy. In a meeting for pouring out grievances, they held their heads and wept bitterly. The two old brothers, estranged from the time of their youth until their hair had turned white, could now be reconciled as they had been in childhood. They said, "It took the Communist Party to clear our eyes and show us who are our loved ones and who are our enemies."

The workers not only recalled the bitterness of the old society but also compared it to the sweetness of the new society.

They discussed the great changes on the docks since the liberation. They discussed how the Party looked after the people without ignoring the slightest detail, how great an improvement there had been in the dock workers' working and living conditions, how their political status had been raised to an unprecedented level, how many dock workers had become cadres, and how the leaders frequently conferred with the workers during the course of the work, paying close attention to the workers' viewpoints. Through these comparisons, the broad masses of dock workers even more keenly appreciated the transformation in their own lives. At the same time they even more clearly recognized their own responsibilities. They said, "Under the old society we were slaves; in the new society we are masters." As a result, the idea of being masters of their own fate was established, and they greatly elevated their work activism.

The victory of the "Democratic Reform" Educational Movement prepared the way for the reform of production on the docks. After the liberation, under the leadership of the Party, many measures were adopted on the docks. Management was strengthened, methods were reformed, and the rate of production was given a definite boost. This all made a great contribution to the transportation of materials in the early part of the liberation, to the support of the Resist America, Aid Korea Movement, and to the promotion of the restoration of the national economy. However, because of the long period during which the docks had been under the control of the evil reactionary powers, the productive forces on the docks had been yoked and trampled underfoot for a long time. Even after going through the period of preliminary reform after the liberation, these productive forces were still terribly backward. The dock management system handed down by history was unsound. The irrational labor organization created obstacles to the development of the productive forces. This meant that the loading and unloading work on the docks could not meet the needs of the high-speed development of the national economy. Especially after the entire nation embarked on the First Five-year Plan, increasing industrial and agricultural production and development of communications and transportation even more urgently demanded that loading and unloading work in the harbor be accelerated. Production costs also had to be cut, and quality guaranteed. This impelled the docks of the whole harbor to advance on all fronts at once in the reform of production, to overcome the backward look of the past, to improve the management system, to overhaul the organization of labor, to accelerate the rate of loading and unloading work, and thereby to meet the needs of the national economy's development.

In the latter half of 1953, the docks of the whole harbor began production reform work on all fronts, the first step being "stationing workers at a fixed point." Before the liberation, the dock workers had been floating laborers, never having a fixed work location. After the liberation, although they had been assigned to teams and had organizations, they still had no direct relationship to the dock enterprises and thus were still floating laborers. This situation meant that the relationship between the dock enterprises and the dock workers was not on a proper foundation. It had a serious effect on the planned and rhythmic conduct of production management and frequently produced great confusion and waste in the loading and unloading work. Because of this, fixing each loading and unloading worker on a particular dock was an important key to the production reform of loading and unloading work.

Stationing workers at a fixed point made progress in reforming labor organization possible. On the docks in the past, because of the irrational division of labor that had been handed down through history, a chain of loading or unloading work was rigidly split up into several stages. Boat carriers only lifted goods while they were on the boat, movers only handled goods on the docks, and stackers were only concerned with what went on inside the warehouse. To weigh the goods, there were also scale operators, and everyone always got in everyone else's way, creating much confusion. If the group responsible for one small link in the chain did not show up, then everyone else had to sit and wait. The loading and unloading work could not proceed smoothly. This created many contradictory and confusing phenomena and had an effect on the acceleration of the rate of work. After workers were stationed at fixed points, the different labor organizations were merged together. Every kind of labor force joined in an across-the-board partnership, grouping the little gangs together as one unit of production. The loading and unloading work became one long dragon, and the rate of production increased greatly.

When the workers were stationed at fixed points, the docks and warehouses of the whole harbor actively prepared to carry out planned management. The workers put into effect a round-the-clock, three-shift loading and unloading system, and a communication system for the entire harbor was established. Beginning in 1954, a planned management system was established and improved on the docks. From then on, the loading and unloading work began planned, coordinated production, even better meeting the national economy's need for planned development.

IV. The Transformation of Dock Enterprises

The series of reforms on the docks revolved around the socialist state-operated economy. After the liberation, the people's government confiscated and took command of the bureaucratic capitalist docks and warehouses, turning them into the basic strength of the socialist state-operated dock and warehouse enterprises. In 1950, the Shanghai District Harbor Affairs Adistrative Office was established, unifying the management of all harbor operations. At this time, not counting the private and foreign commercial dock and warehouse enterprises, they took over a total of 24,910 feet [ch'ih] of docks, warehouse space totaling 3,584,678 square feet and open dumping grounds totaling 6,462,163 square feet. This constituted a strong material base for transforming the whole nonsocialist economic element of the dock and warehouse industry.

The docks and warehouses occupied by the imperialists were all selfish enterprises before the liberation. They were dependent on special privileges, monopolies, and profiteering. On the eve of the liberation when the imperialists saw the strength of the people's armed might and realized that Shanghai would be liberated, they did not stand fast but very early took their huge stocks of capital and left the country. All they left behind was some immovable construction equipment which they had no way to carry. In 1953, after the liberation and after the people's government had taken over the bureaucratic capitalist docks, the government received an application from the foreign docks to cease operations and turn their enterprises over to the government. (The American Commercial Dollar Docks had immediately been taken over after the war to Resist America and Aid Korea had broken out.) Hence these docks that had been occupied by the imperialists for close to a hundred years were finally returned to the hands of the people. Through the government's vigorous improvements and corrections, these docks gained new life and began to serve the great fatherland's socialist construction.

As for the privately operated capitalist dock and warehouse enterprises, they actually occupied only a very small proportion of the industry in the harbor. Moreover, their facilities were inferior and their conditions were very inadequate. Before the liberation, the capitalists depended on strengthening their exploitation of the workers and the abnormal development occurring under widespread profiteering to reap usurious profits. After the liberation, the Party and the people's government adopted a policy of "utilization, restriction, and transformation" in dealing with the privately operated capitalist enterprises. They helped the capitalists overcome difficulties and develop production. The privately operated dock and warehouse industry was also given support and attention. Some boats were appropriately directed to dock, load, and unload at the private docks. Their warehouse areas were leased on a long-term basis by state-operated enterprises and government units for storing goods. This meant that the capitalists could have a guaranteed operating income and meet their expenses. Thus, during the first period of the liberation when the American-Chiang clique was blockading and bombing and the situation for all enterprises in the harbor was poor, the privately operated dock and warehouse industry was able to withstand the difficulties and, when the economic situation improved, was even able to make a profit.

However, the profit-grabbing capitalists, unwilling to give up their rotten capitalist ways of operating, could not honestly accept transformation and voluntarily walk the socialist road. Accordingly, there was a constant struggle between restriction and opposition to restriction. Some capitalists, in order to compete for business, changed dock and warehouse rents and altered organizational relationships at will. Some equipment was consequently put aside and not used or used but not repaired. They even destroyed equipment on a whim. Some capitalists operated thoughtlessly, sluggishly marking time, taking the attitude of "eat everything, sell everything, break everything." They took "giving consideration to both public and private interests" to mean "dividing up everything equally." They referred to the leaders of the state enterprises as "the public interests devouring the private interests." They thus resisted the supervision of the workers and adopted the method of ingratiating themselves with one group against another in carrying out their destructive activities. Some capitalists, in order to compete for boat-docking business, would wheedle and debase state cadres without regard to the consequences. When renting out warehouse space, they would frequently violate government directives and force up the rent in order to make illegal, usurious profits. They would use broken production equipment and tools without repairing them or even secretly dismantle and sell them. Tax evasion and smuggling was commonplace.

These "five poison" activities were exposed and attacked in the "Five-Anti" movement of 1952, and the mad attack of the bourgeoisie was repulsed. The class struggle on the docks was once again victorious, and the progressive transformation of the private capitalist dock and warehouse industry prepared the groundwork for that victory.

After 1953 the nation entered an era of construction on a broad scale. Industrial and agricultural production developed rapidly. The loading and unloading capacity of the harbor increased correspondingly, and the dock-loading and unloading work became more and more strenuous. At this time, the backward production relationships and the rotten operational system in the privately operated capitalist dock and warehouse industry reached a point where it could no longer meet the needs of socialist economic development. Several privately operated docks had ignored the need for repairs for some time. Damage was very severe. Mooring spaces were in such shallow water that steamers could not tie up. Eighty percent of the privately operated warehouses were full of leaks that let in rain and runoff, reflecting poorly on the security of the goods inside. Along the river road and riverbank each company was separated from the others by walls and ditches set up to protect each individual's property, thus hindering the unified utilization of facilities. The roads on the docks were in disrepair, which affected the movement of machinery. All of this explains why the private dock and warehouse ownership system had to undergo a transformation.

An inside look at the privately operated dock and warehouse industry revealed serious contradictions. In the years following the liberation, the state-operated docks and warehouses steadily improved their management. The workers' working conditions improved without a hitch. The amount of machinery and equipment increased day by day, and the docks and warehouses were fully utilized. The workers took command of their own affairs, developed a high degree of activity and creativity in their work, and made a great contribution to the cause of socialist construction. However, the privately operated dock and warehouse industry consisted of unwieldy organizations, corrupt management, worn out equipment, and inadequate operations. Some warehouses that had been rented out for a long time had stacks of disorganized goods. Some equipment that had broken down years before had not been repaired or had been cast away unused. In accordance with the development of the revolutionary state of affairs, the privately operated dock and warehouse industry had already reached the point where it had to undergo a thorough transformation. At the beginning of 1955, the privately operated dock and warehouse industry in Shanghai harbor, under the supervision and impetus of the broad masses of staff and workers, implemented a system of joint private-state management in all enterprises. Throughout the entire harbor, 26 privately operated docks, 105 warehouses, and a large number of dumps joined the joint private-state Shanghai Harbor Dock and Warehouse Company under the leadership of the Shanghai District Harbor Affairs Administrative Office.

Through ceaseless, coordinated transformation and by putting into effect unified management and operations organized by area, Shanghai harbor's dock and warehouse industry ended a confused state of affairs and achieved outstanding development. Under the Party's leadership, the coolies of the past who had worked like beasts of burden on the docks finally became the masters of the docks. Both their labor and their lives achieved a basic transformation.

6

Phenomenal Progress in Loading and Unloading Work

I. Transformation of the Docks' Appearance

The reform of the relations of production on the docks led to a transformation of the docks' appearance. Before the liberation, the docks were all owned by the imperialists, bureaucratic capitalists, and private capitalists. They dictated the docks' objectives, which were either to provide a convenient avenue for their aggression or to seize great wealth. Because they had a single-minded desire to get the greatest possible profit out of the smallest possible investment, dock and warehouse construction in this period was extremely flimsy, and the equipment very inferior. Among the docks, those representing the smallest investment were the floating docks, which made up 42 percent of the dock footage in the harbor. This kind of dock rose and fell with the tide. Not only could large boats not moor there steadily, but the gangplank bridge joining the dock to the land also rose and fell with the tide, often making a steeply inclined slope. This made it even more difficult for the workers to carry goods on and off the dock. Some fixed docks, although they outwardly appeared to be made of concrete, had frameworks that were extremely flimsy. They had limited loading weight capacities and basically could not handle large-scale mechanical equipment. There were also some wooden docks which were decrepit, rotting, soggy, corroded things. They were terribly unsafe and unsuitable for use.

As for the warehouses on the docks, they were all patched together, in a state of scandalous disarray. Some were wood

---

"Chuang-hsieh kung-tso t'u-fei meng-chin."

and brick buildings, tall and short. Some had corrogated iron roofs. They had gone a long time without repair and had broken and corroded so that not even all the doors and windows were there. They were collapsing and leaking, which had a serious effect on the security of the stored goods. The open-air grounds for dumping goods were full of trash and puddles, overgrown with weeds, and had become breeding grounds for destructive insects, mosquitoes, and flies.

The roads on the docks had never been repaired before the liberation. Except for some level, smooth concrete roads built around the foreign bosses' homes and offices, those roads that were not mud roads were made of crushed rock, with high spots and low spots. They were muddy and slippery and hard to travel on. When workers carried heavy goods on them, they often fell. If they were not skillful, they would pay with their lives. If one pulled a metal-wheeled tiger cart on those roads, not only would one fall in the mud, but the cart would shake so much from moving over the crushed rock that one's hands would go numb, as if they had touched an electric charge.

In addition, because the docks before the liberation were privately owned, between each dock there was a ditch, a wall, wire entanglements, or a bamboo fence to divide one from the next and preserve each boss's claim to his own dock. At that time, the land along the two banks of the Whangpoo River was divided into many separate pieces by the obstacles these men put up. It was all in great disarray, one part broken off and separate from another so that there was no mutual communication between docks. Even if there were only a few feet separating one dock from another, one had to twist and turn around a long detour to get from one to the other. This seriously affected the rational utilization of the docks. Moreover, several docks were in areas where the water was not deep enough, where mud, sand, and silt had accumulated and could not be immediately cleared out. This hindered the docking of ships and further confused the general situation, so that some areas had docks but no warehouses or had warehouses but too few docks. Since the traffic capacity was not adaptable, often boats could not dock, or having deposited their goods, there was nowhere to store them. The corrupt dock management, which allowed almost no regularized procedures, created a situation of confusion on the docks before the liberation. Everything was in a hopeless muddle.

The various confused circumstances on the docks before the liberation were entirely created by the irrational system of the old society and were also phenomena which the old society had no way of overcoming. After the liberation, in accordance with the transformation of production relationships on the docks, the appearance of the docks was gradually transformed.

The technical transformation of the docks and warehouses of Shanghai harbor was carried out in accordance with the policy of increasing production and practicing economy, building the nation through hard work and thrift. Although the existing buildings and equipment were old and misused, they had to be fully utilized. The workers thoroughly developed what was hidden in the existing materials, and according to the differing circumstances, they suitably carried out repair, stabilization, reconstruction and expansion, taking the old equipment and using it in new ways. For instance, take the old, undersized, many-pillared warehouses which were unsuitable for mechanized work. They were made bigger by being joined together and higher by ripping out floors. With the high-ceilinged warehouses, raised platforms were used for storing and thus cranes could be used to load and unload. Some of the decrepit, rotting floating docks were converted one after another into concrete docks. The existing concrete docks, with their flimsy frames, inconvenient layout for machinery, sunken foundations, and surfaces easily breeched by water, were all reconstructed, stabilized, and raised. In this way, many of these old-fashioned, aged, and unsuitable buildings and facilities, through repair and reconstruction, were made like new. They were maintained in excellent condition for full utilization and were again thrown into production.

After the transformation of the relations of production on the docks, renovation projects could be completely laid out and executed on a large scale by unified national management. The docks, after they had been thoroughly renovated, were used more efficiently. The ditches, walls, and fences that had separated the individual docks in the past were all done away with one after another, and the docks along the river were all linked together, unifying their utilization and increasing their economic rationality. For instance, at the original Huishan Dock only one boat at the most could tie up at one time. All that remained of the Yangshupoo Dock were a few wooden piles where no boats could dock. Moreover, the two docks were divided by a small stream and a road (I-ho Road). Through renovation, the stream was filled in, and the road removed so that the two docks were joined together. Then the workers added the Huashun Dock on at the side and converted the original floating dock there into a fixed dock of steel and concrete. Through the enlargement of the three docks and the merging of the three into one, five seagoing vessels were able to dock there at one time, and the efficiency of the docks increased tremendously.

While this was going on, the roads on the docks were undergoing a universal reconstruction. This was especially true after the gradual mechanization of the loading and unloading work because mechanized transport put greater demands on the roads. Bumpy roads would not only adversely affect the speed at which carts could travel and easily damage the machinery but would also easily damage the goods being carried by causing much shaking. The fact that on rainy days the roads would be muddy and so slippery that vehicles could not move had to affect production adversely. Therefore, the roads on the dock were completely reconstructed to meet the requirements of mechanization. After the liberation there came to be more than 174,000 square meters of high-grade, recently constructed roads throughout the whole harbor, making up more than 86 percent of the total existing roads. Workers now had no need to sink into "the pool of soft mud" or climb the "razorback mountain." They saw that these level, smooth cement roads were everywhere on the docks, and happiness filled their hearts. The workers said, "Even without mechanization, on roads like these we could carry our goods easily."

The backward condition of the Shanghai harbor docks before the liberation was also illustrated by the dearth of amphibious transshipment docks. Although Shanghai harbor was China's foremost port, a harbor famous throughout the world, each year's loading and unloading capacity was fixed. Many goods were transferred by water, but there was no direct way to transfer goods from steamship to railroad. This gave rise to the great waste of transfer loading and unloading. After the liberation, in 1956 in the upper harbor area around Jih-yun Harbor, the workers began to expand the old K'ai-p'ing and Pei-p'iao docks into the first amphibious transshipment dock. Here the railroad train could run directly to the docks, and the goods could be directly loaded onto the steamships. This cut down the waste of loading and unloading for the intermediate transfer. The efficiency of the docks reached even greater heights. In 1959, after the Jih-yun Harbor amphibious transshipment dock was constructed, the Chang-hua-peng amphibious transfer dock was constructed on an even larger scale in the lower harbor area called the Chang-hua-peng. This was terribly useful, especially in making the docking and loading of foreign vessels more convenient. This dock spread over a wide area and transformed the backward conditions of Shanghai harbor's past in which there had been a lack of amphibious transshipment docks. The loading and unloading facilities of the harbor had become even more modernized.

In addition to this, the docks and warehouses after the liberation carried out quite a few new construction projects. After about ten years, newly constructed docks made up about 21 percent of the total length of all existing fixed docks, and the number of warehouses had also increased. This new construction was very instrumental in the increase of Shanghai harbor's loading and unloading capacity.

Another great transformation was in the implementation of wet weather loading and unloading. On the docks of Shanghai harbor in the past, there generally could be no loading or unloading on rainy days because of the chance of damage to the goods. But it rained in the harbor area approximately a third of all the days in the year, and thus the loading and unloading facilities in the harbor were not used a third of the time. This created serious waste. Before the liberation, when it rained the workers would stop work and suffer. Since the workers lived from day to day at that time, when rainy days came and there was no work, all they could do was go hungry. Life was especially hard during those seasons when there was continual rainy weather. After the liberation, although the workers no longer had to worry about starving on rainy days, they nevertheless saw the waste and loss caused by having to stop work when it rained. This had a bad effect on the turnover of goods and the progress of production and made the workers feel even worse. Under the leadership of the Party, the workers became used to thinking of themselves as the masters of their own house. They developed a collective wisdom. One way or another they overcame the difficulties of carrying out their work on rainy days. They invented movable rain awnings and with other innovations finally solved the problem of working on rainy days.

The movable awning spread out over the steamship, covering the hatch opening. The wind blew it but did not blow it down. The rain hit it but did not seep through. The unloading and loading of goods proceeded as usual without the slightest problem. The efficient use of the facilities consequently increased, and the traffic capacity of the harbor also increased tremendously. By means of this change, the deserted appearance of the docks of Shanghai's past, when all work stopped on each rainy day, was turned into a bustling picture even when it rained.

The greatest transformation in the appearance of the docks lay in the mechanization of the loading and unloading work. The workers in the past, with their waists bent and their backs twisted, formed a long, snakelike line resembling the character "一" [the character for the number "one"] whose end could not be seen. Now, one could see the giant machines and swiftly moving vehicles everywhere. One could hear the rhythmic sound of the machines and the constant honk of horns on the vehicles. The workers wore work clothes and protective headgear. The workers drove the machines and moved the goods. The docks were neat and clean, well ordered, and completely unlike the dirty, noisy, crowded, confused situation before the liberation. It is not surprising that many foreign seamen who had visited Shanghai harbor before the liberation were shocked when they saw this glorious transformation and were full of praise for the changes.

II. Machines Take the Place of Manpower

The operation of the docks in the past relied entirely on human physical strength. When a large ship was at the dock, there were always five or six long, snakelike queues from the holds of the ships to the doors of the warehouses. Each worker was right behind the next. People were all over the docks, a river of people flowing without a stop, crowded and confused. As a result, although the intensity of the workers' labor was very great and they worked themselves to exhaustion, the efficiency of the loading and unloading was very low. For instance, workers had to use an iron shovel to unload coal, shovelful by shovelful. The coal was loaded into baskets and taken by pole bearers up to the shore. A 10,000-ton coal ship would take about a month to completely unload even with over two hundred men working continuously. At that time, the foreign bosses and capitalists were only concerned with their own profits. Who cared if the workers lived or died? When they could exploit this cheap labor, they basically ignored the question of utilizing machinery. Taken all together, there were not over forty pieces of mechanized equipment, large and small, in Shanghai harbor before the liberation, and many of those had been discarded as unusable.

After the liberation, the Party consistently paid attention to cutting down on the physical demands on the dock workers. At the beginning of the liberation, although there was still a temporary lack of mechanized equipment, the Party continued to adopt every means possible to reduce the demands of physical labor and ensure the workers' safety. For instance, the gangplank was widened, and a wooden frame and bottle gourds were used to lift things out of the hold instead of using the "cork-screw leap." The workers made use of wheeled carts for level transportation. At the Yang-ching Harbor Dock and the Tung-chia-tu Dock, which specialized in handling coal, a light-rail railroad was laid down to transport the coal, and so forth. Through these measures, the demands on the dock workers' labor were reduced as a first step, and at the same time the efficiency of the work gangs was increased.

After 1954 production tools on the docks were greatly modernized, and the use of hand trucks and tiger carts to move goods increased. Furthermore, some small-scale loading and unloading machines, such as trailers, shovel carts, wooden-slat conveyors, conveyor belts, and so on began to be introduced. The utilization of conveyor belts played a great role in the liberated dock workers' shoulder-bearing work. In the coal loading and unloading operations, the results were especially spectacular. In 1955 Shanghai Harbor used a conveyor belt for the first time to unload 7,220 tons of coal from the steamship "Ho-p'ing No. 17." The workers used eighty-one fewer man-days than had been necessary in the past; efficiency was increased 2.8 times. They cut costs 60.25 percent on each ton and achieved a great success. Even more important, by using the raised conveyor belt, they could lay the coal directly on top of the coal pile, taking the place of the "over-the-mountain leap" of the past and solving the most severe, most dangerous problem in the unloading and loading of coal. Now that there was a conveyor belt, coal was taken to the coal pile automatically, eliminating the "over-the-mountain leap." The workers were overjoyed and described the conveyor belt like this, "With just a push on a button, the conveyor belt, with all the goods lined up on it, begins to move; but there is no one on the leap, not a soul on the high benches."

In 1955 the warehouses increased their stock of vertical lifting equipment, solving the problem of moving goods upstairs. In the past, workers had to climb stairs with goods on their backs, a terrible drain on their physical strength. Now they had electric lifts, high chain-link conveyors, tower cranes, wall cranes, and electric basket lifts, all of which could take bundles to upper stories without the use of any manpower.

After 1956 they also added a number of floating cranes and huge caterpillar-tread moving cranes, thus solving the problem of mechanical operation in lifting goods from ships' holds and stacking them high on dumping grounds. At the same time, in accordance with the needs of lifting coal out of ships' holds, they manufactured a number of mechanical claws and progressively increased their efficiency in loading and unloading.

Although the stockpile of mechanized equipment increased without interruption and operation techniques steadily improved, up until 1958 there was still not a great deal of mechanized equipment on the docks, and the mechanization of loading and unloading work had not yet reached a very advanced stage. Most of the work still had to rely on human strength. Beginning in 1958, the entire nation on every front entered a new phase of surging, rapid development. Shanghai harbor also set in motion a stirring, seething, clamorous technological transformation and technological revolution and a struggle to realize the mechanization of loading and unloading work. During the high tide of great development, all the staff and workers of the harbor plunged into a mass "Dual Revolution" movement. They each personally took a hand in manufacturing machines, reforming tools, modernizing loading and unloading methods by every means possible, and increasing the efficiency of loading and unloading.

The dock workers' basic cultural level was comparatively low, and they lacked technical knowledge. Generally speaking, none of them had ever manufactured machinery. But under the leadership of the Party, the workers developed the spirit of daring to think, speak, and act. They relied on their collective wisdom, utilized a combination of indigenous and foreign methods and, within a very short time, manufactured a great deal of loading and unloading machinery. Arming themselves, they speedily raised the level of mechanization of loading and unloading work. In 1958 more than 40 percent of the harbor's loading and unloading work was mechanized or semimechanized, and the strenuous physical labor of the dock workers was tremendously reduced.

During the process of the struggle for mechanization, there were a large number of thrilling incidents. For instance, the Yangshupoo Public Service Loading and Unloading Station was originally one of the most rundown units, and although after the liberation the number of tiger carts was increased, the workers there basically still relied on the pure physical labor of pole carrying and shoulder bearing to carry on their operations. Production efficiency was very low. But the staff member and worker comrades of the Yangshupoo Loading and Unloading Station, despite working conditions so bad that they were ready to give up, rose up with even greater vigor, regenerated themselves by their own efforts, and in a situation where they had no technical resources or proper tools or equipment, exhausted every method to bring on a clamorous technological revolution. They moved toward mechanization and finally transformed its poor and blank appearance. In the beginning, they had no technical personnel. All they had were two drivers who knew a little about machinery and an electric light factory worker. They had no charts or plans to speak of, and their only method was to visit fraternal units and inspect their materials. But the workers, by both studying and working, thought out every way to overcome their difficulties. Having no smelting ovens, they turned scrap tea kegs into smelting ovens. Having no lathes or milling machines, they used a file to file an axle and a cogwheel. In this way, the spectacular flower of a technological revolution blossomed in an oilpaper shed at the edge of the docks. In three days and three nights they produced their first jointed crane, which removed the need for physical labor on the three-meter gangplank. This was their first accomplishment. Starting from scratch, they had cleared the way for mechanization. By the beginning of 1960, the whole station had already made thirteen electric cranes, three conveyor belts, and three coal shovels, not counting all the tools and equipment they had made to carry out the technological revolution. Even then they were not satisfied with the achievements they had already attained. In the following years they resolutely took the direction of technological revolution, unceasingly increasing production, constantly modernizing, and continually gaining even better results.

The masses of workers of various other docks also developed soaring enthusiasm and, relying on their own power, advanced toward mechanization. For instance, the workers of the Second Loading and Unloading Area, relying entirely on their own resources, solved problems of equipment, materials, and technique and built the first self-made electric cart. The Soochow River and Harbor Administrative Area originally had no equipment at all, but after more than a year of the technological revolution, the people could all see a forest of cranes over both banks of the Soochow River, and most areas had carried out mechanization or semimechanization.

During the process of the great, clamorous technological revolution, the mood of the working masses was rising, and their enthusiasm was boundless. They said: "An oilcloth sail makes a factory; hammers and files are machine tools. The loading and unloading workers are technical workers, and they do all the work in producing the machines to build a factory." Or they said: "If we can't find materials, we go out the door and hunt for waste material. If there are no blueprints for something, you can still make it by both studying and working."

After the high tide of technological innovation and revolution arose at the docks in 1958, for the next few years there was persistent and continual progress. In 1959 the collective forces applied themselves to two key areas — mechanical claws used in unloading boats and tarps used in covering boat-loading areas on rainy days. The production of these items expanded and increased. Besides this, there was also expanded production of conveyor belts, including the 800-meter-per-minute conveyor used in coal-loading work and the 600-meter-per-minute Hankow-style conveyor used in transporting bagged goods, for a total increase of 401 conveyors. In the "Dual Revolution" movement of 1960, working on the base laid down in the previous two years, the docks entered a stage of great development and progressed on four fronts in solving the important problems of loading and unloading work. First was the overall expansion in the use of mechanical claws, which increased the efficiency of loading and unloading work tremendously. Second was the use of wall cranes, warehouse cranes, slides and other large-scale machines and slides used in transporting goods between upper and lower floors. Third was the increased use of mechanization in raising and lowering things in the warehouses, there being an additional 381 cranes manufactured, plus 440 hoists and other machines. Fourth was the energetic execution of the principle of line planning in operations research in order to improve production, organization, and management. By 1961 development had been consolidated on the basis of the great development in the previous three years. The dock workers had filled in the gaps, made up for deficiencies, and significantly strengthened their inventory of mechanical claws, automatic hooks, lifting cranes, hoists, and six-petaled-flower mechanical claws — altogether 35 separate items — and through their persistent use, the workers had steadfastly researched, modernized, and increased production. At the same time, with the whole harbor switching to the use of mechanical claws, the scope and variety of goods handled by the claws expanded remarkably, and the number of models also increased. In 1960 mechanical claws were only used in 27 percent of the work, but by 1961 this figure had increased to about 36.9 percent. This was comparable to saving the manpower of thirty thousand work crews. After 1962, there came a stage of readjustment and qualitative development. Existing equipment was steadily modernized, and there was a general strengthening and attainment of even more completely satisfactory levels of work. After 1964, technological innovation and revolution on the docks entered a new high tide, and by 1965 there were more than 2,000 machines operating throughout the entire harbor. The degree of mechanization and semimechanization in loading and unloading work had already reached 75 percent, and Shanghai had basically become a mechanized harbor.

III. Faster Loading and Unloading, Increased Efficiency

The many kinds of changes on the docks produced a ceaseless increase in the efficiency of the loading and unloading work. Shanghai is our nation's greatest industrial city, and the amount of commerce it carries on with every part of the nation is tremendous. Every year large amounts of mechanical equipment, hardware, chemical products, and household industrial goods for people's everyday use are sent out from Shanghai to supply other areas. At the same time, every portion of the country has much in the way of industrial raw materials, fuel, and agricultural subsidiary products that are sent to Shanghai. In addition, there is a large quantity of goods which are centrally collected and dispersed at Shanghai, which draws together freight of abundant variety and tremendous volume. Altogether, about 70 percent of that is brought in by boat to be processed at the harbor. All these things presented a glorious yet formidable task for the loading and unloading work at the harbor.

In the approximately ten years following the liberation, our nation's economy speedily developed, industrial and agricultural production and the amount of foreign trade steadily increased, and the amount of material coming through the harbor accordingly increased year by year. By 1965 the amount of goods handled at Shanghai harbor, not including intraharbor commerce, had already reached 14.424 million tons, an increase of 635 percent over 1949. Moreover, this exceeded the 14 million tons recorded in 1936 before the War of Resistance against Japan — the greatest amount ever to pass through Shanghai harbor in a year.

The increasing number of goods handled by the harbor demanded that the loading and unloading work increase its efficiency and provide faster loading and unloading; it required shortening the time that the goods were held up in the harbor and accelerating the vessels' turnaround time in order to preserve unhindered, free-flowing commerce throughout the harbor. Carrying out these demands would provide a powerful support for the speedy development of the national economy.

Owing to the efforts of the dock workers, the accomplishments of the technological revolution, and the modernization of management work and operational methods, the speed of loading and unloading work in Shanghai harbor increased steadily. In 1958 at the beginning of the high tide of the Great Leap Forward, the improvement in the efficiency of loading and unloading was particularly rapid. Although the tasks at that time were terribly difficult, the amount of material handled by the harbor increased 63 percent in 1958 over 1957. It increased another 40 percent in 1959 over 1958. The harbor, from beginning to end, preserved the free flow of commerce. Goods were exchanged and transported in good time, effectively assisting in the leap forward in industrial and agricultural production. Moreover, the costs of loading and unloading steadily decreased. From 1957 to 1958 they declined 14 percent. At the same time, the harbor docking time for ships was also reduced. In 1958 the harbor docking time was cut 13 to 17 percent, and thus the nation's transport capability was greatly increased.

The faster pace of loading and unloading work on the docks not only actively supported the development of the national economy but also won the universal acclaim of the foreign seamen. In 1956, for example, the Japanese steamship "Hsin-nung" was in Shanghai to pick up a load of rice to take to Pakistan. In order to aid the Pakistani people, the Shanghai dock workers took only 38 hours and 45 minutes to load more than nine thousand tons of rice. This set a new record and greatly astonished the Japanese seamen. In 1958 the captain of the Italian ship "Mapolina" [Ma-p'o-lin-na-hao] said: "When we were in the American harbor of 'Sa-na' [Savannah?], it took 20 days in all to unload, but in Shanghai it took only 3½ days to completely unload all our goods. That's really fast!" The captain of the Japanese steamship "Po-shan," showing his astonishment at the fast pace of loading and unloading in Shanghai, said, "We estimated it would take 10 days to unload these goods in Shanghai Harbor, but in fact we were completely unloaded before even 5 days were up." In

1959 the Norwegian ship "Sha Seh Nan," carrying ten thousand tons of goods to Shanghai from Australia, used only 4 days to be completely unloaded. The chief officer on the ship said with surprise: "That's really fast! The Great Leap Forward is truly a great leap forward!" The chief officer of the foreign vessel "Lei-fei-lan" was also startled by the speed with which goods were unloaded, and he said, "They unloaded our goods so fast that we didn't even have to let the steam pressure in our boiler go down before turning around." After the foreign vessel "Ssu-teng-k'o-lo-ssu" arrived in Shanghai, the chief officer telegraphed his wife that he would be kept in Shanghai 20 days. As it turned out, it was not quite 6 days before his cargo was completely unloaded. He said happily, "I had to send another telegram to my family telling them I would be home 14 days ahead of schedule." Then there was the foreign ship that came into Shanghai carrying more than 5,000 tons of goods. When its captain heard that his goods could be completely unloaded in 24 hours, he waved his hand and said: "No, that can't be done. It'll take 4 days to unload this. Unloading it in a day is unthinkable!" The next day he started in to direct the ship's operations. He ran up onto the deck and climbed to the entrance of the ship's hold to have a look. Surprised and dumbfounded, he saw that all the goods had actually been unloaded. It had only taken 23 hours and 50 minutes in all. The captain, unable to hide his amazement, raised his thumb and said: "When the Chinese say they will do something, it's done. It's wonderful! This truly is a great leap forward!"

From 1958 on, the speed of loading and unloading work on the docks accelerated continuously. In March 1965 when the steamship "Ho-p'ing No. 27" unloaded 10,070 tons of coal, it only took $19\frac{1}{2}$ hours to unload 93 percent of the material on the ship. What a tremendous change this was from before the liberation when, relying on the physical labor of human carriers, it would have taken a month to unload 10,000 tons of coal!

The achievement of fast loading and unloading was coordinated with the development of the harbor and guaranteed the rapid distribution of goods. It was a tremendous contribution to the development of the entire national economy. By 1965, the volume of goods handled in Shanghai Harbor had already increased thirteenfold, and trade with Asia, Africa, and Latin America was twenty-six times as great. As the loading and unloading work in the harbor kept pace with the need for an increase in the speed of freight movement, the efficiency of the work crews increased threefold. This guaranteed a steady supply of goods to every part of the country. In particular, it strengthened our nation's mutual aid to the people of Asia, Africa, and Latin America, fortified the solidarity of the anti-imperialist peoples of the world, and profoundly attacked the imperialists headed by the United States.

The achievements in loading and unloading work cannot be separated from the activist efforts of the dock workers. After the liberation, the dock workers, under the leadership of the Party, shook off the feudal yoke. They increased their awareness, liberated their thoughts, and in about ten years made a tremendous achievement. There suddenly appeared a large group of advanced collectives and advanced personalities. The basic transformation in the appearance of the docks in these approximately ten years and the rapid acceleration of the efficiency of loading and unloading sufficiently explain that the human factor is the primary one. These same dock workers, who were persecuted before the liberation, produced a miracle after the liberation. The two different social systems produced two radically different results. It was none other than the superiority of the socialist system which ensured that the activism and creativity of the dock workers could be fully developed and which enabled the docks to become a wide world where the dock workers employed their own wisdom and talent.

7

The Tremendous Transformation of the Dock Workers' Condition

I. The Transformation in Their Political Position and Their Spirit

After the liberation, the Shanghai dock workers shook off the feudal yoke. They all made tremendous changes politically, economically, and culturally. Among these many changes, the most significant was the basic transformation in the dock workers' political position. Before the liberation, dock workers were kept down at the very lowest rung of society and had neither the slightest bit of political influence nor any personal protection. They were severely oppressed and exploited by the imperialists, compradors, feudal bosses, and capitalists and had been no better than slaves for generations. After the liberation, under the leadership of the Party, the power of the state was established under the dictatorship of the proletariat. Laboring people took control of their own lives and became the rulers of the nation. The dock workers took part in the political activities of the nation, putting forward their own representatives and exercising their own political power. After more than a decade, quite a few Shanghai Harbor dock workers had been elected to be people's representatives on the Shanghai People's Joint Representative Council. In fact, a majority of the representatives are people who were dock workers before the liberation. Dock workers not only take part in managing affairs of state, but they also actively take part in the management of the production affairs of the harbor's docks. Every loading and unloading area

"Ma-t'ou kung-jen chuang-k'uang ti chü-ta pien-hua."

on the docks periodically holds a workers' congress. At each congress, the responsible comrades brief all the workers on the achievements in production and the situation in every facet of the work. They receive the supervision of the broad masses of the workers. Moreover, over the past several years, a large group of dock workers have been selected as cadres to directly lead production. Not only are there basic-level cadres in every dock loading and unloading crew in the whole harbor, but the majority of them have been selected from the ranks of the dock workers themselves. In addition, quite a few worker cadres have been promoted to become administrators of the joint unloading and loading areas themselves.

As the broad masses of dock workers have undergone these profound changes from the preliberation to the postliberation era, they have come to deeply appreciate the fact that without the Chinese Communist Party, the dock workers would not have the political position they have today. The class consciousness of all the workers has risen tremendously, and their revolutionary fervor surges forward without a stop. By being outstanding politically and leading the way in their tasks, they have made many remarkable achievements in loading and unloading work. Every year throughout the entire harbor, large groups of outstanding personalities and outstanding collectives appear. Some among them are judged to be the city's outstanding producers, and some are judged to be among the nation's outstanding producers. In addition, there are also many collectives that are selected as outstanding both citywide and nationwide. These outstanding personalities and collectives all provide examples for workers throughout the harbor to emulate. Quite a few dock workers have even had the glorious honor of joining the Chinese Communist Party and the Communist Youth League.

The broad masses of dock workers also closely link their own unloading and loading work with the worldwide revolutionary enterprise. They say: "Standing on the docks, our hearts go out to the world. Loading and unloading work is also for the revolution." When they unload or load goods for the support of the peoples of Asia, Africa, and Latin America, they become doubly careful and highly responsible and consider this a glorious obligation to internationalism. For instance, when loading rice to aid foreign countries, the workers assume an especially accelerated pace and strive to give precedence to transporting it there. Once, when they had more than ten thousand tons of rice to handle, they completely loaded it in two days. Another time they loaded nine thousand tons of rice in only thirty-eight hours. There was also an instance when, in loading complete sets of equipment to aid the nations of Africa, one shift of workers was careless and loaded the heavy goods on top of the light goods. When the next shift of workers discovered this, they immediately decided to start all over again. They said: "Now it doesn't seem like much, but when the ship goes to sea and rocks with the wind and waves, it will be difficult to keep some of the light goods from being crushed. This would adversely affect the installation of this equipment. So if we make a little extra effort now, we can ensure that the African people will be able to complete their construction in time and commence mass production at an early date." Their attitude of great responsibility and their spirit of proletarian internationalism profoundly moved the friendly peoples of the world.

The great masses of Shanghai dock workers, just like all of the nation's people, adore the great Party and its great leader Chairman Mao. From their own experience, they deeply perceive that the revolutionary masses cannot cut themselves off from the Communist Party and that making revolution depends on Mao Tse-tung Thought. Therefore, they adore the works of Chairman Mao and wholeheartedly want to study and grasp Mao Tse-tung Thought. They resolutely read Chairman Mao's books, heed his words, and rely on his instructions to manage their work.

II. The Preservation of Security and Health

At the same time that speed in loading and unloading has developed, the labor and lives of the Shanghai dock workers have also undergone a basic transformation. The dock workers, who had been so completely oppressed and persecuted before the liberation, received the utmost care and sympathy from the Party after the liberation. What most deeply affected the workers first of all was the implementation of all kinds of measures to conserve labor and make labor safer. These measures effectively and reliably ensured safety in their work and well-being in their lives.

In the more than a decade since the liberation, as much of the work on the docks has been steadily mechanized or semi-mechanized, the physical demands on the workers have been greatly reduced. But there are still certain seasonal, exceptional methods used to safeguard the dock workers that are extremely important because of the special nature of their work, it being work that is done outside and often at night. For more than ten years, under the solicitude and leadership of the Party, a great many improvements have been made in this area. Besides the vigorous efforts to soften the effects of the summer heat, the harbor management department has also adopted many safety measures. These have included measures to prevent freezing in order to keep workers from slipping and measures to prevent incidents of accidental poisoning and the like by restricting the movement of dangerous goods. Such measures effectively ensure the safety and health of the workers.

The hot summer is the season when dock work is most troublesome and exhausting. Dock workers in the past, oppressed by Chinese and foreign capitalists and labor contractors, carried on this extremely strenuous work without even stopping for a few minutes. In spite of the sun beating down on their heads and the sweat pouring down their backs, they were denied even one swallow of water. Now, as each summer arrives, awnings are put up all over the docks to shade the workers from the fierce rays of the sun. In addition, many electric fans and large blowing engines are installed so that workers may sit in the cool breeze for a while. On the steamships and transshipment boats, straw mats are laid on the deck near the hold and men are assigned to keep them wet in order to reduce the temperature of the hold and avoid the bad effects the radiated heat can have on the workers' physical health. All the tractors, shovels, cranes, and other moving machinery used in the loading and unloading are equipped with automatic fans and sunshade umbrellas. The cranes are also fitted with heat insulators and electric ventilators to reduce the temperature of the equipment. This protects the workers somewhat from the onslaught of summer heat and reduces fatigue. When working during the summer, the workers on the docks are also supplied with all kinds of cold drinks, such as salt water, salted ice sticks, green bean soup, and salted egg soup, in order to relieve the summer heat, quench the thirst, and refresh the spirits. Many leading cadres not only regularly participate in the labor, working along with the workers, but also frequently bring tea and water to them. They put the bottles of cold drink in the workers' hands and give them cold towels to wipe off the sweat. When some old workers see the leading cadres pushing the cold drink cart toward them, they say with great feeling: "The Party really cares for us even more than our parents do. When the weather turns hot, the cadres immediately bring us ice-cold drinks and tea. One drink and we feel good from head to toe." During rest periods, they say to the young workers: "In the old society when we worked for the capitalists, on very hot summer days a hundred or so of us would chip in to buy a keg of water to quench our thirst. Yet when our labor boss saw us do this, he scolded us for loafing on the job. Think about the past and compare it with the present. Truly, one was hell, and the other is heaven."

Summers are like this, but when the bitter cold winter season arrives, the docks also adopt every kind of measure to ward off the cold and keep people warm. Medical workers at the health stations prepare medicines to prevent cracked skin and other ailments caused by the cold. They distribute them to each work team. The worker dining halls and the night crew dormitories are all equipped with thick hanging screens in front of the doors to hold in the heat. The bedding in the dormitories includes very thick straw quilts and mattresses. Teapots and pots of food are covered to keep them warm, guaranteeing all the workers hot rice, hot vegetables, hot tea, and hot soup. They eat well, sleep well, and are comfortable during their rest periods. The male and female bathhouses are all equipped with stoves or self-controlled water heaters to keep things warm. For those personnel who have to perform work outside, cotton-lined overcoats are provided to ward off the wind and the cold. For the night shift workers there is chiang soup with brown sugar to help keep them warm and withstand the chill of the night. In case of rain, snow, frost, or freezing weather, straw covers and straw mats are spread out and safety nets are added at each operation point to prevent poeple from slipping and falling and hurting themselves. Everything is taken care of; not the slightest detail is overlooked.

The workers have everything that is required in the way of protective gear. The safety of the workers is fully taken into consideration. In daily operations, workers wear protective clothing, protective shoes, and safety hats and gloves to prevent injury. Moreover, life jackets are provided so that if someone loses his footing and falls into the water, it can be kept from becoming a serious accident. Rubber gloves and long rubber boots are distributed to workers handling electrical machinery and equipment so they will not risk electrocution. When loading or unloading rotting or poisonous goods, depending on the different conditions involved, workers use antipoison masks, rubber mouth covers, work clothing, gloves, rubber aprons, and other protective equipment. Moreover, before anything is done, everyone goes through a physical examination, and all those workers who do not meet the requirements are not allowed to unload or load this kind of dangerous cargo. This protects the safety of all the workers.

On the work sites, safety nets are always set up to keep workers from falling and hurting themselves or falling into the water. Any work conducted more than $2\frac{1}{2}$ meters above the ground requires the use of a safety belt. These measures are all carried out with the safety and health of the workers in mind and fully demonstrate the concern of the Party and the nation for the laboring people. When workers think back to what was done on the docks before the liberation, to that time when the capitalists and the labor contractors did not care whether the workers lived or died and when there were basically no labor protection measures at all, they deeply appreciate the warmth of the new society and are deeply grateful for the kindness of the Party. Even some foreign sailors coming into the harbor have heartfelt praise for the many safety measures on the docks. One time a foreign sailor, while boarding a ship, lost his footing and fell off a ladder. He fortunately fell into a safety net and was not injured. After climbing out, he raised his thumb and said, "China, Mao Tse-tung!"

The workers' after-hours life and leisure also receive full attention. They are assured that their fatigue will dissipate quickly and that their vigor and vitality will return in full so they can plunge right back into production. Worker dining halls and bathhouses have been established throughout the docks, and night-shift workers have special dormitories. There are thousands of resting places throughout the harbor, all supplied with mattresses and specially equipped for the relaxation of the night-shift workers. The workers all say, "Now we have a dining hall to eat in, a bathhouse to wash in, and a dormitory to rest in." After a day's work when they have eaten, bathed, and relaxed a bit, with their hearts content, they think back to the days before the liberation when they "ate hsiao-mao soup, bathed in the Whangpoo River, and slept on the side of the road." Truly one is heaven, the other was hell.

In the past when dock workers reached feeble old age or when, because of illness or work injuries, they were no longer able to work, they had nothing left to do but die. No one would interfere. But now the system of laborers' insurance enables workers who are elderly or sick to have effective and dependable protection. In 1964 throughout the harbor area, there were more than four thousand retired workers who each month received retirement income so they could safely pass the twilight of their lives. They thought back to old comrades — those who had been chased off the docks before the liberation and had frozen or starved to death on the road — and they deeply appreciated the differences between what the workers encountered in the old and the new societies. They are deeply grateful to Chairman Mao, and they are grateful to the Chinese Communist Party. One old worker named Wang said: "In the past, with my very own eyes, I saw many brother workers who, although not yet old, could no longer work and were kicked off the docks by the capitalists and the labor contractors. They starved to death on the side of the road. If I were the age I am now and lived in the past, I would have already gotten the short end of the stick and been out begging for food. Now, because the Party and Chairman Mao care and because the nation has shouldered the responsibility for looking after the elderly, I haven't a care in the world. This truly is a dream come true!"

In the past, workers who became ill had no money to buy medicine and so had to grit their teeth and just go on trying to earn their living. Today if someone becomes ill, he can receive the proper rest and the best medical care possible with no worries about medical expenses and no worries about keeping himself fed and clothed. One old retired worker developed a bad ulcer on his leg before the liberation when he was fifty-five years old. He had no money for medicine, so for nearly two years the ulcer just got worse, and he could not work. Life for his family was so extraordinarily difficult that his wife took the children and went out to make a separate living, casting him aside. After the liberation, he retired because of old age, but in 1963 when he was already seventy-five, he contracted another major illness. He had a bad cough, and his whole body had swollen up. He was all alone with no one to look after him. His neighbors all realized that such an old man could not recover on his own, so they notified the loading and unloading district office. When the district office found out about this, it immediately sent someone to take the worker to the Number Two People's Hospital for treatment. The district office production chief and the union cadre both also visited the man. After eight days of the illness, the old man recovered. The costs of the medicine were all paid by the labor insurance system. He himself paid only about three dollars for his meals. The old man was terribly moved. He said the Party had truly shown more consideration for him than even his own relatives had.

On the docks these days, great attention is paid to the health of the workers. If there is sickness, it is treated. If there is no sickness, steps are taken to make sure no sickness breaks out. Each year everyone must be innoculated, and most of the time environmental hygiene is practiced. Dining room utensils are sterilized with steam. Food and water on the job sites are kept in sterilized containers. Each loading area has one professional health worker, and each work team has one member serving concurrently as a health worker. Everyone must have a physical examination each year and must have passed the physical to work in hot weather or in dangerous jobs. Workers judged not to be in good shape are given less demanding work by their leaders. Old workers on the docks who were badly treated in the past and suffer from many ailments can now, through these examinations, receive the proper medicine and care.

As for injuries suffered in work accidents, the attention paid to injured workers is even more comprehensive. Since the liberation, because of the continual strengthening of safety measures and the careful attention of the leadership, the number of injuries from work accidents has been greatly reduced. Yet when a work injury accidentally occurs, the utmost is done to treat it and return the worker to good health as quickly as possible. For instance, in 1963 an old worker named Wu was working in the bottom of a ship's hold when his right leg was smashed. He was immediately taken to a hospital for an operation. After he left the hospital, he went to a convalescent sanitarium to recover from the injury and rested there for a total of three months. All of the medical bills were paid by the state, and he continued to receive his wages. The injury had no ill effect on his life at all. After he returned to work, his leaders assigned him comparatively light work in keeping with his physical condition. Before the liberation, if a worker suffered a work injury, no one would inquire about him, and he would not have the slightest means of dealing with the problem. Comparing these two situations leads the dock workers to appreciate the difference between the old and the new societies and strengthens their love for the new society even more.

In addition to general treatment for illnesses and work injuries, each year some workers are sent away for rest and recuperation. Some old workers go to resort sanitariums in Hangchow or Peitaiho. To visit such fine places and stay in such fine quarters nowadays is a privilege for the workers. They all say that before the liberation they would not have dreamed that this was possible. One old worker sat on his bed at a sanitarium, felt the mattress with his hand, and was so uncontrollably moved that tears ran down his cheeks. Before the liberation, the life of a dock worker was worse than a dog's. After the liberation, the dock worker's health and safety received such considerate and careful attention, how could a man not be moved?

III. Gradual Improvement in Their Material Lives

Only after the liberation did dock workers, who had been treated like beasts of burden before the liberation, really achieve a human existence and really have the material conditions of clothes, food, and housing available to them.

Dock workers had no steady income before the liberation. They lived from day to day, each day poised on the edge between living and dying. Even a single man had great difficulty in making a living. If they stopped working for a moment, they starved, not to mention the famine that hit their families. Since the liberation, dock workers have had steady work and steady incomes. Their material livelihood is assured, so they do not worry about food or clothing. They are in joyful spirits and at ease in their productive work. One old worker said: "Before the liberation, a man had great trouble even providing for himself. I was often out of work, and my children cried with hunger, but all I could do was give them a little water to drink. Now I alone can provide for all five members of my family with what I earn at work. There's no worry about food or clothing, and my three children can even go to school now." This is now the usual situation for dock workers, and they very often reflect on the comparison between how it was and how it is.

Speaking of the food situation, before the liberation there were almost no dock worker families who did not starve. All they had for the main part of their diet was some cracked grain or grain swept up off the ground. Aside from this, they had to rely on other coarse cereals to get through the day, and sometimes they even had to eat wild grass and shrubs to satisfy their hunger. As far as nonstaple foods went, very few people could afford to buy vegetables, and of course there is no need to even talk about meat. Today there is really no problem with dock worker families getting enough food. Their usual diet consists of glutenous rice, common rice, and wheat flour. Their lives are stabilized, and basically they no longer need to worry about getting enough to eat. As for nonstaple foods, normal needs can be satisfied. There is no lack of oil, salt, or vegetables, and people eat fish, meat, and eggs regularly. Some families can even afford to add cow's milk, soybean milk, or other nutritious products to their diets. Truly there is a difference of heaven and earth between this life and the situation before the liberation when people struggled on the edge of starvation for a long time.

The clothing situation is also completely different from what it was in the past. Before the liberation, dock workers wore sacks and torn clothing, and throughout the year they had only straw sandals for their feet. If they did not work for three days, they had to take the shirts off their backs and pawn them. If a worker managed to get a few days' work and accumulate a few days' wages, he could buy an old shirt at the used goods stand. But when the labor contractor or his henchmen saw this, they would say he had stolen the shirt from among the goods on the dock. After all, how could he have enough money to buy clothing? Therefore, the dock workers at that time kept quiet about not having any clothing, and if they had clothing, they could not wear it; they did not dare wear it. In the winter, very few dock workers had cotton-lined garments. On the docks there was water on three sides and open space on the fourth side so that the bone-chilling north wind, without anything to ward it off, hit the workers in their unlined clothing and chilled their bodies so that they shook with the cold. All they could do was grit their teeth, stiffen up, and keep working. Since the liberation, it has become quite common for dock workers to buy cloth and make clothing. Dock workers and their families can now afford to wear a broad range of garments suitable for every season of the year — summer clothing for summer, winter clothing for winter, and cotton-wadded gowns for night so they no longer have to freeze in the cold. Moreover, many people have sweat shirts and knitted woolen sweaters that are insulated, comfortable, and convenient. Tennis shoes and rubber shoes are also extremely common, and some workers have also gotten woolen clothing and leather shoes. The following statistics show how the clothing situation has changed for 277 dock worker families that numbered 1,057 individuals before the liberation and 1,509 individuals after the liberation:

Item	Before liberation		After liberation	
	Total number	Average number per individual	Total number	Average number per individual
Cotton trousers	672	0.64	2,537	1.68
Insulated trousers	46	0.044	1,212	0.80
Knitted woolen trousers	19	0.018	946	0.63
Woolen fabric trousers	5	0.0047	357	0.24
Tennis shoes (pair)	6	0.0057	1,268	0.84
Rubber shoes (pair)	46	0.044	1,014	0.67
Leather shoes (pair)	7	0.0066	412	0.27
Cotton padded gown	347	0.33	1,027	0.68
Woolen blanket	—	—	107	0.71

The numbers listed in the table above for before and after the liberation vividly illustrate the transformation of the dock workers' clothing situation, but this is still merely a quantitative comparison. If we compared the quality of the clothing, the difference would be even more striking. The clothing and padded gowns that dock workers wore before the liberation were full of holes and in scandalously rotten shape. Only most reluctantly can such clothing be included in these statistics for it had already lost most of its capacity to protect someone from the cold. On the other hand, since the liberation, clothing and other effects quite suitably meet the clothing needs. Take shoes, for instance. The straw sandals worn by dock workers in the past quickly wore out, forcing the workers to look continually for bits of straw so they could repair the sandals and wear them again. But now tennis shoes are usually worn, and there are rubber shoes for rainy days and cotton padded shoes for the cold. Each man now has several pairs of shoes. Or, to take another clothing example, the "Eight Trigram cloaks" of the past, consisting of many patches sewn together, served as clothing by day and as a blanket by night, but on rainy days the cloaks got so wet one was better off with nothing on his back. Now coats have an interior lining and an exterior covering. Washable and reversible, they are completely comfortable. From these comparisons, it becomes clear that the situations before and after the liberation are like two different worlds.

The transformation in the dock workers' housing situation is also very remarkable. Before the liberation, dock workers' homes were generally in shanty towns. The shanty towns of that time had garbage heaped up on the ground and disease running rampant. In sum, they were miserable, gloomy slums created by the old man-eating social system. Living in them was like falling into a human hell. Yet there were many dock workers who did not even have this kind of straw shanty to live in and had to live out in the street. During the first period of the liberation, the people's government carried out many work projects to transform the environment of the workers who were congregated in these shanty towns. The government built roads, repaired aqueducts, and installed running water and electric lighting, making great improvements in the environmental sanitation of the shanty towns and making the necessary sanitary conditions available. Then the government also regularly paid out large sums of money to help workers repair and reconstruct their homes. Many dilapidated, broken down straw shacks were completely overhauled and turned into clean, sanitary, well-lighted and well-ventilated houses. The proportion of territory taken up by straw shacks declined greatly, the "dragons rolling on the ground" soon could no longer be seen, and the new construction continued without a letup to bring about a speedy transformation of the appearance of the shanty towns. At the same time, new villages to house large groups of workers rose up all over the city. Many workers moved into new homes where the living conditions had been greatly transformed. By this process, the living conditions of the dock workers were transformed in the same way. Prior to 1965, more than half of the dock workers had already reconstructed or repaired their own dwellings with the assistance of the state administration and their unions. In addition, some worker families moved into existing row houses, and many other worker families moved into new houses.

There has also been quite a substantial transformation in the furniture found inside these houses. In the past, when dock workers did not even have enough food and clothing, how were they going to get any furniture? Some families even lacked such essential utensils as bowls and chopsticks and had to borrow from their neighbors. They slept on the ground covered with straw mats. They had no beds and very few tables and chairs. After the liberation, along with the transformation of living and housing conditions, the dock workers' houses continually added more and more of every kind of furniture and utensil. The table below, based on information from the 277 dock worker families mentioned above, provides a remarkable illustration of what items people were able to acquire before and after the liberation:

Item	Before liberation	After liberation
Bed board	178	374
Bed	18	181
Table	83	376
Chair or stool	149	1,018
Kitchen cupboard	13	136
Chest	129	529
Vehicle	—	15
Clock or watch	10	330
Radio	—	40

To sum up, as far as clothing, food, and housing conditions go, dock workers' lives have already undergone a great transformation since the liberation. Their material lives have reached a general level where they can afford to satisfy the usual demands of life and good health. In addition, some worker families can regularly put away savings and build up a bank account. On the other hand, there are still some families with a comparatively large number of members who have some partial difficulties, but they can all receive aid on a temporary or regular basis, depending on the particular circumstances and, through the solicitude of their leaders and their labor union, be helped to overcome their difficulties and satisfactorily arrange their lives.

IV. The Steady Enrichment of Their Cultural Lives

As the dock workers' material lives improved, their cultural lives were steadily enriched, and their cultural level quickly rose.

Before the liberation, cultural education was designed to serve the exploiting classes. The dock workers and their children, whose poverty had reached an extreme state, basically had no opportunity for an education. At that time, more than

92 percent of the dock workers were illiterate. There were only a very few among their children who could read at all, so there is really no point in even mentioning their cultural life. It was not that the dock workers at that time did not want an education. If they could have found some way to do it, they would all have hoped that their own children could attend school for one or two years and learn to read a little. But in the old society under the control of the exploiting classes, those poor people who wanted an education were simply dreaming. Not only was it economically impossible for them, but people laughed at them for even mentioning it. One old worker named Li studied on his own before the liberation, but he was afraid others would see him so he hid in a dark room when he was reading and as a result became very nearsighted. Clearly, dock workers before the liberation urgently sought education, but all they got was the oppression and restrictions reserved for those in their strata of life and society. Their aspirations could never be realized under the old society. After the liberation, the dock workers shook off the feudal yoke and became masters of their own culture. Many old workers actively and enthusiastically participated in after-hours schooling and movements to wipe out illiteracy. They struggled to overcome the difficulties old people have in memorizing things. They painstakingly reviewed their lessons and took their study seriously so that the great majority eventually took off their illiterate's dunce caps and achieved an elementary or a middle school reading level. Some comparatively young workers studied for several years and made such progress with the encouragement of the Party that they even went to college. This was something that dock workers before the liberation would not have dreamed of in a million years. Only with the advent of a new society under the leadership of the Communist Party could something like this happen.

At the same time, in accordance with the development of mechanization in loading and unloading work, the number of machines being used on the docks was increasing day by day. So the dock workers, on the foundation of mastering culture, also actively studied technology. After a few years, there had built up among the dock workers a large contingent whose technical skills were such that they could operate any piece of loading and unloading equipment with ease and familiarity. In promoting the development of loading and unloading work on the docks, the dock workers have mastered both their culture and their technology.

Even happier are the sons and daughters of the dock workers, for they are now all able to get an education. All children who have reached school age can go to elementary school, about 30 percent can go to middle school, and many can even go to college. For instance, an old worker named Wang had three children, but before the liberation only one could go to a private school to learn to read. After the liberation, he had another child, and in 1965 he had three children attending school — one in elementary school, one in middle school, and one at the Tsingtao University of Marine Studies. The opportunities dock worker children had to receive an education before and after the liberation are terribly different.

As dock workers' material lives have improved and as their cultural level has risen, they have demanded more and more in the way of cultural life. Workers themselves have organized after-hours ensembles and have formed brass bands, folk music groups, song and dance troupes, opera troupes, and even acrobatic groups, magic groups, ballad-singing and storytelling groups, Peking opera groups, Huai [River] opera groups, Shao-hsing opera groups, Shanghai opera groups, and other groups that regularly perform.

Before the liberation, dock workers had basically never had an opportunity to see stage performances, but now they can not only see them, they can make them up and perform in them. On their own, workers have created many short plays, ballads, songs, and poems which they perform themselves. The old workers also have formed chanting groups to perform the dock chants (rhythmic calls to harmonize movements and coordinate breathing when dock workers carry goods). Recreational life throughout the harbor is extremely lively. Several times every year they have recreational festivals or mass songfests. Once a year they have a "spring in the harbor" musical, in which the performers all come from basic-level units. The workers participate enthusiastically, happy to be gathered together. The more active the old workers are, the younger they feel. They sing revolutionary songs, they sing in praise of the Chinese Communist Party, they sing in praise of our great leader Chairman Mao, they sing in praise of the achievements of socialist construction, and they sing in praise of their own new lives.

In addition, physical education activities have developed everywhere. Workers have organized all sorts of ball teams and rowing teams and have developed all sorts of ball game and swimming activities. Each year two sports days are held for the whole harbor.

In the more than ten years since the liberation, the lives of the dock workers have changed completely. They were slaves before; now they have become genuine masters. Old workers who have gone through the hardships of the old society often recall those difficult times before the liberation and feel all the more fortunate in their present lives and all the more thankful for the leadership of the Communist Party and Chairman Mao. At the same time, because of the transformation in their own lives, they are all the more aware of the pain still being suffered throughout the world by their class brothers who are still being oppressed and have not shaken off the feudal yoke. They are terribly concerned about the liberation of these brothers. As a result, they even more resolutely oppose all imperialists and exploiters and even more persistently advance the revolution under the leadership of the Communist Party and Chairman Mao. They have devoted their own strength to the socialist construction of the motherland and the liberation of all the world's laboring people.

II Excerpts from *Historical Materials on the South Seas Brothers Tobacco Factory*

Nan-yang hsiung-ti yen-ts'ao kung-ssu shih-liao [Historical Materials on the South Seas Brothers Tobacco Factory]: Historical Materials on a Model Capitalist Industry in Shanghai. Edited by the Chinese Academy of Sciences, the Shanghai Institute of Economic Research, and the Shanghai Institute of Social Science Research. Shanghai: Jen-min ch'u-pan-she, 1960. These translations are taken, with minor editorial revisions, from Chinese Sociology and Anthropology. Translated by K. C. Ma.

Contents

1

The Living and Working Conditions of the Workers (in Shanghai)

Section I. General Conditions That Concerned the Workers

A. Sectionalization of the Factory

1. The Works Department of the Shanghai factory is directly under the Main Office in Shanghai and comes under the direction and supervision of the manager-in-chief and the submanager.

2. The Works Department of the Shanghai factory is managed by the head of the Works Department and the chief engineer, and these two are in turn under the Main Office in Shanghai and are responsible for the operation of the factory.

3. The head of the Works Department takes his orders from the manager-in-chief and the submanager. His responsbilities include the personnel management of the factory's administrative staff, the appropriation of raw materials, the planning of production, quality control, the appropriation of finance, the receipt of goods, and the management of external affairs.

4. Under the direction of the manager-in-chief and the submanager, the chief engineer is in charge of the improvement of production in the factory, the planning and installations in the factory, the supervision of engineering work, and the discipline of the workers. All external matters are the responsi-

---

"Kung-jen sheng-huo chuang-k'uang ho lao-tung t'iao-chien (Shang-hai fang-mien)." Chapter 6 of Book Two ("The Development and Decline of the Company after Extensive Reorganization [November 1919-1936]) of Nan-yang hsiung-ti yen-ts'ao kung-ssu shih-liao. This translation is taken from Chinese Sociology and Anthropology, VI:1 (Fall 1973), 40-93 (tables omitted).

bility of the head of the Works Department.

5. The Works Department is divided into the cigarette-rolling, tobacco-leaves, packaging, and general duties sections.

6. The cigarette-rolling section is under the charge of one head and his several assistants. They are in turn under the direction of the head of the Works Department and the chief engineer. The head of the cigarette-rolling section and his assistants are in charge of the cigarette-making machines, the unwrapping of poorly-produced cigarettes, and the factory's electricity, water, gas pipings, boiler rooms, and any other maintenance work of the machinery.

(Appended Note: Article 3 of the Work Regulations of the cigarette-rolling section:

Under the direction of the head, the assistants of the cigarette-rolling section are charged with the following duties:

a) the collection of tobacco shreds and the collection and delivery of all raw materials and secondary ingredients;

b) matters related to cigarette-making and cigarette-rolling;

c) the inspection and removal of damp cigarettes and the collection and unwrapping of poorly produced cigarettes;

d) the sharpening of the circular blades;

e) the maintenance of the cigarette-rolling machines; the factory's electricity, water, gas pipings, boiler rooms, and any other repairs of the machinery.)

7. The tobacco-leaves section is under the charge of one head and several assistants. They are in turn under the direction of the head of the Works Department and the chief engineer. The head of this section and his assistants supervise the weighing, treating, steaming and mixing of the leaves. Their responsibilities also include the removal of the veins from the leaves, their grinding and cutting, and the cutting of the stems. Other duties include the preparation and addition of the spices, the cutting of tobacco, the opening of the barrels, crates, or sacks in which the leaves are delivered, the sharpening of the blades, the curing of the tobacco shreds by drying, the weighing of the tobacco shreds, and all other duties arising from the work in this section.

8. The packaging section is under the direction of one head and several assistants. They are in turn under the direction

of the head of the Works Department and the chief engineer. The head of this section and his assistants are responsible for the crating, wrapping, and dry-curing of the cigarettes, the manufacture of large and small packets, crates, round tins, and large tins, the wrapping of the large packets, the hardening of round jars by heating, and all other duties arising from the work in this section.

9. There are a number of security guards in the factory, and these are under the direct supervision of the Works Department.

10. If for any reason either the head of the Works Department or the chief engineer is absent from work, his duties will be taken over by the other.

("Regulations on the Organization of the Works Department of the Shanghai Manufacturing Plant of the South Seas Company" [Nan-yang kung-ssu Shang-hai chih-tso-ch'ang kung-wu-shih tsu-chih kuei ch'eng]; the original document is not dated, but was probably written before November 1, 1931.)

B. Categories of Workers

Classification by Sex: More Than 85 Percent of the Workers in Tobacco Factories Were Females. Throughout all the tobacco factories, the female workers outnumbered the male workers eight times over. But as for their position, they were also eight times worse off than the male workers. This was a great shame and insult to the female workers. Let me give an example by describing the distribution of the work force in the various sections, so that we may better understand the situation.

1. Female workers in the tobacco-leaves section. (The majority of them were between thirty and fifty years old; they worked by hand.)

2. Male workers in the tobacco-shredding section. (They worked with the help of machines.)

3. Male workers in the curing section.

4. Male workers in the cigarette-rolling section. (They worked with the help of machines and were between sixteen and thirty years old.)

5. Female workers in the foil-wrapping section. (The majority of these workers were between sixteen and thirty years old.)

6. Packeting section.

7. Male workers in the crating section.

8. Female workers in the section dealing with poorly produced cigarettes (old women).

In a tobacco factory with ten machines, the distribution of the work force would be as follows:

Tobacco-leaves section	200 female workers
Tobacco-shredding section	10 male workers
Curing section	6 male workers
Cigarette-rolling section	20 male workers
Foil-wrapping section	350-400 female workers
Packeting section	female workers (the number varied, with some factories having none at all)
Miscellaneous duties section	female workers (as above)
Husking section	female workers (as above)
Crating section	6 male workers

In a factory, therefore, female workers would make up at least 85 percent of the work force.

As to classification by age, sixth-tenths of the workers were aged between sixteen and thirty, two-tenths between thirty and fifty, one-tenth between fifty and sixty, and one-tenth between ten and sixteen.

(Chu Pang-hsing et al., eds., <u>Shanghai Industries and the</u>

Shanghai Workers [Shang-hai ch'an-yeh yü Shang-hai chih-kung], first edition, Yüan-tung ch'u-pan-she, July 15, 1939. Chap. 18 for the cigarette industry, pp. 512-514.)

Classification by the Form of Remuneration: Monthly, Daily or by Piece-Rate.

33. The workers in the factory are divided into three kinds: the regularly employed, casual, and piece-rate workers. Those who are paid monthly are considered as regular workers, those who are paid daily are casual workers, and those who are paid by piece-rate are piece-rate workers. All three kinds of workers, on taking up work in the factory, must be processed in accordance with Article 23 of this Detailed Regulations (i.e., entered in the register of workers).

40. All casual and piece-rate workers are hired on a temporary basis, and either party can terminate the employment at any time without paying any compensation. But during the period of employment, if a worker does not report for work for three successive days without any specified reason, this company will consider that he has terminated his employment on his own accord and will proceed with finding a substitute for him. Thereafter, he may only take up his employment again with the permission of this company.

("Detailed Regulations Regarding the Work of the Works Department of the Shanghai Factory of the Chinese South Seas Brothers Company" [Chung-kuo Nan-yang hsiung-ti kung-ssu Shang-hai kung-ch'ang kung-wu-shih pan-shih hsi-tse], the original document is not dated, but was probably written before November 1931.)

Article 4. On taking employment, all monthly and daily workers in the factory must sign a contract of employment, clearly stating the duration of employment, and this must be honored.

("Regulations of the Shanghai Manufacturing Plant of the South Seas Company" [Nan-yang kung-ssu Shang-hai chih-tso-ch'ang kuei-tse], November 3, 1931.)

Classification by the Native Province and Age of the Workers. Half of the workers came from Ningpo and from Kiangsu and Anhwei provinces, while the other half came from various other provinces.

Among the female workers, 50 percent were in the twenty-thirty-five age-group, 20 percent in the twelve-twenty age-group, and those aged under twelve and those over thirty-five together made up 7-8 percent. Among the male workers, most were aged between twenty and forty, and there were very few outside this age-group.

("An Investigation into the Latest Situation in the South Seas Brothers Tobacco Limited Company" [Nan-yang hsiung-ti yen-ts'ao yu-hsien kung-ssu tsui-chin chuang-k'uang chih tiao-ch'a], an investigation carried out in 1928, published in The Industrial and Commercial Fortnightly [Kung-shang pan-yüeh-k'an] Vol. 1 No. 1, January 1, 1929.)

Section II. Working Hours and Working Conditions

A. Working Hours, the Working Day, and Night Shifts

Before November 1931.

34. The first half of the working day in this factory runs from 7:00 a.m. to 12:00 p.m., and the second half runs from 1:00 p.m. to 6:00 p.m. If owing to weather conditions these times have to be changed, one workday unit still comprises ten hours. If a worker continues to work beyond this daytime workday unit of ten hours, his overtime work will be paid at a rate one-third higher than the normal daytime rate, with one overtime work-unit comprising seven and a half hours. However, for those workers on shift-rotation work, Article 35 applies.

35. If for reasons of business this factory has to operate during the nighttime as well, a system of shift-rotation work will be used, and this will be altered once a week. Under this system, the hours of the daytime shift will be as in Article 34, and the nighttime shift will run from when the day-time shift finishes to midnight, and another nighttime shift will run from 11:00 p.m. to when the daytime shift starts the following morning. The rate of pay for the nighttime shift is 50 percent higher than the rate for daytime work.

36. At the beginning of each work shift, a regular worker must sign in on the attendance book in the Works Department, and a casual worker must punch the time clock. No worker may be more than five minutes late. If a regular worker is between five and fifteen minutes late, a deduction of 2 chiao will be made from his wage, and for a casual worker the deduction will be 1 chiao. If any worker is more than fifteen minutes late, he will be considered as absent on that day, and will not be paid.

....

38. The wages in this factory are paid twice a month, in the middle of the month and at the end of the month. There are two rest days every month (on every other Sunday). We also

observe the public holidays laid down by the government. Only the regular workers will receive pay for these rest days.

("Detailed Regulations Regarding Work in the Shanghai Factory of the South Seas Brothers Tobacco Company of China" [Chung-kuo Nan-yang hsiung-ti yen-ts'ao kung-ssu Shang-hai-ch'ang pan-shih hsi-tse], the original document is not dated, but was probably written before November 1931.)

After November 1931.

Article 10. The first half of the working day in this factory runs from 7:00 a.m. to 12:00 noon, and the second half runs from 1:00 p.m. to 6:00 p.m. If owing to weather conditions these times have to be changed, one workday unit still comprises ten hours. If a worker continues to work beyond this daytime workday unit of ten hours, his overtime work will be paid at a rate one-half higher than the normal daytime rate. However, for those fellow workers [kung-yu] on shift-rotation work with specially assigned hours, this overtime rate of pay will not apply.

Article 11. If for reasons of business this factory has to operate during the nighttime as well, a system of shift-rotation work will be used, and this will be altered once a week. The night shift: the first section will run from when the day-time shift finishes to 10:00 p.m., the second from 10:30 p.m. to 2:00 a.m., and the third from 3:00 a.m. to when the daytime shift starts the following morning. The rate of pay for the nighttime shift is 50 percent higher than the rate for the daytime work.

Article 12. At the beginning of each work shift, a monthly worker must sign in on the attendance book in the Works Department, and a daily worker must punch the time clock. No worker may be more than five minutes late. If a worker is between five and fifteen minutes late, this will be considered as tardiness or negligence. If a worker is more than fifteen minutes late, he will be considered as absent on that day, and will not be paid.

Article 13. The five minutes at the end of each shift are to be used for putting the tools away, washing your hands and putting on your clothes. A foreman may not leave the factory until the workers under his charge have all left.

("Regulations of the Shanghai Manufacturing Plant of the South Seas Company.")

B. Atrocious Work Conditions

The Polluted Air and the High Incidence of Pulmonary Consumption. During midsummer, the more oppressive the weather, the more tightly closed were all the windows and doors. The management would not allow them to be open so as to prevent the tobacco from going bad. There were no ventilation facilities on the factory floor, or any safety or protection measures.

The doors on the factory floor were all locked, so that the workers would not be able to move about freely and hamper production. This practice continued through to the time when the factory was on Chiao-chou Road.

The most common illnesses among the workers were pulmonary consumption and ulcers. Wang Yung-sheng once suffered from an acute ulcer, but the company's regulations stated that a sick leave of over three months would mean automatic dismissal from work. Therefore, although his health was failing, Huang continued to work. The fact that his health is still not sound today is the consequence of what took place. Before liberation, Ssu Hsiao-feng could not bear up to the sheer pace of the work, and this, together with her poor living conditions, led to pulmonary consumption. Nothing could be done at the time, and it was only after liberation that she received treatment. This lasted for five years, but under the regulations for the protection of labor, she continued to receive wages throughout this period. The medical expenses, totaling over 1,800 yuan, were also borne by the state.

("A Record of a Conversation with the Old Workers of the Shanghai Factory, Comrades Huang Yung-sheng, Ssu Hsiao-feng, and Others" [Shang-hai-ch'ang lao-kung-jen Huang Yung-sheng, Ssu Hsiao-feng teng t'ung-chih tso-t'an chi-lu], July 11, 1958.)

....The floor of the factory was only washed once every couple of months, and at best once every fortnight. Water was never sprinkled on the floor when it was being swept, and so the air was full of tiny tobacco particles which, when inhaled, brought indescribable unpleasantness. Moreover, cigarettes contain the poisonous substance nicotine, and since the factory was unsanitary, many workers were exposed to it over a long period, and their nasal cavities developed infection and abcess. In a minor case, the effects were headache and the discharge of mucus, but in a serious case, the nose would cease to function altogether, the sufferer would be unable to smell or breathe, and the nose would eventually be blocked up completely and the sufferer would have to rely on his mouth for respiration. We would only need to see the thick yellow nasal mucus in the spittoons used by the workers to realize the high incidence and seriousness of nasal infection among the workers. The nose is an important respiratory organ, and its malfunction will directly affect the lungs. In the factory, the conditions of the workers were further aggravated by the lack and poor quality of food and the abuses and ill-treatment by the management, and so a great number of them contracted pulmonary consumption....

(Chu Pang-hsing et al., eds., Shanghai Industries and the Shanghai Workers, Chap. 18.)

The Absence of Canteens, the Substandard Food, and the High Incidence of Illness during the Summer. Most of the workers brought cold rice to work with them, which they warmed up with hot water during their meals, but it was not always that they could get hold of hot water. During the summer, the rice would turn rancid very quickly, but there was nothing they could do but eat it, and this led to illness in many cases. There was nothing like we have today — a factory running its own canteen where the workers can order what they like.

The plight of the female workers was the worst, since they had no time off for meals at all; they would loose on wages if they took time off to eat. Thus a great many of them would gnaw on biscuits while they were working. When the weather was hot, they would sweat profusely, and when the sweat got on to their faces and into their eyes, they would just wipe it off with their arms, not stopping for a single moment. During busy periods of production, they would have to work from seven in the morning to eleven or twelve at night, and some could just not stand up physically to this pace. But during slack periods of production, they might have just two hours of work to do a day, and so even though they might be in the factory the whole day, they would only be paid for two hours' work.

("A Record of a Conversation with the Old Workers of the Shanghai Factory, Comrades Huang Yung-sheng, Ssu Hsiao-feng, and Others.")

There was no canteen in the factory. The lunch break for the male workers was from 12:00 noon to 1:00 p.m., but only a very few would be able to go home for lunch. The great majority would just buy some pastry from outside the factory gates, or go to nearby eating places. As for the female workers, they were all on piece-rate, and most of the tobacco factories did not give them time off for lunch. . . . Even if there had been time off . . . most of the workers lived so far away from the factories that a return journey would take over an hour, and so many would just buy something to eat outside the factory gates. Every morning, as soon as we got up, we had to hurry off to work, and sometimes we did not even have time to wash our faces. On the way, we would buy a couple of biscuits, millet dumplings, baked sweet potatoes, or some such things to take to the factory to eat. If a member of the staff or a foreman saw what we had, we would suffer their abuse, and a male worker might even receive a bad mark on his record. Inside the factory, everything such as the tables and the wooden boxes were all completely covered with tiny tobacco particles, and since the female workers were all on piece-rate, naturally they would want to do as much as possible to earn a few extra coppers. So when a female worker was taking her food, she would take a bite from whatever it was that she had, then put it down on the table (which was the same as putting it on a pile of tobacco particles), and then she would do a few more packets of cigarettes before she took another bite. Thus a great deal of the tobacco particles was in fact taken in with the food. This was the case with both breakfast and lunch. If a worker brought with him some cold rice in the morning, and then made it hot again with hot water for lunch, this would be considered a first-class meal. But some of the factories did not have hot water, and this would mean having the rice cold. On hot days, none of the workers would bring rice since it would turn sour so easily in the heat of the factory. Most would just buy some pastry, and some would have for lunch cold things such as melons or other fruits, since by the time one finished work at noon, one would feel so thirsty and parched that one could not swallow down any biscuits, and one would want to have some cucumbers, arbutus, or pears to quench one's thirst. But having a breakfast or lunch like this was most harmful to the health of the workers, and so during the summer there were many cases of cholera, vomiting and diarrhea. If it had been possible to keep an estimate of the amount of tobacco dust and tobacco particles that each worker was taking into his system every day, I am sure a considerable quantity would have been revealed.

(Chu Pang-hsing et al., eds., Shanghai Industries and the Shanghai Workers, Chap. 18.)

C. Various Forms of Punishment against the Workers

A Minor "Infringement" of the Factory Regulations Meant a Cash Penalty or a Bad Mark on One's Record, and a Serious One Meant Instant Dismissal. Each section of the factory was under a section-head, a deputy section-head, and several foremen. A worker's every action had to be in accordance with the regulations of the factory. A minor infringement meant a cash penalty or a bad mark on his record, and a serious one meant instant dismissal. No male or female worker in the factory could smoke. No worker could take any cigarettes from the production line. A regular worker discovered to have removed one cigarette would be fined one yuan on his first offense, and a small bad mark would be made on his record; for a piece-rate worker, such an offense would mean instant dismissal. If a worker wished to remove any of his luggage or articles from the factory premises, he had to first have the approval by signature of his section-head, and then his articles had to be inspected by the security guard. If this procedure was not followed, it would be deemed that he was stealing.

("An Investigation into the Latest Situation in the South Seas Brothers Tobacco Company.")

The Regulation on Searching a Worker.
Article 9. Every employee that is leaving the factory prem-

ises, regardless of whether he is carrying any articles, must not refuse a search of his body by a security guard at the gate if the latter deems it necessary.

("Regulations of the Shanghai Manufacturing Plant of the South Seas Company.")

Many of the Factory Regulations Dealt with the Punishment of the Workers. There were many factory regulations, and there were large signs hung up in the work areas which displayed some of these regulations. Most of these regulations dealt with punishment or penalties, and very few dealt with prizes or incentives. The regulations forbade the removal of cigarettes from the production line. If one took between one to five cigarettes, the cash penalty would be 1 yuan, while taking more than five would mean dismissal; and we were also searched on leaving the factory. Brawling or flirting with the female workers would mean dismissal; spitting would mean a cash penalty of 2 chiao, smoking a cash penalty of 1 yuan, being late for work a penalty of 5 fen for a worker and 1 chiao for a member of the administrative staff, while forgetting to punch in would mean a cash penalty of 5 fen for a worker, and forgetting to sign in would mean a penalty of 1 chiao for a member of the staff.

("A Record of a Conversation with Some Old Employees of the Shanghai Factory" [Shang-hai-ch'ang lao chih-kung tso-t'an-hui chi-lu], January 21, 1958.)

The Penalties Laid down before November 1931.

44. Without the permission of the Works Department, no employee may take any cigarettes out of this factory. If anyone is found to have removed from one to five cigarettes, the sum of 1 yuan will be deducted from his wage, while removing

more than five cigarettes will mean dismissal.

....

46. Anyone who commits any of the following will be dismissed:

1) disobedience of the orders of the Works Department;

2) brawling;

3) flirting with the female workers;

4) stealing company property;

5) malicious damage of company property (in addition to dismissal, the cost of the damage will be deducted from the offender's wage);

6) deliberately producing shoddy goods (in addition to dismissal, the cost of the losses will be deducted from the offender's wage);

7) slowdown to the rules;

8) stirring up labor troubles, and sabotaging production;

9) cheating at wages;

10) making a false statement as to the price of a piece of goods for private gain, or secretly making a commission at the company's expense;

11) leaving the factory after signing in or punching in.

47. Anyone who commits any of the following will be penalized in accordance with the seriousness of the offense. Cash penalties will be deducted from the wages of the offenders. Anyone that commits any of the following four times in a month will be dismissed:

1) being absent from one's post,

2) being late for work, or negligent at work,

3) producing shoddy goods,

4) dozing or sleeping at work,

5) being noisy and rowdy,

6) insulting one's fellow workers,

7) spitting indiscriminately.

("Detailed Regulations Regarding the Work of the Works Department of the Shanghai Factory of the Chinese South Seas Brothers Company.")

The Penalties Laid down after November 1931.

Article 29. Without the permission of the factory manager, no employee may take any of the products of the factory. If anyone is found to have removed one to five cigarettes, the sum of 1 yuan will be deducted from his wage, while removing more than five cigarettes will not only mean deduction from the offender's wage but also dismissal from work. If anyone is found to have removed more than a hundred cigarettes, it will mean both dismissal and the total forfeit of his wage. (This sum of money will go to the witness against the offender, or to the person who has discovered the cigarettes.)

Article 30. Anyone who is proved to have committed any of the following will be either dismissed or ordered to pay compensation.

1. disobedience of the factory orders, amidst or leading to serious circumstances;
2. gathering in a crowd and brawling, creating disturbances on the factory floor;
3. flirting with the female workers and hampering work;
4. stealing company property;
5. malicious damage of a piece of company property that is worth more than 5 yuan;
6. deliberately producing shoddy goods, amidst or leading to serious circumstances;
7. stirring up labor troubles, and proven sabotage of production;
8. cheating at wages;
9. making a false statement as to the price of a piece of goods for private gain, or secretly making a commission at the company's expense;
10. leaving the factory after signing in or punching in.

Article 31. Anyone that commits any of the following will be penalized in accordance to the seriousness of the offense. Cash penalties will be deducted from the wages of the offenders.

Anyone that commits any of the following four times in a month will be dismissed.

1. being absent from one's post — cash penalty of 4 chiao;
2. being late for work, or negligence at work — cash penalty of 1 chiao for a daily worker, and 2 chiao for a monthly worker;
3. producing shoddy goods — cash penalty will be based on the extent of the negligence;
4. dozing or sleeping at work — cash penalty of 2 chiao;
5. being noisy and rowdy — cash penalty of 4 chiao;
6. insulting one's fellow workers — cash penalty of 1 yuan;
7. spitting indiscriminately — cash penalty of 1 chiao;
8. forgetting to punch in or punch out — cash penalty of 2 chiao;
9. forgetting to sign in — cash penalty of 2 chiao;
10. stopping work before the shift is over — cash penalty of 2 chiao.

("Regulations of the Shanghai Manufacturing Plant of the Southseas Company.")

Section III. The Livelihood of the Workers

A. The General Situation

1. The Level of Wages

The Level of Wages in the Shanghai Factory in 1920. In 1920 the daily wage of a male worker in the Shanghai Southseas Tobacco Company was between 4 and 5 chiao, with an additional bonus for night work. The daily wage of a female worker was between 200 and 300 wen, with a bonus of 200 wen for night work.

(The First Chinese Labor Year-Book [Ti-i-tz'u Chung-kuo lao-tung nien-chien], edited by Pei-ching she-hui tiao-ch'a-pu, December, 1928, p. 25.)

The Level of Wages in the Shanghai Factory in 1928... Of the regular workers, there were 60 male workers and over 130 female workers in the leaves-mixing section; there were over 20 male workers and the same number of female workers in the spice-adding section; there were about 100 male workers and over 50 female workers in the leaves-cutting section, over 60 male workers in the tobacco-curing section, over 250 male workers and over 10 female workers in the cigarette-making section, over 300 female workers in the cigarette-wrapping section, over 30 female workers in the packet-making section, over 90 female workers in the tin-packing section, over 20 male workers in the blade-sharpening section, over 30 workers in the cement and carpentry section, over 10 clerks in the general affairs section, over 10 clerks in the miscellaneous duties section, about 20 workers in the electrical appliances section, 8 members of the administrative staff in the works section, 5 persons in the disciplinary investigation section, over 120 workers in the machinery section, over 10 accounting clerks, over 40 persons in the security section, and about 10 wages clerks. This makes a total of over 1,500 male and female administrative staff and workers that were regularly employed.... (The Wages of the Regular Workers): The monthly wage of a worker in the leaves-mixing section was between 15 to just over 30 yuan, a worker in the spice-mixing section between 20-odd and 40-odd yuan, a worker in the leaves-cutting section between 15 and 25 yuan, between 20 and 30 yuan in the tobacco-curing section and cigarette-making section, between 20 and 30 yuan in the packet-making section, about 30 yuan in the crate-making section, between 15 and 20-odd yuan in the tin-packing section, and 20-odd yuan in the blade-sharpening section. The daily wage of a cement worker or carpenter was 9 chiao, or a monthly wage of 27 yuan. The monthly wage of the administrative staff in the general affairs section varied between 20 and 100-odd yuan. The monthly wage of a worker in the miscellaneous duties section was about 30 yuan, and about 45 yuan in the electrical appliances section. Those who worked in the Works Department were the senior staff members of the factory, such as the engineers, chemists and the head of the Works Department, and their monthly wages varied between one hundred and several hundred yuan. The members of the disciplinary investigation section received a monthly wage of between 40 and 50 yuan, and members of the inspection section about 20-30 yuan. Workers in the machinery section were divided into several grades: an experienced worker who had worked in the factory over a number of years received a monthly wage of between 70 and 80 yuan, while an ordinary worker in this section received a monthly wage of just 30-odd yuan. The monthly wages of the members of the accounts section and the wages clerks were high, and most of them received a monthly wage of between 40 and 150 yuan. The paydays of each month were the first and the fifteenth on the lunar calendar. . . .

2. Some Supplementary Materials Concerning Wages and Remuneration

The Level of Wages and the Methods of Promotion and Wage Increases in the Early Period. As for the standard of wages in the period 1916-1918, a machine-operator earned 0.80 yuan a day, moving tobacco about earned a worker 0.60 yuan a day, while a child laborer earned 0.40 yuan for a day's work. Most of the workers were daily workers. There were two rest days every month. Prior to 1924 there were two increases in wages every year, and one increase could be as much as three or four yuan, and so wages were getting higher every year.

In 1922 an association of comrade employees [chih-kung t'ung-chih hui] was established, and the system of holidays was modified to one rest day a week. Wages were increased on the average and many short-term workers were promoted to regular employment. A method of promotion was also laid down; it was based on the assumption that there were thirty rest days in a year, and so if a worker worked a whole month without a rest day, two and a half days' of his work would be paid at a higher rate. Since wages were increased every year in the period before the factory was shut down, the daily wage of a machine-operator was now between fifty and sixty yuan, while a worker employed to move tobacco about was earning more than one yuan a day. When the main factory reopened, all workers were taken on as new, and the previous system of wages was abolished.

("A Record of a Conversation with Some Old Administrative Staff of the Shanghai Factory" [Shang-hai-ch'ang lao-chih-yüan tso-t'an chi-lu], June 7, 1957.)

The General Level of Wages and the Methods of Payment of Wages after the Introduction of the Piece-Work System.

The daily wage of a daily worker was 0.65-0.75 yuan, and in general a daily worker earned between 20 and 22 yuan a month.

A regular worker (monthly worker) earned between 28 and 29 yuan a month, and in a few cases, 30 yuan a month. A worker employed to move tobacco about earned 0.60 yuan a day, a machine-operator 0.80-0.90 yuan a day, and a repair worker 1.00-1.10 yuan a day.

The daily wage of a child laborer was between 0.40 and 0.50 yuan.

The rate of pay for night work and overtime work was three times the normal rate.

Before the old factory was shut down and before the founding of the union, there were two wage increases every year. After the establishment of the union, it argued for uniform improvements for all workers. There were two rest days every month, and if these were not taken by a worker, his rate of pay for two and a half days' work in every month would be at a higher rate. After the factory had been reopened, the rate of pay for the day's work after a rest day was doubled, and this meant in effect that the rest day was a paid one.

After the main factory had resumed production, a piece-work system was put into operation, but this was slightly different from the piece-work method at the Ching-hua factory. Every month, the daily workers and the monthly workers (but not the piece-work workers) would receive "prize money" [chiang-chin] of three yuan. During the slack seasons this would be increased to six yuan. In addition, on each of three festivals every year (the Dragon-Boat Festival, the Mid-Autumn Festival, the Winter Solstice), each worker would receive three yuan. The rest of the fund used for this purpose would be distributed at the end of the year. But it was stipulated that part of this year-end "prize money," which was to be equivalent to a month's wage, had to be put aside as savings. At the end of the first five years, a worker could then withdraw every year up to a month's wage from his savings. This meant that a worker always had five years' savings (equivalent to five months' wages). This was an emulation of a method in the factories of the British-American Tobacco Company.

Wages were paid on the fifteenth and thirtieth of each month, and each employee would also receive a number of "welfare cigarettes" [fu-li yen]. A regularly employed worker would receive 50 cigarettes, a member of the administrative staff between 100 to 150, and the head of each section 250, while a piece-rate worker would not receive any.

("A Record of a Conversation with Some Old Employees of the Shanghai Factory.")

Regulations concerning Absence Due to Sickness and Other Causes.

Article 15. Sunday is a rest day, and all regular workers will receive wages as normal.

Article 16. If for any other reason other than sickness an employee has to be absent from work, he must clearly state the reason for his absence and the duration of the absence, and such leave of absence may only be taken with the approval of the factory manager. Wages during the absence will be deducted accordingly. If there is no return to work at the end of the stated period of absence, the employee will be considered as being absent without reason. Two or three successive days of such unexplained absence will be taken to mean a voluntary resignation.

Article 17. Absence due to sickness of any employee must be certified by a doctor to the effect that such a rest is essential to treatment. During an absence due to sickness, a regular worker will be paid his normal wage, and a daily worker will be paid half his normal wage (but wages will not be paid to a piece-rate worker or a temporary casual worker).

....

Article 21. All wages of employees are paid in Shanghai universal silver yuan. Wages are paid out twice a month, on the sixteenth for the first half of the month, and on the first for the second half. Wages for piece-rate workers or temporary short-term daily workers are paid daily or weekly.

("Regulations of the Shanghai Manufacturing Plant of the South Seas Company.")

Treatment at the Branch Factory at P'u-tung. . . . All male and female workers in this factory, after a period of work of six full months, receive a 5 percent increase in their wages. This amount is deposited with the company, and each worker is issued a deposit book, and the monthly interest is 8 percent. If a worker of the factory falls ill, he is treated by the doctors in the factory, and the factory pays for the medical expenses. During the period of illness, the factory pays the worker the full wage during the first half-month, then 50 percent of the full wage during the second half-month. No wage is paid after a month of illness, and a worker is automatically dismissed after three months of illness. The dependants of a worker who dies as a result of an accident at work are paid a compensation equivalent to 10 percent of his total annual wages. This percentage is increased to 12.5 percent for the dependants of a worker who has worked in the factory for a full ten years, and to 15 percent for the dependants of a worker who has worked for a full fifteen years. A female worker who becomes pregnant and who has worked in the factory for a full six months is given a month of leave from work and also a midwifery fee of ten dollars. Sunday is a paid rest day for all regular workers, but piece-work workers are not paid. On public holidays (such as the New Year), all workers receive the sum of 0.35 yuan. Achievement prizes for good workers are presented in December each year, and the sum of this prize for a worker is 4 percent of his total annual wage, regardless of the state of business of the company. (Thus for a worker whose annual total wage comes to 1,000 yuan, his achievement prize would be 40 yuan.)

("An Investigation into the Latest Situation of the South Seas Brothers Tobacco Limited Company.")

The "welfare" treatment [fu-li tai-yü] at "Little South Seas" [Hsiao Nan-yang] was slightly better than that at the old factory. For every yuan of a worker's monthly wage, five fen was put aside by the factory as savings for the worker, and this savings was doubled every five years by the factory. There was no such scheme at the old factory. But there was a catch in this scheme: if a worker was dismissed or made a bad mistake, then all his savings would be forfeited. This was a method of controlling the workers, and the longer a worker had been working in the factory, the more afraid he would be of making a mistake. There was no rest period during the summer, and the wages paid were the same. As for the female workers, their situation was that much worse than that of the male workers. During periods of suspended production, they would not be paid any sort of cash grants to help them cope with the stoppage of work....

("A Record of an Interview with an Old Worker, Comrade Chuang Yü-ch'ing" [Lao-kung-jen Chuang Yü-ch'ing t'ung-chih fang-wen chi-lu], transcribed on May 12, 1958.)

3. The Reminiscences of Some Old Workers concerning the Standard of Wages and the Experiences of Life at the Time

A Cigarette-Rolling Worker and Machine-Operator. I was fifteen years old when I started to work at the South Seas Factory in the second month on the lunar calendar, 1918. On joining the factory, I was assigned as an apprentice in the cigarette-rolling section. My daily wage was 2 chiao, and my working day was ten hours long, divided into a day shift and a night shift. Not long after I joined the factory, the workers went on strike for more pay, and I received an increase of 2 to 3 fen.

Even though I was an apprentice, I was considered as a monthly worker, and this meant that I still could receive my wage during rest days, which were on the fifteenth and thirtieth of each month. Three years later, I was promoted to be a worker in the work of moving tobacco about, and my daily wage was 4 chiao. In 1925 I became a machine operator, and I received 5 chiao a day. By the time the old factory closed, I was receiving 1 yuan a day. When production was resumed, my wage was reduced to 8 chiao a day. Prior to the "August 13 Incident," I was receiving 1.04 yuan a day.

During the period when there were two increases of wages every year, the increases were by no means uniform. Those who obsequiously flattered their superiors would receive bigger increases than those who didn't. In general, the largest increase workers were getting was 7 fen, while the increases for some could be as little as 2-3 fen.

In the past, every year there would be an increase of 1 chiao per day from December 16 on the western calendar, and an increase of 2 chiao per day from the twenty-fourth to the end of the year. This was designed to encourage the workers to work more so that there would not be any decrease in the volume of production. At the end of the year, we would receive some "reward money" [shang-ch'ien] which was put inside an envelope, the amount being at the discretion of the management.

Before 1924, we would each receive 1 yuan on the eve of the Dragon-Boat Festival, the Mid-Autumn Festival, and the Winter Solstice. But this money was only given out to those at work on these particular nights, and if anyone was absent, he would not be able to collect his money on the next working day.

For a time in the beginning, a monthly worker had been able to receive an extra two-and-a-half days' wage for every month's work. But this arrangement was abolished after the union had been reorganized. It was only after a struggle that this was restored, but now this extra amount was paid only to those monthly workers who would work for a full month without any rest days.

In the past, South Seas was described as "a factory of the administrative staff" [chih-yüan ch'ang], since their remuneration was much better than that of the workers. In the beginning, the wages paid to the workers at South Seas were not lower than those paid to workers at the factories of the British-American Tobacco Company. Later on, as South Seas shut down frequently and the workers were taken on again only as new workers at each reopening, the standard of wages at South Seas became lower than that of the factories of the British-American Tobacco Company.

There was a regulation in the factory with regard to the

searching of the workers. If a worker was found to have one cigarette on him, he would have to pay a cash penalty of 1 yuan, and more than five cigarettes would mean dismissal. Brawling would also mean cash penalties or dismissal, while tardiness would mean a cash penalty of 1 chiao. If one forgot to, or did not, extend a leave of absence, it would also mean a cash penalty of 1 chiao. We could not even talk with each other that much, or have too many outside activities, since either would mean a cash penalty or dismissal.

("A Record of an Interview with an Old Worker, Comrade Wu Ping-hou" [Lao-kung-jen Wu Ping-hou t'ung-chih fang-wen chih-lu], transcribed on April 16, 1958.)

Machine-Maintenance Workers. I joined South Seas in 1921 as a maintenance worker on the cigarette-rolling machines. I was a monthly worker from the time I joined, and my wage was 1.2 yuan a day. By the time the factory shut down in 1930, I was earning 55.5 yuan a month. Later on I went to work in the Ching-hua factory and was a temporary worker until the factory was officially opened for production. I was earning 8 chiao a day, and meals were provided at the factory. After the factory had been officially opened for production, I was back on my former wage, and there was no increase in my wage up to the time of the outbreak of the War of Resistance. After the old factory was opened for production, the daily wage of a worker employed to move tobacco about was 6 chiao, while a machine operator earned from 8 chiao to 1 yuan a day.

Prior to the great strike of 1924, there was an annual increase in wages, but this was discontinued after the strike.

The annual bonus was an unpredictable thing: some years we would receive it, and some years we would not. In some years it could be as little as several yuan, in some years as much as 20 to 30 yuan; at most it could be as much as 40 to 50 yuan. In the several years before the "May 30 Incident," the business of the company was bad, and we did not receive any bonuses. In the year of the "May 30 Incident," I received a sum of 37 yuan. After the old factory had resumed production, a piece-work system was put into effect, and apart from an extra three yuan that we received every month, we would receive the equivalent of 45 days' to 100 days' wages at the end of the year.

("A Record of an Interview with an Old Worker, Comrade Ma Kuei-sheng" [Lao Kung-jen Ma Kuei-sheng t'ung-chih fang-wen chi-lu], transcribed on April 24, 1958.)

I went to work in the South Seas Factory in 1921 as a machine-maintenance worker. At the time there were about sixty Japanese-produced cigarette-rolling machines in the factory, producing such brands as "Globe," "Double Happiness," and "Great Patriotism." Business was very good. It wasn't until two years later that the American-produced machines arrived.

When I entered the factory, I was a casual worker and earned one yuan a day. On rest days when there was no production, the regular workers still received their wages, but the casual workers did not. To be eligible for promotion to a regular worker, a casual worker had to have the "essential qualities" [p'ai-t'ou], and only if he had these could he be promoted after two to three months' work.

Prior to 1924, each regular worker was given one month off each year to return to his native village to tend to the graves of his ancestors. If this leave was not taken up by a worker, he would receive a monthly rise equivalent to two-and-a-half days of his wages. This scheme did not apply to a casual worker. During the humid season, although production was only running every other week, we would continue to receive our wages. After 1924, things took a turn for the worse, and there was no welfare to speak of. Only those who had obsequiously flattered the superiors would secretly receive an "annual reward" [nien-shang] at the end of the year. At the end of the first year of the piece-work system, I received 30 yuan. When this "yearly reward" was handed out to us, those who would receive it were called individually into the office where the money had already been prepared. We were also asked not to let the others know, and it was only afterwards that we realized that other people had also received it.

("A Record of an Interview with an Old Worker, Comrade Wu Chiu-chang" [Lao-kun-jen Wu Chiu-chang t'ung-chih fang-wen chi-lu], transcribed on April 29, 1958.)

I went to work in the machine section of the South Seas Tobacco Factory in November 1916 earning 9 chiao a day. At that time the machine-operators had all been sent over from Hong Kong, while most of the workers in the machinery section had been recruited in Shanghai. Those from Hong Kong were receiving cash grants, while those recruited in Shanghai would receive an extra two-and-a-half days' wages every month. A machine-operator would earn 7.5 to 8 chiao a day. There were two increases in wages every year, of 5 fen to 1 chiao while the increase for the administrative staff would be slightly more.

After one or two years' work, I became a monthly worker, and my monthly wage was about 30-odd yuan a month.

In the past we worked for ten hours a day, and there were two rest days every month, in the middle and at the end of the month. The monthly workers were paid for these rest days. If we worked beyond the ten hours on overtime to 9:30 p.m., we would receive an extra half-day's wage, and five hours of overtime would earn an extra day's wage. If in addition a monthly worker worked on the night shift, such overtime would be paid at three times the normal rate.

("A Record of Interviews with Old Employees of the South Seas Shanghai Factory" [Nan-yang Shang-hai-ch'ang lao-chih-yüan fang-wen chih-lu], transcribed on April 22, 1958.)

A Tobacco-Shredding Worker. I started to work for South-Seas in 1927 as a tobacco-shredding worker. At the time I was twenty-eight years old, and had joined the tobacco-shredding section with the help of somebody's introduction. I was a short-term worker, and my daily wage was 4 *chiao*. After three or four years' work, this was increased to 6 *chiao* a day. At the time, some of the workers were earning 6.5 *chiao* a day, the regular workers were earning 7 *chiao* a day, while some other workers were earning as little as 4.5 *chiao* a day.

Two or three years later, the old factory was abruptly closed down. It was only when the workers went to work one morning and found the factory gates closed that we first learned of the shutdown. . . . I was a short-term worker, and I did not receive any shutdown money, just the wage that was owed to me.

Later on when the Ching-hua factory opened, I got a job there through the introduction of somebody who worked there. I earned 5.5 *chiao* a day, and by the time of the "August 13" fighting, I was earning only 6.5 *chiao* a day.

There were ten hours in each working day. During the busy periods, we had to work an extra two or three hours, and for every two hours of such overtime, we were paid the wages of three normal hours.

("A Record of an Interview with an Old Worker, Comrade Huang I" [Lao-kung-jen Huang I t'ung-chih fang-wen chi-lu], transcribed on April 17, 1958.)

A Miscellaneous Duties Worker. I am now fifty-nine years

of age. I started to work for South Seas in 1921 when I was twenty-two years old. On the twelfth of the second month in the lunar calendar of that year, through the introduction of somebody, I joined the miscellaneous duties section as an unskilled laborer. At that time the head of this section was a man by the name of Fang Lo. When I joined the factory, I had to give the section head 5 yuan; it was only after much pleading that I got this reduced to 3 yuan. Even then, in order to secure employment, I had to borrow "a small loan for a short period at an exorbitant interest" [yin-tsu ch'ien] before I was able to give him this present.

An unskilled laborer had to do all sorts of chores: collecting the rubbish, crating, and moving the cigarettes and copper plates about. At that time the factory was using copper coins in its payment of the wages to the casual workers and the female workers. Every day, the company would obtain many boxes of such copper coins from the tram company, and the work of moving these heavy copper coins was a strenuous one.

In my first years of work for the company, my daily wage was 4 mao, and this was paid to me every day. My working day was 10 hours long, the first half from 7:00 a.m. to 12:00 noon, and the second half from 1:00 p.m. to 6:00 p.m. When business was good for the company, we had to work night-shifts till nine in the evening for an extra payment of 2 mao.

All unskilled laborers were considered to be casual workers, and most of them were from northern Kiangsu. They were maltreated and abused practically all the time, sometimes even being punched and kicked. The reason was that the factory could dismiss them at any time, and the unskilled laborers were in constant fear of dismissal, and for this reason, they could never stand up for themselves. For example, the head of the miscellaneous duties section, Fang Lo, would not tolerate for one moment any mistake or shortcoming. Every year, I had to treat him to at least a couple of meals.

Before the union was formed, the suppression of the workers by the factory was truly outrageous. The factory had many security guards of its own, and these could arrest and detain the workers at will. Should they meet up with any resistance from a worker, they would first lock him up in the fire-fighting section of the factory for several hours, and then they would either ask the police to come round to arrest him, or give him a thorough beating. Many of us unskilled workers had been so locked up. The security guards also used to carry axes on them, and once during a brawl with the workers, they used these axes against the workers and wounded some of them. It was only after protest by the workers that the factory did away with the practice of the security guards carrying axes and having the power to lock up the workers.

By the time of the "May 30" movement in 1925, I had been transferred to the packet-making section, where I started doing the work of cutting up the paper for the packet ends. During this time I was earning .65 yuan a day, and my wage was paid twice a month. I was on the night shift, which ran from seven in the evening to seven the next morning. There was a cash penalty of 2 chiao against anybody who was caught dozing, and I was penalized for this two or three times. Later on this section, where large packets were made, was abolished, and it became part of the packaging section. In 1927 I was transferred to the tobacco-cutting section to do the work of tobacco-shredding, and my daily wage was approximately .70-.80 yuan.

After the main factory was shut down, I was unemployed for over a year. In June 1931 I again started working for the factory in the tobacco-cutting section. But when I was taken on, I was classified as a new worker, and my daily wage was decreased to .60 yuan. It wasn't until over a year later that I was again earning .65 yuan a day. At that time there were only two rest days a month, on the fifteenth and the thirtieth, and we were not paid for these two days.

("A Record of an Interview with an Old Worker, Comrade Ch'en Wan-ts'ai" [Lao kung-jen Ch'en Wan-ts'ai t'ung-chih fang-wen chi-lu], transcribed on April 15, 1958.)

B. The Female Workers (Piece-Work) and the Child Workers

1. The Level of Wages

The Classification of the Duties of the Female Workers and the General Level of Wages of the Female Workers in the Cigarette Factories. Apart from those engaged to sweep the factory floors, all female workers were on a piece-work rate. The unskilled female workers engaged in the work of sweeping floors were paid a daily wage of 3-4 chiao. Most of the other female workers were in the foil-wrapping section, in the section where tins of cigarettes were packaged, in the leaves section, in the husking section, and in the packeting section. The work in the foil-wrapping section consisted of wrapping the cigarettes in foil and then putting them in packets [pao]. A box of twenty-five packets of ten cigarettes each was called a carton [t'iao], and the wage for packaging a carton varied from factory to factory, being approximately between 1 fen, 4 li, and 1 fen, 9 li. A larger box of twenty-five packets of twenty cigarettes each was called a canister [chih], and the wage for packaging a canister also varied from factory to factory, being between 2 fen, 7 li, and 3 fen. An even larger box of fifty packets of ten cigarettes each was called a case, [hsia] and the wage for packaging a case was between 2 fen, 4 li, and 3 fen. An average worker, working nonstop for an hour, could earn about 7 fen, and those who were slower could earn only 5 fen. Thus no matter how fast one worked, one could only earn several fen for an hour's work.

The work in the tin-packaging section consisted of wrapping up fifty cigarettes in a thick piece of paper and then placing them in a tin. This was called one tin [t'ing] of cigarettes, and the pay for doing one tin was between 3 li and 4 li. Packaging cigarettes in tins was less common than wrapping them up in foil paper, and there were quite a few factories that did not engage in the former. On the average, the pay for this kind of packaging was better than for foil-wrapping.

The work of the leaves section was to remove the central veins from the tobacco leaves, work of a nature such that all the workers engaged in it had their hands blistered. In the summertime, moreover, the heat and tobacco smell given off by the leaves after they had just been roasted were quite indescribably unbearable. The clothings of the workers were frequently completely soaked through with sweat, and this sweat was yellow, as if one had just taken a bath in a mixture of water and cigarette ash. The pay for this work was based on the number of veins removed from the tobacco leaves, and the rate was 2-3 fen for each pound of such veins. But odd things often happened at the weighing. If the person in charge of it was on good terms with a worker, then the ten pounds of veins that she brought would be weighed in as ten pounds. But the same quantity of veins brought to the weighing by another worker whom the person in charge did not like would be declared at only eight or nine pounds, and there would be nothing that this worker could do. On the average, a worker could remove about two pounds of these tobacco veins in an hour.

In the husking section, the rate of pay was between 2 chiao and 2 chiao, 4 fen, for every thousand cigarettes. The work entailed the removal of the tobacco shreds from cigarettes that were poorly produced. Such cigarettes might have been too loosely rolled, or they might have been soiled by the oil in the machines, and they were generally known respectively as loose cigarettes and stained cigarettes. These could not be put on the market, and their paper had to be torn away and the tobacco retained. The rate of pay was based on the weight of the tobacco shreds so removed, and it was 2-3 t'ung-pan for one pound of tobacco shreds. In one hour a worker could remove about four pounds of shreds.

The above, then, is a discussion of the situation of the piecework workers. They had no regular working hours, and this meant that they did not have a regular income from wages. The work in a tobacco factory was busiest in only three months of the year, and for the other nine months the factory might be open for only half a day or closed altogether. For example, the workers in the foil-wrapping section were earning on the average at the most only 4 chiao a day.

(Chu Pang-hsing et al., eds., Shanghai Industries and the Shanghai Workers.)

The Level of Wages of the Female Workers in the South Seas Factory in 1928. The workers in each section of the factory comprised both regular workers and piece-work workers. The wages of the regular workers were paid out on a monthly basis, while the piece-work workers were paid on the basis of how much work was done every day. In the Southseas factory, the majority of the workers were casual workers and piece-work workers. The casual workers were paid on the basis of the number of hours or days worked, while the piece-work workers were paid on the basis of the number of the articles they worked on. The majority of the piece-work workers were female workers. The factory on Broadway Road had a daily requirement of two thousand piece-work workers, while the P'u-tung factory required fifteen hundred a day. It is difficult to determine the exact number of piece-work workers in the factory on a given day. If the production in the factory was running high, then it would temporarily take on more workers to do the work of wrapping and packaging the cigarettes that were produced in the factory on that day. The piece-work workers were recruited every morning; they would start work at 7:00 a.m., and the pay they received would be based on the number of cigarette packets they packaged that day. Each worker would hand in the packets she had produced to those in charge of the cigarette-packaging section; in return she received her wage. The pay for packaging one thousand stiff-paper packets of ten cigarettes was 6 chiao, 5 fen, and the pay for an equal number of soft-paper packets of ten cigarettes each was 4 chiao, 7 fen. The pay for packaging one thousand packets of twenty cigarettes each was 7 chiao, while the pay for packaging twenty tins of fifty cigarettes each was 3 fen, 5 li. If a female worker engaged in this work could package thirty thousand cigarettes a day, she was considered a most skillful and efficient worker, and a total of twenty thousand a day would be considered a moderate achievement. But in fact most of the workers could package only fifteen thousand cigarettes a day, and their average wage worked out to about 6-7 chiao a day. According to the factory management, only 0.6 to 0.7 percent of these workers could package thirty thousand cigarettes a day, less than 15 percent could package twenty thousand a day, about 60 percent could package fifteen thousand a day, and about 20 percent could package ten thousand a day. According to the workers, the average daily wage for a worker engaged in this work was approximately from 250 to 300 t'ung-pan, and this figure bears out the above estimate for the number of workers that could package fifteen thousand cigarettes a day. As for the female workers engaged in making cigarette boxes [ho] (a large box contained fifty cigarette-packets), their work was also based on the number of articles completed. The pay for making one hundred boxes was 3 chiao, 5 fen, and one worker could make about two hundred boxes a day, earning a wage of between 6 and 7 chiao. As for the machines making such boxes, each of them could make forty thousand boxes a day, and for every ten thousand boxes made, a worker in charge of one of these machines would earn 1 chiao, 7 fen. On the average, therefore, each worker would make about thirty thousand boxes a day, earning just over 5 chiao a day.

("An Investigation into the Latest Situation of the South Seas Company.")

2. The Unequal Treatment Suffered by the Female Workers and the Child Workers

The Female Workers Had No Regular Working Hours. It is unlikely that the extraordinary situation related to the working hours of the female workers existed in other industries. Their working hours were completely geared to the state of the demand for the factory's products. When there was an urgent demand, the workers had to do sixteen to seventeen hours of work a day, that is, from five or six in the morning until eleven or twelve at night. The worst time would be just prior to an increase in the stamp duties. For example, if it was known that the stamp duties would be raised from the first of the next month, then the factory would try to produce as much as possible before that date. This was because the cigarette-paper shops and cigarette shops in other cities, on hearing that the stamp duties would be raised, would place large orders with the tobacco factories so that they could increase their profits after the stamp duties had been raised. The consequence of this would be that the tobacco factories would begin to go into nighttime production, operating a total of sixteen and seventeen hours a day.... But at times when the demand for cigarettes was not urgent, these female workers might have just one or two hours of work a day, or work only every other day, or they might even have no work at all for a week or a month. During the summertime especially, when the tobacco was susceptible to mold, the factory would be disinclined to keep stocks of cigarettes and would thus only manufacture whatever quantity was demanded.... Therefore the workers in the tobacco factory often found themselves in a situation of semiunemployment in which the prospect of going hungry was very real.

(Chu Pang-hsing et al., eds., _Shanghai Industries and the Shanghai Workers_.)

It Was the Child Workers Who Received the Worst Treatment. They Were Frequently Beaten and Abused by the Foremen. The child workers and old workers were frequently beaten and abused by the foremen. The foremen always abused the old workers with such names as "old nothings" [_lao chia-huo_], "walking corpses" [_lao pu-ssu_], or "old hags" [_lao t'ai-p'o_]. Usually nothing more would happen if the old workers would not answer back, but if they did, the foremen would beat them or make them pay out cash penalties. Only very few of the old workers had not received such treatment. As for the child workers, they were always called such names as "little devils" [hsiao-kuei] or "little monkeys" [hsiao-hu], and the foremen would beat and abuse them at will. The youngest workers in the factory were only seven years old. (So long as there were people after the "employment cards" [p'ai-tzu], the factory management was disinclined to notice how old they were.) I used to think about seven- or eight-year-old girls from wealthy families sleeping in their parents' arms. The children of the poor, though poor, were still children. How could their still feeble souls stand up to the coarse voices and stony faces of the foremen and the administrative staff? In the factory, we could often hear the sad crying of the children, to which we wished we could turn a deaf ear. I too was once a child worker, and I have personally lived through the miseries of the child workers....

In the month of July in the year in which I was nine years old, I went to work in the factory, but in actual fact I was not yet eight. At the time my hand was not big enough to take hold of ten cigarettes at a time, and so I had to divide this operation into two stages and place five cigarettes at a time into the copper boxes. On my third day at work, one of the foremen, Ah Hsin, came over to watch me quite a few times. I was so scared that I made the mistake of putting only nine cigarettes in one of the fifty foil-wrappings. Since at that time we were all new at our work, what we had done would have to be checked by the foremen before we could take it to the accounts section to receive our wages. (At the time the South Seas Tobacco Company was paying out cash for wages, and the pay for doing fifty packets was two t'ung-pan.) The sharp eyes of the foreman scrutinized every one of the packets that I had done, and when she discovered that there were only nine cigarettes in one of the packets, she pulled at my pigtail and demanded that I should go with her to the accounts section. I was trembling and speechless; and I was especially afraid of going to the accounts section. I begged her not to take me there, but she kept pulling at my pigtail and insisted that I had to go. The scene at that moment was like that of a policeman dragging a rickshaw-man off to the police station because the rickshaw-man had gone the wrong way. Then I burst into tears and I was dragged to the accounts section, where I was ordered to pay a cash penalty of 200 wen. On that day, I had done only 80 wen's worth of work, and the matter was only settled after I had gone home during the lunch period and brought back 12 t'ung-pan. On returning home that evening, I went into a fever, and I remained in bed with a coma for half a month. I can never forget that particular sickness....

(Chu Pang-hsing et al., eds., Shanghai Industries and the Shanghai Workers.)

3. The Recollections of the Old Workers as to the Standard of Wages and the Living Conditions of the Time

Two Female Cigarette-Packaging Workers. I went to work for the British-American Tobacco Factory when I was eleven years old. I was later dismissed because I was a slow worker.

At the age of fourteen, I went to work in the packaging section of the South Seas Factory. At that time the pay for packaging one hundred packets of cigarettes was 7 t'ung-pan.

At the time of the "May 30" movement, the workers went on strike and called for the promotion of native products and the rejection of foreign tobacco. Many of the workers in the British-American Tobacco Factory went over to the South Seas Factory. At that time the business at South Seas was extremely good, and it had seven or eight thousand workers and over a hundred cigarette-rolling machines. There was also an increase in wages, and the pay for packaging one hundred packets was up to 11 t'ung-pan. Soon after, South Seas established a branch factory at P'u-tung, "Little South Seas," and since my home was in P'u-tung, I went to work at the

the P'u-tung factory when I was seventeen years old.

At the demand of the workers, the P'u-tung factory raised its level of wages to about the same as that of the British-American factory, and the pay for packaging one hundred packets of cigarettes was 3-4 fen, which meant a daily wage of about 3-4 chiao. When business was slack and production was low, the daily pay would be only 1 or 2 chiao. At that time there were no welfare schemes at all. If a female worker had to be off work to have a baby, her leave of absence would be an unpaid one, and consequently many of the female workers would have only three or four days' rest before they would go back to work.

The foremen were all fiercely thorough in their inspection of our work, and they would create trouble and impose cash penalties on us at every opportunity. But they would be a bit more reasonable to anyone who would give them presents at the three festivals of the year. In fact if such presents were not received from a worker, her employment card would be taken away, and she would not be allowed to work. The workers did not even have the freedom to talk, since talking at work would not only mean a cash penalty but also standing in the accounts section for one or two hours to beg for the pardon of the supervisors.

When the P'u-tung factory closed down, I became unemployed. Since my family was poor, I had to go and seek work at the three factories of the British-American Tobacco Company. When they asked me at which factory I had previously worked, I told them the truth, that I had worked in the "Little South Seas." On hearing that they refused to issue an employment card for me, and I could not work at any of them.

Since I had done some work in a British-American factory in the very beginning, I now went to see an acquaintance of mine at one of the British-American factories. Through him I managed to obtain an employment card, and I started to work on the night-shift.

After some time, "Old South Seas" opened the Ching-hua factory, and I went to work there. I had managed to get work there with the help of a friend of my uncle, who was the husband of one of the female foremen in the factory; through him I succeeded in getting an introduction to her. However, she made me promise that I would not get into any sort of trouble in the factory and that I would not oppose the capitalists. Also joining the factory at the same time was the daughter of my great uncle. Her name was Wu San-nan, and she was only nine years old at the time.

My monthly wage at the Ching-hua factory was about 5 yuan. After I had worked there a short time, the female foreman made me lend her five yuan. It was only after my great uncle had pleaded with her that she did not ask me again to lend her money.

The demands on one's life at the Ching-hua factory were very high. There was the manufacture of a "Parker" brand, which was sold solely in Japan, and if any worker could not produce 2 chiao worth of work in a day, she in fact had to pay the factory for machine-money [ch'e-ch'ien]. Life was very difficult indeed; there were hardly enough clothes to wear, and we had no job security at all. Once, the deputy manager of the factory came down to make an inspection, and he made an uncalled-for remark about the work of one of the female workers. That female worker answered him, "My ten fingers are not of the same length." He then promptly asked that the "employment card" of this female worker be removed, that her wage be paid off, and that she be dismissed.

Later on, the Ching-hua factory became part of the old factory, but the oppression of the workers continued as before. The regulations were all laid down by the factory management, and sometimes the workers were not even aware of the existence of some of the regulations. Any minor infringement would mean "interrogation by the accounts section" (i.e., questioning of the worker in the accounts section). A first offense would mean a cash penalty of 2 chiao, and a second one would mean suspension from work for two weeks. For the female workers, such punishment would be a double-barrelled one, since on returning home, they would still have to suffer the beating and abuses of their mother-in-law or stepmother, and very often they would not be given any dinner. As far as the factory was concerned, if any offender still "refused to change his ways," then he would be dismissed. Any workers involved in a brawl would also be dismissed, regardless of the reason for the brawl. When the head of the packaging section came down to the factory floor to make his inspection, none of us would even dare to look at him. We were also not allowed to congregate in groups, and even the frequency of our visits to the toilet was supervised. There was simply no freedom.

A year after the old factory had been reopened, the factory management gave every one (of the female piece-workers) an empty pencil-box of the Great Wall brand. But the management did not want the workers to make a rush for the gifts, and so they thrashed the workers with cane-sticks as the gifts were being given out. In the second year after the old factory had resumed production, we demanded a wage increase, and at the end of the year we asked for a sum of two dollars [2 k'uai ch'ien] for each of us. The head of the packaging section refused, and so the workers went to see him, whereupon the factory management closed down the factory for a time. When work was resumed, there were two kinds of "employment cards" issued to us, one rectangular in shape and the other circular. Those who received the rectangular ones were being dismissed, and these were the ones who had been critical of the foremen, and the ones who had been determined and persistent in their struggle. The purpose of this suspension in production was to get rid of a certain element among the workers. At first I was issued a rectangular card, but my great-uncle, on finding out about this, went to plead with the foremen, and it was only then that I was reissued a circular card. Later on, oiled paper was added to the "Stringed-Pearls" brand of cigarettes, and the pay for doing this work for a hundred packets of ten cigarettes each was 6.5 fen, while the pay for one hundred packets of twenty cigarettes each was 5 fen. During the slack seasons, we worked for only three or four hours a day, but during the busy seasons we had to work till seven or eight in the evening and even on the night-shifts. One evening, after finishing work for the day, some workers who lived in P'u-tung were on their way home by sampan across the river when a large steamer coming downstream collided with and capsized the sampan. There were thirty-odd people on board, and many that were drowned were workers from the South Seas factory.

("A Record of an Interview with an Old Worker, Comrade Wu San-mei" [Lao-kung-jen Wu San-mei t'ung-chih fang-wen chi-lu], dated April 10, 1958.)

Editors' Note: The Shen-pao of April 7, 1932, carried the following report:

> At about 7:00 p.m. on the twenty-ninth of last month, a group of female workers from the South Seas Tobacco Company at Hung-k'ou were on their way home to P'u-tung. They had embarked on a boat at the Chao-feng Pier. When the boat was midway across the river, it was suddenly rammed in the darkness and capsized by the steamer Ching-kuang of the Marine Customs Department. Over thirty of the female workers were drowned. The relatives of the victims have formed themselves into a relatives' association and asked for compensation from both the Marine Customs Department and the South Seas Tobacco Company. Negotiations on several occasions have not produced any results. Details of the negotiations have already been reported.
>
> The latest news is that this case has been taken up by... Fu Ch'ing-huai of the Youth Association who, in a private capacity, has approached the Marine Customs Department and the South Seas Company in the past few days. He has also advised the relatives of the victims not to take any drastic actions. Thus the three parties (i.e., the Marine Customs Department, South Seas, and the relatives' association) have now moved much closer together than before.

> As of yesterday the South Seas Company had already informed the relatives to come and claim the wages due to the victims. This was done as an effort toward a satisfactory settlement of the matter....

When I was twelve or thirteen, I went to work in the P'u-tung factory of South Seas as a packaging worker. My younger sister also started to work for South Seas at that time.

I worked in the P'u-tung factory for three months. On my first day at work, I could only package enough packets to earn 7 t'ung-pan. Later, as my skill improved, I was able to earn more, up to 30 or 40 t'ung-pan a day.

Later on, I found it very inconvenient to go to work each day by taking a boat across to P'u-tung. Furthermore, there was the risk of losing one's life. One time the boat was overloaded and it capsized, killing one person. After this happened, my family was very concerned for my safety, and so my father asked someone to obtain employment for me at the main factory of Southseas. My work was still in packaging.

When I first arrived at the main factory, the pay for packaging fifty packets of cigarettes was 3 t'ung-pan, and 7 t'ung-pan for packaging one hundred packets. When I was sixteen years old, the pay was increased slightly, and fifty packets would pay 5 t'ung-pan, and one hundred packets 11 t'ung-pan. In an effort to earn an extra half t'ung-pan, two workers would pool any parts of fifty packets at the end of the day to make up an extra batch of fifty.

The length of the working day very much depended on the season. The busy season was from September to January. During this period we had to work seventeen or eighteen hours a day, from 6:00 (or 6:30) a.m. to 11:00 (or 12:00) p.m., and there were no breaks for rest. At noon the workers would take out the cakes they had brought, or went out to buy three to five t'ung-pan worth of cakes; then they would have their cakes and work at the same time. The management would not even provide us with boiled water, and so when the workers were thirsty, they had to drink water that had not been boiled. We would only be able to have a proper meal after we had arrived back at home at about eleven or twelve at night. By that time we would be so exhausted that we would fall asleep midway through the meal. The following morning, even before the break of dawn, father would wake us up and ask us to hurry off to work. Since we frequently lacked any proper rest and our eating habits were so irregular, many workers developed ulcers, and I was no exception. But during the slack season between February and August, we could only get two hours' work a day. In order to earn the little pay from this short stint of work, we had to spend two hours every day getting to work.

The wage of 200 t'ung-pan a day which we earned during the busy season was just enough for us to keep our families together. But during the slack season, we could only earn just over 10 t'ung-pan a day, and this was not enough for oneself to live on, let alone to keep a family together with.

There was no welfare system of any sort in the factory. The management would not even provide us with a drink of boiled water. There was no such thing as a sick leave for a female worker, since if she failed to report to work for three days, she would be replaced by someone new. No hardship fund at all was provided for the relatives of a worker who died. The fifteenth and thirtieth of each month were rest days, and we also had a week off over the Spring Festival; but then these holidays were unpaid ones. All that the female workers would receive over the Spring Festival would be 1 chiao and two packets of cigarettes of the "Strong Man" brand. When they became pregnant, many of the female workers would try to conceal the fact by pulling in their stomachs, since they would have to stop work if their pregnancy was discovered.

There were many factory regulations. For example, we were searched from head to toe on leaving work, and if anybody was found to have cigarettes on her, she would be instantly dismissed. Anyone who left out one cigarette in packing a packet would also be dismissed. All those who were involved in any brawling would be fined 20 wen each. If in the wrapping of a packet of cigarettes the glue should seep out of the packet and cause two packets to stick together, the fine would be 10 wen. When handing in our work at the end of the day, we had to stand in line, and anyone who caused any disorder would be fined either five wen or a day's wage. Finally, the foremen were empowered to beat and abuse the workers at any time.

The oppression of the foremen further aggravated the miseries of the workers. Over the new year or any of the festivals, we had to give presents to them. If a worker should fail to give the foremen any presents or money, then even if she did not violate any of the regulations, she would be made to suffer.

("A Record of an Interview with an old Worker, Comrade Lu San-yüan" [Lao-kung-jen Lu San-yüan t'ung-chih fang-wen chi-lu], transcribed on April 13, 1958.)

A Female Leaves-Thrasher. I came to Shanghai in 1921, and with the help of my younger brother's wife, who was then working in the South Seas tobacco factory, I found a job doing the work of removing the veins from tobacco leaves.

At first the pay for one boxful of veins removed was 1 chiao, 5 fen. Each of these boxes weighed between fifty and sixty catties, and we had to haul them up to the third floor. Later on, ten workers would work together on a large box, and the more we worked, the more we would earn.

My wage was paid once every two weeks, and each time I would receive just over 70 chiao.

Work was stopped for one day every two weeks. The working day was from seven in the morning to five in the afternoon. There would be extra shifts if production had to be increased, and there would be an extra 2 chiao in pay for working through the night.

The foremen were all females, and there were just over ten of them, all of them Cantonese. They were extremely fierce, and any mistake by us would cause them to beat and abuse us. We were not permitted to talk while we were walking, and any one who did would have cigarette ashes stuffed inside her mouth. When any of the foremen had a baby, we had to give her presents, such as eggs. If anyone failed to do so, her name would be noted down, and she might not be allowed to work.

("A Record of an Interview with an Old Worker, Comrade Sung Kuei-t'ung" [Lao-kung-jen Sung Kuei-t'ung t'ung-chih fang-wen chi-lu], transcribed on April 11, 1958.)

2

The Great Strike in Shanghai in 1924

. . . .

After the establishment of the union, the capitalists, because they were bound by the agreement they had drawn up with the union, were unable to exploit and oppress the workers at will, and thus they regarded the union with great hostility. For this reason, the capitalists collaborated with a number of the senior members of the administrative staff in an attempt to turn the union into an instrument of their will. The workers were naturally highly dissatisfied with this kind of manipulation and subsequently succeeded in pushing out virtually all of the senior staff members. Hence the capitalists' fiendish Trojan Horse scheme was sabotaged. But they continued to regard the union as a thorn in their side, and relentlessly searched for a way to defeat the union. Their attack on the union was systematic. First, they appointed to important positions those senior staff members to whom the workers objected. Second, they proceeded to sabotage the agreement that had been reached with the workers, with the intention of provoking a strike which would then provide a pretext for them to dissolve the union. Thus in April of this year (1924), K'uang Kung-yao, who had previously

---

"1924 nien Shang-hai ti ta pa-kung." Section II of Chapter 7 ("The Workers' Movement [in Shanghai]), Book Two ("The Development and Decline of the Company after Extensive Reorganization [November 1919-1936]), of Nan-yang hsiung-ti yen-ts'ao kung-ssu shih-liao. This translation is taken from Chinese Sociology and Anthropology, VI:2 (Winter 1973-74), 19-47.

resigned following objections by the workers, was appointed head of the Works Department. (According to a declaration of the workers reproduced in the Republican Daily on September 11, 1924, K'uang was given a new appointment as the inspector of works of the factory.) After his appointment, K'uang proceeded to cut down on the benefits provided by an existing regulation that allowed payment during sick leave, and he further imposed thirty new restrictive regulations on the workers. On several occasions the union held negotiations with the management and made their demands, but without results. Soon after, K'uang dismissed more than ten workers without valid reason, and the union's attempt to restore them to their jobs met with failure. These were all punitive measures that the capitalists applied to the workers in an attempt to provoke them into calling a strike. When the capitalists saw that these measures were ineffective, they went even further and dismissed two representatives of the union, two female workers by the name of Ch'en Ch'ien-ju and Wu Hui-fen. When this happened the workers finally found the situation intolerable, and the great strike was born. With this the capitalists finally realized their long-held and pernicious design; therefore the strike was really a well-planned attack on the workers by the capitalists. For their part, the workers had not made any plans for their defense, and so the strike resulted in their defeat. . . .

(Neng Chih, "The Strike of the South Seas Tobacco Workers.") [Nan-yang yen-ts'ao kung-jen pa-kung ti ching-kuo], in Chinese Worker [Chung-kuo kung-jen] No. 2, November 1924, p. 55.)

After the Chinese Communist Party was founded, it became involved in the workers' movement in Shanghai. . . . In the second half of 1924 the Party was rather active. It took part in the strike of the silk workers, and also led the strike at the South Seas Tobacco Factory.

(Teng Chung-hsia, A Short History of the Chinese Labor Movement (1919-1926) [Chung-kuo chih-kung yün-tung chien-shih], Jen-min ch'u-pan-she, September 1949, p. 136.)

Comrade Hsiang Ching-yü was an outstanding cadre of the Chinese Communist Party. In particular she was loyal to the Party and loyal to the difficult and challenging spirit of work that was part of the cause of the liberation of the Chinese people.... In 1924 she was one of the leaders in both the famous great strike of the female workers in a Shanghai silk factory and in the great strike of the South Seas Tobacco workers.

(Li Ming, "In Remembrance of Comrade Hsiang Ching-yü" [Tao Hsiang Ching-yü t'ung-chih], in Biographies of Glorious Fighters [Lieh-shih chuan], Su-nan hsin-hua shu-tien, August 1949, p. 231.)

Comrade Yang Yin was a member of the T'ung meng hui in his younger days.... When he began to feel that the Kuomintang was in a process of progressive decay, he devoted great energy to a study of various new ideas. In 1923, when he realized the that it was Marxism alone that could save China, he joined the Chinese Communist Party....

In 1924, the year the great strike at the South Seas Brothers Tobacco Company occurred in Shanghai, he formed a backup organization in Canton and Hong Kong. When the Shanghai strike was defeated by the capitalists' suppression, he proceeded to organize a boycott movement against the cigarettes of Southseas Tobacco Company. Several hundred crates of cigarettes were confiscated in Hong Kong, and the proceeds from their auction were given over to help those workers who had been dismissed.

Later he was elected as a representative on a delegation from the backup organization that went to Shanghai. On their arrival, South Seas Tobacco Company first used the tactic of bribery against the representatives. Some of the representatives wavered but, out of fear of Comrade Yang Yin, they dared not carry out any sabotage. For this reason, South Seas Tobacco Company had a deep loathing for Comrade Yang Yin, and they paid some hooligans to assassinate him. Fortunately, Comrade Yang Yin was alert and strong, and the assassination failed. But he suffered a serious head injury, which was the cause of his frequent head pains in later years.

(Li Ming, "A Short Biography of Comrade Yang Yin" [Yang Yin t'ung-chih chuan-lüeh], in Biographies of Glorious Fighters, p. 251.)

A. The Causes of the Strike

The Opposition to Management's Restrictive Regulations, Its Unjustified Dismissal of Female Workers, and Its Plot to Dissolve the Association of Comrade Employees. Since the death of the former manager-in-chief, Chien Chao-nan, his younger brother, Yu-chia, has been the manager-in-chief of the South Seas Tobacco Company Factory, and he has appointed Li Yüan as the deputy head of the Works Department. But Li Yüan made use of his position to bully others, and his countless despicable actions have long been familiar to the public. We workers harbor a deep hatred of him, and it has only been out of concern for our livelihood that we have not voiced our feelings, but have instead kept on working in the hope that we would not cross his path. But now the ruthless Li Yüan has entered into an unholy alliance with K'uang Kung-yao, the newly appointed inspector of works in the factory. Their harsh treatment of the employees has been further intensified, but they are still not satisfied. Without any reason, they transfer members of the administrative staff from section to section. Faced with difficult new duties, these employees either have to follow their instructions or apply to be transferred to more suitable positions. As for their treatment of the workers, these two lowly persons, Li and K'uang, have not only abolished pay for sickness leaves but have also, without cause, fired two officials of our association, Ch'en Ch'ien-ju and Wu Hui-fen. The actions of a person are determined by the circumstances at any given time. Now that Li and K'uang are ruthlessly bullying the workers to an extreme degree, we workers have come to the end of our tolerance. At a plenary session of the association held on the evening of the eighth, we decided to come out on a temporary work stoppage starting on the ninth. We have also written to the manager-in-chief to ask him to investigate our plight and to effect a satisfactory solution.... We have now made a plaintive statement of our situation, and we beg other unions and those who are concerned with the miseries of the workers to come forward and uphold righteousness. Any advice will benefit not only our several thousand workers but also the whole of the world of labor.

("Declaration by the Workers of the South Seas Tobacco Employees' Association" [Nanyang yen-ts'ao chih-kung-hui kung-jen hsüan-yen], Republican Daily, September 11, 1924.)

To all trade unions and other organizations in the country:

Although the reasons for our present work stoppage have been mentioned in our declaration, they may still remain unclear to some. We shall now spell out the reasons in detail, and report on the course of events between the evening of the eighth and the evening of the twelfth.

1. The reasons for the work stoppage. Since its establishment nine years ago, the South Seas Tobacco Factory has grown from having just several machines to having over 170 machines, and

its total profits over the years are in excess of tens of millions of dollars. Whose achievement is it? It is the workers' achievement. The former manager-in-chief, the late Chien Chao-nan, acknowledged this fact, and he came to accept the terms for the setting up of our union. The present manager-in-chief, Chien Yü-chia, does not realize this, and this is why he is plotting to disband the union. He has even gone so far as to impose various harsh measures on the workers (details to follow). This is why we workers have reached the end of our tolerance, and this is the cause of the tragedy of the occurrence of this strike.

2. The scum K'uang Kung-yao has been given the responsibility for the despicable work of implementing the goal of breaking up the union. The scum K'uang once attempted to manipulate the union for his own ends. He tried to capture the union for the management, but when he was exposed, he escaped to Kwangtung. This year he came to an agreement with the company that he would dissolve the union within six months, and that he would receive several tens of thousands of hsien-yang on the completion of his task. Since that time, he has been receiving a monthly salary of several hundred yuan from the company. In July he came to Shanghai and was appointed to the position of the inspector of works in the Works Department. He does not know the first thing about this work, since prior to this he had only been in charge of the warehouse.

3. The scum Li Yüan is the scourge of the workers. The scum Li has been posing as a returned student, although nobody has come forward to substantiate his alleged background. He has unreasonably imposed the most restrictive of regulations, including one which governs the workers' visits to the toilet. A disobedient word from a worker means a fine of 5 yuan, while a failure to greet him politely means a fine of 1 yuan. He rewards and punishes people at his own whim, always without any cause. Scores of workers have already been dismissed simply because he did not like them.

4. There was no cause for the dismissal of our two female fellow workers Ch'en and Wu. The two female workers, Ch'en Ch'ien-ju and Wu Hui-fen, have worked for the company ever

since it was founded and had advanced to the position of foremen. At first, the scum K'uang despicably tried to offer favors to the female workers, but these were refused. These two female workers were conscientious officials of our union (in which only those who work in the factory may hold office), and they were victimized as a warning to others. In his scheme to dissolve the union, the scum K'uang collaborated with the scum Li in a destruction of the good. Our two female fellow workers were first demoted to difficult jobs and then unjustifiably dismissed.

5. Chien Yü-chia went against the terms of the agreement drawn up with the union. (The four terms in question are as follows.)

a) There was no valid cause for the dismissal of our two female fellow workers Ch'en and Wu.
b) The money paid out by the workers in the form of cash penalties, which was intended to be given to the union for welfare work, has in fact been used by the company for its own purposes.
c) New members of the administrative staff were prevented from becoming members of the union.
d) The amount of bonuses owed to the workers was reduced.

("A Most Urgent Plea for Help" [Wan-chi hu-chiu], issued by more than 7,000 male and female workers of the South Seas Tobacco Association of Comrade Employees on September 12, 1924, Republican Daily, September 13, 1924.)

B. The Demands Made by the Workers

Article 1. Both Li Yüan and K'uang Kung-yao, the two enemies of the workers, as well as the strong-arm security guards, must be immediately dismissed and never employed again in the factory.

Article 2. The two female workers Ch'en Ch'ien-ju and Wu Hui-fen are to be asked back by the company and restored to the positions they held in the cigarette-wrapping section. In the future, in considering the transfer of a worker to another section, the company must weigh whether the worker is suitable for the work in question and also obtain the consent of the worker.

Article 3. Abolish new restrictive regulations that apply either to the entire factory or to the individual sections.

Article 4. During the current period of work stoppage, no regular or casual workers, male or female, are to be dismissed or transferred to another section. The company should ask for dismissal of the cases against those workers who have been brought before the court because of the strike (several representatives have been sued by the company).

Article 5. The company is to apply for the release on bail of all those innocent workers that it has wrongly sent to the police station, and the company is to further compensate them for all their losses. The company is also to compensate the union for its losses during the strike.

Article 6. During the current period of work stoppage, the wages of all regular and casual workers, male and female, are to be paid as usual. Each of the casual workers who is on piece rate is to be paid a daily sum of 40 t'ung-yuan.

Article 7. Article 4 in the agreement reached between the company and the union in the eleventh year of the Republic [1922] is to be modified as follows: "No worker of this union may be dismissed except for those who are involved in brawling, stealing, or flirting with the female workers. The cases of those who infringe on the factory regulations should be dealt with in accordance to the seriousness of the offense. If a worker is to be dismissed, such an action may only be taken after consultation with, and the agreement of this union." Article 8 is to be modified as follows: "In the first month of the lunar calendar each year, the company should raise the wages of all those workers who are members of this union, and each increase is to be a minimum of 2 yuan." Article 9 is to be modified as follows: "Five percent of the company's annual profits is to be paid, in the form of bonuses, to the workers of the Shanghai factory, and this amount will be distributed in proportion to the wages of the workers."

Article 8. Recently the level of wages has not kept pace with the increase in the cost of living. Such things as the rent for living quarters have all gone up, and it has been difficult to make ends meet. Starting September 1, the company is to raise the monthly pay of all employees by 3 yuan, while the increase for the casual workers will be decided by negotiation.

These are our eight demands. If in the future, however, the company should do anything detrimental to the workers' interests, further demands will be made.

("Statement by the Workers of the South Seas Tobacco Association of Comrade Employees" [Nan-yang yen-ts'ao chih-kung t'ung-chih hui kung-jen kung-pu], September 10, 1924, Republican Daily, September 14, 1924.)

There is a small group of "restless and dissatisfied" workers in the Shanghai factory, who have been making trouble at the slightest excuse and who have been behind the labor disputes. Recently, on September 8, over the dismissal of the female workers Ch'en Ch'ien-ju and Wu Hui-fen, these people used the name of the Comrade Association to put out printed materials. These materials contain such phrases as "hoping that all fellow workers will struggle together in a spirit of cooperation." The following day, they came up with four demands, and soon made eight more. They incited the cigarette-rolling section to come out on strike first, . . and this brought about a total stoppage of work in the factory for the two days of the ninth and the tenth. . . .

(From the minutes of the fifty-second meeting of the Board of Directors on September 23, 1924.)

C. Management's Despicable Acts against the Strike

1. The Use of Brute Force to Suppress the Workers

The Use of Hooligans, the Impressing of Workers to Return to the Factory, and the Detention of Female Workers Inside the Factory.

6. With the commencement of the work stoppage, the company applied all kinds of pressure against the workers. By 5:00 p.m. on the eighth the workers already had news of the dismissal of Ch'en and Wu, and everyone was incensed, whereupon the company immediately issued its intimidating announcement. On the afternoon of the ninth, a gang of over thirty professional fighters and hooligans openly coerced the workers into returning to work, and beat up those who refused. When over fifty female workers who were not yet aware of the situation arrived at work in the morning, they were detained in the factory. They were given some lunch money at noon, but there was no place where they could buy food. Also worried about their hungry children at home, many broke into tears. It was not until four o'clock in the afternoon that they were released.

. . .

9. On the morning of the twelfth the company sent out over a hundred Shantung thugs, armed with guns, knives, and other weapons. These men forced about a dozen male and female workers to report for work. Those who refused were either sent off to the police or beaten up on the road. There was utter chaos on Chao-feng Road. It was a harrowing scene in which men and women were screaming for help, while passersby turned their eyes away. After the union made public the work stoppage, it had to send out several hundred voluntary marshals to protect the workers on the public roads and to prevent the occurrence of further incidents. . . .

("A Most Urgent Plea for Help," issued by more than 7,000 male and female workers of the South Seas Tobacco Association of Comrade Employees on September 12, 1924, Republican Daily, September 13, 1924.)

The management hired some Shantung thugs and also bribed the police. To entice the workers to return to work, they set up a canteen inside the factory and also used trucks to bring in blankets so that those who would return to work for them could sleep in the factory. At that time the representatives of two of the sections organized a vigilance squad to prevent workers from entering the factory. But there was not much they could do, since the management had trucks driving around in the streets with policemen and informers aboard who would force workers into the trucks and then drive into the factory. There was no way that we could stop them.

("A Record of an Interview with an Old Worker of the Shanghai Factory, Comrade Li Lin" [Shang-hai ch'ang lao kung-jen Li Lin t'ung-chih fang-wen chi-lu], transcribed on April 17, 1958.)

During the great strike in 1924,...the management used the running-dogs Wang Hsing-miao, Wang Tzu-chün, and others, to look for workers from outside. With the help of Shih Hou-ming, who was the chief foreman at the British-American Tobacco Company factory and nicknamed "Little Uncle," and his underlings, the management recruited workers from the British-American factory. They also closed the factory gates, and prevented the workers inside from leaving. At the same time, they cooked a great deal of food to give the striking workers the impression that there were many workers on their jobs. The striking workers organized a vigilance squad which stationed itself on the roads leading to the factory and tried to persuade other workers not to enter the factory. But the management used red police cars to block the roads, and the policemen interfered with what we were doing.

("A Record of an Interview with an Old Worker of the Shanghai Factory, Comrade Wu Ping-hou" [Shang-hai ch'ang lao kung-jen Wu Ping-hou t'ung-chih fang-wen chi-lu], transcribed on April 16, 1958.)

The Bribing of the Police and the Arrests of the Workers' Representatives. . . a representative, a Mr. Ku, was first beaten up by some hoodlums and then sent to the police. The company also arrested four representatives, Sun Kuan-hsiao, Li Pe-t'ing, Kan Shao-lü, and T'an Chin, on the pretext that they were preventing workers from doing their job. In effect, the strike was decided upon by the entire body of workers, and was not stirred up by members of the administrative staff.

("A Most Urgent Plea for Help," issued by more than 7,000 male and female workers of the South Seas Tobacco Association of Comrade Employees on September 12, 1924, and reprinted in Republican Daily, September 13, 1924.)

The Association of Comrade Employees was holding a meeting outside of the factory, and the police and informers were everywhere, arresting the Association's committee members. Committeeman Ch'ang Yüan-ts'an had to move several times in one night. But in the end he was arrested and was involved in a court case that lasted for six months.

("A Record of an Interview with an Old Worker of the Shanghai Factory, Comrade Li Lin," transcribed on April 17, 1958.)

Collaboration with the Concession Courts and the Fines Imposed on the Workers. On the day before yesterday, a coppersmith at the South Seas Brothers Tobacco Company, Yao Pao-fu, in conjunction with other workers — Wang Hsiu-ch'ing, Wang Chin-piao, Tiao Chih-k'uei, and the female workers Wang A-erh, Chou Ts'ai-ying, Chou A-hsiu, Chang Ts'ai-feng, Ku Ts'ai-ai, Yang Wang and others — opposed the new restrictive regulations imposed by the head of the Works Department. After the failure of their demand for the restoration of the two female workers who had been suspended from their positions, the male and female workers joined in an alliance and went on strike. Yao and the others were then arrested by the police and brought before the court yesterday. A Chinese policeman, No. 1406, gave an account of the events that took place. The lawyer Yang Kuo-shu representing the tobacco company, which was the plaintiff in the case, was also in court and gave a description of the circumstances surrounding the case. He claimed that it was the police who had brought charges against the defendants and had accused them of inciting the 5,000-odd male and female workers in the factory to go on strike. Yang asked the court to consider the case carefully. The defendant, Yao Pao-fu, has asked the lawyer Fei Ssu to represent him. Fei denied that his client incited others to go on strike and asked that the case be dismissed. The judge, Sun, after consultation with the American Consul Mr. Ya, passed a lenient sentence on Yao and the two Wangs, fining them 20 yuan each. Tiao Chih-k'uei and the female workers Wong A-erh and others were each asked to write out a statement of the case and were then released after a reprimand.

("Yesterday's Developments in

the South Seas Labor Dispute" [Nan-yang kung-ch'ao tso-hsin], Republican Daily, September 16, 1924.)

The workers T'ang Yung-piao, T'ang A-chin, and the female workers Liang Chou and others, all from the South Seas Brothers Tobacco Company at Broadway Road, were arrested by Liu Wen-hsien, a detective sent by the police. They were brought before the court yesterday morning. The plaintiff, Li Yüan, asked the lawyer Yang Kuo-shu to give an account of the case to the court. Yang stated that there were four or five thousand workers at the South Seas Company and that the defendants, because they were opposed to the manager's action in changing the foremen, adopted threatening tactics and prevented other workers from reporting for work. He further argued that the defendants had in fact committed a criminal offense and should be dealt with accordingly. The defendant, Yang Yung-piao, also acquired the service of a lawyer, who denied in court the charges made against his client. Having heard the case, Judge Han consulted Tao T'ien, the Japanese vice consul. He then sentenced each of the defendants to pay a fine of 20 yuan, or, if they couldn't pay the fine, to submit to fourteen days in detention.

(Republican Daily, September 21, 1924.)

2. The Management's Bribing of the Large Newspapers in Shanghai

(Two Articles Published in the "Guide Weekly" Condemning the Newspapers That Were Bribed by the Capitalists)

"The Strike at the South Seas Tobacco Factory and the Shanghai Newspapers" (by Chün Yü)

We are not at all surprised that the newspapers in Shanghai

have extended no help at all to the present strike of the workers at the South Seas Tobacco factory, since they have all been bribed by the capitalists. But we are singularly astonished by the attitude adopted by the Republican Daily.

Most of the people who read the Republican Daily know that it is an organ of the Kuomintang. The most important duty of the Republican Daily is then of course to support the ideology of the Kuomintang and the interests that the Party represents. However, the materials published in the Republican Daily have often been exceptions to this, and lately there have been a great many such exceptions. The attitude of the newspaper toward the strike at the South Seas tobacco factory is one of these many exceptions.

The present strike of friends at the South Seas Brothers Tobacco Company factory is due to the punitive regulations the company has imposed, the reduction in the size of the bonuses paid to the workers, the unreasonable dismissal of the two female workers Ch'en Ch'ien-ju and Wu Hui-fen, and the plot to dissolve the Association of Comrade Employees. Therefore in order to abolish the punitive regulations, reinstate to their jobs the two female workers who have been dismissed, and increase their wages, seven thousand fellow workers went out on strike on the eighth of this month. The native capitalists have always boasted of their patriotism, of how they have given life to industry in China, and of how they have been fighting against foreign produce. But when it comes to dealing with their less fortunate compatriots, they are as ruthless as the foreign capitalists. In the way they have dealt with the strike, the capitalists have not only issued verbal threats, but have also in fact carried out physical intimidation. On the ninth of this month they sent out over fifty hoodlums, who coerced the workers into reporting for work at the factory and beat up those who refused to do so. At the same time, they dismissed four representatives of the union and moreover had representative Ku beaten before detaining him in the company office. In addition there were fifty-odd female workers who were locked inside the factory; they were not allowed to go home to feed their children or to go out to buy food for themselves. They were only released after they had been crying the whole day. The company thought that in this way it could defeat the workers and break their strike. Apart from what has just been mentioned, the company also took action to mask the public's view of the real situation. Two members of the company, a certain K'uang and a certain Li (i.e., K'uang Kung-yao and Li Yüan, the two running-dogs of the capitalists) issued a statement (in Republican Daily, September 15, 1924), and further bribed ten people who called themselves the "Kwangtung workers in Shanghai" into issuing another statement (in Republican Daily, September 15, 1924). There was yet another statement (in Republican Daily, September 14, 1924) which was purported to have been issued by "fellow-workers at the factory." The gist of all three of these statements was opposition to the strike, and they were intended to destroy public sympathy for the workers. What a shame that it was only in the Republican Daily that these statements were published, and not in any of the reactionary newspapers!

It is curious enough that the Republican Daily has not followed the Kuomintang policy of giving assistance to the strike. But in publishing such things, it has in fact gone against the Party's decision to promote the interests of the workers and peasants. We find this very difficult to understand!

Perhaps some people will say, "What has been published is not news, let alone an editorial comment. It is merely advertising, and the newspaper has published the statements only for reason of revenue. One should not accuse the newspaper of making a mistake on the basis of the advertisements that it carries!" If that is really the case, then perhaps tomorrow the Study Clique [Yen-chiu hsi] can approach the newspaper with a sum of money and then publish in the Republican Daily statements that are insulting to the Kuomintang. And then on the following day, Ts'ao K'un (1) can also pay the Republican Daily to publish statements that condemn Sun Yat-sen!

Where will it all end? So we advise our fellow publication the Republican Daily to think over such matters (as effect the livelihood of 7,000 compatriots) carefully!

(Guide Weekly [Hsiang-tao chou-pao], No. 83, September 17, 1924, pp. 672-673.)

Editors' note: The Guide Weekly was at the time the organ of the Central Committee of the Chinese Communist Party.

"The True Colors of the Shanghai Press as Revealed during the Strike at the South Seas Tobacco Factory"

We have often said that in a capitalist society the bourgeoisie not only have a monopoly of all the means of production and political organs, but also control and the means, such as newspapers, by which public opinion is formed as efficient tools to promote their own class interests and to suppress the laboring class. Although capitalism in China is still in its infancy, it is no exception. This becomes perfectly clear when we look at the attitude adopted by the Shanghai press toward the present strike of the workers at the South Seas Tobacco Company.

Because the more than 7,000 workers of South Seas Tobacco Company have suffered all kinds of cruel treatment and oppression at the hands of the capitalists and their running-dogs, in their own point of view their coming out on strike in unison was inevitable (as mentioned in the communications from the South Seas Tobacco Association of Comrade Employees, which have been carried in the Shanghai Worker). But the capitalists and their running-dogs acquired the services of not only hoodlums to beat the workers on the streets, but also policemen to arrest the workers. In addition to this, they employed all kinds of contemptible and devilish measures, including blatant threats and rumormongering. They have stopped at nothing, and all people of conscience should feel a great sense of outrage over their ruthlessness and cruelty.

The press in Shanghai has always boasted of its efforts to uphold justice and expose the hidden evils in society. However, not one word has been said in support of the strike by the more than 7,000 oppressed workers of South Seas Tobacco Company. On the contrary, it has carried various advertisements for the capitalists which have slandered the workers and created all kinds of rumors. What is this! How can the newspapers carry endless reports of such trivialities as the birthday banquets or new concubines of warlords, or the visits of foreign notables to Shanghai, and yet at the same time say not a single word about a matter of life-or-death importance that concerns the livelihood of over 7,000 workers? What is this!

"It has always been the case that each paper carries the advertisements of the capitalists. Some newspapers receive five or six hundred yuan a month in advertising revenues, while the monthly amount for others is two or three hundred yuan. When the strike started, the capitalists sent people around to the various newspapers with the following messages: 'There is a strike at our factory, and we hope that your newspapers will not carry the news and advertisements brought to you by the workers.' 'We advertise a great deal every month in your newspaper, and we are sure that we can depend on your help now' " (see Shanghai Worker, No. 4).

Ah! This is how it has always been! It turns out that all the newspapers in Shanghai have been bribed by the advertising revenues that they receive from the South Seas Tobacco Company. It turns out that each month a newspaper is getting two or three hundred to five or six hundred yuan from the capitalists, and that this is how the newspapers are run! So! These are the true colors of the Shanghai press!

(Guide Weekly, No. 84, September 24, 1924, p. 685.)

...This time we the more than 7,000 workers are united as one in the effort to save our union, to support our fellow workers, and to struggle for the sacred privilege of freedom. But we are surprised that the Shanghai newspapers have not carried any reports of our struggle. We hereby make a sincere and urgent plea to every sacred trade union and all sections of the community to come forward and uphold justice. Give us your aid, and help us to determine our own fate!

("A Most Urgent Plea for Help," issued by the 7,000-odd male and female workers of the South Seas Tobacco Association of Comrade Employees on September 12, 1924, Republican Daily, September 13, 1924.)

3. Sabotage of the Unity of the Workers

All Kinds of Pressure to Compel the Workers to Return to Work. At present, because the war is greatly inhibiting commerce and the nation's transport system is running in low gear because the method of sending money by drafts is no longer effective, and at the same time there are difficulties in obtaining loans and credit, many of our branch offices have cabled us to either cut down or cancel their orders. It is only because we want to maintain the livelihood of our fellow workers that the manufacturing plant has strived to continue production. But nobody can predict how long the war will last. Should it continue over a long period, then our stocks will build up to such a point that we will have to cut down production in order to balance supply with demand. It seems that during the present dispute a minority of the employees have intentionally stayed away from work to see how the situation will develop. We have already made a clear statement of our intention to regard any employees who have not reported for work by September 14 as having voluntarily dismissed themselves. At present, over 5,000 of the workers have declared their intention to return to work. For those who have yet to return to work, whether they will be taken on again will be decided by consultation and will depend on whether the overall situation settles down and whether goods flow freely again. We therefore hereby issue this public notice and urge all employees to come to the factory as soon as possible between 2:00 and 4:00 each afternoon to register their addresses!

("A Statement from the Manufacturing Plant of the South Seas Brothers Tobacco Company Ltd." [Nan-yang hsiung-ti yen-ts'ao yu-hsien kung-ssu chih-tso-ch'ang ch'i-shih], Republican Daily, September 27, 1924.)

...Following advice from various quarters, the workers have been returning to work, and a small number of new workers have been taken on. Production has now returned to normal....

(From the minutes of the fifty-second meeting of the Board of Directors on September 23, 1924.)

The Use of Traitors among the Workers to Gain Control of the Union and Sabotage the Workers' Unity. We have just read "A Statement from the Fellow Workers and Association of Comrade Employees at the Manufacturing Plant of the South Seas Tobacco Company"; we are utterly amazed. This union has now been in existence for two years. In October last year, T'ang Yüan-ts'an, Ma Wei-ch'ing, Li Pai-t'ing, T'an Chin, and others were elected to be union officials at a general meeting of the union. In February this year, after the resignation of Yung, Hsü, Liang, and others, T'ang, Ma, Li, T'an, Sun, and others were elected to succeed to the posts of chairman and vice chairman of the committee, committee member in charge of financial matters, and to other positions. With respect to the present situation, what happened was that the company first broke the agreement it had with the union by the unreasonable dismissal of our fellow workers. This action outraged the entire union membership, and it was on the evening of the eighth that we decided unanimously to go out on strike. Furthermore we issued eight demands, and it was agreed that we would not give in until these demands were met. Such a decision was supported without objection by Liang T'ai, Ch'en Wen-piao, P'ang Ch'i, Ch'en Hung-kuang, Ch'ien Shao-mei, Feng Fu, Wei Hsien-sheng, Ch'en Yo-nan, Ch'en Li-kuang, Ch'en Hsiu-jan, Li Ch'i-nung, Teng Shao-ming, Feng Jih-tung, and others, who were all present at the meeting. The strike has been on for more than ten days now, and during this time the company has employed all sorts of measures to sabotage the unity of our union. It has applied all kinds of pressure on our fellow workers, and a small number of them succumbed to such enticements. Liang T'ai, Ch'en Wen-piao, P'ang Ch'i, Ch'en Hung-kuang, Ch'ien Shao-mei, Feng Fu, Wei Hsien-sheng, Ch'en Yo-nan, Ch'en Li-kuang, Ch'en Hsiu-jan, Li Ch'i-nung, Teng Shao-ming, Feng Jih-tung, and others are among those who have been lured away. These people changed their allegiance midway through the struggle and willingly became running-dogs. They are by now totally rejected by the other union members. It does not take much substantiation to prove that the various points in the statement have all been fabricated. For instance, the dismissal of Wu and Ch'en was not due to the fact that they broke any of the factory regulations but was the result of a retaliatory action taken by Li and K'uang. All the 7,000-odd fellow workers in the factory knew that such an action went against Article 4 of the agreement that was concluded between the company and this union, and this was the reason why the entire body of fellow workers went on strike in indignant protest. So far the company has only succeeded in enticing or compelling about a thousand workers into returning to work. The majority of these workers are children and female workers, and only thirty-odd regular workers have been lured back to work. These facts are borne out in the accounts issued by the other unions which have made an attempt at mediation, and they cannot be nullified by the rumormongering of a small group of people. The statement concerned is but yet another act of sabotage directed at this union by the management. This union has now not only left this matter in the hands of a solicitor with the intention of litigation but is also publishing this statement in the press to clarify the situation.

("An Urgent Statement from the South Seas Tobacco Association of Comrade Employees" [Nan-yang yen-ts'ao chih-kung t'ung-chih hui chin-chi ch'i-shih], Republican Daily, September 27, 1924.)

[Appended note]: A Statement from the Fellow Workers and Association of Comrade Employees at the Manufacturing Plant of South Seas Tobacco Company.

To the Public and All Organizations:

Two years have now passed since this union was established. An account of the history of the union has already been published in the weekly magazine. Since February this year, T'ang Yüan-ts'an, Ma Wei-ch'ing, Li Pai-t'ing, T'an Chin, Sun Kuan-hsiao, and others have taken advantage of a changeover in the office-holders of the union and seized the posts of the committee chairman, committee members, etc., usurped control of union affairs, and done whatever they liked, thus alienating our fellow workers over a long period of time. Following the management's dismissal of two female workers who broke the factory regulations, T'ang Yüan-ts'an and the others, without the consent of a general meeting, conspired with a small number of workers to incite a strike. They assaulted our fellow workers who were returning to the factory, and further, without any legitimate authority, sent off cables and statements to the press in an effort to create malicious rumors and confuse the public. Now, over five thousand of our fellow workers have reported back to the factory for work, and they have all expressed the opinion that T'ang Yüan-ts'an and the others have gone too far, and ever since inciting the strike they have used the union's name to create trouble everywhere, ruining the good name of this union. Therefore a special meeting of temporary representatives from the various sections was convened inside the factory at 9:00 a.m. on the twenty-fifth. At this meeting the following were made temporary representatives of the union: Wang Ch'i-fa, Lo Ta-fu, Cheng Sheng, Yung Man, Huo Wei, Lin K'ang, Li Hsün, P'an T'ien, Li Ping-chün, Feng Fu, Ch'ien Shao-mei, Wei T'ien-sheng, Hsü Ping, Huang Pi, Liang T'ai, P'ang Ch'i, Ch'en Hung-kuang, Ch'en Yo-nan, Chien Shao-ch'ing, Yung Yün-hsien, Teng Shao-ming, Ch'en Wen-piao, Ts'eng Ch'i, Lu Hui-yüan, Feng Jih-tung, Wang Hsing-miao, Ch'en Li-kuang, Wang Tzu-chün, Chien Chen-sheng, Ch'en Hsiu-jan, T'an Hsiu-yün, K'ung Chiao, Chiang Shun-ti, Wang Fu-sheng, Shih Chia-ming, Li Ch'i-nung, Huo To, Ku A-hsin, Ou Lai, Ch'ien Chieh-ch'u, and others. The above persons have assumed collective responsibility and will now conduct the union's affairs. A general meeting will be held to formally elect the committee chairman, the committee members, etc. From the moment this statement is published in the press, all financial dealings of the union will be declared null and void unless they are handled by Wang Ch'i-fa. Furthermore, the members of the union do not recognize the various cables and mimeographed materials that have been issued in the last few days. We hereby make this collective statement with the hope that all will take note.

(Republican Daily, September 26, 1924.)

4. "Guide Weekly" Exposed the Capitalists' Efforts to Sabotage the Strike

"The Ruthless Actions Taken by the South Seas Tobacco Capitalists to Destroy the Strike"
(by Chen Yü)

If a worker stops work for just one day, he will go hungry

right away. When we see a factory in which more than 7,000 workers opt to strike and suffer hunger in an effort to eradicate harsh treatment, we can well imagine the harshness of that treatment. The capitalists of South Seas Tobacco have always been even craftier than other capitalists, and their "intelligent eyes" have long perceived that "the strength of the solidarity of the workers' organization is capable of sealing their fate. So their first tactic against the strike was to disband the workers' organization. They paid double wages to those who returned to the factory, promoted casual workers to become regular workers, used dismissal as a threat against the striking workers, employed Shantung bullies to waylay the striking workers, and bribed policemen to arrest them.

After going hungry for more than ten days, and with no news of a possible settlement, the workers became apprehensive and could no longer bear up to the deceit and the threats. Thus those workers who were the weakest were the first to enter the factory, albeit grudgingly and with great resentment and bitterness. The capitalist then jumped on this to publicize widely: A number of workers have already returned to work; anyone who does not return to the factory before September 14 will be fined. After this threat had been made, more and more workers were compelled to return to work grudgingly and resentfully. But even then there were still as many as two thousand workers who were resolute to the end, and their strength was considerable. Then the capitalists produced another trick. On the one hand, they bribed two lawyers, Mu An-su and Fei Ssu, to take part in the mediation and to give the workers false hope of a legal victory, so that the workers' feelings would simmer down a bit, making it easier for the capitalists to move in for the kill.... On the other hand, they bribed a small number of workers to intimidate the majority of workers into issuing a statement in the name of 5,000 workers, alleging that the strike had been incited by a small number of workers. This small number of workers further intimidated the majority of workers into electing them as the officials of the Association of Comrade Employees. Thus the capitalists not only turned this struggle between themselves and the workers into a struggle among the workers, but also, with the aid of a legal code that protected the capitalists, totally wiped out the basis of this strike.

By this time, those workers who opposed harsh treatment to the very end and were still fighting had become innocent victims, isolated and helpless. They were further framed with the trumped-up charge of "robbing the union of miscellaneous items," and all the former officials of the union were being sought by the police. For news of these events see the statement of the South Seas Association of Comrade Employees and the statement from the new committee chairman of the Association; such news was also extensively reported on the second and third of this month in the Republican Daily and the Daily Report [Shen-pao]. The poor and helpless workers, who had already suffered during this strike the misfortunes of imprisonment and fines, were like birds startled by the twang of a bowstring when they heard this latest news; . . . the capitalists, however, were in a position to sing out their triumphant song!

Having come to this act in this drama of ruthlessness and deceit, we can well imagine the tragedy that is to be unfolded by the final curtain! If we carefully examine the contents of the September 12 leaflet ["A Most Urgent Plea for Help"] issued by the South Seas tobacco workers, we can see that the development of this evil drama has been no accident. It was all the doing of K'uang Kung-yao and Li Yüan, both backed by heavy bribes from the capitalists. These two plotted to abrogate the seventeen-article agreement and to dissolve the union, and they successfully manufactured a deliberate provocation (by the groundless dismissal of the two female workers). All these pernicious actions had been thought out and planned in advance, . . . and the workers walked unwittingly into the trap as if by invitation! Now the new officials of the Association of Comrade Employees are all the personal slaves of the capitalists, and the union has been transformed into an instrument of the capitalists. From now on the workers can only guard against being slaughtered; they can no longer depend on the union to promote their welfare!

...

To those resolute and courageous fellow workers who are fighting to the very end! The newspapers, courts, lawyers, law, and police in the present society...whom do they really serve, and whom do they really protect? ... The courageous and combative spirit with which you fight for the workers' interests can never be destroyed! In having people like you, it is like the working class having their own bodyguard to protect them, and the liberation of the working class depends entirely on you. The capitalists' oppression of the workers is a common occurrence, so do not attach too much importance to the failure of one particular strike. Do not be disheartened, but work to unite these more than 2,000 resolute and courageous elements. Position them throughout all the various cigarette factories in Shanghai, and tell the people of the lesson that has been learned from the failure of this strike. Organize an even stronger army of heroes, and when the opportunity arises for another life-and-death struggle with the capitalists, I dare say that "the final victory is yours."

On this occasion we also want to issue a warning to the Kuomintang's Executive Department [Chih-hsing pu] in Shanghai and to the Republican Daily, the organ of the Kuomintang: In the Manifesto and Constitution worked out after the reorganization of the Kuomintang, it is clearly written that the Party should protect and fight to promote the interests of the workers and peasants. But now Kuang Kung-yao and Li Yüan, two right-wing members of the Kuomintang, have assisted the capitalists in bringing great suffering to righteous workers who are resolute in their resistance and struggle. The Executive Department in Shanghai not only refused to expel these traitors who have gone against the policy of the Party, but also allowed the Republican Daily to continue to publish advertisements that ever more vehemently aided and abetted the abuses of the capitalists. This clearly proves that by violating the article in the Kuomintang's Manifesto and Constitution that states that the

Party should protect and fight to promote the interests of the workers and peasants, the Kuomintang Executive Department in Shanghai and the Republican Daily have declared themselves to be traitors!

(Guide Weekly, No. 85, October 1, 1924, p. 695.)

"The Shameless Sabotage of the Organization of the Unemployed Workers by the South Seas Company and Its Running-Dogs"
(by Lung Chih)

After the capitalists' suppression had brought about the failure of the strike by the more than 7,000 workers at South Seas Tobacco Company, the workers continued their struggle without respite, on the one hand consolidating their organization, and on the other sending representatives to the various trade unions in Hong Kong, Macao, and Canton to spread the word of how the capitalists had suppressed the workers. All these unions were outraged at this, and they were not only forthcoming in their offers of assistance to the workers but also most active in a boycott of the company's cigarettes. As Kwangtung was the largest market for the company, when its sales there began to suffer greatly, the company sent Chang Wei-ch'uan and three other representatives to Kwangtung in an attempt to bring disunity to the unions. After their arrival in Hong Kong, they proceeded to sabotage the unity of the Hong Kong Federation of Trade Unions [Hsiang-kang tsung-kung-hui]. But the Kwangtung representatives of the South Seas workers found out what they were up to, and they reported it to a special committee. The committee then sent its representatives to Hong Kong, and the scheme of Chang and the others was completely thwarted. It has also been reported that a vigilance squad came upon a consignment of cigarettes of the "Hundred Birds" brand which was on its way to Kwangtung. The squad confiscated over 400 crates of the cigarettes. These were first deposited at the office of the workers' representatives and later auctioned off, with the proceeds going to compensate the workers for their losses.

After this blow, the capitalists of the company adopted the tactic of feigning peace in Hong Kong and Macao while at the same time fomenting yet another fiendish plot against the several thousand unemployed workers in Shanghai. Under the pretext of taking back these unemployed workers, the company ordered the running-dogs they had bought off to sabotage the organization of the workers. Please look at the following urgent statement that was issued by the provisional executive committee of the South Seas Tobacco Association of Comrade Employees and reprinted in this paper on the twenty-first of this month: "We are very baffled indeed by the news in the papers today concerning the meeting of the Confederation of Trade Unions [Kung-t'uan lien-ho-hui] and the statement issued by it. It is reported that one of the organizations that participated in the meeting was the South Seas Tobacco Association of Comrade Employees, but we in fact did not send any representatives to the meeting. It is reported that among those who attended the meeting were the two persons Wang Kuang-hui and Kuo Chi-sheng. It was these two who, at the height of the struggle between the fellow workers of this union and the capitalists, collaborated with Wang Ch'i-fa and others who were in the services of the capitalists, in a deliberate sabotage of the work of this union. Furthermore, when the capitalists took the pernicious action of dissolving this union and creating a new one under their control, these two persons, Kuo and Wang, were appointed as secretaries of the new union with monthly salaries of 80 yuan each. From then on they have been doing their best to sabotage our union. Now our union has the assistance of the trade unions in Canton, Hong Kong and throughout the rest of the country, and we are conducting a boycott of the company's cigarettes. The day before yesterday the newspapers reported the seizure of more than 200 crates of the company's cigarettes; this shows that there is still a sense of justice in people's hearts. Now Wang, Kuo, and the others have suddenly advertised in the newspapers the registering of fellow workers who are unemployed. This is clearly an act of sabotage against our organization, and our fellow workers will not fall into their trap. But we are concerned that other organizations and compatriots in all walks of life may be hoodwinked by this. We therefore are hereby making public the true situation and hope that our labor circles and all compatriots will take note."

From the way in which Wang Kuang-hui and Kuo Chi-sheng collaborated with the capitalists to oppress the workers, we can see that there are many who may sell out their own class for their own profit. Fellow workers, we must be even more careful!

From the enthusiastic way assistance has been given to the unemployed workers of South Seas by the trade unions in Canton, we can see that the vital interests of working classes everywhere are the same. Only if the working classes unite as one can they resist the capitalists and win a final victory!

(Guide Weekly, No. 96, December 24, 1924, p. 807.)

Editor's note: At the Second National Labor Conference [Ch'üan-kuo lao-tung ta-hui] convened in Canton on May 1, 1925, the "Resolution to Eradicate All Traitors among the Workers" was passed, and this contained a list of the names of the most infamous traitors among the workers. Wang Kuang-hui and Kuo Chi-sheng were among the four names given for Shanghai. See Teng Chung-hsia, A Short History of the Chinese Labor Movement (1919-1926) [Chung-kuo chih-kung yun-tung chien-shih].

III Five Documents on Revolutionary Management and Development

Contents

1

An Important Reform of Management of Industrial Enterprises

Wang Hao-feng

Summation of a Speech Delivered to a Heilungkiang Provincial Conference of Industrial Cadres

The current conference is a success. Five units, namely, the state-owned Ching-hua Machine Tools Plant, Chien-hua Machinery Plant, Harbin Locomotive and Carriage Repair Works, First Engineering Bureau of the Third Engineering Corporation of the Northeast, and Sung-kiang Metal Works, have given accounts of their experiences at the conference. The experience of each of the units is distinctive. Ching-hua Machine Tools Plant has given an account of its experience in three aspects of its work — participation by cadres in labor, direct participation by workers in the management, and reform of management work. Participation in labor by cadres of this factory is more general in this factory than in any other, and the hours of their participation in labor are longer (all workshop cadres do half a day's labor every day). Some experience has been gained in this way. Direct participation in the management by the workers began only recently, but very good results have been achieved. The revolutionary reform of management work in conjunction with the participation in labor by cadres and direct participation in the management by the workers was never

Wang Hao-feng, "Ch'i-yeh kuan-li ti ch'ung-ta kai ke." Jen-min jih-pao [People's Daily], April 26, 1958. This translation is taken, with minor editorial revisions, from SCMP, No. 1774 (May 19, 1958), 4-13.

attempted before in the province. Chien-hua Machinery Plant has given an account mainly of experience in the direct participation by the workers in its management. They have spent a longer time on the matter than any other factory, and have gone through a process of trial and error. The spirit in which they tackled problems during the process deserves to be imitated. Their ideological work, too, was done with considerable attention to detail. The experience of the First Engineering Bureau of the Third Engineering Corporation of the Northeast in assimilating cadres to the workers, making the cadres live the same life as the masses and regularizing their labor, and in the "five togethers" (the cadres' eating together, living together, laboring together, and taking recreation together with the workers, and so on), is also quite remarkable. It shows a high degree of determination on the part of the leadership of the bureau and the thoroughness with which the cadres changed their style of work. The Harbin Locomotive and Carriage Repair Works has given an account of how, in accordance with the directive of the central leadership concerning the cultivation of experimental fields, they have produced "two dragons," and how they have learned later the experience of Chien-hua Machinery Plant in letting their workers take a direct part in the management. The local state-operated Sung-kiang Metal Works of Harbin has given an account of experience principally in the participation of their cadres in labor. In short, the experience recounted by these units is quite valuable and deserves to be learned by all other industries and enterprises in the province. At the same time, all this experience is new and of some fundamental character. Wider application of such experience in earnest will be of great importance to the current rectification and double-anti movement, the big leap forward in production, or to future improvement of work in all branches of our industries and enterprises.

The experience exchanged at the current conference on three subjects — participation of cadres in labor, direct participation by the workers in the management and reform of management work — represents in essence revolutionary measures for the fundamental improvement of the leadership and management of enterprises, a revolution in the style of work and method of work of the leadership of the enterprises, and an important reform of management work. Participation of cadres in labor assimilates them to the workers; direct participation of the workers in the management makes them producers and managers at the same time; revolutionary reform of management work thoroughly revises those regulations and systems that restrict the activism of the masses and the development of their productivity. As a method of work, all this is the kind of method that will produce quick and good results, the method of progress, as has been mentioned by Chairman Mao Tse-tung. Therefore, if such experience is carried out in all our industries and enterprises, we shall be able to overcome thoroughly bureaucratism and subjectivism in their leadership, fully carry out the mass line of the Party, greatly elevate the level of the leadership of the enterprises and the level of management, and effectively promote the development of productivity. If our enterprises can truly enforce the two fundamental systems of leadership for enterprises decided upon by the central leadership, i.e., the system of making factory managers responsible under the leadership of the Party committees and the system of workers' congresses under the leadership of Party committees, if the mass line method of work ("blooming and contending," wall newspapers, and mass debates) developed during the rectification is really applied to our regular work, and if a sound system is gradually developed by earnestly applying the three kinds of experience recounted at the current conference, then in our industries and enterprises there will be:

1) Strong Party leadership and political-ideological work.
2) A system of management of democratic centralism that combines a high degree of democracy with a high degree of centralization.
3) A systematic mass line method of work.
4) An army of cadres both red and expert, which will be formed within a short space of time.

Under these conditions, we shall be able fully to carry out the

Party's principle of relying on the workers for the proper operation of our enterprises and the mass line method of work, and further solve the unity of politics and technique. A "lively political situation where centralism is combined with democracy, discipline with freedom, and unified will with individual facility" will then be brought about.

Over the past several years, we have gained a lot of experience in, and learned many lessons about, the leadership and management of enterprises. They may be summed up into this conclusion: In the final analysis, the most fundamental question in socialist enterprises is the strengthening of Party leadership and carrying out of the mass line, regardless of whatever special character the industries and enterprises may have. In these industries and enterprises, as in our revolutionary movement of the past, practice has proved once more that work can be well done through creative application of Marxism (in other words, through combination of theory with practice), and that work can never be done properly through rigid adherence to dogmas. This is a lesson which we must never forget.

After several years of groping about, we now deeply realize the decisiveness of the role played by the masses in a socialist enterprise. At any time and in any kind of work, so long as we really and fully mobilize and rely on the masses, we shall be able to solve problems which the leadership cannot solve alone, overcome difficulties that have arisen in our work, and work miracles in production and our work. This may be clearly seen in the current rectification and double-anti movement and the big leap forward in production. Let us ask: If we had not freely mobilized the masses through "blooming and contending" and wall newspapers in accordance with a directive from the central leadership of the Party and Chairman Mao Tse-tung, could we have so thoroughly exposed the contradictions and problems in our enterprises? If we had not fully relied on the masses and carried out rectification and improvement by adopting the mass line method of work, how could we have dealt with so quickly and properly the thousands of suggestions put forward by the masses during the "blooming and contending"? If the masses had not been fully mobilized politically and ideologically during the rectification and the political consciousness of the masses and their activism for production had not been increased, how could the present high tide of production and big leap forward in production have been possible? All this proves once more the complete correctness of the principle, laid down at the Second Plenum of the Seventh Central Committee of the Party, of relying on the working class for the proper management of our enterprises. It also effectively proves that the method of work adopted by many enterprises in the past, in which management organs were expanded without any restriction, nonproductive personnel were increased, reliance was placed solely on the index system, on organizational discipline and a system of heavy rewards and punishment, and in which nothing was done to increase the consciousness of the masses and reliance was never placed on their activism, was wrong and was contrary to the Party's spirit of relying on the working class for proper management of enterprises.

As a result of the rectification, we are able to understand better the internal contradictions of our enterprises and the substance and cause of their problems. In socialist enterprises, although means of production is owned collectively by the people, the working class is the master of these enterprises, and contradictions within the working class are nonantagonistic contradictions arising on the basis of unanimity of basic interests, contradictions still really exist between productivity and relationship of production and between the superstructure and the economic basis. Various kinds of contradiction also exist within the working class, between the advanced and the backward elements, between those with the right views and attitude and those with erroneous views and attitude, between different parts of the masses, and between the worker masses and the leadership of the enterprises. Most of these contradictions concern the relationship between the leadership and the masses, and they arise principally from the three "isms" of the leadership and its rightist conservatism. This is quite clear from the thousands of suggestions put forward by the masses during the rectification and double-anti movements. The rightist conservatism and three "isms" of the leadership are manifested not only in the implementation of the Party's principles and policies, but also in the style and method of work of the leadership and the system of management. Therefore, the thorough exposure and criticism of rightist conservatism and all kinds of wasteful and conservative practice through the rectification and double-anti movements and revolutionary reform of the management of enterprises with respect to the style and method of work of the leadership are of great significance not only to the adjustment of the internal contradictions of the enterprises (contradictions between productivity and relationship of production, between the superstructure and the economic basis, between the leadership and the masses, and between one part of the masses and another), but also to the further implementation of the Party's principle of relying on the working class for the proper management of enterprises, the carrying out of the policy of "quantity, speed, quality and economy" and of striving for advance with the utmost vigor, the radical reform of the whole aspect of the enterprises, the effective promotion of productivity, and the bringing about of an overall leap forward from the leadership down to the masses and from ideology to actual production. The experience in these respects recounted by Ching-hua Machine Tools Plant and other units suggests some concrete measures and measures in principle for the solution of our problems. That is why their experience is so valuable.

In the past years, many cadres have not properly solved, cognitionally and in their work, the question of coordination of political with economic work and the question of simultaneous achievement of redness and expertness. As a result of the rectification and participation of cadres in labor, these questions are now better understood, and new experience has been gained with regard to their solution. It should be pointed out that we have acquired a good deal of experience during the rectification concerning the coordination of political and economic work. Cases of political work throughout the whole Party and among all cadres (including administrative cadres and technical cadres of all levels) and different forms of self-education by the masses may be said to be a great development of political work in our enterprises. As regards the question of redness and expertness, our experience is still scanty, but owing to the participation of cadres in labor during the rectification movement and the subsequent thorough improvement of their style of work, and to the considerable increase in the political consciousness of all technical personnel through the rectification and anti-rightist struggle, we may be said to have already found a correct means of solving the question. Is it not pointed out positively in the circular issued by the central leadership on the cultivation of "experimental fields" that the cultivation of experimental fields is "the way that will enable cadres to achieve both 'redness and expertness'" and a very good means of "achieving unity of politics with techniques"? Are not many of our enterprises energetically carrying out this directive from the central leadership?

In short, the recent rectification has further solved, ideologically and in actual work, some of the fundamental problems of the leadership and management of enterprises. We have already acquired considerable new experience as to how we should rely on the working class for the proper management of enterprises and how we should fully adopt the mass line method of work in all branches of our work (including administrative and managerial work). We should seriously study and sum up such experience.

I am now going to discuss the following three questions.

I. The Question of Direct Participation of Workers in Management

If the production team is taken as a unit and the workers who make up the team are made responsible for the management of the team, can that be said to be a form of direct participation of the worker masses in the management? Yes, it can. Because the workers truly take part in the management. It is different from the participation by some workers in the workers' congress that in turn takes part in the management and supervision of the administration — a form previously adopted — in that it is a further expansion of democracy in the management of enterprises. It is in fact a new form of direct participation of the workers in the management, a form which is not in conflict with the form of workers' congresses in the least. The new form represents a creative development of the mass line in the management of enterprises, and it places such management work on an even broader mass basis. It is an unprecedented attempt to improve fundamentally the management of enterprises. Its significance is great and manifold. First of all, it attracts the worker masses on the broadest possible basis to participation in the management, fully promoting the activism of the masses in production and management and greatly strengthening their sense of responsibility as masters of the country and their collectivist thought. Next, it is a fundamental measure for thoroughly overcoming bureaucratism in the management of enterprises. Moreover, it is also an excellent means of cultivating the management abilities of the worker masses and creates exceedingly favorable conditions for the selection of cadres from among the ranks of the workers. Combined with the participation of cadres in labor, the measure is also of great significance to the removal of the contradiction between mental labor and physical labor and the contradiction between the leadership and the masses. One of the main causes of the contradiction between the leaders of enterprises and the worker masses is the different position occupied by the two in production. The worker masses directly participate in productive labor (principally physical labor) and generally do not directly exercise their powers of management. On the other hand, the leaders of enterprises directly exercise administrative powers and generally do not take part in any physical labor. That imposes certain restrictions on the understanding of the two sides. The participation by cadres in labor and direct participation by workers in the management will largely eliminate such restrictions on the two sides, rationally adjust the mutual relations between the leadership and the masses as well as within the ranks of the workers themselves in production, and effectively promote the development of productivity. Practice has shown that direct participation of the workers in the management produces excellent political and economic results, and that these results are evident. Some comrades have said that the carrying out of the measure has made both the cadres and the masses happy and production and other branches of work easier. I think that the statement is justified and true. So, we must understand fully the significance of the experience. It should be affirmed that the experience is completely correct in principle, but that owing to its recent acquisition it is not yet perfect and mature, and that many problems still remain to be further studied and solved in practice. Here I shall discuss some of the questions raised during the conference and make suggestions for your consideration.

1) What should be the character of the (production) team? Does it belong to the Party, the trade union, or the Young Communist League? No, it does not belong to any of these. It appears that the team should be more aptly called a mass production management team. It is an administrative organization in character. Its relationship with the Party, trade union and Young Communist League should be determined according to its character. So, it cannot take the place of the Party, the trade union, or the Young Communist League organization.

2) In principle, the size and scope of a team should be determined principally by the characteristics and needs of production and the time that the worker masses can spare. In other words, the size and scope of a team should be determined by its usefulness to production. Participation of the worker masses in the production management must not take them away from their production work; they should take part in the management only in their spare time. Therefore, no member of a team should be given too much to do. There should not be too many kinds of management teams. I think it is enough to have one kind — the production management team.

3) With regard to the creation of the team leader, a method should be adopted which combines election by the worker masses

and appointment by a superior authority. In this way the principle of democratic centralism will be observed. In accordance with the needs of work, a superior administrative authority may transfer the leader of a team elsewhere and may also directly appoint someone to take this place.

4) As to the division of labor within a team, that should be based on the suitability and aptitude of every member of the team. The principle of volition should also be observed. While each worker should have something to do, no one should be burdened with too much work. Participation in the management by the worker masses should not take too much of their spare time, so that they may still have time for spare-time studies and participation in Party or other mass activities.

How should the experience be applied extensively?

First, ideological work must be done well in order to dispel various worries of the cadres and the masses and to correct their erroneous impressions. The experience of Ching-hua Machine Tools Plant and Chien-hua Machinery Plant shows that the cadres are worried mainly through their distrust of the masses. They are afraid that the workers, who are "coarse and clumsy," may make a mess of everything and so hamper production. These cadres should be taught to trust the majority of the workers. They should be convinced that today's worker masses are quite different from what they used to be, that they are at a higher level not only politically and technically, but culturally too, that the workers who take a direct part in production management are not required to do highly complicated work, that each member of the team has only very little to do and what they are required to do is already familiar to them, and that most of the management procedures and systems have been simplified as a result of the management reform. Then, what is there which is beyond the abilities of the worker masses? Have not the results of experiments carried out in certain units proved that the workers are adept in management too? Some of the workers may find management work strange at first, but they will learn to do it soon enough. In the case of the worker masses, their worries are mainly the fear of making mistakes, of too much responsibility, of too much trouble, and of a reduction in wages where they are paid on piecework basis. So, it is necessary to strengthen the inculcation in them of the idea that they are masters of the country. Experience shows that most of the workers are eager to take part in management work, believing that such participation implies a high degree of trust reposed in them by the leadership and that it is an opportunity to assert themselves as masters of themselves. So they show an earnest attitude toward such work and redouble their enthusiasm for production. Meanwhile, mass self-criticism and mutual criticism is extensively developed as a result, and mutual supervision among the masses is greatly strengthened.

Second, a certain amount of training in the business of management will be necessary for the worker masses at the beginning, and constant attention should be paid to training their management capabilities. At the same time, management procedures and systems should be reformed and leadership methods improved in order to facilitate direct participation of the workers in the management.

Third, leadership for this work by the Party, government, trade unions, and the Young Communist League should be strengthened. Experience should be summed up in time and problems should be studied and solved as they arise, so that the system may be gradually perfected. It is wrong to think that since the masses are eager to take part in administrative work, Party and other mass organizations would have little or nothing to do and that ideological and organizational work may be relaxed. The Party and the trade unions should also try to find out how they could help in this work, and to build up experience in this respect.

II. The Question of Participation of Cadres in Labor

In industrial enterprises, the participation by cadres in labor and in the cultivation of "experimental fields" has the same significance as the participation of agricultural cadres in the cultivation of experimental fields so far as improvement of leadership style and method of work and the achievement by the cadres of both redness and expertness are concerned. That is what the provincial Party committee has said in its comment on a report by Harbin Locomotive and Carriage Repair Works concerning cultivation of "experimental fields." In the industries, capital construction, forestry industry, and communications and transport enterprises in this province, more and more cadres are now taking part in labor in accordance with the directives from the central leadership concerning participation by leadership cadres in labor and cultivation of "experimental fields." Some preliminary experience in this respect has also been acquired. This is shown by the accounts given during the current conference by Ching-hua Machine Tools Plant, the First Engineering Bureau of the Third Engineering Corporation of the Northeast, Harbin Locomotive and Carriage Repair Works, Sung-kiang Metal Works, and other units. It is clear from the experience of these units (actually similar experience is also acquired by other units in the province) that earnestly carrying out the directives from the central leadership concerning the participation of cadres in labor and cultivation of experimental fields is of great significance to the improving of leadership style and method of work and the establishment of closer ties between the cadres and the masses. But a careful examination reveals many problems in this branch of work. These principally are:

1) Leadership cadres of many units who take part in labor have not properly correlated such labor with their leadership of production, and are quite vague about the object of their own participation in labor. They seem to be taking part in production for the sake of production alone. As a result, they are not yet united with the masses and their labor does little to help their leadership of production, although they have taken part in actual production. It shows that they have not yet properly understood the meaning of the directive from the central leadership about this matter. In some units, the participation of leadership cadres in production has produced some effect on the improvement

of leadership for production management, but relations between the Party and the masses remain the same. They (including the secretaries of Party committees) are not skillful enough at (and some do not even pay attention to) closely coordinating, from their participation in production, the improvement of leadership of economic work with the improvement of leadership of political work.

2) We have not yet discovered a method of determining the different needs, forms and methods of participation in labor in accordance with the special circumstances of the cadres and the requirements of production. Ching-hua Machine Tools Plant and other units have acquired some experience in this respect, but have not completely solved the question. On the proper solution to this question depends not only the correct and full exploitation of the effects of participation by cadres in labor, but also the regularization and systematization of such participation in labor. Improper solution of the question is one of the principal causes of our failure to regularize and systematize the participation of cadres in labor, although there are other causes.

3) The question of how cadres may purposefully go in the direction of "redness and expertness at the same time" through their participation in labor, that is to say, how the plan for their participation in labor should be combined with their own plans for becoming "both red and expert" (including the study of political theories and of techniques connected with their work), has also not yet been solved. Of course, this question is closely related to the second question above.

In addition, there are leadership cadres of certain enterprises who have not yet begun to take part in labor. How should the situation be dealt with?

In view of the circumstances mentioned above, how should the directive on this matter from the central leadership be carried out further, and how should the work of participation of cadres in labor be advanced? I think that, apart from continuing to solve the ideological problems of the cadres, the answer depends on the solution of the three questions mentioned above.

With regard to the question of determining the different needs, forms and methods of participation in labor in accordance with the special circumstances of the cadres and the requirements of production, you are asked to consider the following plan in principle. First, with regard to the principal leadership cadres of the enterprises, their participation in labor must have as its object improvement of leadership for production. Therefore, the form and method of their participation in labor should be determined in accordance with that object. Units to take part in labor may or may not be specified but, in general, they should not include too many at the same time. The time of such participation should in general be one half day to two half days a week. Too long a time may not necessarily be good for production and other work. Moreover, when taking part in labor, leadership cadres should do so together with some technical personnel and Party-masses liaison cadres, if that is possible, and form a group with them (as is being done in some units). This may prove helpful to the solution of certain problems and to the combination of political with economic work. Second, with regard to the technical personnel, their participation in labor should in general be based on the principle of further combining technique with labor and of making management work better serve production. The duration, form and method of their participation in labor should be determined not only by the need for training in labor, but first of all by the need of improvement of technical and business leadership. Third, the principal purpose of participation in labor by other nonproductive personnel apart from those two classes already mentioned is training in labor. To a certain extent it is similar to the sending of cadres to the countryside or to lower levels, but the duration of participation in labor in this case is different.

III. The Question of Business Reform

During the rectification, various enterprises have generally made improvements in the regulations, systems, and procedures of their management, but none so thoroughly as Ching-hua

Machine Tools Plant. Theirs is a revolutionary measure aimed to solve all problems basically. The principal features of their business reform are:

1) The business reform was undertaken in conjunction with the participation of cadres in labor and direct participation of the workers in management. On the one hand, the cadres have taken part in labor in order to overcome bureaucratism and subjectivism (principally dogmatism) in the leadership and management, and reforms have been made of the regulations and systems. On the other hand, the workers have taken a direct part in the management, laying a foundation for the business reform and, in conjunction with the participation of cadres in labor, basically overcoming bureaucratism in the management. The three are organically related to one another and act upon one another. The three are products of the rectification and double-anti movement. Their common basis is the thorough reform of the style of work of the leadership through masses and technical personnel. Had it not been for these changes, particularly the change in the style of work of the leadership, the three things would not have been brought about, and even if brought about, it would not have been easy to make a success of them.

2) As a result of the business reform, the principle of turning management work toward production and making management serve production is carried out, and business and production, as well as technique and labor, are further unified.

3) The business reform also fully embodies the spirit of trusting the masses, relying on the masses, and making things easier for them. This is clear from their bold reduction of operation, simplification of reports, improvement of management systems, delegation of authority to the lower levels, simplification of procedures, and their plan to further retrench their structure. Should we run our business by simply relying on the complicated and formal regulations and systems? Or should we resolutely and thoroughly revise all unjustifiable regulations and systems in accordance with the principle of freely promoting the activism of the huge masses and developing productiveness?

It appears that Ching-hua Machine Tools Plant has already solved the question ideologically and in actual work.

Because the business reform of the factory was conducted in accordance with the policies and principles mentioned above, it has not only been enthusiastically welcomed by the cadres and masses, but has also proved effective. Of course, as the reform was only recently undertaken, and as the character of the business is quite extensive and involves wide spheres of activity, many problems still remain to be solved. Many of the things done have yet to be studied and to be tried in practice. But no matter what the final outcome, we think that they have taken the completely right direction in carrying out the reform. We actively support their action, and hope that other enterprises in the province will study and make use of their experience. But before taking action on revising the regulations and systems laid down by a superior authority, a report should be made to the authority concerned and its approval obtained. Some systems may be adopted only after a period of trial.

Our comrades who attend the current conference attach great importance to the experience recounted at the conference and are prepared to follow it actively and with speed. The seventy-nine enterprises taking part in this conference have proposed to all industrial, communications, and transport enterprises in the province to resolutely carry out (the resolutions adopted at) the conference. The district Party committees and hsien Party committees directly under the provincial committee have also challenged one another to friendly contests. All this shows the success of the current conference and also reflects the high degree of revolutionary fervor of the comrade participants. The question now is how to correlate the application of the experience recounted at the conference with the current rectification and double-anti movement and the big leap forward in production. That is to say, we shall have to make overall arrangements for all these things. When applying the experience, action should be based on the actual circumstances of different areas and units, and slavish following of the experience must be avoided. We must not only learn this experience, but also develop and perfect it, because, although the experience is in the correct direction, its actual application still leaves many problems which must be further studied and solved. Moreover, each unit has its own different circumstances, and application by one unit of another's experience may not help to solve problems, but may even lead to errors. It is hoped that you will remember that. As I have said before, the experience recounted at this conference is a product of the rectification movement, which is its root and its common basis. So, in order to apply this experience well throughout the province, it is necessary first of all to insist on carrying the rectification to the very end, and not to call a halt before complete victory is won. Specifically, we must carry out the double-anti movement intensively and thoroughly. We must closely correlate the double-anti movement with the double contest (contest of advancement and of "quantity, speed, quality, and economy"), and the big leap forward in thinking with the big leap forward in production. We must also closely correlate the improvement of style and method of work on the part of the leadership and the determined effort to carry out business reform and improve regulations and systems with the strengthening of the socialist education for the masses, their full mobilization for active participation in the management of enterprises, the promotion of their activism and creativeness in production and work, and the working up of a massive high tide of technical innovations. We must work up an extensive and overall high tide from the leadership to the masses of competing with one another for advancement, learning from the advanced, and catching up with the advanced throughout the province — in all municipalities and hsien, all industries, capital construction projects, the forestry industry, and communications and transport enterprises. We shall see which of us has carried out the rectification and double-anti movement most thoroughly, which has made the most rapid leap forward in production, which has made the most technical innovations, and which has made the best plans for the leap forward and carried them out. We must compete with one another not only in revolutionary fervor, but also in the art of leadership, so that we may improve the style and method of work of leadership. We should make the application of the experience recounted at the current conference (that is, improvement of the style and method of work of leadership and improvement of the system of management) the "big watermelon" of the current rectification and improvement campaign. We should make technical innovation the principal content of the movement of advanced producers. We should make the improvement of the level of leadership for the enterprises a pivotal point on which all other work revolves. Through the solution of all these basic problems we may guarantee the proper execution of all work and of the big leap forward in production.

The provincial Party committee plans to call a conference in May-June to examine and sum up the carrying out of the experience recounted at the current conference. It will also be a conference of comparing and appraising the art of leadership as practiced throughout the province. It is hoped that you will prepare for that conference with the utmost revolutionary fervor, by organizing a fighting, revolutionary contest between different areas and different enterprises.

2

An Important Beginning for Reform of Industrial Management

People's Daily Editorial

The bold reform of industrial management initiated by the worker masses of the Ching-hua Machine Tools Plant in Heilungkiang on the basis of the rectification campaign, as reported in our April 25 issue, is a beginning of important significance. The experiences acquired by the plant consist of three aspects:

1) Administrative cadres of departments and workshops take part in half-day physical labor every day, and the leading cadres of the plant take part in one-day physical labor every week.

2) Under the leadership of the shop administration the workmen take a direct part in some of the everyday administrative work of the production teams.

3) We must improve industrial management and operation, i.e., reform irrational rules and systems. Coordination of the work in these three spheres will fundamentally improve the relations between the leading cadres and the worker masses and enhance the workers' sense of responsibility and activity, thereby setting in motion a leap forward in production.

With cadres performing half-day physical labor and the work-

"Kai-ke ch'i-yeh kuan-li kung-tso ti ch'ung-ta chuang-hsing." Jen-min jih-pao [People's Daily], May 7, 1958. This translation is taken, with minor editorial revisions, from SCMP, No. 1774 (May 19, 1958), 1-4.

men taking a direct part in the everyday administrative work of production teams, a profound change will take place in the relations between the administrative cadres and the worker masses. As we know, in our socialist enterprises the means of production belong to all the people, and both the administrative personnel and the workmen strive for one great common objective — building socialism. Politically they are absolutely equal and their relations in work are comradely relations which are fundamentally different from the relations of exploitation and oppression between the administrative personnel and workmen of the old society. But this does not mean that no problem exists between them at all. Certain survivals of old relations of production are still constantly found between them. For instance, some administrative personnel, standing head and shoulders above others and not treating the workmen as equals, regard themselves as persons exclusively charged with the task of directing and controlling others; they merely issue orders from the top, seldom going to the production sites and taking no part in physical labor. In their opinion, an enterprise can be managed well if only they set up a huge machinery with multifarious rules and systems and issue administrative orders. For this reason, they disregard the position and role of the worker masses as masters and run the enterprise without relying on the creativeness and consciousness of the masses. They disregard the fine Party tradition of following the mass line. And the result is that they divorce themselves from the masses and reality. This is what we call official airs. The worker masses are not satisfied with this, and certain workmen even get the impression that administration is a business concerning only the cadres and that workers are only concerned with work. This gives expression to some remnants of the old relations of production, remnants which hamper the political activity and production activity of the worker masses to a certain extent and hinder the rapid development of the productive forces. The main aim of the Party Center in directing cadres to take part in physical labor and in launching a rectification campaign in enterprises is to change radically the thinking and work style of cadres and heighten the consciousness of the worker masses so as to overcome such remnants of old relations of production, achieve socialist equality, mutual help and cooperation in the relations between the leader and the led, thereby to develop further the productive forces.

In this respect, the leading cadres and worker masses of the Ching-hua Machine Tools Plant manifested a revolutionary creativeness. This plant has not only introduced a system whereby the leading cadres perform physical labor for one to one and a half days each week but also introduced a system whereby the administrative cadres of departments and workshops take part in half-day physical labor every day; simultaneous with this, the workmen under the leadership of the shop administration take a direct part in some of the everyday administrative work of production teams. The practical action taken by cadres in performing physical labor, and particularly the practical action taken by the workmen in doing the administrative work of production teams, are strong proof that in a socialist enterprise there is only a difference in division of labor and duties and no difference in social status between the leader and the led, between administrative personnel and workmen. Thus, the administrative cadres should not only do administrative work but should also take part in certain physical labor; the workmen should not only engage in production but should also do certain administrative work. This will bring about a new change in one's thinking, heighten the workers' sense of responsibility, form a habit of loving the factory and taking good care of state property, develop criticism and self-criticism, and manifest collectivism. The workmen of the Ching-hua Machine Tools Plant gave the following description of the change that had taken place since cadres took part in physical labor: "Formerly, papers in hand, they ran away from difficulties and sat in their offices despite urgent production tasks; now, cadres come down and work with us, and integration of theory with practice can solve any problem." At present, the workmen of this plant affectionately call the working cadres "Master Chang" or "Master Li" as the case may be in the same way as they address fellow workmen. This enables the cadres and workmen to help each other, understand each other, divide labor, and maintain intimate relations. These new relations go a step further to promote the big leap forward in production. The Heilungkiang Chien-hua Machinery Plant (which introduced, before the Ching-hua Machine Tools Plant, a system whereby the workmen took part in the everyday administrative work of production teams) surpasses the leap forward targets every day and revises its targets constantly; the workmen take good care of their plant and products, interest themselves in the collective body, cooperate with each other, and do their jobs to their best ability. Their watchwords are: "Everything under proper care and everybody gets things to do" and "Good production and good management." Their enthusiasm in production, work, and study is heightened as never before. This gives the administrative cadres a greater initiative in their work and makes it possible to set themselves free from routine and to concentrate on important problems. They are enabled to go into the thick of reality, contact the masses, and create favorable conditions for becoming both red and expert.

The measures taken by the Ching-hua Machines Tools Plant and the Chien-hua Machinery Plant to enable their workmen to take a direct part in the everyday administrative work of production teams has enriched our experiences in industrial management and made it possible to bring our system of industrial management to greater perfection. Democratic centralism is a fundamental principle of our socialist industrial management. Unified and centralized management of enterprises by their leaders under the leadership of the state organs of industrial management is dictated by the planned economy of socialism and the characteristics of modern production. But, as repeatedly instructed by the Party Center, a high degree of centralization must rest on a high degree of democracy. Simultaneous with the strengthening of centralized leadership, we must constantly expand democratic life and resolutely carry out the mass line of the Party in industrial management. With a view to carrying out the Party policy of wholeheartedly relying on the working class for industrial management, we have taken many successful measures over the past years. In particular, we have introduced two basic systems — the superintendent responsibility system and the workers' council under Party leadership. These measures and systems have much changed the internal relations and activities and markedly raised the level of management. But how to enable the worker masses to take a direct part in the everyday management of sections and teams so as to acquire a more extensive mass foundation for democratic centralism remains a problem to be properly resolved. Experiences of the Ching-hua and Chien-hua factories have opened a new path for us in this respect. By integrating the superintendent responsibility system with the workers' council system and by constantly acquiring new experiences in their application, a set of socialist industrial systems relatively integral and capable of ensuring the mass line can gradually be established.

The Ching-hua and Chien-hua factories also successfully carried out reform designed to change the irrational rules and systems. In these two factories, as in other factories, there existed some out-of-date rules and systems and multifarious procedures that restricted the mass activity and hindered the development of production and the improvement of management. The obstruction of these out-of-date rules and systems to production was brought into more striking relief after cadres took part in physical labor and the workmen took part in administration. Without immediate change of these irrational rules and systems, it would have been impossible to introduce the above two measures. Comrades of these two factories, relying on the masses and with leaders combined with the masses, boldly broke down many out-of-date rules and systems and instituted some new and rational systems which both facilitated production and made it convenient for the masses to take part in administration. Relying on the wisdom and creativeness of the masses, the Ching-hua Machine Tools Plant did away with and simplified 263 kinds of forms and revised 158 systems in a few days. Moreover, they instituted a "delivery" system whereby the functional departments concerned delivered materials, medicines, and money to the production sites. This system is of great convenience to the masses and has been well received by the worker masses. As a matter of fact, without a set of scientific rules and systems it is impossible to manage modern enterprises. Many of the rules and systems worked out by the administrative organs over the past years are still applicable but a considerable part of these rules and systems have become obstacles to mass enthusiasm and productive force and must be revised or done away with. The rules and systems for socialist enterprises must be in keeping with the socialist principle of industrial management and must be such as to promote the development of productive forces and enable the workmen to carry on with production activities and production management. It is thus not only essential but also possible to reform the rules and systems along the line of quantity, speed, quality and economy, on the basis of the awakening of the masses through the rectification campaign and along the mass line.

The reform of industrial management carried out by the Ching-hua Machine Tools Plant and the Chien-hua Machinery Plant is a result obtained during the rectification campaign, under Party leadership and on the basis of the rising Communist spirit of cadres and workmen. This indicates once more that Party leadership, ideological work, and political work are guarantees of economic work. Ideology and politics are the "general" and "soul." It is very obvious that without this great socialist revolution on the political and ideological fronts during the rectification campaign and without the ideological liberation of the cadres and worker masses, such a creative action based on ideological awakening could have not appeared. To strengthen Party leadership and intensify political and ideological work is an important guarantee of better industrial management. This is true of the period of reform and even more so of the period in which reform has been carried out and new measures and new systems are put into effect.

The experiences of the Ching-hua and Chien-hua factories in reforming industrial management represent a new development of our experiences in industrial management and are fully in keeping with the socialist principle of industrial management. These experiences have been popularized with marked results among the industrial enterprises of Heilungkiang. These experiences should be studied by all areas, and a group of enterprises should be selected to try out the experiences before they are gradually popularized. In the course of experiment and popularization, leadership must be strengthened, problems should be uncovered and solved on time, and new experiences should be summed up so that the experiences can be enriched and brought to more perfection.

3

Raise High the Great Red Banner of Mao Tse-tung Thought and Continuously Deepen the Revolutionization of Enterprises

Hsü Chin-ch'iang

Basic Experience in Revolutionizing the Tach'ing Oil Field

Under Party leadership and thanks to the concern and support of various related quarters, workers of the Tach'ing Oil Field in the 1960-63 period overcame innumerable difficulties and succeeded in completing this huge oil field at a very high speed. Since 1964, holding even higher the great red banners of the Thought of Mao Tse-tung and of the General Line for socialist construction, taking class struggle and the struggle between the road of socialism and the road of capitalism as the key link, and using the "one dividing into two" theory as a weapon, the oil field has been learning from the Liberation Army and other advanced units, and has continued to revolutionize its operations.

The broad masses of workers, high in fighting morale and exuberant, have gone on improving their spiritual outlook. Work in various respects has continued to report substantial progress. And new victories have been won in the construction and production of the oil field. A first-class, modern and huge petroleum base has been built, a force of revolutionized workers

---

Hsü Chin-ch'iang, "Kao-chü Mao Tse-tung ssu-hsiang wei-ta hung-ch'i pu-tuan chia-shen ch'i-yeh ko-ming-hua — Ta-ch'ing yu-t'ien ch'i-yeh ko-ming-hua ti chi-pen ching-yen." Ching-chi yen-chiu [Economic Research], No. 4 (April 20, 1966), 8-21. This translation is taken, with minor editorial revisions, from SCMM, No. 538 (August 22, 1966), 8-27.

armed with the Thought of Mao Tse-tung trained and tempered and, at the same time, a socialist mining area of a new type combining town and countryside, industry and agriculture, and government and enterprise initially established.

The victory of the battle for building Tach'ing Oil Field is a victory for the Thought of Mao Tse-tung, a victory for the Party's General Line.

The road along which Tach'ing Oil Field has traveled is a road for the operation of socialist enterprises according to the Thought of Mao Tse-tung. For the past several years Tach'ing has always used the Thought of Mao Tse-tung as its guide, persevered in the Party's General Line for socialist construction, and taken class struggle and the struggle between the two roads as the key link. It has learned from the PLA in a big way, brought politics to the fore, and opened up a road for China's industrialization.

As a result of prolonged practice and recurrent struggle, we have profoundly realized that in operating a socialist enterprise it is necessary to hold high the great red banner of the Thought of Mao Tse-tung, put politics first, regard the Thought of Mao Tse-tung as the supreme directive for all work and as the criterion for all action, and act on Chairman Mao's instructions honestly. This is the direction for an enterprise's revolutionization; this is the way for its revolutionization.

In order to persist in this correct direction and way, it is imperative to draw a line of demarcation with capitalism and revisionism. This is the struggle between two ideas and two roads for running a socialist enterprise. Only by drawing a line of demarcation with capitalism and revisionism can the Thought of Mao Tse-tung take root in the enterprise and can the enterprise be revolutionized. Slight wavering in this direction and way would lead to blunders and cause us to take the wrong track.

After six years of hard work, we have gained, in the main, the following nine points of understanding with respect to the realization and continual deepening of the revolutionization of the enterprise:

I. Class Struggle Must Be Used as the Key Link

In order to revolutionize an enterprise, we must, in accordance with Chairman Mao's instructions on classes and class struggle, firmly grasp class struggle as the key link as well as the struggle between the socialist and capitalist roads which is also a key link. Our enterprise is a socialist enterprise. It is one where the proletariat makes revolution and undertakes construction. It is a ground for the Three Great Revolutionary Movements — class struggle, production struggle, and scientific experiment. This ground must be occupied by us employing the proletarian stand, viewpoint and method and proletarian ideas and style of work. We must intensify the revolution and promote production by integrating the socialist revolution with socialist construction, class struggle with the struggle for production and scientific experiment. Extremely fallacious are the viewpoint and practice which hold that an enterprise is engaged in nothing but production and which separate revolution from construction and class struggle from the production struggle and scientific experiment. Without carrying out class struggle, there will be revolution; instead, there will be capitalism and revisionism.

The road for Tach'ing's revolutionization is a road for class struggle. The six years of battle fought by Tach'ing have been six years of class struggle. In this period, whatever class struggle that was waged in society would invariably be reflected among our ranks. Class struggle is grasped every year and a new political situation emerges every year. Our ranks will continue to deepen their revolutionization. The production upsurge will be sustained and developed in a healthy way from beginning to end.

To carry out class struggle, we must rely on the masses, ferret out the landlords, rich peasants, counterrevolutionaries and wicked elements hidden among the workers, and isolate them politically. We must strengthen the supervision of them by the masses and reform them through labor. Moreover, we must use them as teachers by negative example in order to heighten the revolutionary vigilance of our ranks and arouse a class hatred for them among the broad masses.

To carry out class struggle, we must give attention to preventing the emergence among certain cadres of the ideas of bureaucracy, graft, and abuse of authority, ideas which cause one to degenerate.

To carry out class struggle, we must wage a resolute struggle against the exploiting classes' idea among a number of intellectuals that "those who work with their brains should rule those who work with their hands."

To carry out class struggle, we must criticize the bourgeois individualist ideology of various shades and colorings and promote the socialist spirit which takes the principle of integration of collective interests with personal interests as the criterion for all words and deeds.

The first kind of struggle mentioned above represents contradictions between the enemy and us. To the majority of people, the latter three kinds of struggle represent contradictions among the people, and it is necessary to step up persuasion and education, continue to reform their thought, and raise their class consciousness. Only thus can the atmosphere of righteousness prevail and the foul wind and evil atmosphere be subdued, and ogres of all kinds will have no hiding place.

How can we carry out class struggle and conduct class education well? The practice adopted by Tach'ing in this regard over the past several years is as follows:

First, in accordance with the Party Central Committee's directive concerning the conduct of the socialist education movement, we concentrated time and leadership on prosecuting the movement in depth and fighting a good battle of annihilation to promote proletarian ideology and eradicate bourgeois ideology.

Second, every year, two or three months were set aside in winter for general five-good assessment. In the course of the general assessment, a period was specially set aside for the conduct of class education, having regard for the tendentious problems present among the ranks.

Third, in the course of day-to-day political and ideological work, we consciously applied the class viewpoint and the method of class analysis and conducted regular class education. Class education was carried out at all times, for every important political event, and everywhere. In this way, the broad masses of workers have been steeled and tempered in the course of class struggle, their class consciousness continuously enhanced, and their proletarian stand made firmer still. Mastering the method of class analysis, they are good at using the viewpoint of class struggle to analyze and handle problems.

II. Learn from the PLA and Bring Politics to the Fore

In the operation of an enterprise, whether or not we should bring proletarian politics to the fore is a basic question of whether we should take the socialist road or the capitalist road. An enterprise run by the bourgeoisie exploits the workers by depending on the discipline of hunger and the policy of buying off [union leaders], while an enterprise run by the revisionists relies on material incentives and actually takes the road of capitalist restoration. In operating our socialist enterprises, we must rely on bringing proletarian politics and the Thought of Mao Tse-tung to the fore. That is to say, we must put political and ideological work in the first position and chiefly rely on the workers' class consciousness and sense of responsibility as masters for giving full play to their enthusiasm and creativeness and developing productivity. This is a sharp struggle between the proletarian and bourgeois ideas, between the socialist and capitalist roads.

In order to put politics to the fore, we must wholeheartedly, honestly and unreservedly learn from the experience of the Liberation Army in bringing politics to the fore, and like the Liberation Army, put the Thought of Mao Tse-tung in command of all work.

In learning from the PLA and bringing politics to the fore, we have concentrated on doing the following things well:

1) Primarily we grasped the creative study and application of Chairman Mao's works.

To bring politics to the fore is to bring the Thought of Mao Tse-tung to the front, that is, to arm the people with the Thought of Mao Tse-tung. Hence, it is the primary task of all to get the workers organized to study and apply Chairman Mao's works creatively. We must persistently and untiringly turn the creative study and application of Chairman Mao's works into a regular mass movement, continuously raise the people's consciousness, and gradually turn the study of Chairman Mao's works into conscious action. In this connection, the most fundamental thing is to study Chairman Mao's theory on class struggle and his philosophical thought, transform the objective world while transforming the subjective world, and solidly establish the revolutionary outlook on life and on the world. In studying Chairman Mao's works, we must make a special effort to apply them and to achieve five combinations: the combination of the study of Chairman Mao's works with the study of the Party's policies and guidelines; the combination of the study of Chairman Mao's works with the study of the PLA's experience; the combination of the study of Chairman Mao's works with the analysis of the situation and the task of one's unit; the combination of the study of Chairman Mao's works with criticism and self-criticism as well as thought reform; the combination of the study of Chairman Mao's works with the summing up of work experience.

2) It is necessary to place consciously politico-ideological leadership above all work.

Politics is the commander and the soul; it must be used to command work and techniques. For this reason, in talking about leadership, we must first of all talk about politico-ideological leadership and leadership by the Thought of Mao Tse-tung. Whether you are in charge of administrative work or technical work, you must first of all grasp politico-ideological leadership and through it give leadership to administrative or technical work. Whether you are a political cadre, an administrator, a professional cadre or a technical cadre, you must put politico-ideological work in the first place. Only in this way can work and techniques pass the test. If you ignore politico-ideological leadership and do not put politico-ideological work in the first place, then you will lose your bearings and eventually fall into the mire of capitalism and revisionism, while in work and technically you will be useless.

3) It is necessary to make the political work organ really a command headquarters for politico-ideological work under the leadership of the Party committee.

In putting politics first and strengthening politico-ideological work, we must establish an effective political work organ and institute a set of political work systems. All personnel of the political work organ must be model pacesetters for revolutionization. Only thus can full play be given to the functions of the political work organ and can it really be turned into a command headquarters under the leadership of the Party committee on the politico-ideological front.

4) Everybody must grasp living ideas and implement the "four firsts."

An enterprise is faced with a host of problems which fall into two categories: Ideological and production problems. But production problems often are caused by ideological problems. It would not be enough to depend for the prompt solution of these problems on the political work organ and political cadres alone. It is imperative to trust and rely on the masses; to mobilize everyone to do politico-ideological work and grasp living ideas; and to grasp the living ideas of everyone. Living ideas must be grasped not only by leading cadres but also by the worker masses and their dependents; not only by political cadres but also by technical and administrative cadres. Moreover, living ideas must be grasped at all times, on all occasions, and by one and all, so that a strong mass contingent for politico-ideological work may be formed.

The task of the political work organ and that of the political cadres are chiefly to mobilize and organize all concerned to take part in politico-ideological work. It is only by having everyone take part in politico-ideological work that politico-ideological work can be really put in the first position, that the "four firsts" can be implemented, that politico-ideological work can be effective a hundred percent of the time, that politico-ideological work can be implemented in all fields, and that politics can be brought to the fore.

Work of grasping living ideas consists of two aspects. One is to be good at carrying out ideological work for one particular person or event. This is the basic requirement for doing ideological work well. In carrying out ideological work for one particular person or event, we must opportunely discover living ideas, make them clear earnestly, and solve them correctly. The other aspect is that we must be adept in grasping problems of a universal nature by seeing through their phenomena and concentrate our strength on solving them. We must fight a battle of annihilation for establishing proletarian ideology and eradicating bourgeois ideology. This is particularly important to the leadership.

In grasping living ideas, we must master the laws of thinking and carry out politico-ideological work as the first and not the last thing. Some basic-level units in Tach'ing have explored some of these laws.

For instance, when one wins a battle, one is liable to slacken; so it is necessary to educate the workers to advance from victory to victory. When one finds the going smooth, one is liable to benumb oneself; so it is important to teach the workers to raise their vigilance. When the going is rough, one is likely to show fear of difficulties and hope for luck; so it is necessary to educate the workers in the need for hard work and plain living and to establish their confidence in their ability to win. When one is commended, one is likely to feel complacent; that is why we must energetically seek out the gaps and continuously raise the standards and requirements. When one suffers setbacks, one is liable to succumb to despair; that is why we must do everything to encourage exertion of big efforts. When a contest is on, one is likely to chase after big and quick results without paying attention to quality; and this is the reason why we give top priority to quality. When there are many new hands, accidents are liable to occur; so it is necessary to unfold technical training and pay heed to safety. And so on and so forth.

5) Grasp the five-good movement and intensify basic-level construction. The five-good movement (for five-good workshops and five-good workers) has as its principal content the following basic-level work in an enterprise: to bring politics to the fore and strengthen regular politico-ideological work in coordination with the enterprise's tasks at various periods; to better develop the role of the Party branch as the fighting fortress and reinforce Party building; to provide a greater scope for the enthusiasm and creativeness of the workers in the enterprise and set in motion the mass activities of comparing with, learning from, catching up with, and surpassing the advanced and helping the backward; to strengthen the single leadership of the enterprise's Party committee, to pay attention to the basic level, improve the style of leadership, and train cadres. Hence, the Party committee must provide stronger leadership over the five-good movement.

In developing the five-good movement, we must set up standard-bearers, provide examples, create images of the proletariat, establish proletarian ideas, fill the political atmosphere with vigor, and let more good people and good things emerge. Living examples are most convincing and are something that the masses can see or touch. Standard-bearers and examples must be set up clearly and the Thought of Mao Tse-tung given expression in conjunction with the Three Great Revolutionary Movements in the enterprise. We must make clear what must be promoted and what must be opposed. We must set an example in a honest way for only when examples are well set and experience well introduced can they command people's attention.

The central problem for launching the five-good movement is to intensify basic-level construction and strengthen the building of the Party branch. The enterprise's Party branch must be the core of leadership and unity for the workshop and for the basic-level production team; it is a fighting fortress. How can we give full play to the role of this fighting fortress?

First of all, there must be a revolutionary and staunch group of leadership. This group is the committee of the Party branch.

The committee must persevere in the system which combines collective leadership with division of work and responsibility and must handle properly the relationships between the Party branch secretary and the committee, between the Party branch secretary and the committeemen, and between the political instructors and team leaders. We must support and care for each other; be brave in upholding principles and bearing responsibilities, and constantly make criticism and self-criticism. Every member of this group must first devote himself to the revolution and be free from selfishness; he must show a high degree of revolutionary zeal and be the first to suffer and the last to enjoy and take part in labor; when problems crop up he must consult with the masses and cadres at the same level, and he must not become self-righteous or subjective and one-sided.

In order to really play the role as a fighting fortress, the Party branch must seriously attend to important problems. First, it must put the creative study and application of Chairman Mao's works in the first position; second, it must step up class struggle and class education; third, it must grasp living ideas on a large scale; fourth, it must conduct the five-good movement; and fifth, it must let the Party member play an exemplary role and must give play to the organizational functions of the trade union and the Communist Youth League.

The Party branch can do the work of revolutionization well and make a success of production only when it attends to these major problems.

6) Select young and outstanding cadres and foster red and expert successors to the revolution.

How to select young and outstanding cadres? The most important thing is to test, understand, and select cadres in the course of the Three Great Revolutionary Movements. A cadre must be judged on the basis of his basic qualities and the principal aspect of his character. We must boldly promote truly outstanding cadres to positions of responsibility in strict accordance with the five conditions laid down by Chairman Mao for fostering successors to the proletarian revolution. This is a major strategic measure for ensuring that our ranks will forever be loyal to the Thought of Mao Tse-tung. Five-good standard-bearers and five-good cadres who have been tested many times provide the main and inexhaustible source for the selection of cadres. Those who are good politically and ideologically must be selected first.

Newly promoted cadres must be fully trusted and boldly assigned to work. Strict demands must be made on and warm assistance given to them. They must be allowed to take up heavy burdens in the Three Great Revolutionary Movements; they must be given a free hand to work and positively supported in their ventures and work. But strict political and ideological demands must be made on them.

In the case of technical cadres, the policy of uniting with them, educating them, and reforming them must be conscientiously pursued. They should be treated on the same basis as the broad masses of workers in respect to politics, work, and livelihood. They must not be given any special privileges.

It is necessary to place the cadres under the supervision of the masses before we can guarantee that they will not degenerate. We should enable them to live and work alongside the masses.

III. It Is Essential to Follow the Mass Line and Conduct a Large-Scale Mass Movement

A socialist enterprise is an enterprise of the laboring people. An enterprise of the laboring people must be run by the masses of the people, by the working class. The revisionists turn an enterprise practically into the private property of the bourgeois privileged stratum; they manage an enterprise by dictatorial means and control the masses by commandism, the imposition of penalities and the enforcement of rigid systems. These are two kinds of ideas and two kinds of roads for operating an enterprise. In operating an enterprise we respect, trust, and rely on the masses, we take the mass line and conduct the mass movement on a grand scale. In this way the enterprise will be run efficiently and a vigorous revolutionary situation will be brought about. Whether we must follow the mass line, mobilize the masses with a free hand, and conduct the mass movement on a grand scale in an enterprise is definitely not a question of method but a question of basic attitude toward the masses of the people. It is a boundary line between a proletarian revolutionary and a bourgeois one.

The battle at the Tach'ing Oil Field has been a large-scale mass movement. For the past several years, we have consistently abided by Chairman Mao's teachings, persevered in the mass movement, and consequently maintained a favorable revolutionary situation throughout.

How to carry out a large-scale mass movement?

A. Mobilize and Rely on the Masses

In order to conduct the mass movement with success, we must really let the masses run their own house. To this end, we must:

1) Opportunely reform those rules and systems which bind the hands and feet of the masses and impede the development of productivity. Appropriate rules and systems are needed, for they can unify our actions and help us to work according to the objective laws. It is for this reason that rules and systems must come from reality and the masses, and must be revised and perfected in keeping with the changes in production. Such rules and systems are flexible as they are capable of giving full play to the enthusiasm and creativeness of the masses and promoting the development of productivity. Those rules and systems which restrict man's action and reduce him to being a slave must necessarily bind the masses and productivity, and must be eliminated.

2) Prevent the bureaucratic style of organs. An organ must serve production, the basic level and the masses, making the cadres and workers at the basic level devote themselves wholly to winning the battle in production. Hence, we should pay heed to overcoming the bureaucratic practice among certain organ cadres of sitting high above, issuing orders, and demanding service from the basic level.

3) Get rid of the bourgeois authoritative complex of some of the intellectuals. The practice of the Three Great Revolutionary Movements among the masses of people is the source of all knowledge. However, in an enterprise there are often some people who, influenced by the ideology of the exploiting class, think they are superior to others because they have a little knowledge, use this little knowledge to frighten the masses, and look down upon labor. Such ideas must be criticized and their influence eliminated.

B. Unreservedly Promote Democracy in Politics, Production, and Economy

Promoting political democracy is aimed principally at ensuring that the whole body of workers, led by the Party, will continue to enhance their proletarian political consciousness and fully exercise "five major rights":

1) the right to struggle against all acts which run counter to the policies and guidelines of the Party and the state and against foul wind and evil atmosphere;

2) the right to examine the revolutionization of leading organs and the observance of rules and regulations by the leading cadres;

3) the right to criticize the cadres at any conference;

4) the right to hear and discuss reports by leading cadres on work;

5) the right to elect basic-level cadres through the democratic process.

Giving free rein to production democracy is aimed at ensuring that the workers will participate in production and technical management, combining specialized management with management by the masses. Whether it is the formulation of production plans, the drafting and execution of rules and systems, or the solution of major production and technical problems, opinions must be extensively solicited from the masses and the masses should be encouraged to devise methods. Their wisdom should be centralized and they must be relied upon in doing things.

In order to safeguard the right of the workers to run their own house, Tach'ing has provided for workers at production posts "five big functional rights":

1) the right to refuse to take orders having nothing to do with their production posts;

2) the right to refuse to operate a machine which is due for overhaul;

3) the right to refuse to let unqualified personnel operate a machine;

4) the right to report immediately to the higher level on hidden dangers in production and, should the higher level fail to give any instruction or take any action, to suspend production when suspension is the only way to avoid accidents;

5) the right to refuse to commence production where there are no working regulations, quality standards, and safety measures.

As for capital construction workers, they are also empowered not to carry out construction under five conditions; namely,

1) they may not start operation if their task is not clearly defined and the construction blueprints are not clear;

2) they may not start operation if the quality, specifications, and technical measures are not clear;

3) they may not start operation when the materials necessary for construction are not well prepared;

4) they may not start operation if the construction equipment is not in good condition;

5) they may not start the next operation sequence if the quality of the previous operation sequence is not up to standard.

Promotion of economic democracy is designed to ensure that the masses will take part in the economic and food management of the enterprise and exercise four rights:

1) the right to fight against all phenomena of extravagance and waste;

2) the right to participate in the economic accounting of the enterprise;

3) the right to participate in the mess hall management and to examine the accounts of the mess hall;

4) the right to participate in the distribution of farm and subsidiary production.

C. Carry out a Mass Movement on a Large Scale in Combination with the Strengthening of Centralized Leadership

It is necessary to use the Thought of Mao Tse-tung as the highest guiding principle for leading the mass movement. Only thus can the movement develop healthily in a correct direction from beginning to end.

It is necessary to do things in accordance with the Party's line, policies, and guidelines. It is also necessary to work out a concrete lever for thorough implementation of the Party's policies and guidelines. We must make clear what must be done and what must not be done.

The movement must have a key. During various periods the work of the enterprise must have a center and a clearly defined fighting goal. Only thus will it be possible to achieve unity of thinking and objectives.

In the course of the movement clear-cut examples must be set up in good time. Only thus can we have clear-cut banners and slogans, can we have concrete policies and experiences, and can we convince the masses and give them general guidance. And only thus can the movement develop in vigor and depth and will it be possible to achieve centralization and unity of action.

D. Foundation Work Must Be Realistically Done

In conducting the mass movement on a grand scale, we must do realistic and practical work in the light of objective laws. We must not adopt a rough attitude and commit ourselves to formalism. It is not easy to mobilize the masses, and after they have been mobilized it is not easy to lead them well. Before the masses are mobilized, we must encourage them to go all out and work hard; after they have been mobilized, we must calmly urge them to go forward.

As we see it, in the course of the vigorous mass movement, it is necessary to take a firm grip on foundation work in the following five respects:

1) secure firsthand data and master the laws of production;

2) improve the quality of work and work to ensure success in the revolution;

3) streamline the management of equipment and see to it that every machine is in perfect working order;

4) intensify technical training in order to acquire real, tough skills;

5) adhere strictly to the system of responsibility at individual posts.

Work in the above five respects constitutes the foundation for successful production. No matter what movement we carry out and what "wind" is blowing, we must not let anything undermine this foundation. Only by making success of foundation work in these five respects will the mass movement have a sound foundation and become powerful as a mass movement should.

IV. It Is Necessary to Develop the Party's Revolutionary Traditions of Hard Work and Plain Living

Chairman Mao has taught us, saying: "It will take several decades of hard work to make our country rich and strong. Among other things, we must adopt the policy of practicing austerity and opposing waste, a policy of building the nation along industrious and economical lines" ("On the Correct Handling of Contradictions among the People," People's Publishing House, 1957 ed., p. 36).

Therefore, the revolutionary tradition of hard work and plain living must not be abandoned at any time. Ideologically we must acquire the viewpoint of hard work and plain living; in day-to-day work and living we must form the habit of industry and frugality. When the going is tough we must prepare to work hard; when the going is smooth we must all the more prepare for hard work. Not only must we work hard during our lifetime, but we must also educate our children to work hard. Whether one can work hard and persist in frugal living is an important indication of whether a cadre has revolutionary awareness or not.

In order to promote the Party's revolutionary traditions of hard work and plain living, we must oppose those who put industry in a privileged position because they think they have more workers, more funds, and more things to work with; those who one-sidedly seek modern, tall, large, and novel projects and indulge in extravagance; those who spend money carelessly, give no attention to the upkeep of equipment and materials, and carry out production and construction regardless of cost; and those who cling to the bourgeois ideas of extravagance and waste, pursuit of material comforts, and fear of hardships and fatigue. Failure to get rid of these ideas and practices would make it impossible to promote the Party's revolutionary traditions of hard work and plain living, to implement the policy of operating an enterprise with industry and economy, or to revolutionize the enterprise.

How to promote the Party's revolutionary traditions of hard work and plain living? Our way is:

To promote the spirit of "storming a fortress." That is, with regard to production and construction we must seek new techniques and high quality, while our living facilities should be simple and indigenous. Whether it is plant construction or living facilities, we must give attention to practicality and must not chase after formalism and grandeur. We should not build tall buildings, including office buildings, auditoriums, hostels, and reception houses. Size should be determined by local conditions and local materials must be used. We must save construction funds for the state and establish the idea of taking pride in plain living among the workers.

To promote the spirit of "mending." We must develop the spirit of unsewing, washing, and mending old clothes, repairing the old and utilizing the waste. In the matter of livelihood, we must "wear a new dress for three years, wear it as an old dress for three years, and then mend it and wear it for three more years." In the field of production, we must put small materials to maximum use, make the best use of fine materials, find substitutes where materials are lacking, and utilize waste materials.

To promote the "one penny" spirit. That is, we must not waste one drop of oil, one unit of electricity, one tael of coal, one inch of steel or timber. Everybody must practice austerity. Austerity must be practiced everywhere, in everything, and at all times.

To promote the spirit of never letting a flaw in quality pass unnoticed. We must give top priority to quality.

V. It Is Essential to Integrate Revolutionary Zeal with a Scientific Attitude

How to integrate a high degree of revolutionary zeal with a strict scientific attitude? The most fundamental thing is for all of us to study and apply Chairman Mao's philosophy creatively. Chairman Mao's philosophy is the philosophy of the worker and peasant masses, the philosophy of the proletariat, and the broad masses of workers must be organized to study and master it. Throughout the battle at Tach'ing, "On Practice," "On Contradiction," and the "Law of One Dividing into Two" were studied and applied in a big way to oppose metaphysics and scholastic philosophy. When people understand materialist dialectics, they will attach first importance to revolutionary zeal at any time and give full play to man's subjective conscious activity. At the same time they will also correctly understand the objective laws and handle problems and use their zeal with a scientific attitude. In this way the spiritual force can be transformed into a material force.

From the battle itself we have gained the following points of understanding:

We must grasp the principal contradictions and concentrate forces for fighting a battle of annihilation. At all times we must grasp the principal contradictions correctly and concentrate forces for fighting a battle of annihilation. In the early days of the battle, since the foundation of the petroleum industry was weak, manpower, material and financial resources from various petroleum plants, mines, institutions and schools in the whole country were concentrated on this main battlefield of Tach'ing so that this battle of annihilation could be fought to a successful conclusion.

Thus, by turning the relative inferiority of the whole situation into an absolute superiority in a partial situation, we enabled the workers to bring their skyrocketing zeal into full play so as to eliminate the backwardness of the petroleum industry. We won the time and the victory. When a quick victory was won on the main battlefield, the whole situation was turned into an active situation, and a favorable prospect was opened up for the petroleum industry for the whole country.

We must advance against difficulties. That is, we must meet and overcome difficulties, regarding them as the motive power of advance. We must advance where conditions permit; where conditions are lacking we must create them. We must not soften our hearts or relax our hands in face of difficulties. If we do, it means retreat.

We must dare to fight and be good at fighting. We must not only have ambitious revolutionary goals but also carry out "stupid" and "foolish" work, seriously conduct investigation and research and make our work more refined and realistic. Just as the well-drilling workers said: "Strategically we must despise five thousand meters — we must dare to fight. Tactically we must respect one millimeter — we must be good at fighting."

It is necessary to sum up our experiences continuously so that we may be brave and resourceful. All newborn things must be tested. We must gradually know the objective laws by engaging in repeated practice and continuously summing up experiences. Only by doing so can we find out the conditions, have a great determination and the right methods of work; can we be brave and resourceful, make inventions and discoveries, and go on creating and advancing.

We must divide one into two and continue to advance. In dealing with anything we must divide one into two. Particularly in dealing with victories and difficulties, we must all the more divide one into two. In this way we shall stand high and see far, neither feeling conceited when we win nor feeling despondent when we lose. We must carry on the revolution and go on advancing forever.

VI. It Is Necessary to Launch the Technical Innovation and Technical Revolution Movement on a Large Scale and Catch up with and Surpass the Advanced World Levels

In revolutionizing an enterprise, we must also launch the technical innovation and technical revolution movement on a large scale and continuously raise the level of modernization. This requires us to follow Chairman Mao's teachings, liberate our minds, break down superstitions, give full play to the wisdom and creative spirit of the working class, and catch up with and surpass the advanced world levels.

How to carry out a technical innovation and technical revolution movement?

A. We Must Be Brave in Practice and Daring in Creation

The purpose of carrying out a technical innovation and technical revolution movement is to make creations. If we just copy from others and follow others' examples, there will be no innovation and revolution to speak of, and we can only claim to be the second best.

To create things, we must wrestle with difficult technical problems and with the most advanced levels in foreign countries. We must dare to touch the hindquarters of a tiger and never concede defeat. There is no technical problem we cannot tackle because we have the leadership of the Party, the guidance of the Thought of Mao Tse-tung, the superior socialist system, and the wisdom of the masses.

To create things, we must fight for time and strive to raise our standards. We must dare to scale the pinnacle and produce the newest things. New techniques are new because they are fast in application; otherwise, they become old techniques. Hence, technically we must catch up with and surpass others in one stride and not in two strides.

To create things, we must break down conventions and eliminate those outmoded rules which retard man's creativity. We must discard all conservative policies. We must provide full scope for man's subjective conscious activity. It is necessary to rely on the masses, effect the triple-combination [combining the leadership, the technical staff and the masses of workers], and so organize everybody for large-scale cooperation.

To create things, we must not have selfish ideas and must not be afraid of taking risks. Things which can be done well must be done well. Where mistakes can be avoided, they must be avoided. We must be bold in doing those things which have not been attempted before. Even if we encounter some shortcomings and mistakes on the road of advance, we must not be afraid.

To create things, we must acquire a strict scientific attitude. We must seek truth from facts, start from reality in doing everything, and subject everything to test. In face of scientific problems, we must be honest men who do honest things; we must carry out arduous research and do things according to the laws of objective things. We cannot accomplish anything if we are careless, impetuous, and subjective.

To create things, we must have tough basic skills. We must master the fundamental theories and have a specialized knowledge. We must commit to memory basic data, formulae in common use, and technical rules and apply them with flexibility so as to pass the test when called upon to do so. This calls for strenuous study and training based on reality in the course of ordinary practical work.

To create things, we must seriously study the strong points of others. We must master all advanced techniques, no matter who possesses them. The purpose of studying techniques is to apply them, to catch up with and surpass them.

B. In Catching up with and Surpassing the World Levels, We Must Have a Strategic Objective

Only when we have a strategic objective can we be farsighted, can we encourage the masses to have the ambition of catching up with and surpassing the advanced world levels, and can we increase our foresight, reduce our blindness, and strengthen our initiative. Only thus can we concentrate forces, fight a war of annihilation by separate stages, and accomplish spectacular results.

In order to realize the strategic objective, we must aim accurately at the most advanced levels of the world, map out short-range action plans, use long-range plans to guide present plans, use present plans to guarantee the fulfillment of long-range plans, combine long-range plans with short-range plans, and advance in a gradual course.

In order to realize the strategic objective, we must undertake not only large projects but also small projects, proceeding with them simultaneously. We must use the advanced standards to lead the general standards and use the latter to promote the former.

In order to realize the strategic objective, we must also promptly evaluate and sum up the results of technical innovations and technical revolution, systematize them, and incorporate them into planning, technological processes, and working regulations. Only in this way will the results of innovation not be lost and scattered but be consolidated, popularized, developed, and improved in the course of production.

C. We Must Direct Our Attention toward Production and Serve Production

Our purpose in carrying out technical innovations and technical revolution is to promote and develop production. Therefore, all subjects relating to technical innovations and technical revolution must originate from production. When results have been gained, they must be tested, summed up, modified and improved in the course of production.

It is best for scientific and research personnel to come from production fields. Because they have participated in production practice, carried heavy burdens in production, been more or less familiar with production, and shared common feelings and a common language with the workers, they are likely to think in terms of production and work in the best interests of production.

D. "Triple Combination" Is the Most Effective Way for Technical Innovations and Technical Revolution

In effecting this "triple combination," it is essential to bring into full play the roles of the leading cadres, workers, and technicians. "Triple combination" must be effected from investigation and study, formulation of plans, drafting of designs, organization of supply of equipment and materials, manufacture of equipment, experiments on the spot and application of results of experiments in production all the way to the summarization and popularization of results of experiments. The workers call this "a dragon's triple combination."

VII. It Is Necessary to Establish a Revolutionary Style of Work

From the moment the joint battle at Tach'ing began, we have been following a set of instructions of Chairman Mao and the successive directives of the Party Center regarding the style of work. We have learned from the "three-eight" style of the PLA. Taking Tach'ing's concrete conditions into account, we have established the following style of work: We must be honest men, speak honest words, and do honest deeds; we must make exacting demands on ourselves, have a strict organization, a serious attitude, and strict discipline; and we must work in the same way whether at night or in the daytime, whether the weather is inclement or favorable, whether the leadership is absent or present on the spot, and whether or not our work is inspected by some people. For the past several years, the working style of our ranks has been improving and their fighting power has been growing stronger and stronger.

In forming the above-mentioned revolutionary style, the most crucial question is for us to be strict, careful, correct, and energetic.

By being strict we mean first of all being strict politically and ideologically, doing things according to the Party's principles and not making any concession on questions of principle.

By being strict we mean that in doing all work we must not be perfunctory or leave things to luck. We must work seriously and well.

Being strict means that for all work there must be a high standard, which must not be lowered. We should not be satisfied with existing levels. We should not consider our tasks fulfilled when the quality of our products and engineering projects measures up to the prescribed standard. Instead we must seek greater perfection and really satisfy the needs of the users. When problems arise, we must solemnly carry out education and must not compromise.

By being strict we mean that we must first be strict with ourselves. We must set ourselves as examples and be strict with ourselves in every respect and everything before we can cultivate a good style of work. If we are not strict with ourselves, and if we are muddleheaded, then the people below will slacken.

By having a strict style of work, people will become the motive power to push work forward. When the leadership is strict, everyone will also be strict, work energetically, have a sense of responsibility, and display fighting power. Being strict is a prerequisite for making specifications, producing techniques, imposing high standards, and producing good products. Being strict is the requirement of the revolution, of class interests, and of socialist construction. Being strict does not mean that we should open our eyes wide and look stern and resort to the imposition of penalties and to commandism, but that we should conduct ideological education regularly, continuously, and patiently.

Being careful means that we must, in accordance with

Chairman Mao's teachings, do economic work with increasing care. We must do all work in a very careful and highly meticulous manner. In producing petroleum, we carry out a great many underground operations in high temperature and at high atmospheric pressure. Many projects are undertaken below the ground surface. The production processes are highly complicated, and the solution of many problems has to depend on the analysis of large amounts of data and on our judgments of them. All this calls for great care. When we work carefully, we will get a complete and true picture of the conditions, our work will conform more to the objective realities, and we will succeed in achieving high quality and a high level. Should we approach our work in a rough and crude attitude, we will be unable to stand an inspection and will do harm to the state.

Being correct means that we must look at problems correctly and do our work correctly. This is the foundation for correctly solving problems and correctly directing production. To be correct, we must make a serious study of the Thought of Mao Tse-tung and the policies and guidelines of the Party Center, conduct arduous research, do penetrating thinking, and strive to solve problems thoroughly. We must go to the basic level, penetrate reality, and go deep among the masses to conduct investigations and studies seriously so as to find out the conditions below as they are. If we fail to see and grasp a problem correctly, we will commit subjectivism and issue commands with closed eyes.

Being energetic means that we must work with great vigor to the end and will not stop until results are produced. In dealing with a problem or a piece of work, if we find out the conditions clearly, we will then have to make up our minds to tackle it boldly and persistently. If we are afraid of the dragon in front and the tiger behind, if we hesitate and let opportunities slip by, then we will accomplish nothing in our lives.

We must also be energetic in rectifying shortcomings and mistakes. We must adhere to the correct things to the end. When we make a mistake, we must correct it quickly. We must bravely acknowledge and promptly correct our shortcomings and mistakes.

These four points constitute the principal content of the style of work mentioned above. They reflect the objective demands for modernized production and construction at Tach'ing Oil Field, giving expression to the integration of the revolutionary spirit with the scientific attitude and to the aspirations of the broad masses of the workers. If we do our work correctly, carefully, strictly, and energetically, then, with the passage of time the style of our ranks will be further improved, their outlook will undergo a new change, their organization and discipline will be further strengthened, and their fighting power will be still greater. They will improve their work further as an industrial army should.

VIII. It Is Necessary to Revolutionize the Leadership and Organs

The key to the revolutionization of an enterprise lies in the revolutionization of its leadership. It is only when we have a revolutionized core of leadership that we can have revolutionized organs, revolutionized workers, and revolutionized enterprises. The most fundamental question for the revolutionization of leadership is to bring politics to the fore, to dare to hold high the great red banner of the Thought of Mao Tse-tung, and to dare to make revolution, wage struggles, seek truth from facts, and win victories. Only thus can we at any time and under any conditions size up the general situation, see the mainstream, discern the current situation, master the direction, and enable our ranks to advance in a correct political direction. Otherwise, the leadership will become feeble, powerless, and incapable of leading the ranks to the broad path of revolutionization. Nor will the enterprise be revolutionized.

In revolutionizing the leadership and the organs during these years, our way has been to:

A. Go to the Front in Person and Go to Stay at the Basic Level

Leading cadres must persist in staying at selected spots and regard this as a system. Through staying at selected spots, they must continuously seek to understand the work the masses are doing, what they think and what they want. They must grasp thinking, not the signs and trends, set examples, cite typical cases, and sum up experiences. We must combine centralized leadership with mobilization of the broad masses and general calls with specific guidance, so that the opinions of the masses may be gathered together and any decision reached on the basis of these opinions may be implemented among the masses. In this way, correct leadership can be realized.

B. Adopt the Work Methods of "First and Second Lines," "3-3 System" and Face-to-Face Leadership

Tach'ing has upheld the principle laid down by Chairman Mao to the effect that "big power must be centralized while small power must be decentralized. Decisions reached at the Party committee must be implemented by various quarters, and they must be implemented resolutely and on the basis of principles. The Party committee should be responsible for inspection of work." It has persistently executed the system of division of work and responsibility under the collective leadership of the Party committee. We have introduced the work methods of "first and second lines," "3-3 system," and face-to-face leadership in a way consistent with the fact that Tach'ing is a large modern enterprise.

The "second line" of the "first and second lines" is composed of the principal leading cadres of the Party committee of the oilfield. They do not command production directly and do not concern themselves with complicated routine affairs. Instead, they attach special importance to bringing politics to the fore. In the main they are faced with five tasks: They must acquaint themselves with the Thought of Mao Tse-tung, the policies and guidelines of the Party Center, and the directives of the higher authorities concerned; they must go to the basic level to stay at selected spots and carry out investigations and research; they must size up the general situation, see the mainstream, point out the direction, and grasp the central issues; they must examine and assist in the work of the "first line," seek out the shortcomings and mistakes, and sum up experiences.

The "first line" is composed of three units – the political headquarters, the production office, and the livelihood office. Leading comrades of the "first line" are to organize concretely the execution of the decisions made by the Party committee in various fields – political, production, and livelihood. They exercise unified command over daily production.

Introduction of the division of work of the "first and second lines" gives everyone a clear goal to work for and urges him to work hard. In this way, work may be done well with uniform steps. This avoids division of work according to departments and types of operation, for such division would lead to competition for selfish reasons.

The "3-3 system" is that one-third of the working personnel of an organ stay in the office to handle routine work, another one-third do field work, and still another one-third stay and work at selected basic-level spots. In this way, the higher and lower levels, and the points and the whole area, are connected.

For introduction of face-to-face leadership, there are the following forms:

1) To handle office work on the spot, "five things are done on the spot": political work is carried out on the spot, production command is exercised on the spot, designing work is done on the spot, supplies are arranged on the spot, and livelihood service is rendered on the spot.

2) To organize a command structure at the front so as to direct operations on the spot.

3) To assign personnel to the spot to solve problems there.

4) To simplify organs, reduce intermediary levels, and command the basic level directly.

C. Insist That Leading Cadres Abide by "Three Agreements"

These "three agreements" are as follows:

1) To persevere in the fine traditions of hard work and

plain living without claiming any special privileges.

They will not build office buildings, auditoriums, hostels, and reception houses; they will live in "makeshift dwellings" or single-story houses. They will hold no parties and present no gifts; they will neither dance nor put a sofa in their office. They will eat in collective dining rooms. And they will teach their children not to seek privileges for themselves.

2) They must persist in participating in physical labor and must never be bureaucrats sitting high above the people.

Cadres should participate in labor at fixed hours. They must submit to the leadership of team and group leaders. They must create material wealth. Moreover, they must effect "five combinations": combination of participation in labor with leadership work, with work on experimental plots, with the carrying out of investigations and studies and the solution of problems, with the learning of operating techniques, and with their own administrative work.

3) Persist in being "honest" and "strict"; never feel conceited or tell lies.

They must persist in staying at selected spots and step up investigations and studies, consult with the masses when common problems arise; insist on using the "law of one dividing into two" as a weapon for summing up work continuously; and regularly call meetings of Party groups, examine the conditions of execution of "three agreements," make criticism and self-criticism, and oppose liberalism.

In order to execute the "three agreements" satisfactorily, we must persist in the system of examination. Apart from the leading cadres at various levels conducting examinations at meetings of Party groups, every year the workers and their dependents should be organized to conduct such examinations.

D. Organs Must Serve Production, the Basic Level, and the Masses

The basic question of revolutionization is a question of the service viewpoint. After several years of practice in revolutionization of organs, we have gradually made clear five relationships concerning the work of organs.

The relationship between administrative work and production. All administrative work in an enterprise must proceed from production; all the work is for winning the battle at the production front. Therefore, the administrative work of organs must be subordinated to production requirements.

The relationship between organs and the basic level. An organ must establish the idea of serving the basic level and through this service make a success of management.

The relationship between strictness and flexibility. In the enforcement of systems, the principle must be strict while the concrete methods must be flexible.

The relationship between restraint and promotion. Rules and systems must have a restraining force, aimed at mobilizing the initiative and creativeness of the workers and promoting production.

The relationship between targets and work. A target is a fighting goal, showing the result to be achieved from doing a large amount of practical work. The realization of targets must depend on the implementation of work. Therefore, an organ must direct all its efforts to grasping work; it must not spend the whole day making target calculations.

After these relationships are clearly defined, the service viewpoint of an organ will be strengthened. It will enable the organ to rely on the masses, break the old framework of "management," and establish an integral set of work systems with service to the basic level and the masses as the core. The organ will tackle difficulties and give conveniences to the basic level. It will think on behalf of the basic level in every respect and serve production.

As we see it, as the organ attends to more affairs of the basic level, its routine work tends to be reduced, and the more conveniences it gives to the basic level, the greater the benefit will be brought to production and to the revolutionization of the organ itself.

E. Energetically Step up the Work of Summing up

When it comes to the arrangement, examination and summing up of work, we put special emphasis on attaching first importance to summing up. That is, we grasp work in the order of summing up — arrangement — examination. By so doing we can correctly arrange work and conduct timely and penetrating examination of work through summing up.

The work of summing up at Tach'ing has produced a set of systems: a monthly big examination and summing up is carried out for the system of responsibility at individual posts and for the five-good movement. When a drilling team completes a well or a construction team completes an engineering project, it invariably makes a summing up. A big examination and a big summing up of work and a five-good preliminary assessment are carried out once each half year. At the end of each year, a general summing up and five-good general assessments are made.

While experiences must be summed up, they must not be regarded as being good for all time. Experiences are of two kinds: One is basic experience which must be followed and talked about every year and repeatedly. It must not be modified or lost. It must be perfected and developed in the course of practice. The other is concrete experience. It changes in keeping with concrete conditions. It must be summed up and revised in good time. When basic experience is lost, people will lose their direction; when concrete experience is rigidly followed, it will restrict the action of man.

IX. Combine Industry with Agriculture and Town with Countryside, and Progressively Reduce the Three Differences

When an enterprise is built by us, it means a new ground for socialism is added. We must give full play to the leading role of the working class, pursue the general policy of developing the national economy with industry as the leading factor and agriculture as the foundation, strengthen the ties between industry and agriculture, use industry to support agriculture and hasten its development, and speed up socialist construction in an overall manner. Therefore, a socialist industrial enterprise does not merely produce products for the state; it must also develop its role as a socialist position fully — politically, ideologically, and economically.

If we build an industrial or mining enterprise on a foreign model, we shall have to build or expand a city; we shall have to build a welfare district with tall buildings and use walls to keep the peasants away. This is bound to lead to separation from the masses to a serious extent and to expansion of the differences between industry and agriculture and between town and countryside; it will jeopardize the worker-peasant alliance and be harmful to socialist construction and the transition to a communist society. From the very beginning Tach'ing Oil Field has firmly refused to do things on such a foreign model.

In the course of an inspection tour of Wuhan Steel Works in 1958, Chairman Mao had directed that such a large enterprise as Wuhan Steel Works could be gradually expanded into a comprehensive complex. Apart from producing a greater variety of iron and steel products, it should also produce some machines, chemicals, and building materials. Such a large enterprise, in addition to industrial production, should also engage, on a modest scale, in agriculture, trading, education, and military training. When other leading comrades of the Party Center visited Tach'ing Oil Field for an inspection, they also indicated that the construction of the mining district must be based on the principle of integrating industry with agriculture and town with countryside for the benefit of production and the people's livelihood. Workers' living quarters should be scattered and not concentrated in one area. A large city should not be built. The dependents of the workers must be properly organized to take part in labor and develop production.

It is by following these directives of Chairman Mao and other leading comrades of the Party Center that we have proceeded with the construction of the mining district. At present, Tach'ing has preliminarily built a new socialist mining district where town and countryside, industry and agriculture, and government and enterprise are integrated.

Tach'ing has not built a concentrated urban area; instead it has built residential points in scattered places. At the moment, it has completed three workers' towns and several dozen central residential points (each consisting of 300-400 households) and residential points (each with 100-200 households). Every central residential point with four or five residential points surrounding it becomes a livelihood base. Within this base are set up a mechanized farming station, an agricultural technical research station, a primary school, a part-work (farming) and part-study middle school, a bookstore, a health clinic, a nursery, a mess hall, a food shop, a flour mill, a commercial store, a barbershop, a bathhouse, a shoe repair shop, a sewing and mending unit, a post and telecommunications agency, and a savings office. These are establishments for production, livelihood, culture, education, and health. Their presence contributes to production and to the improvement of living standards. Within residential points all houses built are single-story houses of earth.

Tach'ing Oil Field does not mean to move the dependents of workers into a city from the countryside or turn them from producers into consumers. Instead, it organizes them to take the path of revolutionization and to participate in productive labor.

At present, the dependents whom the oil field has organized to take part in various kinds of collective productive labor represent 95 percent of the total number of dependents with labor capacity. They are engaged in farm and subsidiary production in the entire mining district. In addition, they are also charged with the task of maintaining several hundred kilometers of highways; they work in industry as auxiliary laborers and are engaged in service trades. Today, the residential points and production teams are managed by the dependents themselves — and are managed well. The dependents constitute an important force for the construction of the mining district. Their spiritual outlook has undergone a marked change. The overwhelming majority of the dependents, who formerly were concerned only with their small families, are now concerned with the important affairs of the state and the world. They are concerned with the cause of the revolution. Because they have revolutionized their thinking, large groups of five-good dependents and five-good production teams have emerged. In 1965, among the dependents 192 joined the Party and 162 joined the League. Revolutionized, the dependents become an important force for politico-ideological work.

In organizing the dependents to engage in productive labor, Tach'ing has put into force the principle of "taking the team as the foundation, practicing unified accounting, assessing work performance and recording work points, and paying according to work." All products are without exception delivered to the proper authorities. Whether they are engaged in industry or agriculture or engage in service work or work as teachers, the dependents do not receive salaries; their work is assessed and work points are recorded for them, and those who work more are paid more. Cadres engaged in work looking after the dependents also participate in labor and their work is assessed and work points are recorded for them in the same way. There will be year-end summing up, assessment, comparison, and distribution.

Tach'ing Oil Field is actively enforcing two systems of labor and two systems of education. Today, it has introduced universal primary education and lower-middle school education and established an education network ranging from primary school to university, including primary schools, part-farming and part-study junior middle schools, part-work and part-study schools, and a part-work and part-study petroleum college. Whatever school is needed has been established, and personnel have been trained to meet the requirements of production. Since the oil field is in need of well drilling and extraction personnel, it has established a school for training such kinds of personnel. Since medical and health personnel are short in the oil field, a medical school has been set up, where not only Chinese traditional medicine but also Western medicine are studied. In this school, the students, besides studying medicine, also study nursing. In order to meet the needs of mechanization of farm production, it has established a tractor drivers' training school for the dependents, who study during slack seasons and farm during busy seasons.

In order to strengthen centralized and unified leadership in the mining district, Tach'ing has established a government in the mining district so as to effect integration of government with enterprise. The Party committee of the oil field is the Party committee of the mining district. The work of the government and that of the enterprise are carried out under the unified leadership of the Party committee.

Through the construction of the Tach'ing mining district, we have gained the following points of understanding with respect to reduction in the differences between town and countryside, between industry and agriculture, and between mental and physical labor:

1. We must develop the Yenan spirit. Using simple and indigenous equipment and local materials, Tach'ing has built residential points in scattered places. It builds no walls and no welfare zone with tall buildings. Thus it has inherited and developed the Yenan spirit. By so doing, the living standards of the workers and dependents are similar to those of the local peasants. Having no special privileges in living, the oil field has been able to maintain and develop the Party's glorious traditions of hard work and plain living and to resist corrosion by bourgeois ideology. By so doing, it has been able to strengthen the ties between the workers and peasants and further consolidated the worker-peasant alliance. By so doing, it has built a city according to lower standards and at faster speed and lower costs than if it had concentrated its efforts on building a real city. This conforms to the spirit of the General Line for socialist construction.

2. We must develop the Nan-ni-wan spirit and the working style of the old Eighth Route Army. Utilizing the favorable

conditions created by the large size of the oil field and by plenty of wasteland, Tach'ing has reclaimed the wasteland and put it under the plow, thereby achieving an abundance of food and clothing. While putting the wasteland under cultivation, it has educated the dependents of workers and organized them to participate in collective productive labor, thereby promoting their revolutionization. In this way, with the thinking of the workers and dependents revolutionized, the relations of the workers to the state have changed, and so have the relations of the workers to the enterprise. Some workers said: "We have two homes. In the past we were mainly concerned with our own small families. Now we are mainly concerned with the oil field as our home." This is the reason why the workers are able to devote themselves to revolution completely.

3. We must develop the spirit of K'angta [Resist Japan University]. We must operate schools arduously by relying on our own efforts. We must enforce two systems of education and set up part-work and part-study, part-farming and part-study schools on a large scale. We must train new-type laborers who can write and labor so as to create conditions for the gradual reduction of the differences between mental and physical labor.

4. We must develop the working style of old hsien chiefs in revolutionary base areas. After having integrated government with enterprise, the working personnel of the government for the mining district have promoted the working style of old hsien chiefs in revolutionary base areas. They have gone deep among the masses and into the basic level to serve the masses and production in every way, thus further cementing the ties between the government and the masses in coordination with the development of the production and construction of the oil field.

In short, the Yenan spirit, the K'angta spirit, the Nan-ni-wan spirit, the working style of the old Eighth Route Army, and the working style of old hsien chiefs are revolutionary styles of work and the revolutionary spirit. If only we run the enterprise in such revolutionary spirit, and if we construct the mining district in such revolutionary spirit, we shall be able to turn the enterprise into an ideological position for the proletariat, a scientific and technical position for industry and agriculture, and a position for socialist culture and education. We shall integrate town with countryside and industry with agriculture and progressively reduce the three big differences.

Although Tach'ing has obtained definite results in its work these years, it still has many shortcomings. Now, the whole country is learning from Tach'ing, but what should Tach'ing do? We feel the enormity of the pressure. We are determined to continue to hold high the great red banner of the Thought of Mao Tse-tung and the red banner of the General Line, bring politics to the fore, and take class struggle as the key link. We must learn from the PLA, Tachai, and other advanced units. Using the law of one dividing into two as a weapon, we must promote the achievements and overcome the shortcomings. Prudent and humble, we must continue to deepen our revolutionization and march forward bravely to win greater victories.

4

The Basic Law of Operation of Enterprises by the Proletariat

Hung Hang-hsiang

Study the "Anshan Steel Constitution" and Thoroughly Eradicate the Remnant Poison of the Counterrevolutionary Revisionist Line Pursued by Liu Shao-ch'i in the Sphere of the Economy

"Anshan Steel Constitution," which the great leader Chairman Mao personally commented on ten years ago, is the basic law of operation of enterprises by the proletariat. Its five brilliant principles are:

— Firmly insist on putting politics in command.
— Strengthen leadership by the Party.
— Carry on mass movements in a big way.
— Put into effect two-participation, one transformation, and three combination.
— Carry out technical revolution in a big way.

The constitution is Chairman Mao's creative development of the Marxist-Leninist doctrine of continuing revolution under the dictatorship of the proletariat, a beacon light that illuminates the socialist direction of advance by industrial enterprises, a powerful ideological weapon to stop and prevent socialist enter-

---

Hung Hang-hsiang, "Wu-ch'an-chieh-chi pan ch'i-yeh ti ken-pen ta-fa — Hsüeh-hsi 'An kang hsien-fa,' ch'e-ti su-ch'ing Liu Shao-ch'i tsai ching-chi ling-yü li t'ui-hsing ti fan-ko-ming hsiu-cheng-chu-i lu-hsien ti yü tu. <u>Kuang-ming jih-pao</u> [Kuang-ming Daily], March 21, 1970. This translation is taken, with minor editorial revisions, from SCMP, No. 4627 (April 1, 1970), 78-88.

prises from degenerating and becoming capitalist enterprises.

Today, when a great victory has already been won in the Great Proletarian Cultural Revolution and the struggle between the two classes, the two roads, and the two lines is developing in depth on our economic front, a renewed study of "Anshan Steel Constitution" — the basic law of the operation of enterprises by the proletariat personally commented on by the great leader Chairman Mao — is of great practical significance.

I

The principle of "firmly insisting on putting politics in command" in "Anshan Steel Constitution" is a concrete embodiment in a socialist enterprise of the great leader Chairman Mao's great idea "Politics is the supreme commander and the soul." It is the lifeblood of all economic work and the basic guarantee of our successful operation of socialist enterprise.

Firmly insisting on putting politics in command means putting Mao Tse-tung's Thought in command of everything and reforming and directing everything with it. It means the observation, analyzing, and actuating of everything through the viewpoint of classes, class contradiction and class struggle, and the method of class analysis. It means putting everything under the total political leadership of the proletariat and reforming the world in accordance with the image of the proletariat.

On the socialist industrial front, the concrete content of insisting on putting politics in command is to uphold firmly from beginning to end the position of supreme commander of proletarian politics in relation to all production, economic and technological activities of an enterprise and correctly know and solve the relations between politics and production, politics and the economy, and politics and technology.

Marxism holds that revolution is the locomotive that pulls history forward. Ever since mankind was divided into classes, the history of mankind has been a history of class struggle. All social progress, the supersession of old systems by new ones, and the leap forward of productivity have been accomplished by means of revolution. Revolution is the greatest political activity, while production is promoted by revolution and in turn serves politics.

Ours is a socialist country led by the working class on the basis of the worker-peasant alliance. The dictatorship of the proletariat and the superior socialist system has opened a wide world for the development of productive forces and is a powerful force that pushes forward the development of productivity. Therefore, socialist enterprises must be subservient to and serve proletarian politics and must never be separated from the political leadership of the proletariat for a single moment. The relationship between politics and production, politics and the economy, and politics and technology — i.e., between politics and the total operational activity of an enterprise — is always a relationship between the commander and the commanded.

To follow Chairman Mao's teaching, firmly insisting on putting proletarian politics in command, firmly upholding the great guideline of "grasping revolution and stimulating production," and opposing any interference with and sabotage of enterprises by Right or "Left" opportunism are a question of political orientation for enterprises and a matter of fundamental importance in firmly following the socialist direction and the socialist road.

By trumpeting "production first," "technique first," "profit in command," and such preposterous views, renegade, hidden traitor, and scab Liu Shao-ch'i and his gang tried to radically extract the "soul" from our socialist enterprises, reverse the relationship between politics and production, negate the absolute leadership of the proletariat and its political party over the enterprises, abolish the position of supreme commander of proletarian politics in relation to production, and so change the socialist nature of industrial enterprises, demolish the economic basis of the dictatorship of the proletariat, and restore capitalism. Their effort must be resolutely struck down and thoroughly criticized.

Here it should be pointed out that the idea of "good in production is good in politics" which confuses the relationship between politics and production, the Rightist idea that "we have done nearly all that should be done in revolution and it is now time to pay attention to construction," and the compromise that politics and business should be "emphasized by turns" and revolution and production should alternate are all metaphysical viewpoints that put revolution and production in opposite positions. They are radically in conflict with the great guideline of "grasping revolution and stimulating production" and in essence an expression of the remnant poison of Liu Shao-ch'i's counterrevolutionary revisionism.

Similarly, the view that "My job is to grasp revolution, not production" and "To grasp production is to go back to the old road of bringing production to the fore" essentially negates and abolishes politics. It does not bear proletarian politics in mind. Those who hold this view do not try to know and solve the relations between politics and production by grasping the law of unity of opposites, and do not let politics take command of production, promote production and set production in motion. The view itself is an ideological expression that is "Left" in form but Right in essence.

As for those who hold up the banner of "bringing politics to the fore" but have ulterior motives, who ignore production costs and economic accounting and spend money extravagantly and wastefully, and who moreover spread the preposterous view that "economic accounting will not bring politics to the fore," these are class enemies who are deliberately muddying the water so they may undermine the socialist economy and dig at the root of the dictatorship of the proletariat.

All these must rouse our vigilance to a high degree of serious attention.

Chairman Mao's teaching that "the economy is the foundation, while politics is a concentrated expression of the economy" most penetratingly and thoroughly explains the relationship between politics and the economy. Socialist economy is the solid basis for the proletarian dictatorship, which in turn is the most concentrated expression of socialist economy and the basic guarantee of the building, consolidation, and development of socialist economy.

In developing production and the socialist economy, in

successfully carrying out economic accounting in our enterprises, increasing production and practicing economy, delivering profit to the state, and accumulating capital for expanded socialist reproduction — in a word, in all our business activities — we have only one object, and that is to consolidate and strengthen the dictatorship of the proletariat.

To promote the development of production, it is in turn necessary to bring proletarian politics to the fore, firmly insist on putting politics in command, and consolidate and strengthen the dictatorship of the proletariat. Only when the dialectical relationship between politics and economy is understood will it be possible to understand why weakening or abolition of the position of proletarian politics as supreme commander over the economy will amount to weakening or abolition of socialist economy and also means weakening or abolition of the proletarian dictatorship. Only then will it be possible to thoroughly remove the remnant poison of Liu Shao-ch'i's "management of the economy with economic methods" and "Do what is profitable."

It should also be pointed out that great importance should be attached to correct understanding and solution of the question of relationship between politics and technology. The proletariat attaches great importance to the role of technology in the development of production. However, technology is mastered by man. It is mastered by men of a particular class and serves the politics of that particular class. In order to make technology serve proletarian politics, it is necessary to insist firmly on putting proletarian politics in command, arm people's mind with Mao Tse-tung Thought, and carry out successfully man's ideological revolutionization. Only then will people who have mastered technology follow a firm and correct political orientation, develop the thoroughly revolutionary spirit of "fearing neither hardship nor death," and dedicate technology to the socialist cause. Only then will they be able to know and solve correctly the question of the relationship between revolutionization and mechanization, lead mechanization with revolution, and promote the continuous development of technology.

Liu Shao-ch'i advocated "technique first" and pursued the counterrevolutionary revisionist line of "experts run factories." His object was to oppose our great leader Chairman Mao's teaching on relations between politics and economy, oppose man's ideological revolutionization, oppose revolutionization's leadership over mechanization.

The Great Proletarian Cultural Revolution has now dealt a fatal blow to Liu Shao-ch'i's "technique first," "experts run factories," and such counterrevolutionary revisionist trash. However, the view that "technicians are not wanted" is still current among some technicians who are deeply affected by "Liu's poison." This shows that there are still people who "think longingly of the old days" in their hearts, when they sat in their office or study and sketched capitalist blueprints. It shows that the remnant poison of Liu Shao-ch'i's counterrevolutionary revisionism is still doing harm to some people, and that its poisonous influence cannot be completely eliminated overnight.

Marxism is developed in its struggle against various shades and schools of opportunism and opportunist thought trends. To establish the brilliant principle of "firmly insisting on putting politics in command" contained in "Anshan Steel Constitution" and correctly know and solve the relations between politics and production, politics and economy, and politics and technology, socialist enterprises must also be formed and consolidated in the midst of struggle. To firmly uphold politics as the commander in enterprises, we must study still better the "Anshan Steel Constitution," hold still higher the great red banner of Mao Tse-tung Thought, and wage a resolute, protracted struggle against Liu Shao-ch'i's counterrevolutionary revisionism and all kinds of opportunist thought trends.

II

The great leader Chairman Mao teaches us: "In carrying out socialist revolution and socialist construction, it is necessary to persevere in the mass line, freely rouse the masses, and launch mass movements in a big way." To trust the masses, rely on the masses and respect their revolutionary pioneering spirit is the essence of Chairman Mao's proletarian revolutionary line. The mass line is the basic line for all work of our Party. The revolutionary principle of "launching mass movements in a big way" and "two participations, one transformation, and three combination" as laid down in the "Anshan Steel Constitution" is built on the basis of trust in the masses and reliance on the masses and embodies in a most concentrated way Chairman Mao's great idea of the mass line.

The formulation of the revolutionary principle of "two participations, one transformation, and three combination" is a great pioneering act in the history of the international proletarian movement. In theory it enriches the Marxist-Leninist doctrine of continuing revolution under the dictatorship of the proletariat, and in practice it solves the question of "The working class must exercise leadership over everything."

History was made by the masses of people. Direct management of enterprises by the working class is to set right the history that has been put upside down by the exploiting classes, ensure that power over the enterprises will forever be in the hands of the working class, and guide the enterprises forward always in the correct political direction. All revolutionary people support this great pioneering measure, but all reactionaries oppose it.

Taking the stand of landlords and the bourgeoisie, archrenegade Liu Shao-ch'i has consistently and madly opposed the great truth that "the masses of people are the creators of history" and the exercise of power over enterprises by the working class. Early in the days of the democratic revolution, he already slanderously called the Chinese working class "backward" and "puerile." After the liberation, he even more maliciously attacked the working class, calling them "unreliable."

In 1961 Liu Shao-ch'i asked his black general Po I-po to produce a black document designed to oppose the great "Anshan Steel Constitution." In it he resorted to counterrevolutionary dual tactics, saying, "Enterprises should sum up the experience of workers in their participation in the management of production groups, so as to formulate a system gradually." That is downright deception and utter hypocrisy.

Participation by workers in the management of enterprises was positively laid down by the great leader Chairman Mao. There is no need for any "exploration" and "summing up" on this basic line; what is needed is practice. Chairman Mao wanted workers to participate in the management of enterprises, but the black document limited worker participation in management only to "production groups" so as to resist and oppose the exercise of power over enterprises by the working class and their political leadership over enterprises. Here Liu Shao-ch'i completely revealed his character of a renegade, hidden traitor, and scab!

Participation by cadres in collective productive labor is Chairman Mao's greatest concern and affection for the broad masses of cadres and effective criticism against Liu Shao-ch'i's "Labor in order to gain a veneer of gold." By taking part in collective productive labor, cadres will place themselves under the supervision, assistance, and education of the masses, imbibe from them their vigorous, revolutionary feeling, constantly wash away the dirt in their thought, and forever preserve the revolutionary youth of the proletariat. The cadres will be able to go deep into reality, understand and master the objective laws of class struggle, production struggle and scientific experiment, solve problems that practically exist, and better transform the objective world and hence the subjective world. As Chairman Mao has taught us: "This is an important thing of fundamental character under the socialist system. It helps to overcome bureaucratism and prevent revisionism and dogmatism."

The superstructure must conform to and serve the economic base because that will help to promote the development of productivity. With the continuing intensification of the socialist revolution, some of the regulations and systems — an integral part of the superstructure — regularly become unconformable with the economic base and the needs of development of productivity. The breaking and reforming of outdated and irrational regulations and systems is a regular task for industrial enterprises and an important part of the content of struggle-criticism-transformation in enterprises.

"Without destruction, there can be no construction. Destruction means criticism and revolution." Only when "daring" and "destruction" takes the lead will there be discovery, invention, creation, and progress. The view that "destruction is now more or less complete, and it is time mainly to construct" directly contravenes Marxism-Leninism-Mao Tsetung Thought.

Lenin pointed out: "Marx believed that the entire value of his theory lay in its being 'essentially critical and revolutionary.'" Only with criticism can there be progress. The world and society makes progress amid criticism. Without intensive revolutionary mass criticism and eradication of the poisonous influence of feudalism, capitalism and revisionism in enterprises, there will be no true "construction" in which proletarian politics is brought to the fore. New things can be discovered and established only through criticism of old things.

The relationship between "destruction" and "construction" is a dialectical relationship. Thus the view that refuses to "seek construction through destruction" and that "destruction is more or less complete" is against science and against dialectics. Views that "systems are universally applicable" and "systems are useless," which have emerged during the reform of regulations and systems, are similarly antidialectical. The former fails to see the human factor, does not believe in the great power of proletarian politics, and blindly believes in the universal applicability of systems. It is a variation of bourgeois fetishism. The latter, on the other hand, negates and refuses to admit anything, whatever it is or whether it is right or wrong. It is an anarchistic thought trend. Both are metaphysical viewpoints.

In reforming regulations and systems in socialist enterprises, it is necessary to follow Chairman Mao's teachings by fully rousing the masses and earnestly developing revolutionary mass criticism, so the masses themselves may distinguish fragrant flowers from poisonous weeds in the course of criticism, rise to abolish the foreigner's slave type of systems transplanted bodily from capitalist and revisionist countries, reform overcomplicated and irrational regulations, and establish scientific and new regulations and systems of socialist enterprises that serve proletarian politics, the masses and production, so as to enable the superstructure to serve the socialist economic base better.

The method of "three-in-one combination" of revolutionary workers, revolutionary cadres, and revolutionary technicians is a new form of organization enabling industrial enterprises to follow the mass line under the banner of Mao Tse-tung Thought. It helps to pool together the experience and wisdom of the revolutionary workers, revolutionary cadres, and revolutionary technicians to form a powerful force to win new victory in greater breadth and depth. It helps revolutionary leading cadres go deeper into reality and the masses to lead them forward. It helps to break up the domination by bourgeois intellectuals over the scientific and technological domain, and the reeducation by workers, peasants, and soldiers of intellectuals graduated from old schools to thoroughly change their old way of thinking. It also helps workers and fighters with rich practical experience to enter the stage of science and technology, puts science and technology under the leadership of the working class, and allows the masses of workers to develop their talents fully. It is an important measure for the proletariat to exercise total leadership over socialist science and technology, a revolutionary crucible for turning workers and peasants into intellectuals and intellectuals into laborers, a good way to organize and mobilize the masses for building socialism with greater, quicker, better and more economical results.

"The proletariat wants to transform the world according to its world outlook. So does the bourgeoisie according to its."

In the "three-in-one combination" serious class struggle still goes on to decide who will lead and reform whom, and the remnant poison of Liu Shao-ch'i's "experts run factories" and "technique first" still occasionally plays the devil.

Some people shout: "You lead in political matters, but let us take charge of technical matters." In "three-in-one combination" groups, some people discriminate against and reject the worker masses, harass and hit them, deny them technical know-how, make things difficult for them, sow dissension among them, and corrupt them in an effort to take their place and reform the "three-in-one combination" groups according to the bourgeois image. We must follow Chairman Mao's teachings, take hold of the key of class struggle, and carry out class analysis everywhere and on everything. In dealing with technicians we must take pains to reeducate them, unite with them, and rouse their activism. In dealing with the class enemy we must wage resolute struggle against them.

Chairman Mao teaches us: "It is necessary to conduct mass movement in every kind of work. It won't do not to have mass movement." Without mass mobilization, there will be no true revolutionary movement. Without mass participation, it will be impossible to carry on proletarian revolution. The mud and sludge left by capitalism, revisionism, and feudalism can be washed away only in a tremendous revolutionary mass movement. The struggle-criticism-transformation movement that is to change heaven and earth can accomplish its purpose only by relying on the broad masses and with their participation.

The rich experience of our socialist revolution and socialist construction fully demonstrates that in order to run socialist industrial enterprises successfully, it is necessary to follow Chairman Mao's great directive in the "Anshan Steel Constitution," follow the mass line, conduct mass movements in a big way, thoroughly criticize Liu Shao-ch'i's crime of resisting the mass line and opposing the conducting of mass movements in a big way, rouse the masses in the broadest and deepest manner, and let the masses most fully and enthusiastically demonstrate their creative wisdom, so they may join forces in a powerful, irresistible torrent of mass movement and rush forward courageously in the direction indicated by Chairman Mao.

III

Chairman Mao teaches us: "We cannot go the old way of technological development of other countries of the world and crawl slowly step by step behind them. We must set aside normal rules and procedures, adopt advanced technique where necessary, and build our country as a modern socialist power in not too long an historical period." The principle of "carrying out technical revolution in a big way" laid down in the "Anshan Steel Constitution" is a brilliant embodiment of this farsighted great thought of Chairman Mao.

The principle of "carrying out technical revolution in a big way" is the most resolute proletarian principle of trusting and relying on the working class in the development of science and technology.

Since the advent of the new China, a vehement struggle between the two lines has always existed with regard to the question of on whom we should rely for the development of science and technology. Our great leader Chairman Mao firmly trusts and relies on the working class. Liu Shao-ch'i and his gang, on the other hand, have lain prostrate at the feet of the bourgeois technical "authorities" and consistently advocated reliance on the bourgeoisie.

The working class has the thoroughly revolutionary spirit, rich practical experience, and infinite creative power. Countless facts show that so long as we follow Chairman Mao's teachings, implement the principle of "carrying out technical revolution" in a big way, thoroughly criticize and bring to utter disrepute Liu Shao-ch'i's doctrine of crawling at a snail's pace and foreigner's slave philosophy, and conduct in a big way mass activities of technical revolution and technical innovation, the working class will dare to think and act, dare to make revolution, dare to break and do away with foreign rules and regulations, dare to look down on the bourgeois technological and scientific "authorities," develop the communist spirit in the domain of science and technology, and open a revolutionary way for the development of socialist science and technology. They will be able to solve all problems of productive activity most resolutely in accordance with Mao Tse-tung Thought. What foreign countries have we shall also have, and what foreign countries have not we shall create. The appearance of science and technology in our country will change continuously. Flowers of science and technology of brilliant colors will bloom one after another. We shall scale pinnacles never before scaled by man.

The principle of "carrying out technical revolution in a big way" is the most thorough revolutionary guideline for the defense of national independence and national sovereignty, and for building socialism in an independent, self-determined, and self-reliant manner. To conduct in a big way mass activities of technical revolution and technical innovation is to place the guideline for development of science and technology on the basis of our own strength.

With regard to learning from foreign countries, we must "strike down the slavish way of thinking and bury dogmatism," strike down Liu Shao-ch'i's traitorous guideline of "relying on foreigners for everything," combine learning from foreign countries with a pioneering spirit in a critical attitude, "use foreign things for Chinese purposes," and, relying on the strength of the masses of our own people, rehabilitate and develop national economic construction and science and technology, so as to build socialism with greater, quicker, better and more economical results.

The principle of "carrying out technical revolution in a big way" is also a guideline of continuing revolution of Marxism-Leninism-Mao Tsetung Thought.

Chairman Mao teaches us: "In the sphere of production struggle and scientific experiment, mankind develops continuously and so does Nature. They never stop permanently at a certain level."

Vigorous carrying out of technical revolution, exploration of scientific and technological domains unknown to man, and ceaseless development from the kingdom of necessity to the kingdom of freedom is a law that conforms to the development of science and technology and social economy, as well as to man's conquest, utilization and transformation of Nature.

Social progress needs continuous revolution in order to enable society to advance from one stage to another. Similarly, development of science and technology also needs continuous revolution in order to enable science and technology to reach from one peak to a newer peak. The proletariat is the greatest, strongest class. To carry out mass activities of technical revolution and technical innovation, to reform Nature, society and the world and push history forward with the spirit of continuous revolution — this is a task entrusted to the proletariat by history. Only the proletariat dares to undertake and can undertake such a great task.

"The core of the force that leads our cause is the Chinese Communist Party." "Without the leadership of the Chinese Communist Party, no revolution can succeed." The principle of "strengthening Party leadership" in the "Anshan Steel Constitution" is the basic guarantee of all our victories.

The Chinese Communist Party is the vanguard of the proletariat. The basic principles of the operation of enterprises outlined in the "Anshan Steel Constitution" are realized through leadership by the Party. Only by strengthening Party leadership can we advance in triumph along the splendid road pointed out in the "Anshan Steel Constitution."

Marxism-Leninism-Mao Tsetung Thought constitutes the theoretical basis of the ideology of the Chinese Communist Party. Strengthening Party leadership means strengthening leadership by Mao Tse-tung Thought, relying on the hardcore role of the Party organization, and using Mao Tse-tung Thought to command all work in enterprises, reform all departments of an enterprise, occupy all positions in an enterprise, and direct the struggle-criticism-transformation movement in all enterprises.

Chairman Mao teaches us, saying, "China should make greater contributions to mankind." The "Anshan Steel Constitution" which Chairman Mao personally commented on is an ingenious, creative development of the doctrine of the proletarian revolution. It provides the international proletariat a splendid example and effective guarantee in respect to the consolidation and strengthening of the socialist economic basis, the prevention of capitalist restoration, and the continuing revolution under the dictatorship of the proletariat. It has also opened a splendid way for reforming Nature and society and pushing history forward by mankind.

Let us hold high the great red banner of the Thought of Mao Tse-tung, rally around the Party Center headed by Chairman Mao with Vice Chairman Lin as the deputy, and operate our enterprises as bright-red big schools of Mao Tse-tung Thought along the splendid road pointed out by the "Anshan Steel Constitution," so as to make still greater contribution to the Chinese revolution and world revolution.

5

Closely Rely on the Masses for the Successful Running of Socialist Enterprises

Investigation of the Condition of Struggle-Criticism-Transformation in Enterprise Management Conducted by the Small Parts Section of the Diesel Engine Workshop of Peking Internal Combustion Engine General Works

The small parts section of the diesel engine workshop of Peking Internal Combustion Engine General Works is specialized in the production of diesel engine parts. It has six workers' squads comprising 258 workers, of whom 55 percent are women. It owns 97 machine tools, producing 213 kinds of spare parts.

The revolutionary workers of the small parts section exerted their earth-shaking efforts during the Great Proletarian Cultural Revolution, greatly changing the backwardness in the production of diesel engine parts that existed before the Great Cultural Revolution. Since 1970, under the leadership of the revolutionary committee of this works and the PLA's propaganda team stationed in this works, they have gone further to implement the "Anshan Steel Constitution" approved by Chairman Mao, to carry out Chairman Mao's directive "In industry, learn from Tach'ing," to learn the experience of the six factories and

---

"Chin-chin i-k'ao ch'ün-chung pan-hao she-hui-chu-i ch'i-yeh — Pei-ching nei-jan-chi tsung-ch'ang ch'ai-yu chi-ch'e chien-hsiao chien-kung tuan k'ai-chan ch'i-yeh kuan-li tou, p'i, kai ti ch'ing-k'uan tiao-ch'a." Jen-min jih-pao [People's Daily], February 10, 1971. This translation is taken, with minor editorial revisions, from SCMP, No. 4852 (March 8, 1971), 1-12.

two schools in Peking and to insist on giving prominence to proletarian politics. Taking a firm hold of class struggle and having revolutionized their thinking, they conducted a struggle-criticism-transformation movement in enterprise management in depth, thereby providing some experience in relying on the workers for the successful operation of a socialist enterprise and realization of revolutionization in enterprise management.

At present, in the whole section, the workers take on a completely new mental outlook, management is in good order, and production increases with each passing day. The annual production plan for 1970 was overfulfilled by 10 percent some four months ahead of schedule, and new achievements were made in the fourth quarter. The production tasks of the first month in 1971 were also accomplished with excellent results.

In the course of penetratingly conducting a struggle-criticism-transformation campaign in enterprise management in accordance with Chairman Mao's revolutionary line, the workers of the small parts section have learned deeply:

1) In the last analysis, the aim of struggle-criticism-transformation in enterprise management is to put Mao Tse-tung Thought in command of all work of an enterprise and to put all work on the track of Chairman Mao's revolutionary line. Therefore, it is necessary to constantly carry out education on the struggle between the two lines, to continuously conduct revolutionary mass criticism against renegade, hidden traitor and scab Liu Shao-ch'i's counterrevolutionary revisionist line in running an enterprise, and to eliminate the pernicious influence of this revisionist line. If we are contented only with the superficial breaking of the old rules and regulations laid down by the revisionist line in running an enterprise and yet do not let Chairman Mao's revolutionary line take root deep in our minds, the socialist enterprise can gradually go wrong.

2) Running an enterprise in accordance with Chairman Mao's revolutionary line means that we must trust and rely on the masses and persevere in launching a mass campaign in doing all tasks. We cannot run a socialist enterprise well if we trust only ourselves. Neither can we run it well if we rely on only a

few. To follow the mass line, we must thoroughly "go" to the masses of workers and take them really as masters of the enterprise. Only in this way will it be possible to bring the wisdom and talent of the masses into full play, exploit all positive factors, and really put the Party's various directives and policies of industrial construction on a solid basis at the grass-roots level.

3) Revolutionization of man's thinking is the basis of the realization of revolutionization of enterprise management. The revolutionization of enterprise management in return can further consolidate and step up the revolutionary vigor of the masses and tap the potentials of manpower and equipment. The leading squad must be good at closely linking these two factors together and lead the broad masses to advance continuously on the road of revolutionization of the thinking of the masses and revolutionization of enterprise management.

A Mass Movement Must Be Launched Perseveringly in All Work; to Do without a Mass Movement Would Be Unthinkable

In conducting the struggle-criticism-transformation campaign in enterprise management, the small parts section proceeded from revolutionary mass criticism and enforced a deep-going reform in planned management, thereby making the broad masses the real masters in the planning, greatly arousing the enthusiasm of the masses and carrying out great leader Chairman Mao's teaching "In drawing up plans, it is necessary to mobilize the masses and see to it that there is enough leeway."

Early last year, the small parts section only consulted the leaders of various squads on the production plans assigned by the higher level and stuck to the old method. Returning to their squads, the squad leaders transmitted to the masses exactly what was told them. Superficially, they called meetings and let the masses discuss the problems but, actually, the cadres mounted the rostrum and made speeches and the masses below the rostrum expressed their agreement, and so the matter was settled. The plan was still in the pockets of the cadres and was not yet revealed to the workers. The cadres at the two levels of the work section and the workers' squad came early in the morning and went off their work late in the evening, making arrangements for production. They were so very busy that they could spare no time to take part in manual labor. But various branches of work were still in confusion.

As soon as he attended to his work, a squad leader was busy distributing the tasks to the workers and then ran to the warehouse to fetch a blank and to the workshop to get a cutting tool. He moved round the whole day. The masses criticized him, saying, "You had better not wear the working clothes. A pair of working shoes is sufficient for you." Yet the masses still did not know by how much their tasks had been accomplished, what had to be done with priority and what else might be delayed. There often appeared the situation in which work was done loosely at an earlier stage and hurriedly at a later stage and carried out desultorily at some moments and intensively at other moments. The masses were deeply dissatisfied with such a state of affairs.

After all, what problems existed in the planned management of the small parts section? The leading squad aroused the masses to make an analysis in accordance with Chairman Mao's revolutionary line. The workers pointed out sharply that the planned management was in disorder at the basic level but this was caused by the failure of the leadership to take the mass line. They criticized the three erroneous ideas cherished by some comrades.

First, they did not believe that the masses could draw up a good plan of management. They feared that too many people together would produce too many opinions and that the plan would be in a mess if it was assigned to the masses. Accordingly, a squad which had fifty to sixty workers and which was responsible for production of a few dozen spare parts had to rely on its leader to arrange production. As a result, the squad leader was busily engaged in work and yet could not put things in order.

Second, they held that this work section had to produce many varieties and great quantities of spare parts which required long work processes, so that planned management had long remained a "hard spot" of this works and it was not strange at all that management was somewhat in a mess. The workers criticized them, saying: "These comrades do not find this strange because, first of all, they only see the complexity in planning and arranging production in this work section and do not see that man is the decisive factor. A plan is arranged by man and the workers are by no means 'old, big troubles.' The working class can master the destiny of history. Once all are aroused, is it impossible to arrange production plans properly ?"

Third, they dared not take hold of enterprise management, fearing that they would make the mistake of "giving prominence to work." They were always afraid that the masses would criticize them for failing to give prominence to proletarian politics. They did not understand that to put Chairman Mao's revolutionary line in command of enterprise management was a form of giving prominence to proletarian politics. In the last analysis, they still did not trust the masses.

After analysis and criticism, the leading group of the work section deeply realized that a fierce struggle between the two lines was still under way in enterprise management. Before the Great Proletarian Cultural Revolution, a few people of this plant sat high above and drew up plans and issued "work orders" to the lower levels. The revisionist method that the workers did their jobs under "orders" was broken down superficially but it actually was still influential; the bourgeois concept that "the lofty are intelligent and the lowly are stupid" had not been eradicated from the people's minds. In this way, they would not really regard the broad revolutionary masses as masters of a socialist enterprise, work would be in a mess and production invariably could not be conducted well.

Accordingly, obeying Chairman Mao's teaching "The mass movement is necessary in all work; it would not do without mass movement," they gave the masses free rein and let them take part in planning management. When transmitting the productive tasks assigned by the higher level, they first explained clearly to the masses the situation in the international sphere, at home and in the whole works, so that the masses closely linked the part where they were with the revolution as a whole. Meanwhile, they told them the objective conditions and the existing problems in the course of accomplishing the tasks. The squad leaders also took the production plans out of their pockets, going from the annual plan to the weekly plan and organizing the masses to discuss them in depth, so that all knew clearly what jobs each machine tool had to do, whether the arrangements were made properly, what hardships they would meet in accomplishing the tasks, how they should help each other, and how one procedure of work should be linked with the following procedure.

Taking into consideration the situation as a whole and the opinions of the masses on the amendments of the plan, the work section effected balance in various fields and promptly informed the masses of the results of this balance. The masses were aroused every week to sum up and examine the conditions of accomplishment of the plan, so that they constantly kept a clear view of what had been done and what had to be done.

In drawing up a plan, once a mass movement had been launched, it was possible to exploit the positive factors in various fields. First, various contradictions in production had been exposed: There was insufficient manpower to operate the machine tools in some work processes but surplus manpower in some other processes; some workers' groups lacked cutting tools while some others did not have blanks; the contradiction between a procedure of work and the following procedure often concerned two workers' groups and some contradictions even concerned other plants or other workshops. If the masses were aroused to resolve these contradictions, production would increase in a bigger margin.

In the second place, those who participated in the discussion were people with the richest practical experience in this works, so that the things which seemed unfeasible were done after the workers thought on the problems, drew up plans and tapped the potentials; some irrational arrangements were corrected after they were discussed by the workers. The plan thus drawn up had the least conservative ideas, was most compatible with the objective realities, and had enough margin.

Knowing what they should do at present and in the next steps, the workers had the initiative in production, so that they found it convenient to make preparations beforehand and to greatly shorten the time spent on nonproductive work.

On one occasion, the workers of a certain squad saw that they had to produce a machine part at once in accordance with the plan, but the other workshop had not yet delivered the blanks to them. They went on their own initiative to press for the delivery of the blanks. In the other workshop, they discovered that because the technical requirements were impractical, some of these blanks which did not affect processing of the products were taken as rejects, so that they could not be supplied on time. Accordingly, they explained this matter to this workshop, avoiding suspension of work caused by failure of supply.

The leading groups of the work section and the workers' squads also liberated themselves from the confinement of day-to-day work and worked together with the workers on shifts. In the course of manual labor, they kept in more practical contact with the conditions of the accomplishment of the plan and could exercise command more vividly over production.

A certain workers' squad was known as a "hard spot" in the works in 1969. It was responsible for the production of spare parts of many varieties but its management was in a mess. It often produced too many of the spare parts of one variety but did not produce enough of other varieties, so that it always worked passively. Its output in 1969 was only 40 percent of that in 1970; it had to rely on the aid by other units and still failed to accomplish the plans of production of spare parts of a few varieties. In 1971, the people remained the same and the equipment also remained the same, but man's thinking had changed, so that the method of planned management also changed. The annual plan was overfulfilled in only eight months.

The leading group of the small parts section learned an

impressive lesson of the power of the mass movement from the change in planned management. After that, whatever it did, it persisted in giving free rein to the masses, vigorously launched a mass movement and, in the course of mass struggle, gradually trained a backbone force comprising about one-third of the total number of workers in this section and with the old workers as the mainstay. With this force leading the masses, there was a solid foundation for all items of work in this section.

Only When the Masses Have Enhanced Their Consciousness Will It Be Possible to Establish and Consolidate the Rational Regulations and Systems

After assigning the plan to the masses, the small parts section again aroused the masses to gradually establish the rational regulations and systems governing work norm, registration of score (registration of a worker's daily output), examination of quality of products, and keeping of finished products.

Each of the regulations and systems of this work section was formulated in the course of carrying out education on the line struggle and unfolding the ideological struggle for destroying selfishness and establishing devotion to the public, on the basis of the enhanced ideological consciousness of the masses and after being summed up by the masses.

In early 1970, when the plan was assigned to the masses, the workers felt that if there was no norm of work hours and no record of output, it would be difficult to calculate how much work one could do, how much work one had done, and how much work one should do, and this would lead to confusion. They hoped that corresponding systems governing the norm, etc., could be established. But a few people could not distinguish between the right and the wrong, saying: "Here comes again Liu Shao-ch'i's method of 'supervision, control and suppression!'" Some people feared that the regulations and systems would mean restrictions on them. They said: "Now the workers have enhanced their consciousness. Establishing such regulations and systems again means distrusting the masses and upholding perplexing trifles."

After all, are the rational regulations and systems means of "supervision, control and suppression" and "perplexing trifles"? Are the systems unnecessary once the masses have heightened their consciousness? The work section held a study class for the purpose of helping all heighten their consciousness. In the study class, the workers applied the viewpoint of the line struggle and compared the "supervision, control and suppression" by Liu Shao-ch'i's counterrevolutionary revisionist line with the rational regulations and systems. They made concrete analysis of the differences between the new and the old systems governing the norm:

The norm before the Great Cultural Revolution was fixed by those who were specially charged with the task of secretly calculating by means of a stopwatch how much time a worker needed to produce a spare part. In putting this norm into effect, the capitalist-roaders in the plant again used "material incentives" and "cash awards in command" to corrupt the workers' innermost being. This system meant basically distrusting the masses, was a typical case of "supervision, control and suppression" of the masses, and was a tool used by the bourgeoisie to exercise dictatorship over the proletariat.

The new norm drawn up now by the workers on the basis of conscious manual labor for the revolutionary cause is for the purpose of further consolidating and arousing the enthusiasm of the masses and obtaining data for arranging production plans. In this way, a foundation is laid for doing business accounting in a better way for a socialist enterprise.

After this analysis and comparison, the workers realized that the new and the old systems governing the norm reflected two different lines and two different goals. They said: "The rational regulations and systems are neither means of 'supervision, control and suppression' nor 'perplexing trifles' whatsoever. They are entirely compatible with Chairman Mao's revolutionary line. They are not unnecessary but are essential!"

The rational regulations and systems set up in the course of the struggle between the two ideologies and between the two lines in the small parts section have the following characteristics:

1) They manifest the revolutionary spirit of "going all out and aiming high." The new norm system takes into consideration the technical and physical conditions of the majority of the workers and maintains the work at a relatively advanced level. The new norm is on the average 35 percent higher than the old norm before the Great Cultural Revolution. Some workers might not reach the new norm at the time, but they perseveringly demanded fixing the norm according to the advanced target. Many workers went on their own initiative to teach the workers who could not reach the norm for the time being their experience in carrying out production and to help them overcome difficulties, so that they might, under the concern shown by the collective and through their selfless labor and creative work, speed up and reach the norm very quickly. All the workers of this work section have now surpassed the new norm; the new norms for various products have also been surpassed by 29 percent on the average.

2) There is an extensive mass basis; the masses can observe these norms consciously and make continuous efforts to improve these new systems in the course of practice. They also set up the system of examining the quality of their own products and of each other's products and charging some people especially with the task of examining the quality of the products.

Before setting up this system, the workers carried out a deep-going revolutionary mass criticism against Liu Shao-ch'i's counterrevolutionary revisionist line and criticized the erroneous ideas of some people who held that "it is invariable that we may turn out some rejects since we have produced such a great quantity of spare parts." This educated all on the struggle between the two lines, enhanced their consciousness of giving a high yield after achieving fine quality of products, and made them ensure good quality of products in the spirit of a high degree of responsibility for the people.

On one occasion, when some workers examined the quality of one another's products, they discovered that a woman worker turned out a few rejects because she did not examine and adjust the measuring instrument. This woman worker was afraid that other people might fall into a similar situation. She went on her own initiative to report the matter to the workers' management group, which called a meeting on the spot. She got together with other workers at the meeting to sum up experience and lessons, so that when one made a mistake, others would learn a lesson.

Not long ago, in view of the fact that some new workers did not understand the important meaning of ensuring the quality of products, the workers proposed holding meetings once a month to talk about the problems of quality of products, thereby further improving the system of examining the quality of products.

3) These regulations and systems further step up the revolutionary vigor of the masses and propel the revolutionization of man's thinking.

After the new norm system and the system of registration of results were set up, the masses felt that there was a clearer target for their daily production tasks and they had a target for comparison among themselves. The workers of the whole work section caught up with and surpassed one another. Very soon they touched off a new upsurge of grasping revolution and promoting production. The register of scores became a silent propagandist and promoter. The workers vied with one another in reporting their best scores to great leader Chairman Mao. Production was carried out enthusiastically.

Helped patiently by their teachers, some apprentices surpassed their norms in production and also surpassed the norms for their teachers. The teachers patiently taught their pupils and the apprentices dared to surpass their teachers. All workers were firmer ideologically in doing manual labor for the revolutionary cause.

Organize the Strength of the Masses, So That They Can Direct Their Efforts to the Point

The leading group of the small parts section realized that when the masses worked vigorously, it would be the task of the leadership to give the masses further help in developing their potentials and to rationally organize the strength of the masses, so that their revolutionary enthusiasm could be combined with their scientific attitude and they could direct their efforts to the point.

Before the Great Proletarian Cultural Revolution, as a result of the influence by the counterrevolutionary revisionist line of running an enterprise, this works laid down a rule that the workers could only work at the machine tools for which they had been held responsible, the workers of different branches of work, such as turning, grinding and milling, were forbidden to help one another and to change their work with one another, and even when a worker was shifted to another machine tool doing the same kind of work, he also had to pass a test and obtain a "working permit." For this reason, some workers were able to do only one job with one particular machine tool after working for some ten years in this works and could not do anything when help was needed on other machine tools. These revisionist rules and conventions, called by the workers "a system isolating one branch of work from another," tied the workers hand and foot to one particular machine tool, seriously dampening the enthusiasm of the masses and hindering the development of productive forces.

This time they made a deep-going criticism of this system. The leading group of the work section adopted methods, organizing the masses to help and learn from one another, to learn while working, and to learn and work simultaneously, so as to train the masses into versatile laborers versed in one job while being capable of doing many others and to help them tap their potentials to a further extent.

Now, in the whole work section, 52 percent of the workers have mastered the operational skills of two and more branches of work, and some workers are able to operate all 11 types of machine tools.

A certain woman worker could operate only one type of lathe after working for more than ten years in this works. Last year, breaking down the barrier between different branches of work, she learned to operate four types of machine tools. She said: "Everyone knows work is tiresome. But when we have the idea of serving the people, we are eager to do more work for building socialism. We can work with all-out efforts once we have broken down the barrier between different branches of work!"

After breaking down the barrier between different branches of work, the workers fought wherever they were, bringing man's strength into vivid play. The leading group scientifically organized this strength and helped the workers direct their efforts to the point and form a powerful force. Since May 1970, after breaking down the barrier between different branches of work, they put Mao Tse-tung Thought in command of production, took the whole work section as a game of chess, strengthened co-ordination, and concentrated forces to fight a battle of annihilation.

At the moment, inspired by great leader Chairman Mao's solemn statement "People of the world, unite and defeat the U.S. aggressors and all their running dogs!" the revolutionary workers of the small parts section worked with earth-shaking efforts and were determined to accomplish the annual production plan ahead of schedule. To win this victory, the leading group of this section first aroused the masses to make a concrete analysis of the current conditions.

This work section had six squads then. Its annual plan of producing spare parts of some 140 varieties had not been fulfilled, and blanks for some 40 varieties of these spare parts had to be supplied by other workshops. Judging from the state of various squads, the No. 2 and No. 5 squads did not have to produce many varieties of these spare parts. With a few excepted, these spare parts were not produced in large quantities and the supply of relevant blanks was reliable. Working with strenuous efforts, these squads could possibly be the first to accomplish the annual plan. The No. 3 and No. 4 squads did not have heavy tasks, but some of the blanks needed had to be supplied by other factories, so that they could not work actively. The No. 1 and No. 6 squads had to produce many varieties and large quantities of spare parts. They were the units of this work section with the greatest hardships in accomplishing their plans ahead of schedule.

Applying Chairman Mao's teachings of the "ten major principles of operation," they decided that the No. 2 and No. 5 squads should first win a victory and then concentrate forces to tackle the key points and help the No. 1 and No. 6 squads accomplish their tasks ahead of schedule. The No. 3 and No. 4 squads should observe the objective conditions and win a victory at a favorable moment. Each squad should first "clean the surroundings," accomplishing the easy tasks first and at the same time making preparations for solving the key problems in the accomplishment of the major tasks.

A key problem for the No. 2 and No. 5 squads was that they had to do in a month what they usually did in six months in producing a certain variety of the spare parts. They improvised a technical innovation, improved a tool, and adopted the method of joining forces in a fight. Eventually, they accomplished their task very quickly. Immediately after that, the whole work section concentrated forces to help the No. 1 and No. 6 squads. In the course of production, they broke down the barrier between different branches of work.

The workers went any place they were needed. In this way, some sections which formerly had little hope of fulfilling the annual plan ahead of schedule because they were relatively poor in manpower and equipment now concentrated their forces, "paid attention to the major aspects concerning the situation as a whole," and solved the problems one after another, thereby changing the poor conditions into absolute superiority and gaining confidence of winning a victory.

As a result, by mid-July, they overfulfilled the annual plans of production of all spare parts, with one excepted because of failure of supplies of blanks from another locality. It was not until August 27 that the blanks were delivered to this works. The workers processed them through day and night and achieved all-round overfulfillment of the production plan for 1970 four months and three days ahead of schedule.

Only When Technical Innovation Becomes the Wish and the Cause of the Masses Will There Be Strong Vitality

The output of the small parts section in 1970 was more than double that in 1969. In winning this victory, the workers chiefly relied on tapping their potentials. They said: "It is not a real increase if we increase production by asking for supply of manpower and equipment from the state."

The technical innovation carried out on this ideological basis became a wish and a cause of the masses. Every worker thought of making any possible innovation on the machine tool he was operating, in the parts to be produced and in the work processes for which they were responsible, so as to increase production. Many old workers thought of technical innovation even when they were sitting or walking. They drew up diagrams on paper and on the ground. Activities of technical innovation were carried out everywhere and had extensive mass basis and strong vitality. Now this work section has trained a backbone force of technical innovation comprising more than 40 people with old workers as the mainstay and with sent-down technicians and members of the leading group taking part in it. Under their leadership, 135 items of technical innovation were realized in 1970 in the small parts section, which meant that an average of every two workers could achieve one item of technical innovation.

The strong vitality of the technical innovation in this work section was shown in these aspects:

1) The workers put the all-round viewpoint of placing revolution in command of technical innovation. They perseveringly do whatever is profitable to the development of socialist production. Their items of innovation include the making of some parts by powder metallurgy or precision casting instead of forging, and some parts are made of plastic instead of metal.

The molds of these innovated parts should be made by the tools workshop and the pressure casting done by the casting workshop. But these workshops had many tasks to do and could hardly handle these items in a short period of time. Some comrades said that the making of molds and the casting of spare parts by pressure were beyond the limits of duty of the small parts section. The workers criticized them, saying: "What are the limits of one's duty? The making of molds is not within the limits of our duty nor is the making of plastic parts. But, increasing production is within the limits of duty of the working class." They worked and learned simultaneously and perseveringly worked with their hands. The whole section has already made and produced sixteen sets of molds for making the spare parts and one machine for making plastic parts by pressure casting.

2) They persist in the policy of "self-reliance" and "hard struggle." The two major items of innovation — one jet-flow control boring machine and one plastic parts pressure-casting machine — have been achieved by them by working with their hands and making use of rejects and used materials.

When making the plastic parts pressure-casting machine, they went three times to other localities to learn lessons: The first time, they went to a factory and saw that the modern equipment needed would cost some 29,000 yuan and take more than a year's time to complete. The workers said: "We cannot build this modern equipment. Time is pressing. Extravagance is abominable." The second time, they went to another factory and saw that the equipment there was relatively complicated. The third time, they visited a small factory and saw an indigenous pressure-casting machine, which had simple structure and was easy to build. They were greatly enlightened. Returning to their works, they took an old hydraulic press which had been discarded for many years, and processed it with materials obtained on the spot. After fighting arduously for twenty-one days, they rebuilt this machine at a cost of only some 1,000 yuan.

3) They not only pay close attention to the major items of innovation, such as automation of a machine tool, but also attach importance to and lay emphasis on various items of minor innovation in the course of production. They not only consider the needs of a long-range development in production, but also proceed from the current needs of production and lay emphasis on reinforcing the weak links in production at present. They hold

that if they pay close attention to the minor items of innovation, the small victories will add up to a major victory and some minor innovations will lead to a major victory, and that if they lay emphasis on solving the current needs of production, they can arouse the masses more extensively and the technical innovations will bring fast results.

In the past, a milling machine could process only one spare part at a time, so it could not meet the current needs. The workers improved it by every possible means. In a few days they made a new mold, by means of which the milling machine could process eleven spare parts at a time, thereby greatly heightening productivity and solving a major problem in production.

The blank for making another spare part was big and clumsy. The workers have now changed it to be a small and handy blank made by precision casting.

According to the planned output for 1971, two tons of rolled steel may be saved. Moreover, because some work processes have been canceled, it is possible to save more than 10,000 man-hours of work.

At present, the revolutionary workers of the small parts section of the diesel engine workshop of Peking Internal Combustion Engine General Works are going further to learn the advanced experience of Tach'ing Oil Field and the six factories and two schools in Peking. They continue to tightly grasp class struggle and the struggle between the two lines and to carry out the struggle-criticism-transformation movement in depth in the economic field. They are high in spirit and firm in determination. They are resolved to win a new and greater victory in 1971!

Investigation Group of First Ministry
of Machine Building,

Investigation Group of Revolutionary
Committee of Peking Internal Combustion
Engine General Works, and

NCNA reporter

IV On The Management of Socialist Enterprises

by Kung Hsiao-wen et al.

Quotation from Chairman Mao

The correctness or incorrectness of the ideological and political line decides everything.

Our objective is to create a political situation in which there are both centralization and democracy, both discipline and freedom, and both unity of will and personal ease of mind and liveliness in order to facilitate our socialist revolution and socialist construction, to make it easier to overcome difficulties, to enable our country to build modern industry and agriculture at a fairly rapid pace, and to consolidate our Party and state and make them better able to weather storms and stress. The general theme is to correctly handle the contradictions among the people, and the approach is to adhere to the mass line and work in a practical and realistic way.

Kung Hsiao-wen teng, T'an-t'an she-hui chu-i ch'i-yeh kuan-li [On the Management of Socialist Enterprises]. Shanghai: Jen-min ch'u-pan-she, 1974. This complete translation is taken, with minor editorial revisions, from Chinese Economic Studies, IX:1 (Fall 1975). Translated by Ai Ping.

Contents

1

Workers Are the Masters of Socialist Enterprises

Kung Hsiao-wen

In enterprise administration work, we often come upon many concrete problems relating to quantity and quality of products, as well as to equipment, tools, and raw materials. Handling these problems merely seems to be a question of dealing with the relationships among objects, or among men and objects. Marxist political economy shows, however, that behind all these lie the relationships among men, that is, certain production relations.

In analyzing capitalist business administration, Marx pointed out that all large-scale, direct social labor or communal labor more or less needs some direction in order to coordinate individual activities and to exercise the functions which are called for in the implementation of general production. A violinist can act as his own director, but an orchestra needs a conductor. Right after this statement, Marx pointed out: "If the labor associated with capital becomes cooperative labor, the functions of administration, supervision, and regulation are transformed into the functions of capital. As a special function of capital, administration acquires a special character." (1) This means that capitalist management reflects the function of capital. It is a capitalist relationship of production. "What the capitalists are concerned with is how to manage business for robbing and how to rob through management." (2) A capitalist enterprise,

---

Kung Hsiao-wen, "Kung-jen shih she-hui-chu-i ch'i-yeh ti chu-jen." [This essay originally appeared in Hsüeh-hsi-yü p'i-p'an (Study and Criticism), No. 4 (December 16, 1973), 11-13, under the title "T'an-t'an ch'i-yeh kuan-li" (On Enterprise Management)].

no matter whether it is managed by the capitalist himself or by his agent, operates for the sole purpose of extracting more surplus value from the workers. Hence, the relationship between the capitalist and the worker is absolutely one between the ruling and the ruled, between the exploiting and the exploited.

A socialist enterprise also exercises the functions of administration, supervision, and regulation. However, these functions reflect the relations between man and man in a socialist undertaking, that is, they reflect a relationship of socialist production. The means of production in a socialist enterprise are owned by all the working people, and the worker masses are the masters of the enterprise. In this fact lies a fundamental difference between socialist management and capitalist management. In all kinds of work of running socialist enterprises, if we divorce ourselves from socialist production relations in discussing enterprise management, then we are bound to depart from the basic Party line and be unable to draw a distinction between the different natures of socialist and capitalist management, even running the danger of slipping into the mire of capitalism and revisionism.

Whom should we rely on for management? On the eve of the nationwide victory of the Chinese People's Revolutionary War, Chairman Mao pointed out to the whole Party that we "must wholeheartedly rely on the working class." (3) After liberation, Chairman Mao summed up more than once the experience of the worker masses participating in management and gave it his personal confirmation. The "Anshan Steel Constitution," ratified by Chairman Mao himself, laid down a series of principles: persisting in putting proletarian politics in command, strengthening the Party's leadership, launching large-scale mass movements, implementing the two participations, one transformation, and three-in-one-combination*, and going in for tech-

*"Two participations" is the cadres' participation in manual labor and the workers' participation in management. "One transformation" is the revision of regulations. And the "three-in-one-combination" is the coordination among the leading cadres, workers, and technical personnel. — Tr.

nical innovation and revolution in a big way. At the time that the Great Proletarian Cultural Revolution was scoring great victories, Chairman Mao once more taught us that leadership in a factory or enterprise must be kept in the hands of genuine Marxists and the working masses. It is noted in the Political Report to the Tenth National Congress of the Chinese Communist Party that "the basic experience learned from our socialist construction during more than two decades is to rely on the masses." This is a fact: Enterprises seethe with enthusiasm and liveliness when we have faith in and rely on the masses and are good at mobilizing and organizing them to participate in management. Enterprises fall into a dreary and lifeless state whenever we rely on a few administrative staff and technicians for management to the neglect of the masses. It is only by relying wholeheartedly on the working class for the strengthening of management and by putting the leadership of a socialist enterprise in the grip of the proletariat that we can improve and incessantly develop the relations of socialist production. Thus, the task of consolidating and strengthening the dictatorship of the proletariat can be carried out in every unit at the basic level, and the productive forces can be advanced incessantly.

Specific professional managerial personnel are needed for socialist management, and it is necessary to bring their role into full play. However, they must always remember: Bearing the mandate of the Party and state, we are here to administer the enterprise on behalf of the working class. Therefore, we should rely on the toiling masses at all times and on no account be separated from them. In the revisionist, social-imperialist Soviet Union, the socialist public ownership of the means of production has degenerated into ownership by a handful of bureaucrat monopoly capitalists. The administrative staff in factories have become sharply antagonistic toward the worker masses, to the extent that they discharge workers at will. The so-called "Shurkino Experiment" is in fact a disguised system of hire-labor. (4) In our country, workers are the real masters of socialist enterprises. They resolutely implement Chairman Mao's revolutionary line, grasp the leadership of enterprises, and administer socialist enterprises. Practice has proved that by firmly relying on the broad masses of workers we can resolve all contradicitions and difficulties in production and work wonders in the mundane world.

Since the Great Proletarian Cultural Revolution, the relations among the workers, cadres, and technical personnel have undergone great changes. In the process of identifying themselves with the worker masses, cadres and technicians have remolded their own thinking and feelings and have elevated their consciousness of the political line. The broad masses of workers have enhanced their sense of duty as masters of their own affairs and have accumulated certain experience in participating in management. Many industrial enterprises have also acquired experience by practicing relying on the workers to strengthen management under the leadership of the Party. The worker masses not only take part in the various squad and section administrations but also choose representatives to participate in the three-in-one revolutionary committees and other leading organs at different levels. The worker masses conduct enthusiastic discussions concerning production, technology, finance, and plans for their enterprises. They constantly make use of weapons such as the big-character posters to exercise effective supervision over the cadres' implementation of the Party's line and its general and specific policies. In this way, they ensure consistent adherence to Chairman Mao's proletarian revolutionary line and greatly enhance the Party's leadership over their enterprises.

In a socialist enterprise, there exist a great many contradictions, of which the contradiction between the proletariat and the bourgeoisie — between the roads of socialism and capitalism — plays the decisive role. This contradiction, when reflected inside the Party, takes the form of a struggle between two lines. Lin Piao adopted Confucius' precept of "restrain oneself and restore the rites" as his own reactionary program in a vain attempt to subvert the proletarian dictatorship and reinstate capitalism. One of Lin's objectives was to demote the workers from being masters of socialist enterprises to being hired slaves of capitalist enterprises. Therefore, to do well in managing our enterprises, we must rely on the broad masses of workers and grasp the key link of class struggle and two-line struggle. We must thoroughly repudiate the ultra-Right essence of Lin Piao's revisionist line and put the basic Party line in command over all our work, including management work.

In order to run a socialist enterprise well, we must have proper rules and regulations. Rules and regulations are indispensable in organizing and coordinating modern industrial production. However, they always have a class character; they represent the will and interests of this or that class. Chairman Mao teaches us: "The system must benefit the masses." (5) The rules and regulations of socialist enterprises should correctly reflect the ever-improving socialist production relations and facilitate the strengthening of the Party's leadership. They should be conducive to stimulating the initiative of the broad numbers of cadres and masses. It is entirely wrong to assert that regulations can only benefit production and not the masses. If the regulations in a socialist enterprise embody the workers' experience of practice and are formulated through adequate discussion by the masses, they will certainly not affect the workers' socialist enthusiasm but, on the contrary, will be even more beneficial to stimulating their initiative. Of course, there are regulations that are fetters to the masses, but they are the regulations of capitalism and revisionism, regulations advocated by Liu Shao-ch'i and Lin Piao. During the Great Proletarian Cultural Revolution, the vast numbers of cadres and masses rose to break down irrational regulations and, by summing up their experience, formulated new and rational regulations. This was a great revolutionary creation of the working class. It symbolized their high revolutionary consciousness of being masters of socialist enterprises.

The high sense of revolutionary consciousness displayed by the worker masses is most precious. Once it is stimulated, it will serve as a great material force for boosting both revolution and production. What should we do to stimulate this consciousness? Use material incentives? No. The worker masses cast off this kind of revisionist "incentive" long ago. In the "money-is-all-powerful" capitalist society, the capitalists brandish clubs at the workers and at the same time use money to bribe and rear a handful of labor aristocrats. In fact, the revisionists introduce the material incentive because they want to use it as a means to enslave and employ the workers as hired laborers. Today in our country, workers are the masters of socialist enterprises. They are engaged in creative labor for the cause of revolution and socialism. Their socialist enthusiasm stems from their class awareness and consciousness of the two-line struggle. It is by no means the fruition of "material incentives." Chairman Mao has consistently taught us: "Political work is the lifeblood of all economic work." (6) For the more than twenty years since liberation, we have been continuously strengthening the Party's leadership, arming the worker masses with Marxism-Leninism-Mao Tsetung Thought and raising their class awareness and consciousness of the two-line struggle. And we have been relying on these measures to run socialist enterprises well and to develop the socialist economy. Some comrades always have blind faith in rewards and punishments and think they are the most convenient way to stimulate mass initiative. These comrades ignore the fundamental difference between socialist enterprise and capitalist enterprise and forget that our workers have been elevated from being hired laborers to being masters of the enterprises. Compared with political and ideological work, rewards and punishments may be much easier approaches. However, if such measures really worked, the capitalist system would not be doomed to extinction.

"The important thing is to be good at learning." (7) To do a good job in managing socialist enterprises, we must study Marxist political economy and constantly explore and grasp the law governing the development of socialist economy. Not only the leading cadres and administrative personnel in an industrial enterprise should study conscientiously, but the broad masses of workers should also study earnestly. By studying Marxist political economy, the worker masses will further realize the historical mission of the working class and become aware of the position they occupy in the socialist enterprise. Thus, they will even more consciously participate in the management of enterprises. Having acquired a good grasp of the law governing the development of socialist economy and a clear understanding of the Party's basic line, the worker masses will be better able to assist and supervise the cadres in implementing Chairman Mao's revolutionary line. Any deviation from this line on the part of the leading cadres and administrative personnel will be quickly spotted, and the masses will put a stop to it. In this way, we will make fewer mistakes and avoid gross blunders.

Marx pointed out: "Once theory is grasped by the masses, it will become a material force." (8) Since the Great Proletarian Cultural Revolution, political economy has been liberated from the scholars' studies and has become a theoretical weapon of the masses for criticizing revisionism. During the mass movement to "Learn from Tach'ing in Industry," the broad masses of cadres and workers in many industrial enterprises studied Marxist political economy and made concrete analyses concerning the expression of the contradictions between socialist production relations and productive forces and between the superstructure and the economic base in their respective units. They made timely readjustments of the mutual relations among men in production, strengthened management, and consolidated the economic base of socialism. In the current campaign to criticize Lin Piao and Confucius, the movement among the broad masses of cadres and workers to study Marxism-Leninism-Mao Tsetung Thought is forging ahead. It can be expected that the study movement will bring about an even greater development in socialist revolution and socialist construction.

Notes

1) Marx, "Capital," Vol. 1, Complete Works of Marx and Engels, Vol. 23, pp. 367-368.

2) Lenin, "How to Organize Competition?" Selected Works of Lenin, Vol. 3, Jen-min ch'u-pan-she, p. 395.

3) "Tsai chung-kuo kung-ch'an-tang ti ch'i chieh chung-yang wei-yüan-hui ti-erh-tz'u ch'üan-t'i hui-i shang te pao-kao" [Report to the Second Plenary Session of the Seventh Central Committee of the Communist Party of China], Mao Tse-tung hsüan-chi [Selected Works of Mao Tse-tung], Vol. 4, p. 1318.

4) Shurkino is a Soviet chemical alloy plant located in the city of Tula near Moscow. In the plant, the Soviet revisionists have conducted a so-called "economic experiment to enhance the staff's concern for increasing production, to boost the productivity of labor, and to reduce the number of working personnel." Its objective is to raise the productivity of labor and cut down the number of workers by strengthening labor intensity. Meanwhile, it is stipulated that the total amount of wages of the plant will remain unchanged over several years. The funds saved through dismissal of workers will be put at the disposal of a handful of privileged persons in the plant. Up to June 1971, the plant had discharged more than 1,000 workers out of a total of over 7,000. Brezhnev, the chieftain of the Soviet revisionists, spared no effort in ballyhooing the "experiment" and ordered it to be popularized on a large scale. At present, the so-called "Shurkino Experiment" has become a major form of exploitation of the working people by the Soviet revisionists.

5) Reprinted from Jen-min jih-pao [People's Daily], May 31, 1972.

6) "'Yen-chung ti chiao-hsün' i wen an-yü" [Introductory Note to "A Serious Lesson"], Chung-kuo nung-ts'un ti she-hui-chu-i kao-ch'ao [The Socialist Upsurge in China's Countryside], Vol. 1, p. 123.

7) "Chung-kuo ke-ming chan-cheng ti chan-lüeh wen-t'i" [Problems of Strategy in China's Revolutionary War], Mao Tse-tung hsüan-chi [Selected Works of Mao Tse-tung], Vol. 1, p. 162.

8) "Introductory Notes to the Critique of Hegel's Philosophy," Complete Works of Marx and Engels, Vol. 1, p. 460.

2

Enterprise Management Has a Class Character

Chiang Yang-nan
(The Wu-sung Chemical Plant)

Why must there be management in a factory? Some comrades believe that with so many people working together, each with his own task yet mutually linked, production could not proceed in an orderly fashion without management. Some comrades also believe that management is nothing but the organizing principle for production. It is a prerequisite for any sizable labor project and a means for organizing and coordinating production. Are these views correct?

Marx remarked in Capital that "any comparatively large-scale direct social labor or communal labor requires varying degrees of direction to coordinate individual activities and perform all the general functions stemming from the overall movement of production, a movement which is different from the overall movement of independent sensory organs." Citing the example of an orchestra's need for a conductor, Marx explained that management is an objective necessity in communal labor, and it is closely connected with the development of production. However, Marx subsequently noted: "If labor which is related to capital becomes cooperative labor, this kind of administrative, supervisory, and adjustment function then becomes a function of capital. And this kind of management function enables the special function of capital to acquire a special character."

Chiang Yang-nan, "Ch'i-yeh kuan-li shih yu chieh-chi-hsing ti."

Here Marx clearly points out that the class character of capitalist management is the function of capital, that is, the function of capitalists exploiting hired laborers by using the means of production they possess. This nature of capitalist management is determined by capitalist production relations. Capitalist industry has developed through several historical periods, comprising the periods of simple coordination and cooperation, handicraft workshops and big, mechanized industry. There have been a great many changes with respect to production skills, coordination of production, and organization of labor. The level of productivity has been greatly enhanced, and the form of management has undergone various corresponding changes. However, the class character of capitalist management remains unchanged. It has always been as Lenin described: "What the capitalists are concerned with is how to manage business by robbing and how to rob through management." Therefore, the management in a capitalist enterprise is nothing more than the means by which capitalists exploit workers.

Analyses of capitalist management by the revolutionary teachers of the proletariat convince us that in a class society there is no management which rises above classes; management of an enterprise always bears a class character. The question is which class possesses and exercises the power of administration and which class benefits from it. The nature of the production relations determines the nature of an enterprise. In different kinds of enterprises, management has different characters. This is a basic starting point for studying the issues of management. We cannot depart from this principle when we analyze capitalist management, and we must not deviate from the same principle if we intend to comprehend socialist management.

In socialist enterprises, the proletariat and the laboring masses have become masters, and they hold the power of administration. Under these circumstances, can we define socialist management as only a question of strengthening the specialized organizations, carrying out the "five principles of administration" well, and improving the "seven systems"? No, we cannot. "Marxists should on no account depart from the correct position of analyzing class relations." (1) Take the "five principles of administration" and the "seven systems" for example. Some of these administrative regulations directly reflect the relations between man and man, that is, they are connected with production relations. Some regulations stem from the need for production skills, representing the demand of the productive forces. However, the questions of who makes these regulations and who carries them out are certainly involved with the relations between man and man. In a socialist society classes, class contradictions, and class struggle exist. Every kind of human relationship bears the imprint of a class and represents certain class relations. If we view the management of socialist enterprises only from the question of how to organize and direct the production, we will surely leave out the class character of the management. Consequently, we will be unable to distinguish the class characters of the two entirely different systems of management, those of socialism and capitalism, and are likely to lead the management of socialist enterprises astray.

Starting from the basic viewpoint that management always bears a class character, we must adhere to the Party's basic line in running socialist enterprises. We must wage struggles between the two classes, two roads, and two political lines in order to consolidate the leadership of the proletariat and ensure that the enterprises will have a socialist orientation. Historical facts have shown us that with the basic accomplishment of the socialist transformation of the ownership of capital goods, the proletariat endeavors to consolidate and improve socialist production relations while the bourgeoisie attempts to erode and destroy them. This struggle goes on ceaselessly. The old social system has been smashed, but "remnants of old ideas reflecting the old system remain in people's minds for a long time, and they do not easily give way." (2) This is the environment in which socialist enterprises find themselves, and it is under the condition of still prevailing class struggle that socialist production is being conducted. This fact invariably finds its expression in management.

Since the liberation, revisionists like Liu Shao-ch'i, Lin Piao, and their followers have made repeated, frenzied attacks against the proletariat on the issue of enterprise management. They have been selling revisionist black commodities such as the "system of directorship," "administering the factory by experts," "material incentives," "profits in command," and so forth. They have attempted to start with management, usurping the leadership of the administration and tampering with the socialist principles guiding management, and finally to achieve their end of making the socialist enterprises degenerate into capitalist enterprises. Emulating the fallacy of Confucius that "the superior man minds the law, the inferior man minds the benefit," Lin Piao advocated that he and his gang were lawmakers and the broad masses were persons coveting small gains, fit only to be dominated. This was an undisguised advertisement of the nonsense that "oppression is justified." Poisoned by the counterrevolutionary revisionist line enforced by Liu Shao-ch'i and Lin Piao, leadership in part of the industrial enterprises had been usurped over a period of time by the bourgeoisie and their agents within the Party. These units maintained the socialist ownership in form, but were virtually in the process of degeneration. During the Great Proletarian Cultural Revolution, the proletariat recaptured the leadership in these units and correctly reoriented their management. This was a great victory.

However, has the problem of the proletariat exercising leadership over the management of industrial enterprises been fully solved? Has the two-line struggle reflected in the management been brought to an end? No, not yet. As long as classes and class struggle exist, there can never be an end to the two-line struggle in managing enterprises. Under these circumstances, the management of socialist enterprises bears a distinct class character. It openly proclaims that it works in the interests of the proletariat and laboring masses and serves the consolidation of the proletariat dictatorship. The "Anshan Steel Constitution," formulated by Chairman Mao himself, indicates the correct direction for the management of socialist enterprises. In the final analysis, socialist management is nothing but a specific means for the proletariat to consolidate the public ownership of socialism and develop socialist production. Through socialist management, the proletariat exercises its own power and, in accordance with socialist principles, correctly handles the relations between man and man in order to unite all the forces that can be united in a common struggle against the bourgeoisie.

With the movement to criticize Lin Piao and Confucius developing in greater depth, the issue of political line involves all fronts, whether political, economic, or cultural. Adhere to Marxism or practice revisionism? Proceed along the road of socialism or revert to the path of capitalism? These are questions of paramount importance and hold true in all cases, including enterprise management. Consolidating and strengthening the leadership of the proletariat in socialist enterprises and criticizing capitalism and revisionism should be taken as the fundamental factors in socialist management. If we deal with production and the enterprise merely from the point of view of production and the enterprise, neglecting fundamental factors, we are bound to ignore the proletarian character embodied in the management of socialist enterprises and lead management astray.

In socialist management we must primarily grasp the political line and orientation of the enterprise. But this does not mean to say that we can relax our hold on the concrete work of management. With the two-line struggles as the key link and adherence to the socialist orientation as a prerequisite, we must conscientiously grasp the specific work of management. The management of socialist enterprises comprises many aspects, such as plan control, management of production, labor control, technical supervision, financial administration, supply service, care for life and welfare, and so forth. These are obligatory tasks, and must be fulfilled. However, if we do not attach priority to the question of which political line we carry out and which road we follow when performing these tasks, we certainly cannot do them well.

Whether a socialist enterprise fully implements the plan set by the state or one-sidedly seeks profits and value of output;

whether it holds a responsible attitude toward the people and improves the quality of its products incessantly or turns out crude and inferior products to the neglect of quality; whether it persists in economical accounting and is industrious and thrifty or runs the business in a rough way, being extravagant and wasteful; whether it fosters the spirit of socialist coordination, yielding to the convenience of others, or practices selfish departmentalism, disregarding the common interests of the whole nation — all these are not purely business questions but relate to the political line being pursued. It is the same with the implementation of various regulations in management. When enforcing the regulations, whether to have faith in the masses, rely on the masses, and correctly handle the relations among the people in an enterprise or whether to have an eye on material factors to the neglect of human factors, grasping regulations from the viewpoint of regulations and doing things by resorting only to administrative orders; this is also not purely a business question. It involves the political line being executed. These are all vital issues concerning the two political lines and the two roads. It is only by using the Party's basic line for guidance and by seizing the plan of struggle between the two classes and the two lines that we can grasp the essentials of enterprise management, things governing the whole situation, and matters of paramount importance. We must correctly tackle issues concerning class contradictions and class struggle. At present, we must grasp especially well the campaign to criticize Lin Piao and Confucius, which is a matter of primary importance. Only thus can we correctly settle all the contradictions existing in the enterprises and help bring about a lively and thriving outlook in both revolution and production.

Notes

1) "On Strategy," Complete Works of Lenin, Vol. 24, p. 26.

2) Chairman Mao, "'Yen-chung ti chiao-hsün' i wen an-yü" [Introductory Note to "A Serious Lesson"], Chung-kuo nung-ts'un she-hui-chu-i kao-ch'ao [The Socialist Upsurge in China's Countryside], Vol. 1, p. 123.

3

Management Is also Socialist Education

I Miao-chang
(Shanghai Electronic Machine Plant)

Chairman Mao has issued an important directive on the management of socialist enterprises: "Management is also socialist education." (1) Based on the objective law governing class struggle in the socialist era, Chairman Mao's directive presents the nature of management in socialist enterprises and clearly shows us the directions of socialist management.

It is only when the management of a socialist enterprise embodies socialist production relations that it can help boost the development of productive forces. The management of socialist enterprises cannot do without the role of the socialist superstructure. Chairman Mao's directive about administration teaches us that we must attach importance to the role of the superstructure. We must have an understanding of the superstructure when we do work relating to the economic base. We must strengthen the management of our enterprises through socialist education so that we can push the productive forces forward.

Chairman Mao teaches us: "The basic contradictions in a socialist society continue to be the contradiction between production relations and productive forces and that between the superstructure and the economic base." (2) In our country, the socialist transformation of the ownership of the means of production has basically been accomplished. Ever since, the main aspect of the situation has been conformity between the production relations and productive forces and between the super-

---

I Miao-chang, "Kuan-li yeh shih she-hui chiao-yü."

structure and the economic base. Aside from this, there is still the question of contradiction. The basic contradiction in a socialist society finds its class expression in the contradictions and struggles between the proletariat and bourgeoisie. Such contradictions and struggles will certainly find their expression in the management of enterprises. "Management is also socialist eduction" is a precept teaching us that we must grasp the class struggle and the two-line struggle in the sphere of enterprise management and draw a distinction between the management of socialist enterprises and that of capitalist enterprises. Socialist enterprises are the battlefront for the proletariat and working people to carry on the Three Great Revolutionary Movements of class struggle, production struggle, and scientific experiment. By making use of the battlefront, the proletariat strives to create the material and mental conditions for the realization of communism; the bourgeoisie attempts to realize in our enterprises their scheme of capitalist restoration. In the course of the Great Proletarian Cultural Revolution, there emerged in enterprise management a great many new revolutionary things. Lin Piao, the capitalist careerist and conspirator, maliciously swore at the new things coming forward during the Great Proletarian Cultural Revolution in his vain attempt to "restrain oneself and restore the rites," retrogression, and restoration. Therefore in managing an enterprise, no matter whether dealing with a problem relating to production skills or solving a business issue, we should consider whether the management will lead to the affirmation or the negation of the fruit of the Great Proletarian Cultural Revolution and whether it will serve to support or oppose the new things which emerged during the Great Proletarian Cultural Revolution. That is to say, it is a question of which class will benefit, which road will be pursued, and which political line will be executed. When we grasp the management of an enterprise, we should on no account tackle problems in a "business-is-business" way but must grasp the superstructure and keep a firm hold on class struggle and two-line struggle. We must organize the cadres and workers to study Marxism-

Leninism-Mao Tsetung Thought and strengthen their education in ideology and the political line to enable everyone to distinguish socialism from capitalism and differentiate between the proletarian and the capitalist way of running enterprises. It is only by doing this that we can resist the erosion of the bourgeoisie and ensure that the leadership of socialist enterprises is in the firm grip of Marxists and the worker masses. In this way, we can continuously consolidate the economic base of socialism and expand the productive forces of the whole society.

One of the major components of socialist production relations is the relations among people in production. In a socialist industrial enterprise, apart from the relations between the broad masses of working people and a handful of members of the exploiting class, the relations among people in production are mostly the relations among the laboring people. The precept "management is also socialist education" requires us to unite the working people in our management of the enterprises and wage a struggle against those capitalist-roaders and all other monsters and freaks who conspire and perpetrate capitalist and revisionist activities. It requires us to gradually reform the handful of members of the exploiting class, turning them into workers who live on their own toil, and correctly handle the contradictions between the working people and these few exploiting elements. It requires us to correctly handle the contradictions among the working people in the same enterprise and bring into full play their enthusiasm for socialism in order to boost socialist production with greater, faster, better, and more economical results.

In a socialist industrial enterprise, the relations among the working people mainly take the form of the relationship between the leaders and the masses and that between administrative and technical personnel and the workers. With the establishment of socialist public ownership of the means of production, the relations between the leaders and the masses and those between the staff and the workers are an ever-improving comradely relationship underlying which is a basic identity of interests.

However, this cannot be explained by saying there are no contradictions among them. Because of the influence of bourgeois ideology and the different positions functionaries and workers hold, it is likely that some leading members may deviate from socialist principles in their handling of the relations between the masses and themselves. They may avail themselves of their positions and power to seek privileges; they may take no part in physical work, remaining high above the masses with an arrogant, lordly air; and they may act arbitrary and despotic, suppressing democracy, treating people unequally, and turning the relations among comrades into relations between the ruling and the ruled. Some administrative and technical personnel have not remolded their bourgeois world outlook completely. They may lack faith in the masses and conduct their work without relying on the masses, and when something happens, they may ignore the advice of the masses. All this can give rise to contradictions between the leadership and the masses, between the staff and the workers. Generally speaking, these contradictions fall into the category of contradictions among the people and are nonantagonistic. Nevertheless, if these contradictions are not resolved correctly and in time, they may confound and subjugate the revolutionary spirit of the masses to assume the role of masters of their own affairs. If this situation persists, the workers may not consider the factory as their own but may consider it to belong to the leading members or administrative personnel. The workers will be brought into sharp antagonism with their leaders and other functionaries.

During the Socialist Education Campaign, and especially during the Great Proletarian Cultural Revolution, some cadres were criticized by the masses. One of the reasons for the criticism was that they had carried out a reactionary capitalist line, which angered the masses. Another reason was that they had seriously estranged themselves from the masses and had violated socialist principles when dealing with the masses, and the masses objected. The criticism served as a profound education in socialism. With criticism and education, the majority of the cadres changed for the better. They earnestly improved their relations with the masses and modestly accepted the supervision of the masses. In many enterprises there appeared a lively situation of "cadres and masses being of one mind, those above and below rallying together." Many business heads, administrative staff, and technical personnel, as well as the worker masses, have greatly enhanced their consciousness of socialism and have further improved the relations among themselves. Consequently, they have managed the socialist enterprises more successfully.

This has proved that we are able to run our socialist enterprises better if we merely follow Chairman Mao's instruction that "management is also socialist education" and correctly handle the relationships among people. However, there is also a small number of people who are hostile to the new revolutionary things which emerged during the Great Proletarian Cultural Revolution and who attempt to negate its achievements. Such persons will certainly lead management down the wrong road of restoration and retrogression. This is a question of principle and should be solved through the movement to criticize Lin Piao and Confucius so that we can ensure the continual progress of our enterprises along the track of revolution.

Historical experience shows us that enterprise management comprises a good many special lines of work. These include planned management, management of production, labor control, technical supervision, financing, supply service, livelihood and so forth. And in every category of administration, there are dozens or hundreds of concrete tasks. All these tasks must be fulfilled and done well. However, in the final analysis, all these matters are by no means confined to the relations between material objects and human beings, but are connected with the relations among people. Thus, in strengthening the management of socialist enterprises, we must not merely keep our eyes on material factors and lose sight of the human elements, that is, we must incessantly improve the relations among people in accordance with the principles of socialism, especially the relations between cadres and masses. For the purpose of establishing and developing socialist relationships among people within our enterprises, we must consistently implement in our management all the principles set down in the "Anshan Steel Constitution." These include the constant participation of cadres in productive labor, the participation of the masses in management, the transformation of irrational codes and conventions, and the implementation of the three-in-one combination of workers, cadres, and technical personnel.

The Socialist Education Movement embraced not only the problem of class struggle and issues of the cadres' participation in productive labor, but also the job of assuming a strict scientific attitude in conducting experiments and thus learning to solve several problems in our enterprises and undertakings. Through socialist education we must "enable our cadres to become good cadres who understand not only politics but also business, who are both red and expert, who do not float above, lording it over the people and divorced from the masses, but who identify themselves with the masses and are supported by the masses." (3) It is only by implementing the spirit of socialist education in our enterprise management that we can resist and weed out bourgeois influence, incessantly strengthen the militant solidarity among the cadres and masses, overcome bureaucracy, and guard against revisionism and dogmatism. All systems of administration can be easily dealt with if the relations between the cadres and masses are handled well. But if the relations are not handled well, the systems will be of no use no matter how good they are. By the same token, the leadership and administrative and technical personnel in an enterprise must frequently participate in productive labor. They must go down to the workshops and sections, identifying themselves with the workers and treating the workers as their teachers. They must learn some technical skills from the workers. If they do not work in this way, if they know nothing about technology but remain inexperienced all the time, they certainly cannot manage the enterprise.

In sum, socialist management means managing enterprises under the guidance of the Party's basic line. It requires us to grasp the superstructure and ideology, to correctly handle the relations among people in production in order to consolidate and push forward the economic basis of socialism. It is certain that with socialist production relations continually developing and improving, we will propel the socialist productive forces forward.

Notes

1) Reprinted from Jen-min jih-pao [People's Daily], August 14, 1972.

2) "Kuan-yü cheng-ch'üeh ch'u-li jen-min nei-pu mao-tun te wen-t'i" [On the Correct Handling of Contradictions among the People], Mao Tse-tung chu-tso hsüan-tu [Selected Readings from Mao Tse-tung's Works], Anthology A, Jen-min ch'u-pan-she, 1966, p. 336.

3) Reprinted from Jen-min jih-pao [People's Daily], July 24, 1973.

4

The System Must Beneficially Stimulate Mass Initiative

Yang Ying-shun

To transform irrational rules and regulations and formulate and improve rational ones is a major task in the management of a socialist enterprise. But how are we to judge whether or not the rules and regulations are rational? Chairman Mao has summed it up incisively: "The system must benefit the masses." That is to say, whether the rules and regulations are beneficial to stimulating mass initiative is the criterion for judging their rationality.

The rules and regulations in an enterprise should help develop the masses' enthusiasm for socialism. This requirement is determined by the nature of socialist production relations. Any enterprise in which production is socialized must lay down a set of rules and regulations; and any set of rules and regulations is drawn up on the basis of certain production relations and must finally give expression to those relations. In capitalist enterprises, the sole motive and aim of the capitalists is to extract as much of the surplus value created by the workers as possible. The relationship between the capitalists and the workers is absolutely one between the ruling and the ruled, between the exploiting and the exploited. The rules and regulations in a capitalist enterprise are therefore the means by which the capitalists dominate and exploit the workers. They are invisible

---

Yang Ying-shun, "Chih-tu yao yu li yü fa-hui ch'ün-chung chi-chi hsing."

ropes binding the workers. Hence, they can only benefit the capitalists and not the workers. In a socialist society, the proletariat and working people are the masters of the state and the enterprises. Their status in society has undergone a fundamental change. "The masses have a potentially inexhaustible enthusiasm for socialism." (1) The rules and regulations in a socialist enterprise must mirror the wishes and requirements of the broad masses so that their initiative can be brought into full play. In the past, cadres of some enterprises were affected by the influence of Liu Shao-ch'i's revisionist line. Relying on a small number of administrative and technical personnel, "behind closed doors," they worked out a set of trivial rules and regulations, intending to exercise "supervision" over workmen and production by resorting to regulations. For example, in some foundry factories, it was provided in the operation regulations that "heated iron had to be picked up with a clasp." This is simply rubbish! One transportation unit drew up for the maintenance of its trucks a whole set of "maintenance procedures accompanied by music" which required the workers to go through 360 procedures in accordance with the tempo of some musical records. Could this be defined as being anything other than a barrier to the workers? Such rules and regulations in essence are nothing but variations of regulations in the capitalist enterprises. They are entirely contradictory to socialist production relations. There also existed in the past some other rules and regulations which, judging by their contents, were basically in conformity with the requirements of production. But they were frequently not fully implemented and were even opposed by the worker masses. What brought this about? This was because some cadres lacked faith in the awareness of the masses. Focusing their attention on the material factor to the neglect of the human element, they did not regard the workers as the masters of regulations but took them to be objects for their supervision. They did not consult the masses beforehand when mapping out the rules and regulations; nor did they conduct ideological and political work when implementing them, but attempted to tie down the workers by continually resorting to a certain regulation. In this way, they seriously confounded the masses' enthusiasm for socialism, and the regulations they drew up invariably met opposition from the workers. Hence, the formulation and implementation of rules and regulations must be a process of mobilizing the masses, relying on the masses, and "from the masses, to the masses." Only in this way can the various rules and regulations take deep root among the masses.

Whether the rules and regulations in an enterprise facilitate bringing forth mass enthusiasm for socialism is a major gauge in judging whether the nature of the rules and regulations is socialistic or capitalistic. Concerning the issue of what kind of rules and regulations were to be enforced, there had always existed the struggle between the revolutionary line represented by Chairman Mao and the revisionist line pursued by Liu Shao-ch'i, Lin Piao, and the like. Lin Piao advocated the idealist historical concept of "the sage and the dullard." He had all along cast aspersions on the working people, picturing them as "occupying themselves with how to make money, how to gain rice, oil, salt, sauce, vinegar, and firewood." The struggle in this respect is in essence a question of having faith in the masses or treating the masses as imbecile children, of relying on the masses or "running the factory by experts." To get to the grassroots, it is a question of proceeding along the road of socialism or regressing to the road of capitalism. Obviously, whether the regulations are beneficial to the masses is not a question of working method but one of political line.

Rules and regulations can benefit production only when they are beneficial to the masses. Benefiting the masses and benefiting production are the same thing. It is wrong to assume that since regulations are binding, they can only benefit production and not the masses and thus set benefit to the masses in opposition to benefit to production. Production is always undertaken by the masses. Without the masses there can be no production. "The people, and the people alone, are the motive force in the making of world history." (2) Rules and regulations in a socialist enterprise have a certain binding capacity. Once they are laid down and before they are revised, they must be consciously observed by everyone. The binding quality of the regulations mainly serves as a check to bourgeois thoughts and actions. It is also a necessity in coordinating the activities of production. Rational rules and regulations can relatively accurately reflect the relations between the parts and the whole, between department and department, enabling all production activities to be coordinated. The broad masses observe these regulations, regarding them as binding on themselves, because they want to build socialism with greater, faster, better and more economical results, an undertaking which in the end will benefit the broad masses themselves.

"The lowly are the most intelligent; the elite are the most ignorant." (3) Rational rules and regulations are the summing up of the masses' experience in practice. They are the reflection of laws governing the techniques of production. They conform to the requirements of the masses, and the masses are willing to observe them. However, rules and regulations of any kind stem from the subjective views of man, and man cannot bring them in line with objective laws by going through one process of cognition only. Moreover, objective matters are continuously progressing, and man's cognition of them must develop correspondingly. The rationality of rules and regulations is not absolute but relative. With the masses gaining more experience in practice, their cognition deepening, and objective matters developing further, regulations which were previously rational may become irrational or partly irrational and disadvantageous to stimulating mass enthusiasm for socialism. Consequently, they need proper revision. It is necessary to mobilize the masses incessantly, earnestly sum up their experience, and keep improving the rules and regulations not yet perfect in order to continually improve the relations among men in socialist production and thus expedite the development of production.

Rational rules and regulations are formulated by man and are carried into effect by man. In the relationship between man and system, man always occupies the primary position. Even when we have rational rules and regulations, we cannot rest assured that there will be no problems. "Political work is the lifeblood of all economic work." It is only by strengthening political and ideological work that rational rules and regulations can have vitality and be made to play their appropriate role.

Notes

1) Chairman Mao, "'Chei ke hsiang liang nien chiu ho-tso hua le' i wen an-yü" [Introductory Note to "The Township Went Cooperative in Two Years"], Chung-kuo nung-ts'un ti she-hui chu-i kao-ch'ao [The Socialist Upsurge in China's Countryside], Vol. 2, p. 587.

2) "Lun lien-ho cheng-fu" [On Coalition Government], Mao Tse-tung hsüan-chi [Selected Works of Mao Tse-tung], Vol. 3, p. 932.

3) Quotation from Chairman Mao, reprinted from Jen-min jih-pao [People's Daily], June 4, 1970.

5

Take a Correct View of the Elimination and the Establishment of Rules and Regulations

Huang Lai-chi
(Shanghai Diesel Engine Plant)

How to correctly view the elimination and establishment of regulations is a frequent issue in enterprise management. To sum up experience in this connection in good faith is imperative if we are to do well in the management of socialist enterprises.

For over twenty years, there has been a phenomenon deserving our notice, namely, during each high tide of socialist revolution, the rules and regulations in our enterprises came under attack in either a big or small way. After the socialist transformation of the ownership of the means of production was basically accomplished, such attacks occurred several times. The bigger attacks included the one during the Great Leap Forward in 1958, the one during the "four cleans" [Socialist Education Campaign], and particularly the one during the Great Proletarian Cultural Revolution, which was broader and more thorough. The spearhead of the revolutionary mass movement was directed against all aspects of the hackneyed rules and regulations, piercing them without resistance and breaking them like rotten wood.

Why was it that whenever a revolutionary mass movement surged forward there would be an attack on the old rules and regulations of our enterprises? Was this coincidental? Obviously not.

Huang Lai-chi, "Cheng-ch'üeh k'an-tai kuei-chang chih-tu ti p'o ho li."

Chairman Mao teaches us: "The basic contradictions in a socialist society continue to be the contradiction between production relations and productive forces and that between the superstructure and the economic base." Most of the rules and regulations fall into the categories of production relations and superstructure. There exist both conformity and contradiction in the relationship between the regulations of socialist enterprises and the socialist economic base or the development of productive forces. The impact that the revolutionary mass movement has on the irrational regulations precisely reflects the development of this contradiction.

The rules and regulations in our enterprises do not drop from the skies but gradually take shape in the process of transforming the old economy and during the acute struggle between the two classes and the two lines. On the whole, such regulations reflect socialist production relations and can serve as an impetus to the development of socialist production. However, some of them retain traditions and vestiges of the old, handicapping the progress of production. Under the guidance of a correct line, an enterprise, by relying on the masses, can ceaselessly overcome the irrational part and develop the rational part of its regulations, getting rid of the old and introducing the new. In this way it can make the regulations catch up with the requirements of increasing production, facilitate the consolidation and development of socialist production relations, and help the broad masses bring forth their enthusiasm for socialism. But if an enterprise is disturbed by a wrong line, the negative part of its rules and regulations will grow dominant, which can wreak havoc on socialist production and frustrate mass enthusiasm for socialism. Under these circumstances, it is possible that the rules and regulations in this enterprise could become entirely incompatible with the socialist economic base and would surely be cast off by the masses in the end.

Why did the masses attack some old administrative regulations during the Great Proletarian Cultural Revolution? The fundamental cause was that in some enterprises affected by the revisionist line of Liu Shao-ch'i and Lin Piao the administrative regulations contained things which did not conform with socialist reasoning and failed to fully embody the status of the worker masses as masters of these enterprises. The major target of the attack was the irrational regulations seriously hampering the socialist initiative of the masses. These regulations brought the cadres and technicians into sharp opposition against the workmen, grossly damaged unity within the ranks of the working class, and were an extremely corrosive agent among the workers. These regulations must be abolished. Without eliminating revisionist regulations, it is impossible to establish correct relations among men in accordance with socialist principles, and it is impossible to bring into play the consciousness and enthusiasm of the worker masses for being masters of their own affairs. Some rules and regulations which had been in keeping with the needs of production were also swept away. However, it did not happen for no reason. It happened because the rules and regulations were either associated with material incentives or did not follow the mass line when formulated, thus lacking a genuine mass basis. However, any rational regulations, if actually established in keeping with the ideas of the masses, cannot be swept away even if you want to do so; and if they were swept away for the moment, the masses would revive them voluntarily. Analyzing the above phenomena from a revolutionary point of view, you can see that the masses' impact on the old administrative regulations was precisely their expression of opposing the revisionist management in their enterprises. It was a necessity in boosting socialist production.

"There is no construction without destruction, no flowing without damming, and no moving without halting." (1) New rules and regulations can only be established when old ones are removed. During the process of struggle-criticism-transformation in the Great Proletarian Cultural Revolution, we criticized the revisionist line of enterprise management symbolized in "running the factory by experts," "material incentive," and "supervision, control, and suppression"; and at the same time, we gave fuller support to the spirit of the "Anshan Steel Constitution." Compared with the situation prior to the Great Proletarian Cultural Revolution, basic systems in socialist enterprises such as the unified leadership of the Party, the system of democratic centralism, cadres participating in labor, workers participating in management, cadres, technicians and workers forming a three-in-one combination, and so forth have all made great progress. The system of the masses studying works of Marx, Lenin, and Chairman Mao has been universally set up, which makes the enterprises more politicized than ever. All this demonstrates that with the drastic destruction and construction during the Great Proletarian Cultural Revolution, the management of our enterprises has been greatly strengthened, which provides a more favorable condition for the rapid development of production.

Once the rules and regulations are laid down, they should have relative stability and be taken seriously. We must not repudiate them lightly, especially in the case of regulations reflecting the objective laws of production. If they are violated at will, the violation will cause grave damage to production. However, production struggle, class struggle, and scientific experiment continuously move forward, and man's cognition of objective laws is also heightened step by step. Limited by various conditions, rules and regulations previously formulated will wholly or partially get out of step with reality and wholly or partially fall short of the requirements of the masses. This is a common phenomenon. Some regulations are correct and rational at a given time or under given conditions but become incorrect and irrational when the time and conditions change. And it is possible that things which once benefit the stimulation of mass initiative and serve as an impetus to the expansion of the productive forces may one day stand in the way of mass initiative and the productive forces. Therefore, we must constantly and consciously readjust the existing rules and regulations and make them fit in with the development of revolution and production. To regard regulations as unchangeable once they are laid down will stalemate their reform and revisions, which is very harmful. In the factories there frequently emerge some phenomena which are "rational but illegal, or legal but irrational."

There are things created or innovated by the masses and beneficial to production but regarded as illegal or out of keeping with existing regulations. To conduct business in accordance with old rules and regulations is legal, though it only brings about fewer, slower, inferior, and expensive results. Such strange situations often spring up when the reform of regulations comes to a standstill.

The smashing of old rules and regulations and the setting up of new ones is a process of struggle. Old ideology upholds hackneyed rules and regulations, which in turn become evidence justifying old ideology. Without eliminating the old and bringing forth the new in ideology there can be no discarding of the old and setting up of the new. Influenced by the revisionist line, all kinds of nonproletarian thoughts such as bureaucratism, departure from the masses, separation from labor, ignoring reality, slighting the creativity of the masses, the philosophy of being a slave to foreigners and worshiping things foreign, and so forth often find their expression in the management of our enterprises. And under certain conditions, things criticized during the Great Proletarian Cultural Revolution may crop up again in disguised form. There are people who do not assume a responsible attitude or who are afraid of taking responsibilities. They tend to conduct business according to regulations so that they can be justified by rules and formalities if something goes wrong. It is their belief that the more regulations the better, the more stamps and signatures the safer. If we let such erroneous ideas go unchecked, it will be difficult for us to eliminate old and set up new systems on the right track. Therefore, in the whole process of reforming irrational rules and regulations, we must pay attention to the struggle in the ideological sphere and grasp well people's education concerning thought and political line, ceaselessly criticizing revisionism and the bourgeois world outlook. This has become a most essential requirment for systems reform. We must particularly focus our attention on Lin Piao's reactionary program of "cultivating oneself and restoring the rites," criticizing the expressions of Lin Piao's revisionist line in all respects, including regulations in the enterprises, so that we can eliminate all its remnant poison.

In the final analysis, the smashing of old and setting up of new systems is a question of how to run our affairs in conformity with the objective law. We must adhere consistently to the principle of "arousing the masses fully, with everything undergoing experimentation." (2) The practice of the broad masses is the only criterion for judging the rationality of regulations. As to which regulations are to be abolished and which instituted, the masses are the most qualified to decide. We must persist in the mass line of "from the masses, to the masses," rely on the masses, and engage in mass movements in order to bring into full play the energy, wisdom, and creativeness of the masses. We must constantly mobilize the masses to expose contradictions and rely on them to resolve the contradictions. As our more than two decades of experience in practice has shown, the aforementioned is the only approach for revising rules and regulations. Pursuing this path, the systems in our enterprises can be continually improved and forged into a mighty weapon for enhancing productive forces and consolidating and bettering socialist production relations.

Notes

1) "Hsin min-chu-chu-i lun" [On New Democracy], Mao Tse-tung hsüan-chi [Selected Works of Mao Tse-tung], Vol. 2, p. 655.

2) A quotation of Chairman Mao, reprinted from Hung-ch'i [Red Flag], No. 11, 1959.

6

Discipline Must Be Established on the Basis of the Masses' Consciousness

Wu Yüeh-hua
(Hu-chiang Engineering Plant)

"Strengthen discipline, and the revolution is invincible." (1) Discipline ensures the implementation of the political line; hence it is a prerequisite for the victory of the revolution. To carry on production effectively in a socialist enterprise, we need a revolutionary discipline. But what kind of discipline is it, and how do we maintain it? This is a question we must straighten out first.

Marxism tells us that under different social systems discipline has an entirely different nature and the ways to maintain it also vary. Lenin pointed out: "The system of serfdom depends on the clubs to maintain the organization of society's labor, ... capitalism relies on hunger to maintain the organization of society's labor, ... communism (its first stage being socialism) maintains the organization of society's labor through the voluntary and conscious discipline of the laboring masses who have ridded themselves of the landlords' and capitalists' oppression." (2) The three types of discipline in the three social orders reflect in depth the class characters of the disciplines and mirror the different relations among people in the different social systems. In the serf and capitalist societies, landlords and capitalists formulate their discipline for the exploitation and oppression of the laboring people and the suppression of

---

Wu Yüeh-hua, "Chi-lü yao chien-li tsai ch'ün-chung ti tzu-chüeh-hsing shang."

their resistance. Their ways of maintaining discipline have to be compulsory and arbitrary, and their reactionary discipline is bound to arouse resistance among the masses of workers and peasants.

Socialist society has established socialist public ownership of the means of production, and discipline in socialist enterprises has also undergone a fundamental change. For the few exploiters, discipline is a weapon forcing them to accept socialist reform. As for the broad masses of workers and peasants, it is an important measure for correctly handling contradictions among the people, mobilizing socialist enthusiasm, developing socialist production with greater, faster, better, and more economical results, and for creating the conditions to eliminate all classes and erase all the differences among them. In a socialist industrial enterprise, the worker masses are the masters of the factory. Labor has become a glorious career, and fulfilling the task assigned by the state has become the broad masses of workers' own demand. Hence, it is natural for them to voluntarily observe revolutionary discipline, which is an expression of the superiority of the socialist system. The task of managing a socialist enterprise simply requires giving full play to the superiority of the socialist system. It means relying on the broad masses of workers, arousing their sense of duty as masters of their own affairs, and bringing forth their enthusiasm for socialism in order to push forward the development of both revolution and production. Thus, although the rules and regulations are definitely binding on each producer, this binding power can only really be effective when it is based on the consciousness of the masses. To implement the regulations merely by administrative coercion frequently will not work. Lin Piao advocated, "One has to implement not only the portion of the Chairman's directives which one comprehends, but also the portion which one does not understand." Lin's idea was nothing but a replica of what Confucius once said, "If you want to lead people to work for you, you should not let them have a great deal of knowledge." Prior to the Great Proletarian Cultural Revolution, some units, influenced by the revisionist line of Liu Shao-ch'i and Lin Piao, had no faith in arousing the workers' consciousness. They practiced the so-called "leadership instituting the rules, administrative staff implementing the rules, and the masses observing the rules," exercising "supervision, control, and suppression" over the workers. Rules and regulations formulated under these circumstances failed to reflect correctly the socialist production relations and the superiority of the socialist system. This handicapped the development of production. The contents of certain rules, such as the system of quality inspection and regulations for operation, might correspond to the practical requirements of production; but as they were not founded on a mass basis, they too failed to become the voluntary behavior of the masses. Since the Cultural Revolution, many units, guided by Chairman Mao's revolutionary line, have mobilized the masses to stage revolutionary mass criticism. In this way, they have deliniated the two lines of management, summed up the experience of production, reformed irrational rules and regulations, and set up rational ones. And the masses have also greatly enhanced their consciousness of observing revolutionary discipline.

In socialist society, "the people enjoy extensive democracy and freedom, but at the same time, they have to keep within the bounds of socialist discipline." (3) The broad masses are fully aware that socialist discipline is entirely different from the discipline enforced by the exploiting classes. They consciously regard the observance of socialist discipline, as well as rational regulations, as a necessity in the drive to grasp revolution and promote production. In this way, their enthusiasm and creative spirit are further brought into play, and production is propelled forward at great speed. Chairman Mao has pointed out, "Unless the masses are conscious and willing, any kind of work that requires their participation will turn out to be a mere formality and will fail." (4) Only when socialist discipline and socialist regulations strike root among the masses and become their conscious behavior can Chairman Mao's revolutionary line be ensured of implementation.

As a matter of fact, the masses do not all have the same

level of socialist awareness. Owing to the erosion of bourgeois thinking, a small number of workers may not have a high level of class consciousness, and they may demand freedom to the neglect of discipline. What is the correct attitude we should adopt regarding this problem?

The socialist consciousness of the proletariat has never arisen spontaneously. It grows out of the leadership of the Party and education in Marxism-Leninism-Mao Tsetung Thought. The fact that there is still a small number of workers who do not have a high level of consciousness demonstrates the need for strengthening the Party's ideological and political work. By conducting thorough and meticulous education in socialism, we will awaken their class awareness, help them acquire a correct understanding of the dialectical relation between freedom and discipline as well as of the significance of socialist discipline. When they come to know that the observance of socialist discipline has important bearing on the revolutionary cause of the proletariat, they will consciously keep themselves within the bounds of socialist discipline. "Our discipline is founded on the basis of consciousness. This is the fruition of our Party's leadership and education." (5) It is likely that there may be some people who do not give in for the time being. However, if we distinguish between the two different types of contradictions and resolve the contradictions among the people by sticking to the formula of unity-criticism-unity, we will be able to bring into play the socialist initiative of the broad masses and create a political situation in which there are both centralism and democracy, both discipline and freedom, both unity of will and personal ease of mind and liveliness. If we shut our eyes to the majority of the masses and only see the shortcomings of a small number of persons, we will fail to perceive in essence the mass initiative for socialism. And when some relaxation in discipline appears, if we do not focus our effort on political and ideological work but resort to rules and regulations for a solution, or even go so far as to indulge in the implementation of irrational regulations, we will never be able to bring about a political situation with ease of mind and liveliness as required.

As for those very few who have made repeated gross violations of discipline and do not repent after education, it is necessary to couple serious criticism with disciplinary measures to correct them. However, these measures can become effective only when discipline is based on the consciousness of the majority.

The Political Report to the Tenth National Party Congress pointed out, "The basic experience learned from our socialist construction during more than two decades is to rely on the masses." We must take this as our starting point in the formulation and implementation of regulations so that we can achieve the expected results. Furthermore, there are a lot of problems which cannot be solved by regulations alone. In the great undertaking of building socialism, the broad masses display great energy, working day and night without regard for rewards. They also give play to a revolutionary style of work, contending for the heavy loads and taking the initiative in coordination. All this cannot be attained by rules and regulations alone, but by exercising the Party's leadership and arming the masses with Marxism-Leninism-Mao Tsetung Thought. "Political work is the lifeblood of all economic work." Whenever the Party's ideological and political work is being strengthened and the masses' enthusiasm for socialism is being brought into full play, our enterprises will be full of vigor, and our undertakings will thrive. Whenever the Party's political and ideological work is being weakened and the socialist initiative of the masses is being held down, the management of our enterprises will deviate from the socialist orientation, and our undertakings will suffer a setback. This is an historical experience we should always bear in mind.

Notes

1) Quotation from Chairman Mao, reprinted from Hung-ch'i [Red Flag], 1967, No. 3.

2) "The Great Creation," Complete Works of Lenin, Vol. 29, p. 381.

3) "Kuan-yü cheng-ch'üeh ch'u-li jen-min nei-pu mao-tun ti wen-t'i" [On the Correct Handling of Contradictions among

the People], Mao Tse-tung chu-tso hsüan-tu [Selected Readings of Mao Tse-tung's Works], Anthology A, Jen-min ch'u-pan-she, 1966, p. 332.

4) "Wen-hua kung-tso chung ti t'ung-i chan-hsien" [The United Front in Cultural Work], Mao Tse-tung hsüan-chi [Selected Works of Mao Tse-tung], Vol. 3, p. 913.

5) Quotation from Chairman Mao, reprinted from the joint editorial of Jen-min jih-pao [People's Daily], Hung-ch'i [Red Flag], and Chieh-fang-chün pao [Liberation Army News], August 1, 1972.

7

The Big-Character Poster Is a Weapon for Mass Participation in Management

Ts'ao Pao-mei

In our socialist industrial enterprises, the worker masses often use the big-character poster as a medium to put forward their opinions and suggestions concerning the problems of enterprise management to the leaders. You put up a poster, and I follow suit. With more people taking part, contention abounds. The enterprises are seething with enthusiasm, and the masses are dashing forward with great energy. Spurred on by the posters, many age-old problems are quickly solved with the backing of the masses and the leadership's concern. During the Great Proletarian Cultural Revolution and the Campaign to Criticize Lin Piao and Rectify the Style of Work, and especially in the current struggle to criticize Lin Piao and Confucius, more and more leading cadres of industrial enterprises have further elevated their cognition of the role of the big-character poster and have voluntarily taken it to be a mighty weapon for elucidating the political line, disclosing contradiction, gauging discrepancy, expediting transformation, and strengthening business management by relying on the workers.

Chairman Mao teaches us: "The big-character poster is an extremely useful new weapon. It can be used in cities, villages, factories, cooperatives, shops, government organs, schools, army units, and streets; in short, in all the places where there are

---

Ts'ao Pao-mei, "Ta-tzu-pao shih ch'ün-chung ts'an-chia kuan-li ti wu-ch'i."

masses. It has been used everywhere and should be used forever." (1) In mobilizing the masses to participate in enterprise management, the big-character poster also serves as "an extremely useful weapon," playing a very important role.

Revolutionary wall-posters can arouse the socialist enthusiasm of the masses widely for participating in management. Since the Great Proletarian Cultural Revolution, the mass participation in the management of industrial enterprises, in both its content and form, has made great progress. Representatives from the worker masses have become members of revolutionary committees at various levels in factories. This has notably aroused the initiative and creativity of the vast masses and has fostered the revolutionary spirit of the worker masses as masters of their own affairs. It has further improved the relations among men in production within the enterprise itself and has helped develop socialist production with greater, faster, better, and more economical results. However, those workers who directly participate in the leadership at various levels in a factory are, after all, limited in number. Mass management, as well as worker masses assuming leadership in an enterprise, does not mean that every worker should occupy a leading post. The decisive factor is how to develop democracy to the fullest extent and enable every worker to have a say in the management of the enterprise as a whole. The broad masses take delight in reading and talking about the big-character poster. It is a good medium for fostering democracy. Everybody can write a big-character poster and put it up at any time, regardless of form or length. If the worker masses have any opinions or suggestions regarding issues of management, they may state them directly using the wall-posters. Thus, they provide a possibility for every worker to take a part in managing his enterprise. Making full use of the weapon of the big-character poster will create an even wider mass basis for mass participation in management and workers assuming leadership in their enterprises.

Our country is a socialist state of proletarian dictatorship. The working class is the master of our country, and workers have the right to exercise revolutionary supervision over cadres of different ranks in our Party and the state. And the revolutionary wall-poster is a mighty weapon for the worker masses to fully exercise their revolutionary supervision. The management of socialist enterprises does not grow spontaneously. It takes shape through the repeated struggle between the two classes, two roads, and two lines. In their attempt to restore capitalism, the bourgeoisie and its agents always try to guide enterprise management down the vicious road of revisionism. Some of our comrades know little about Marxism and do not rely on the masses. They frequently fail to distinguish between Marxism and revisionism and to differentiate between socialism and capitalism. They are likely to judge and deal with the contradictions and problems in their work from a metaphysical point of view. When the dynamic mass movement makes an assault on the outdated rules and regulations, some people are there "sticking to antiquity," and when the broad masses further improve the new regulations, they are there advocating "following the old rules." They confuse the regulations formulated under the guidance of the proletarian revolutionary line with those laid down when the revisionist line interferes. When the state requires the industrial enterprises to turn out more products, some people keep their eye on the quantity and value of the output and ignore the quality of their products; when the state demands the improvement of quality, they lower quantity and raise the costs of production. Thus, they sever the two aspects of production which are originally closely connected. Such ideological trends may sometimes take the wind out of some people and affect the consistent implementation of Chairman Mao's revolutionary line, causing damage to both revolution and production. This is a reflection of class struggle and the two-line struggle in real life. In dealing with the struggle between the two classes, two lines, and two roads as expressed in enterprise management, we must not only make a strict distinction between the two entirely different types of contradictions, but must also conduct criticism and struggle against all kinds of erroneous thought. The big-character poster is definitely a powerful weapon in the struggle against all mistaken ideas. The wall-posters make public the existing contradictions and invite everyone's participation in deliberating, judging, and criticizing them. Usually when a few wall-posters are put up, one poster will be followed by ten more, and ten will be followed by a hundred. In this way, they will soon grow into a strong revolutionary force making a fierce assault on the various erroneous views. Confronting the big-character posters, things with a revisionist brand can no longer retain their foothold, comrades who entertain wrong ideas become sober-minded, and those age-old problems cannot drag on unsolved forever. Consequently, the revolutionary torrent of the proletariat will rapidly beat back the reverse current of the bourgeoisie and constantly push our undertakings forward in the socialist direction.

Some comrades are not quite used to managing their enterprises through the medium of big-character posters. They tend to regard it as a good sign if no wall-posters are put up in their units. Whenever they see a few posters being stuck to the wall, they become panic-stricken and think the situation is bad. They are afraid that big-character posters might make a mess of the "normal order" in their management. But, in fact, realities often run contrary to what they expect. When the worker masses put up their revolutionary wall-posters, they change the dreary and deathly silent situation prevailing in their units and bring about a political situation filled with vigor and liveliness.

"Management is also socialist education." To do a good job in the management of socialist enterprises is, in fact, to conduct revolution in the superstructure, including the sphere of ideology. In order to press socialist revolution and the undertakings of socialist construction forward, it is a must for the proletariat to use the weapon of the big-character poster and struggle against all kinds of erroneous views. All mistakes must be exposed and criticized. Needless to say, such criticism should be made by "applying the dialectical method with great effort," and "what is needed is scientific analysis and convincing argument." (2) Hence it is groundless to assume that when the masses put up posters it is a sign of a bad situation and to even go so far as to exclude the use of wall-posters from enterprise management. The masses write wall-posters to disclose problems existing in management, their objective being to adhere to truth and rectify mistakes. The more of this kind of wall-posters that come up, the more concern the broad masses will show for management. It is a sign of a good situation and a matter to be delighted in. Contradictions can only be resolved when they are brought to light. For fear of the wall-posters written by the masses, some people do not actively guide the masses in uncovering the contradictions but cover them up unresolved. This so-called "normal order" of theirs is actually abnormal. It will not benefit mass mobilization and will constitute a barrier to the struggle the proletariat launches against the capitalists. Everything in this world is in motion, and there is no such thing as a static "order" in management. To congeal management work means to cease progress. We must mobilize the masses to bring to light all contradictions and solve them constantly, our objective being to create a dynamic and lively political situation. Only when we have grasped the law that things develop through struggle can we ceaselessly propel our work forward; and while watching a certain major tendency, we should keep our sight on an alternative tendency that might be concealed.

The key to fully bringing into play the role of the big-character poster in managing socialist enterprises lies with the leadership. We must stand with the proletariat and, guided by the Party's basic line, extend warm support to the revolutionary mass movement, encouraging the masses to use the mighty weapon of wall-posters. In the current struggle to criticize Lin Piao and Confucius, it is especially necessary to deeply criticize the precept of "cultivating oneself and returning to the rites" as advocated by Lin Piao. Through the medium of wall-posters, we must conduct criticism regarding the major issues related to class struggle and the two-line struggle in real life. In this way, we can continuously improve socialist production relations and their superstructure in line with the orientation pointed out by Chairman Mao, expedite the consolidation of the socialist economic base, and boost the productive forces immensely.

Notes

1) "Chieh-shao i ke he-tso-she" [Introducing a Cooperative], Mao Tse-tung chu-tso hsüan-tu [Selected Readings of Mao Tse-tung's Works], Anthology A, Jen-min ch'u-pan-she, 1966, p. 381.

2) "Kuan-yü cheng-ch'üeh ch'u-li jen-min nei-pu mao-tun te wen-t'i" [On the Correct Handling of Contradictions among the People], Mao Tse-tung chu-tso hsüan-tu, Anthology A, 1966, p. 354.

8

Adhere to the Socialist Principle of Economic Accounting

Tan Hsi

Chairman Mao teaches us: "Any economic undertaking in socialist society must pay attention to making the fullest possible use of the labor force and equipment. It must do its utmost to improve labor organization, renovate management, raise labor productivity, and economize as much as possible on manpower and material resources. It must also launch labor emulation and practice economic accounting." (1) Economic accounting is one of the major contents in the management of socialist enterprises. To do it well is of great importance to a socialist enterprise in its effort to implement the Party's General Line for Building Socialism and carrying out the policy of running the enterprise through diligence and frugality.

According to the popular explanation, economic accounting is keeping accounts and preparing accounts to record, calculate, analyze, and compare the consumption and yields of labor in the course of production. Calculating a product's output, variety, quality, and consumption of material is called calculation in kind, and calculating a product's output value, production cost, profit, and capital turnover is termed calculation in value. We must do a good job of economic accounting and strive to achieve greater, faster, better, and more economical results in developing socialist production with the least possible funds,

---

Tan Hsi, "Chien-ch'ih ching-chi he-suan ti she-hui-chu-i yüan-tse."

manpower, and material resources. This will facilitate the ceaseless consolidation and improvement of socialist production relations, that is, the economic base of the proletarian dictatorship.

To do economic accounting well in a socialist enterprise, it is necessary to set up and improve a variety of administrative systems governing planning, technology, labor, material supply, and financial affairs. It is also imperative to do a good job in controlling quotas, recording primary data, maintaining good statistics, and measuring quantity. Obviously, economic accounting is fairly meticulous and complicated work, embracing a great deal of business transactions and calculations. However, economic accounting is not just simple addition, subtraction, multiplication, and division in a purely technical sense. How to settle an account, which account is rational and which one is not — all lead to the question of whether it is in conformity with the socialist principle.

What is the socialist principle of economic accounting? It is that economic accounting in a socialist enterprise must subordinate itself to the objective of socialist production. The objective of socialist production is to meet the ever-growing requirements of the socialist state and the broad masses of working people. It aims at strengthening and developing the economic base of socialism, consolidating the proletarian dictatorship, and creating the conditions for the realization of communism. To be in conformity with the objective of socialist production is to be in keeping with the principle of socialism. But to attain this there must be a process of struggle.

When a socialist enterprise manufactures a certain product, the amount of steel, electricity, and other materials consumed may be figured out through calculation in kind. Based on the calculation, we can tell whether the material consumption is economical or wasteful so that necessary measures can be taken to prevent waste and ensure frugality. However, calculation in kind in socialist society is expressed through the form of calculation in value, including in the figuring how much value of output is produced, how much the cost is, how much profit is earned, and so forth. To conduct economic accounting through the medium of value is still indispensable in socialist society. However, value is an economic category molded under the conditions of commodity economy. Although the category of value in a socialist society reflects the socialist production relations, it is a category subordinate to commodity economy. Invariably, it retains the remnants and traces left over from the old society. The existence of the category of value marks the existence of commodity production. And the existence of commodity production manifests the contradiction between the value and the use value of a commodity. Thus, given a certain condition, it is possible for the bourgeoisie and its agents inside the Party to avail themselves of this contradiction to sabotage socialist construction and lead socialist economy down the vicious road of capitalism. Influenced by bourgeois ideas of management and the revisionist line enforced by Liu Shao-ch'i and Lin Piao which called for "the greater the profit, the larger is the investment; the smaller the profit, the smaller is the investment; and there will be no investment where there is no profit," some enterprises fail to produce according to the needs of the state and the people. They tend to turn out more products of high value and big profit and manufacture less of those with low value and small profit and even blindly seek value of output and profit. Chasing one-sidedly after [exchange] value to the neglect of use-value is an erroneous practice which runs counter to the objective of socialist production.

Under the influence of bourgeois ideas of management, the economic accounting in an enterprise may for a time turn out products of high value at low cost with big profits and quick capital turnover. It may give the impression that the enterprise has done a fairly good job of economic accounting. But in fact it deviates from the objective of socialist production, being short on supplies of goods which the state and the people need, while being long on supplies of goods which the state and the people do not need. Consequently, neither the targets fixed in exchange value nor the targets fixed in use-value can be fulfilled. This will certainly damage the national economic plan and entail waste in the productive forces of the society. From this it can be seen that economic accounting is by no means just a matter of bookkeeping; it reflects the serious struggle between the two ideologies and two roads of socialism and capitalism. To adhere to the socialist principle of economic accounting, it is necessary to correctly understand and handle the contradictions and struggles emerging in the process of economic accounting. And to achieve this, we must take the Party's basic line as the key link, drawing a clear distinction between the right and the wrong line, resolutely struggling against the ideologies and influences of the revisionists and capitalists, and consciously working in accordance with the directions, policies, and unified plans laid down by the Party and the state in order to obtain an overall fulfillment of the targets planned by the state. Only in this way can we achieve the objectives of socialist production.

In a socialist society, the economic relations among socialist enterprises must also be subordinated to the objective of socialist production. The very nature of socialist public ownership of the means of production provides a potential for all enterprises to conduct extensive coordination and cooperation among themselves. With the same goal, all enterprises should support and help each other. However, all socialist enterprises are relatively independent units for economic accounting, and business transactions among them must be reflected by their accounts. The relationship of economic accounting among enterprises benefits the strengthening of the sense of duty of each enterprise with respect to enterprise management. Therefore, this relationship must be adhered to. On the other hand, the contradictions of economic interests among the enterprises may, under certain conditions, affect the coordination and cooperation among them. Suppose there is a factory specializing in producing spare parts and mechanical equipment. With appropriate innovation and improvement of its products, it will help promote immensely the labor productivity of the factories which use its spare parts and mechanical equipment. As for the factory itself, during the process of innovating and improving its products, it temporarily may have to sustain higher costs of production and lower labor productivity. What should we do to resolve this contradiction?

All socialist enterprises are components of a unified socialist economy. They have their basic common interests, and there is no fundamental clash of interests among them. This is entirely different from the relationship of mutual contending and benefiting oneself at the expense of others that prevails among the capitalist enterprises. Thanks to this nature, socialist economy does not practice economic accounting within the scope of a single enterprise only but practices it in the sphere of the society as a whole. An enterprise is a part, and society is the whole. The economic accounting of an individual enterprise should be subordinated to the economic accounting of the whole society; that is to say, every individual enterprise should start from the common interests of the national economy and subordinate its partial interests to those of the whole. Anything which is of advantage to the production of the society as a whole, though it may entail temporary loss to a single enterprise, should be performed with enthusiasm, and the departments concerned should give their active support. Nevertheless, as each enterprise must conduct independent calculations, accounts must be kept and settled among the enterprises. Each enterprise should figure out its own gains and losses. But the primary concern is mutual assistance and cooperation and the cultivation of the communist style of work. Relinquishing coordination and cooperation, discarding the communist style of work, and placing partial interests of individual enterprises above the common interests of the whole society, such tendencies, if developed and unchecked, would invariably lead to degeneration of the socialist enterprises. What is involved here is an acute struggle between the two classes, two roads, and two lines regarding the interrelations of socialist enterprises. It is only by cultivating the communist style and correctly handling and continually improving the relations between the enterprises according to the socialist principle that we can fully develop the superiority of the socialist system, boost socialist production with greater, faster, better, and more economical results, and persist in the socialist orientation of the enterprises.

Economic accounting in the socialist enterprise reflects socialist production relations and will certainly enlist the support and approval of the broad masses. The masses are fighters on the front line of production, and they are the ones who have the most say about issues of how to economize manpower, funds, and material resources in promoting socialist production with greater, faster, better, and more economical results. Many industrial enterprises have instituted a cost-accounting system by section or squad, which is also a form of conducting enterprise accounting by the masses. Only by relying on the masses and keeping close ties with the masses can the financial personnel find out the various problems in management and administration work, fully develop their expertise, and with the masses, increasingly improve their practice of economic accounting.

Note

1) "'Chen-ju ch'ü Li-tzu-yüan nung-yeh sheng-ch'an ho-tso-she chieh-yüeh sheng-ch'an fei yung te ching-yen' i wen an-yü" [An Introduction to "Experience of Li-tzu-yüan Agricultural Cooperative of Chen-ju District in Economizing on Costs of Production], Chung-kuo nung-ts'un te she-hui chu-i kao-ch'ao [The Socialist Upsurge in China's Countryside], Vol. 2, p. 768.

9

Set up an Administrative Structure That Forges Close Ties with the Masses

Kung Ching
(Department of Political Economy, Futan University)

To establish in industrial enterprises a revolutionized administrative structure which forges close ties with the masses is a major element in strengthening enterprise management. It will play an important role in ensuring the Party's unified leadership, effectively organizing and mobilizing the enthusiasm of the broad masses for socialism as well as boosting socialist production.

Since the founding of our state, there has always existed a struggle between two lines and two ideologies over the issue of how to set up an administrative structure in industrial enterprises. A lot of experience, both positive and negative, has been accumulated in this respect. To establish a good administrative structure it is imperative to take the two-line struggle as the key link and earnestly sum up the experience so that we can get hold of the essence of administration and discover the laws governing it.

From the early days of the postliberation period to the beginning of the First Five-Year Plan, most factories, through democratic reform, eliminated capitalist administrative structures and rules such as the system of having foremen and supervisors, the system of searching the workers entering or

---

Kung Ching, "Chien-li i ke lien-hsi ch'ün-chung ti kuan-li chi-kou."

leaving a factory, and so forth. All these were intended for the oppression of the workers, and their extermination greatly enhanced the workers' revolutionary spirit of being masters of their own affairs. After 1953, many places introduced some foreign systems of administration without any modification. They instituted the revisionist system of "running the factory under one director" and set up enormous administrative structures, which seriously handicapped the workers' enthusiasm for socialism. In 1958, the worker masses rose to strike down these revisionist goods and began the dynamic and vigorous situation of the Great Leap Forward. In the years 1961 and 1962, because of Liu Shao-ch'i's revisionist line, administrative structures in some enterprises retrogressed to the old path of the minute divisions of labor and overlapping levels. Consequently, the administration divorced itself from the masses and impeded the development of production. During the Great Proletarian Cultural Revolution, the broad masses, guided by Chairman Mao's revolutionary line, rose once again to storm the rules and regulations shackling mass initiative and smash the overlapping structures divorced from the masses. Many industrial enterprises, under the leadership of revolutionary committees, have set up compact and unified command systems of production and have extensively realized the "three-in-one combination." The cadres there persistently take part in collective labor, forge close ties with the masses, and foster a vigorous revolutionary style of work. Administrative organs closely associated with the masses as such help promote both ideological and organizational revolutionization, bring into play the enthusiasm of the broad masses, and thus serve as a great impetus to the development of production.

Since liberation, the administrative organs have gone through a course of repeated progress and reverses. From this it can be seen that the setting up of administrative organs in the industrial enterprises is not routine work, but an acute and profound two-line struggle. From these rich historical experiences we have learned very deep lessons.

With regard to the issue of how to establish an administrative structure in the industrial enterprises, the primary requisite is to set a basic guiding thought. Chairman Mao teaches us: "To reform the state organs, the basic requirement is to maintain close contact with the masses." (1) Chairman Mao's brilliant directive is the basic guiding thought for the reformation of state organs. It is also the basic guiding thought for setting up administrative structures in our industrial enterprises.

The nature of our socialist enterprises determines that the administrative structures in the factories must facilitate association with the masses. This is a major feature that distinguishes socialist from capitalist and revisionist enterprises. The administrative structure in a capitalist enterprise can display a lot of variety, but the capitalists neither will nor can ever turn out an administrative structure which maintains ties with the masses. In their enterprises, the nature of the production relations is one of capitalists exploiting hired laborers. Administrative structures which are determined by this kind of production relations and are set up to uphold such relations cannot be anything but instruments by which the capitalists rule the workers. They are absolutely opposed to the workers. Contrary to the capitalist enterprises, socialist enterprises are founded on the socialist public ownership of the means of production. To rely on the conscious initiative of the worker masses for socialism is the essential approach to run a socialist enterprise well and to develop socialist production. Taking over the fallacy of Confucius and Mencius that "the mean men cannot be ruled without gentlemen," Lin Piao advocated the idea of "the sage and the dullard." His attempt was to thoroughly negate the fact that workers and other laboring people are the masters of socialist enterprises. The administrative organs of our socialist enterprises must take the opposite direction from the road followed by Lin Piao and Confucius and Mencius. We must forge close ties with the masses, "from the masses to the masses." Although administrations of different enterprises cannot be uniform because of differences in concrete conditions, they should all be beneficial to maintaining close contact with the masses. If there is any deviation from this, should one merely concentrate one's efforts on the forms and titles of enterprise administration, one would "not see the woods for the trees" and would lose direction.

How can the administrative structure of an enterprise provide free access to and maintain close ties with the masses? One of the most important factors for this is reliance on the participation of the toiling masses in enterprise management.

Chairman Mao has all along attached importance to the participation of the worker masses in enterprise management. He has often personally summed up and confirmed their experiences in management. In the "Anshan Steel Constitution" he has listed the worker masses' participation in management as a basic principle for running socialist enterprises well. Over the past two decades, guided by Chairman Mao's revolutionary line, many industrial enterprises have created various approaches relying on the worker masses for management and have scored great achievements. Revolutionary committees made up by the three-in-one combination came into being during the Great Proletarian Cultural Revolution. They further realized the principle of associating with the masses. As practice has shown, under the unified leadership of the Party, worker masses have directly participated in the administration of factories. They are "both officials and common folk." (2) As they are not divorced from productive labor, they can maintain direct and close ties with the broad masses. In this way, they can duly transmit the opinions and demands of the masses upward and also exercise mass supervision over all levels of leadership from the bottom to the top. Besides, they can also quickly pass down the tasks and policies of the Party and turn them into voluntary actions on the part of the masses. This provides the Party's leadership and administrative structures at different levels with a more extensive and solid mass basis and ensures that the leaders and administrative personnel in an enterprise will persist in the mass line and keep close contact with the masses.

Apart from the above, we must practice the principle of "maintaining fewer but crack troops and streamlining administration" when we set up administrative structures in our enterprises. Chairman Mao has taught us many times: We must "simplify organizational structure, reform irrational rules and regulations, and transfer office personnel down to the lower level." (3) We must also "break up overlapping administrative structures, practice the principle of maintaining fewer but crack troops and streamlining administration, and organize a revolutionized leading body which keeps close contact with the masses." (4) The idea that "with more people, work can be done better" should be understood in this connection: A good many tasks can only be done well by relying on the joint effort of the masses. With fewer and better administrative staff, their contacts with the masses will become closer, and work can surely be done well. Even if there are a great many administrative staff members, they are still a minority when compared with the broad masses. If they fail to keep contact with the masses and do not rely on the masses, they still cannot do the work well.

However, simplifying organizational structure does not mean merging organs and laying off personnel without discrimination. Simplification must be coupled with effectiveness, its objective being to keep close ties with the masses and to raise efficiency. When we have fewer but crack troops, everyone will actively assume responsibility and conscientiously do the things that must be done. Consequently, everything will be taken care of and nobody will stand idle. Owing to the rapid development of production and the gradual deepening of the drive of struggle-criticism-transformation, the structural layout in some enterprises will fail to keep pace with the new situation. It must be strengthened and readjusted in time in order to further consolidate the victorious result of simplification achieved during the Great Proletarian Cultural Revolution. We must not negate the revolutionary actions of the masses in assaulting the old administrative structures; nor should we revive without discrimination all the institutions and structures set up in the past.

In readjusting the administrative organs in our industrial enterprises, the common objective is to attain "simplification, unification, effectiveness, economy, and opposition to bureaucratism."(5) Generally speaking, attention must be paid to handling well the relationship between centralized and decentralized management, between coordination and division of labor. Taking the convenience of the masses as our starting point, we must pursue the principle of combining unified leadership with administration at different levels. We should not centralize everything when centralization is the word; nor should we decentralize everything if decentralization is stressed. Each functionary organ in an industrial enterprise must have a definite duty and a division of labor; but division of labor does not mean the division of everything with everyone hoeing only his own row. Ours are socialist enterprises, and we should emphasize mutual support and coordination with the same goal. Overstressing mutual restriction will result in squabbles if it is not handled well. In the final analysis, too much restriction will end up in restricting the masses, hampering the masses' enthusiasm for socialism. To exercise administration by relying on the so-called role of restriction is in essence to rule over the masses and not to rely on them. As a result, you cannot rule over the masses; nor can you rule them well. Without a revolutionary style of work and an attitude of wholeheartedly serving the people, even a rationalized administrative structure cannot achieve the aim of maintaining contact with the masses. Therefore, the leading cadres and administrative personnel must face the masses, face production, go deep into reality, conduct study and investigation, persistently take part in labor, and do a good job of ideological revolutionization.

Finally, it is also necessary to have a developing point of view when dealing with the establishment of administrative structures for industrial enterprises. Administrative structures of any kind are not unchangeable and they will evolve following the progress of revolution and production. Administrative structures conforming to revolution and production may, under given conditions, partially or completely grow out of line with revolution and production. And then it is necessary to readjust them. This is a dialectical process of growth and stagnation. When an organizational structure needs adjustments, the broad masses must be consulted and decisions should not be made by a few people behind closed doors. To depart from the mass line and set up administrative organs maintaining no contact with the masses is bound to meet mass opposition. And it is likely that after a few years the masses will rise again to attack those overstaffed administrative organs which maintain no ties with them. The broad masses stand on the forefront of the Three Great Revolutionary Movements of class struggle, production struggle, and scientific experiment. They have the best understanding of the real situation. They have clear ideas about what organs should be set up in their factories and how the organs should be staffed. It is only by fully mobilizing the masses and fostering democracy that administrative organs can be set up in keeping with reality and be brought into genuine association with the masses.

Notes

1) Reprinted from Jen-min jih-pao [People's Daily], March 30, 1968.

2) Quotation of Chairman Mao, reprinted from Jen-min jih-pao [People's Daily], June 8, 1967.

3) Reprinted from Hung-ch'i [Red Flag], 1968, No. 2.

4) Reprinted from Jen-min jih-pao [People's Daily], March 30, 1968.

5) "K'ang Jih shih-ch'i ti ching-chi wen-t'i ho ts'ai-cheng wen-t'i" [Economic and Finance Problems during the Anti-Japanese Period]. Mao Tse-tung hsüan-chi [Selected Works of Mao Tse-tung], Vol. 3, p. 850.

10

Bring into Full Play the Role of the Revolutionary Committees under the Leadership of the Party

Fu P'ei-tzu

The documents of the Tenth National Congress of the Party indicate that the Party committees at various levels should further strengthen the unified leadership of the Party and at the same time bring into full play the role of the revolutionary committees. Through study we are deeply aware that to conscientiously implement this directive in our socialist enterprises is the fundamental guarantee of running socialist business management well and consolidating the economic base of the proletarian dictatorship.

Socialist economy is based on public ownership. In the state enterprises, the means of production are owned by the proletariat and the working people. In the collective enterprises, the means of production are owned by collectivized working people. However, be it a state enterprise or a collective enterprise, they are all under the unified leadership of the Communist Party, the vanguard of the proletariat. These enterprises conduct productive activities and enterprise management in agreement with the interests of the proletariat and the vast working people. To depart from or weaken the Party's unified leadership is to lead socialist enterprises astray. Chairman Mao says: "Of the seven sectors — industry,

---

Fu P'ei-tzu, "Tsai tang ti ling-tao hsia fa-hui ke-wei-hui ti tso-yung."

agriculture, commerce, culture and education, the army, the government, and the Party — it is the Party that exercises overall leadership." (1) The Party must strengthen its unified leadership over all sectors of the socialist economy.

In what context can the unified leadership be regarded as strengthened in a socialist enterprise? We have plenty of experience and lessons deserving summation concerning this question. Before the Great Proletarian Cultural Revolution, comrades in some enterprises thought that to strengthen the Party's leadership was to monopolize all activities, big or small, by the Party organs. They would often pick up the sesame seeds and forget the melons, grasping trivial matters to the neglect of major issues. As a result, they lost the ability to distinguish between the right and the wrong lines and even went so far as to pursue the revisionist line. They not only failed to boost production but even led the enterprises down the vicious road of capitalism. The Political Report to the Tenth National Congress of the Party further summed up the experience of strengthening the Party's unified leadership and emphatically pointed out: "Quite a few Party committees are engrossed in daily routines and minor matters, paying no attention to major issues. This is very dangerous. If they do not change, they will inevitably go down the road of revisionism." To grasp major issues is to grasp the ideological and political line, persevering in implementing the Party's basic line and resolutely resisting the revisionist line so that the management work of our enterprises can proceed continuously in the socialist direction. This is the basic issue in bringing about the unified leadership of the Party.

At the same time as strengthening the Party's unified leadership, it is necessary to bring into full play the role of the revolutionary committees in the industrial enterprises. "The three-in-one revolutionary committee is a creation of the working class and the masses of people during the Cultural Revolution." (2) The revolutionary committee is a new thing which emerged during the Great Proletarian Cultural Revolution. In the storm of the "January Revolution" in 1967 when the revolutionary committee first appeared, our great leader Chairman Mao immediately backed and confirmed with wholehearted eagerness this great creation of the working class and the masses of people. Farsightedly he pointed out that "the revolutionary committee is good."

The reason why revolutionary committees are good is first of all that representatives of the worker masses participate in the leading bodies at various levels in the enterprise so that enterprise management can further embody the leadership of the working class. The participation of the worker masses in the revolutionary committees is a major organizational assurance for the Marxists and worker masses to grasp the leadership of the enterprises. Prior to the Great Proletarian Cultural Revolution, many enterprises had, in varying degrees, implemented the participation of workers in administration, setting up various systems such as the workers' congress, meetings analyzing economic activities, administration by squads and sections, and so forth, which had been useful. But as the worker masses had not maintained their leadership, some enterprises had for a time deviated from the socialist direction, and some even had their leadership usurped by a handful of villains. Since the Great Proletarian Cultural Revolution, our enterprises have undergone a profound change. The worker masses have chosen representatives to participate directly in the leading bodies at various levels in their enterprises. This is a new dimension in mass management. It has great significance for the consistent implementation of Chairman Mao's proletarian revolutionary line as well as for resisting the revisionist line. The broad worker masses fight on the forefront of the Three Great Revolutionary Movements of class struggle, production struggle, and scientific experiment. They best understand the Party's policy and are the most resolute in its implementation. They are the most capable in discerning the revisionist line, and they are the most forceful when fighting against it. The direct participation of representatives from the worker masses in leading bodies has made it possible for the masses to effectively take an active role in the overall work of their enterprises, assisting and supervising the cadres in their implementation of the Party's line. Take the drawing up of the production plan for example. In some enterprises in the past, a few cadres mapped out plans in the headquarters and brought these fixed plans to the masses for discussion. The worker masses commented: "This is consultation in form and arbitrariness in fact." Consequently, the cadres were unable to fully arouse the workers' enthusiasm for socialism. And as a few cadres regarded themselves as "wise" and entertained a blind faith in the "experts," they even prevented workers from having their correct proposals adopted. But things are quite different now that the worker masses have participated in the revolutionary committees. Take for instance the Shanghai No. 23 Radio Factory. At the beginning of 1973, when the revolutionary committee in the factory conducted study and discussion concerning the annual plan, those committee members who were not divorced from productive labor fully reflected the opinions of the masses and put forward many proposals for increasing production, practicing economy, and bringing out latent power. Quite a few times they vetoed the low plan targets suggested by the department of production, ending up by working out a production plan exceeding that of 1972 by 21 percent. The plan won the support of the masses, and as a matter of fact, it was fulfilled two months ahead of schedule, and the quality of the products was notably improved. The evolution of planning as noted above indicates that since the representatives of the worker masses have directly participated in the leadership of the factory, they have had more say over the major issues in the factory, and the status of the worker masses as masters of the factory has stood out more conspicuously than ever. Clearly it is entirely wrong to regard as negligible the direct participation of worker masses in the leadership over the factory.

With the participation of representatives from the worker masses, the revolutionary committees not only realize the leadership of the working class but also enable the leading body in an industrial enterprise to take root among the masses, providing the leading body with a reliable assurance of pursuing the mass line and forging close ties with the masses. Mass representatives in the revolutionary committees are generally not divorced from productive labor. They are "both officials and common folk," connected with the broad masses like flesh and blood. In this way, they can duly relay the opinions and requirements of the masses upward and simultaneously pass the general and specific policies of the Party downward, turning them into voluntary actions of the masses. Numerous facts have proved that the three-in-one revolutionary committees are superior in maintaining close ties with the masses, which is a powerful assurance for doing all kinds of work well and a major factor in strengthening the unified leadership of the Party. However, some people have the idea that with Party organs reestablished in the enterprises, the historical task of the revolutionary committee has been accomplished and that from now on what the revolutionary committee must do is to merely "hang up its signboard and stamp its name on the documents." Some people even hold that having the revolutionary committees debate problems discussed and decided by the Party organs is redundant. Thus, more problems would be directly decided by the Party organs and fewer meetings would be held by the revolutionary committees, resulting in turning the unified leadership of the Party into a monopoly and reducing the role of the revolutionary committees to a formality. In fact, neglecting the role of the revolutionary committees will invariably affect the links between the Party and the masses, being disadvantageous to revolutionizing the leading body as well as to strengthening the Party's leadership. To strengthen the unified leadership of the Party does not mean substituting Party organs for the revolutionary committee, which in fact cannot be replaced. It is only by bringing into full play the role of the revolutionary committees and paying attention to forging close ties with the masses through the revolutionary committee that the Party organ can really strengthen its unified leadership.

During the Great Proletarian Cultural Revolution, the broad masses founded the principle of combining the old, the middle-aged, and the young in the leading body. It provides favorable conditions for us to train, in accordance with the five requirements laid down by Chairman Mao, millions of successors to the cause of the proletarian revolution. The three-in-one revolutionary committee is the most useful for the upbringing and growth of new cadres. According to incomplete statistics, in the six years since the founding of the revolutionary committees, new cadres at various levels brought up from among the workers in some enterprises in Shanghai generally exceeded the total number of cadres promoted from among the workers during the seventeen years prior to the Great Proletarian Cultural Revolution. In some cases the ratio is more than double the previous figure. The development of new cadres from among the workers is a major result of the Cultural Revolution. Having taken leading posts in revolutionary committees at various levels, the new cadres assume heavier loads of responsibility and have more opportunities for tempering themselves. Besides, with the new and old cadres working side by side in the revolutionary committee, they learn from each other, overcoming their weaknesses by acquiring each other's strong points, with the old bringing up the new and the new urging the old onward. All this ensures organizationally the fulfillment of the important task of training successors to the proletarian revolutionary cause. Old cadres in many enterprises are aware of the responsibilities on their shoulders. They not only modestly learn from the new cadres but also enthusiastically show concern for their growth. This is in line with Chairman Mao's teaching that we should enable "the seniors to keep contact with the masses and the youths to be seasoned." (3) By bringing into full play the role of the three-in-one revolutionary committee, we can enable the ranks of our cadres to flourish, thus ensuring that there will be successors and rejuvenating our Party.

It is not an easy thing for the revolutionary committees to acquire a deep and solid mass foundation. The broad masses of workers and staff were dancing with joy when revolutionary committees were set up in their units. Therefore, we must wholeheartedly cherish the revolutionary committees, uphold, consolidate, and develop them. The revolutionary committee was a new thing which came into being during the Great Proletarian Cultural Revolution. Lin Piao and his like were dead set against all the newly emerging revolutionary things. In the struggle to criticize Lin Piao and Confucius, we must make a thorough repudiation of the various fallacious abuses which the Lin Piao anti-Party clique maliciously poured on the new socialist things so we can ensure that the revolutionary committees made up by the three-in-one combination of the young, the middle-aged, and the old will grow more sturdy and thrive. This is a major issue relating to the consolidation and development of the fruits of the Great Proletarian Cultural Revolution. It has an important bearing on how to do an earnest job of struggle-criticism-transformation in the industrial enterprises. By bringing into full play the role of revolutionary committees under the unified leadership of the Party, we can surely further socialist management and ensure that socialist enterprises will ceaselessly march forward along the track of the Party's basic line.

Notes

1) Reprinted from Chou En-lai, "Tsai Chung-kuo kung-ch'an-tang ti shih tz'u ch'üan kuo tai-piao hui shang ti pao-kao" [Report to the Tenth National Congress of the Communist Party of China].

2) Quotation of Chairman Mao, reprinted from Jen-min jih-pao [People's Daily], March 30, 1968.

3) Reprinted from Jen-min jih-pao [People's Daily], March 30, 1968.

Editors' Postscript

To run enterprise management well is a question about which the vast workers and cadres in the industrial enterprises are always concerned. However, in correctly handling enterprise management, one must study and have a good grasp of the principles of Marxist political economy, adhere consistently to the Party's basic line in our work, integrate theory with practice, and distinguish between the two lines in running our enterprises. To satisfy the need for study and discussion of problems in this connection, we compiled this pamphlet for everyone's reference. It contains the article entitled "On Enterprise Management" [T'an-t'an ch'i-yeh kuan-li] which was carried by the journal Hsüeh-hsi yü p'i-p'an [Study and Criticism], 1973, No. 4 [December 16, 1973, pp. 11-13] (the title has been changed to "Workers Are the Masters of Socialist Enterprises" in this book) and other articles dealing with enterprise management which appeared in the column entitled "Learn Something about Political Economy" [Hsüeh i-tien cheng-chih ching-chi hsüeh] of the Liberation Daily [Chieh-fang jih-pao] during July, August, and December 1973. These articles were written by comrades from some industrial enterprises and the departments concerned and were based on their study of theory, investigation, and research as well as the experience they have summed up. Minor revisions have been made in wording and phraseology when they were put into book form.

January 1974

V Two Documents on Workers' Participation in Management on the Shanghai Harbor Docks in the 1970s

Contents

1

Be the Masters of the Wharf, Not the Slaves of Tonnage

A Revolutionary Big-Character Poster from the Workers of the No. 5 Loading and Unloading District of the Shanghai Harbor Affairs Bureau

"People's Daily" Editor's Note

This revolutionary big-character poster from workers of the No. 5 loading and unloading district of the Shanghai Harbor Affairs Bureau lays hold of the current vital problems in enterprise management. It carries universal realistic significance.

What does a socialist enterprise rely on after all to arouse mass activism and to step up production? This question is not a minor but a major issue. The big-character poster sounds a bell of warning to us: If the Party committee does not grasp major issues, those things criticized in the Great Cultural Revolution may appear once again and there is still a possibility for socialist enterprises to step onto the revisionist road!

The workers of the No. 5 district of the Shanghai Harbor Affairs Bureau aptly say: We must not only take care of production but especially take care of the line.

"Yao tang ma-t'ou ti chu-jen, pu-tso tun-wei ti nu-li — Shang-hai kang wu-chü ti-wu chuang-hsieh ch'ü kung-jen i-chang ko-ming ta-tzu pao." Jen-min jih-pao [People's Daily], February 1, 1974. This translation is taken, with minor editorial revisions, from SCMP, No. 5561 (February 27, 1974), 88-91

> The leading comrades of all enterprises must doggedly put proletarian politics in command and humbly receive the supervision of the worker masses. They must arouse the worker masses to help the leadership keep a proper grip on the line, grasp revolution and promote production, so that our enterprises can at all times advance along Chairman Mao's revolutionary line.

* * *

Chairman Mao teaches us, "The people, and the people alone, are the motive force in the making of world history." "A fundamental communist rule is to place direct reliance on the broad masses of revolutionary people." One important experience of the Yang-shu-p'u Loading and Unloading Station is to take wharf workers as the masters of the wharf and wholeheartedly rely on the broad masses of workers. The leadership of our district always talks about relying on the masses, but the masses are forgotten when work is carried out. Herein lies the cause of not much change in the features of our district over the past few years. The leadership has looked upon the workers not as masters of the wharf but as slaves of tonnage. This is a reflection of the revisionist enterprise-operation line in our district.

1. Two Different Kinds of Reliance Reflect Two Different Lines

What should be relied upon to fulfill state plans? The experience of the Yan-shu-p'u Loading and Unloading Station is to arm the worker masses with Marxism-Leninism-Mao Tsetung Thought and fully trust and rely upon the broad masses of workers. With the leadership relying on them, the workers raise their consciousness as masters of the house. The broad masses of workers glory in suffering and take contributing a bit more to the revolution as conscious action. But the leadership of our district relies not on political-ideological work to arouse the masses but on "incentives" and on pressure. It can often be heard that the leadership of the team mobilizes the workers in this way: "Finish the job and be free." "Take your bath after fulfilling the plan." Sometimes, when the loading and unloading pace slows down a bit, the leadership applies pressure, saying, "You people cannot practice anarchism!" To fulfill an assignment, to "take the shortcut" with all ways and means. They rely not on workers' activism but on "pressing in tonnage" and "overloading." Why has our district failed to curb working against regulations? The key lies in that the leadership has not correctly implemented the line.

2. Two Different Things in Command Reflect Two Different Lines

How should we handle the relations between revolution and production? The experience of the Yang-shu-p'u Loading and Unloading Station is that we must put proletarian politics in command, keep a proper grip on the revolution in the superstructure and on the transformation of production relations, and give a boost to the development of productive forces. However, the leadership of our district adopts a "purely military viewpoint" and puts "tonnage in command." It forgets what is primary when attention is paid to tonnage. It forgets what line is taken when attention is paid to opening up several routes.

When loading rice on one occasion, to ensure the quality of rice loading by other squads, a squad made arrangements for preparatory work and thus caused some delay in rice-loading time. At the squad-level meeting the following day, the leadership cited the squad credited with high tonnage but mentioned not a word about that squad which carried forward the style of work. The masses said indignantly, "Style or no style, tonnage is all that counts!" "A lofty style does not count as much as a high tonnage!"

To pursue tonnage, the leadership does not think far ahead and does not divert some people toward mechanization. Instead, it rests content with the manual hauling of pig iron piece by piece. To bring about the early mechanization of the harbor, a worker suggested the adoption of an iron-handling machine fitted with a lotus-type of magnetic ladle (荷花抓斗式). Hearing this, the team leader voiced no support but put on a hard expression and chided him, saying, "You are dreaming!" Mass activism for transforming the outlook of the harbor was thus repressed by heavy tonnage.

3. Two Different Starting Points Reflect Two Different Lines

In fulfilling a plan, should we just keep an eye on our own department or a part thereof, or take the whole situation into consideration and proceed from coordination as in a "chess game"? The experience of the Yang-shu-p'u Loading and Unloading Station is that though we are charged with different types of work, our thoughts must be linked together like a chain, and we must properly handle the relations between the loads on both sides of a shoulder-carrying pole, act in coordination and fight in concert. However, the leadership of our district is mindful only of itself but not of others, the part but not the whole. At times there even appears the strange phenomenon of a slowdown in the general pace of loading and unloading despite the overfulfillment of tonnage targets by some squads. To hurry through the unloading of weighty goods, some squads even leave the light pieces buried beneath, thus "leaving behind a mound of earth in the course of sinking a well." They themselves claim a higher tonnage, but others are required to duplicate the same job by digging up the buried light pieces, thus causing the pace of loading and unloading to slow down. For the sake of convenience, some squads even just throw to one side those floor cushion boards, and as a result the next shift has to take the trouble of removing them. Work speed thus suffers further.

We must be the masters of the wharf and not the slaves of tonnage. As wharf caretakers, we must take care of not only production but also the loading of more goods and the unloading of goods at a faster rate, and especially take care of the line.

We must swing into action, emphasize the line, expose contradictions, look for gaps, promote transformation and properly handle the affairs of our No. 5 district, of our harbor, and of China.

Some Workers of the No. 5 District of
the Shanghai Harbor Affairs Bureau

January 7, 1974

Investigation Report Attached

According to our understanding, the problems exposed by the workers of the No. 5 district are completely true. This shows that the struggle between two ways of thinking and the two lines is very acute in the economic sphere. The leadership of the No. 5 district does not insist on putting proletarian politics in command. It does not rely on and trust the masses but puts tonnage in command with no thought given to the line and the style of work. So long as the specified tonnage is fulfilled, those involved are cited and can leave earlier. This approach brings in its wake serious consequences. It abandons the style of cooperation and encourages departmentalism. It pays no attention to safety and quality and makes no effort toward mechanization. The loading and unloading teams compete for the handling of heavy pieces and are unwilling to handle the light ones. In a word, mass socialist activism is dampened. Under the influence of this erroneous approach of the leadership, some squads of the No. 5 loading and unloading team are more salient in their scramble for tonnage and overloading. They have been praised by the leadership of the district for this. However, the worker masses have hit the nail on the head, pointing out that this is the remnant pernicious influence of the theory that only productivity counts. On the wall of the coordination office of the No. 5 district there is hung a blackboard for recording work progress. A big-character poster put up by the workers demands a change of this way of putting tonnage in command. It points out, "The blackboard is innocent, but the line is not in order!" At a forum, the workers said: We want to be masters of the wharf and not slaves of tonnage. We do loading and unloading for the Chinese revolution and the world revolution. We do it with speed for the sake of socialist tonnage and not departmentalist tonnage.

After the appearance of the big-character poster, the Party committee of the No. 5 district called a meeting. It pledged to sincerely accept the workers' criticism, and expressed the determination to further study the New Year's Day editorial, to emulate the experience of the Yang-shu-p'u Loading and Unloading Station, to vigorously criticize the theory that only productivity counts, and to further arouse the masses of the whole district in exposing contradictions, promoting transformation, and swiftly changing the outlook.

By Chieh-fang jih-pao [Liberation Daily] and Wen-hui Pao Correspondents

2

With Criticism of Lin Piao and Confucius Bearing Abundant Fruit, One Hundred Large Vessels Race Upstream against the Current

A Tour of the Battlefront of the Shipbuilding Industry in Shanghai

Like a strong east wind, the movement to criticize Lin Piao and Confucius is sweeping the banks of the Whangpoo River.

Everywhere can be seen a scene of a lively and vigorous political situation and sustained leaps in the shipbuilding industry of Shanghai. The broad masses of shipbuilding workers are assiduously reading the works of Marx and Lenin as well as the writings of Chairman Mao, and contingents of theorists are springing up like bamboo shoots after a spring rain. Vessels of 10,000 tons are launched one after another, and 10,000-horsepower diesel engines are started in close succession. In the first ten months of the year, they have already fulfilled the state plans in toto. The broad masses of shipbuilding workers, by adhering to the policy of "maintaining independence and keeping the initiative in our own hands and relying on our own efforts," have waged a resolute struggle against the worship of foreign things and blind faith in things foreign, rolled the war drum for "building more ships, bigger ships and better ships," and composed one splendorous battle song after another.

"P'i Lin p'i K'ung chieh shih-kuo, pai ko ching-liu ching shang-yu — Shang-hai tsao-ch'uan kung-yeh chan-hsien hsün-li." Kuang-ming jih-pao [Kuang-ming Daily], December 18, 1974. This translation is taken, with minor editorial revisions, from SCMP, No. 5779 (January 23, 1975), 104-113.

On the eve of the 25th anniversary of the founding of the Chinese People's Republic, the oceangoing freighter "Feng Ch'ing," designed and built by China and completely fitted out with equipment made in China, returned from her first voyage from the Mediterranean Sea. Recently, another oceangoing freighter, "Feng Kuang," designed and built by China and fitted with Chinese-made equipment victoriously returned along "Feng Ch'ing's" route. The return of the "Feng Ch'ing" and the "Feng Kuang" one after the other has brought a new vigor to the battlefront of the shipbuilding industry in Shanghai and pushed the already dynamic and impressive upsurge in revolution and production to a new plateau.

Contemplating the Present and Recalling the Past Fills the Heart with Exhilaration

After the victorious return of the "Feng Ch'ing," the Party committee of the Chiang-nan Shipyard which built the vessel held a meeting that night. The topic under discussion at the meeting was: "What new contributions has the century-old shipyard made?" The people cast "the accounts of transformation": Before liberation, the old "Chiang-nan," over the course of 85 years after its founding, had built only one 2,000-ton vessel. This vessel was built with foreign materials under foreign supervision, and although work began in 1946, it was still not completed up to the eve of the liberation of Shanghai. After liberation and particularly since the Great Proletarian Cultural Revolution, earth-shaking changes have taken place in the Chiang-nan Shipyard. The production capacity of the new "Chiang-nan" today is equivalent to more than a hundred old "Chiang-nans" before the liberation. A retired old shipbuilder walked up to the deck of the ship with the help of a walking stick, and stroking the brand-new steel plates of the 10,000-ton vessel, said emotionally, "How fast and how new! Before liberation by the time a small vessel was launched, the steel plates had become so rotten that they could hardly be used. Now, in just one year, several 10,000-ton vessels have been launched.

There is really no comparison!" The casting of "the accounts of transformation" was well done. The more accounts were cast, the more people were inspired and the more people realized that the proletarian revolutionary line of Chairman Mao is the guarantee for victory. Their resolution was: To sail on the correct course, discover the gap, be modest and prudent, and continue to make progress. As soon as the Party committee meeting of the shipyard was over, the several secretaries of the Party committee promptly led the cadres at all levels to the forefront of production to labor alongside the broad masses of workers and to battle at the key posts where work was most formidable.

A tense battle was going on aboard the 16,000-ton coal-carrying vessel "Ch'ang-ch'un." The project of installing the main engine, the auxiliary engine, and navigation instruments was underway and the ship was ready for a trial-run and delivery. The responsible members of the combat group onboard "Ch'ang-ch'un" set up a command post on the open deck. They erected a wooden shed, installed a telephone, and began to work. When we came there for a visit, the whole ship was vibrating under the blows of hammers, and sparks from welding torches were flying everywhere. People went into and came out of the command post in great haste. The workers said to us with justifiable pride, "Comfort will not win the battle and make the shipbuilding industry stand on its own feet, and slackness in work will not build socialism. We shipbuilding workers prefer the philosophy of struggle."

How aptly said! The more than 1,000 shipbuilding workers fighting onboard the vessel "Ch'ang-ch'un" actively took part in the struggle to criticize Lin Piao and Confucius and the criticism of the slavish comprador philosophy. Working under the blazing sun in daytime and battling under the lamps at night, they were determined to deliver this 10,000-ton vessel which was outside the annual quota to the maritime transport department for putting into navigation. We asked the responsible member of this combat group where such drive came from. This responsible member thought deeply for a while. Following this, he wiped the sweat from his face, and pointing to the Whangpoo River, solemnly said, "The Whangpoo River is a witness to history. In the dark years before the liberation, vessels flying the Stars and Stripes bumped right and left here, and the Chinese shipbuilding workers and seamen suffered endlessly from humiliation and insult." He then told us of the story of an old seaman. Before liberation, for the sake of making a living, this old seaman went aboard a foreign vessel to serve as an apprentice. The foreign capitalist took him to the stern of the vessel and arrogantly asked him to look at the flag flying there, and ferociously told him, "You Chinese will never be able to build a ship, and as you have no ships, your Chinese flag will never fly on any ship. If you want to work on my ship, you must obey all my instructions!" At that time, this old seaman was so angry that he could hardly speak. How he hoped that one day China could build her own ships.

However, in the old China where "for hundreds of years have demons and monsters swept in a swirling dance, and the 500 million people were disunited," as we were bullied by others politically and had to rely on others economically, how could big ships be built? Moreover, the reactionary rulers basically had no intention of building their own ships. The Chiang-nan Manufacturing Bureau founded by Li Hung-chang and the Chiang-nan Shipyard under the rule of Chiang Kai-shek were both tools for repairing ships for the imperialists and for providing the imperialists with a market for dumping their surplus materials. The economic aggression of the imperialists had seriously stifled China's shipbuilding industry. Of the 37 private shipyards in Shanghai at that time, 33 were forced to shut down. Liu Shao-ch'i and Lin Piao were also a pair of lackeys. Because they pushed the counterrevolutionary line that "it is better to buy ships than to build ships, and it is better to charter ships than to buy ships," in the 17 years before the Great Proletarian Cultural Revolution, Shanghai had built only one 10,000-ton vessel.

"Today, everything has changed." Pointing at the two 10,000-ton vessels, the "Feng Ying" and the "Feng Yen," which were moored alongside the Bund and under construction, this responsible member of the combat group of the coal-carrying "Ch'ang-ch'un" said with infinite pride, "These are built in China! In the first ten months of this year, our shipyard has completed several ships of the 10,000-ton class. We still intend to build larger ships. Whenever I think of the new contributions made by this century-old shipyard, our drive surges forth!"

The high hopes and great ambition of the "century-old shipyard which aspires to make new contributions" have today been translated into practical action by the workers of the whole shipyard. For the sake of making new contributions, the members of the spare-time assault team of a work section in the hull workshop, after fulfilling their own work in daytime, also took part at night in the heroic battle for the launching of the "Ch'ang Yang," another 16,000-ton coal-carrying vessel, within the year. For the sake of making new contributions, the ten groups of the shipbuilding installation workshop jointly proposed that the "Ch'ang-ch'un" must break away from the old convention which required a new vessel to make two trial runs in the past, and they resolutely strove to ensure "the success of one well-integrated trial run."

The return of the "Feng Ch'ing" from her long journey against the current not only drew forth a strong response from the Chiang-nan Shipyard, but also brought about a chain reaction in the whole shipbuilding system of Shanghai. The workers of the Hu-tung Shipyard, under the battle cry that "the main engine must be able to stand the test and the new vessel must make long voyages," shortened the shipway period, thus enabling two 10,000-ton class freighters to be delivered for trial-run ahead of schedule. They also resolved to launch another 25,000-ton freighter, which was already on the shipway, ahead of schedule. The Shanghai Shipyard, which built the "Feng Kuang," ushered in the "Feng Kuang" and also fought for the "Feng Ming." Working as one man, the workers of the whole shipyard were resolved to deliver the "Feng Ming" at an earlier date. The Party committee of the Chung-hua Shipyard which is battling fiercely for the "Feng Ko" has moved its command post to the scene of action. They resolve to go all out and capture this 10,000-ton vessel. The Tung-hai Shipyard has stepped up the tempo of production and installation of diesel engines, and from the engine workshop of Ch'in-hsin Shipyard there has come a report of success on ushering in 1975 ahead of schedule.... A stirring and seething upsurge of production marked by giving pursuit to each other is still growing on the whole battlefront of the shipbuilding industry. The broad masses of shipbuilding workers are resolved to write a new chapter in China's shipbuilding industry with their diligent labor.

Continuing the Revolution without Marking Time

One day in the early part of winter, alongside the wharf of the Hu-tung Shipyard, two brand new cream-color 10,000-ton passenger-cargo ships, decked in festive colors, were set for sail. On the wharf, the sound of gongs and drums shook the sky and red flags were fluttering. The people were joyously sending off their comrades-in-arms taking part in the trial run. The long blasts from the sirens shook the divine country, and the splendid scene on the Whangpoo River was indeed a gladdening sight to behold. The S. S. "Ch'ang Chin" and the S. S. "Ch'ang Hsiu" slowly sailed away from the wharf amidst ringing cheers. They cut through the waves and vanished gradually into the distant horizon of the river. As the people stared at the river rolling eastward, they were astir with thoughts, and the stirring scene of the battle for the "Ch'ang Chin" and the "Ch'ang Hsiu" in July and August this year was again conjured up before their eyes.

July and August in Shanghai are the hot summer months. On the 10,000-ton slipway, the hulls of a pair of sister ships stood imposingly side by side. Under the hot scorching sun, the workers working on the steel plates were sweating profusely, and their work clothes were soaked with sweat and almost seemed to drip water. Fighting the battle to make the shipbuilding industry stand on its own feet, they had to bond the sweat from hard work with a thousand steel plates.... As the workers were working cheerfully, the responsible member of the Party committee of the shipyard appeared on the deck with the cadres and handed each of the workers a bowl of a cool refreshing drink. Although the workers were drinking the cool drink with their mouths, the sweetness they felt was in their hearts. Everybody expressed, "The more the leadership shows concern for us, the more we must exert ourselves to triumph over the high temperature and win high production. We shall launch the 'Ch'ang Chin' and the 'Ch'ang Hsiu' for trial run at an earlier date."

This new type of relationship between the cadres and the masses with the cadres taking good care of the masses and the masses cherishing and helping the cadres is a new atmosphere which has appeared in the Hu-tung Shipyard in the movement to criticize Lin Piao and Confucius after the Great Proletarian Cultural Revolution. In the past, owing to pressure of work, some cadres of this shipyard had become estranged from the broad masses of workers. The workers opportunely sent in revolutionary big-character posters. At first, some cadres were unwilling to accept some of the sharp criticisms. Following the gradual deepening of the movement, through the warm help of the working masses, they raised the criticisms contained in the big-character posters to the level of the line. They examined their own words and deeds and found these criticisms in the big-character posters to be extremely valuable. Together with the workers, the cadres criticized thoroughly the fallacy of "the wise of the highest class and the stupid of the lowest class" of Confucius, and eliminated the pernicious influence of "the theory that the masses are backward" of Liu Shao-ch'i and Lin Piao. The broad masses of cadres rose with greater revolutionary spirit and marched with bigger strides in continuing the revolution.

The revolutionary big-character posters have enabled the old cadres to glow with vitality. The revolutionary big-character posters have brought a new radiance to the lively and vigorous political situation of the shipbuilding industry in Shanghai.

People remember that in 1970 it was in this Hu-tung Shipyard that the first big-character poster put up by the workers of the No. 22 squad of the casting workshop which rolled the war drum for the battle to make the Shanghai shipbuilding industry stand on its own feet.

In the early part of this year, in the process of taking the vessel "Feng Ch'ing" built by the Chiang-nan Shipyard out for trial run before delivery, countless obstacles were encountered from people who worshiped and had blind faith in things foreign. Under the excuse that the cylinder valve should be changed, they refused to accept the main engine that was up to standard after inspection in an attempt to deprive this 10,000-ton Chinese-built vessel of the right to take up sea navigation. The shipbuilding workers put up a big-character poster with the spearhead directed straight at the slavish comprador philosophy of Liu Shao-ch'i and the revisionist line of capitulation and national betrayal of Liu Shao-ch'i and Lin Piao, thus unveiling the prelude to a struggle centered around the sailing of the "Feng Ch'ing." This big-character poster received strong support from the CCP Shanghai Municipal Committee as well as the enthusiastic response of the broad masses of seamen. The "Feng Ch'ing" in the end sailed gloriously away and victoriously returned.

Although a victory has been won in the struggle, there are still struggles after the victory. In the Shanghai Shipyard, we again witnessed the living example of how, encouraged by the happy tidings of the return of the "Feng Ch'ing" from her long voyage, the workers put up big-character posters to struggle resolutely against the worship of and blind faith in things foreign. As the workers of the shipyard were waging a heroic struggle for building more 10,000-ton vessels, an individual member of the production command group of the shipyard suddenly sent down an "amended notification" demanding that the Chinese-made "three major parts," including the gyro-compass and the electric generator, be replaced with imported goods onboard the "Feng Ch'ih" scheduled to be put into the water next year. The comrades of the combat group for the "Feng" class vessels in the technical unit of the shipyard immediately noticed something very funny in this "notice." After further investigation, they got a clear picture of things. Actually, some of the "three major parts" which certain people wanted to change were still in foreign ports and there was no way to know when they would arrive, and some were still unfinished. However, the practice of navigation by the "Feng Ch'ing" had proved that the quality of the Chinese-made "three major parts" was fully in conformity with the demand when put to use, and the supply was also able to meet the demand. The workers and technicians of the technical unit and the hull workshop of the shipyard in succession put up revolutionary big-character posters to express their resolute opposition to this "amended notification." They also pointed out, "This is not merely a question of production, but a question of which line is being implemented. What the notification wants is to do away through the change with the revolutionary will of the working class, and to replace it with blind faith in foreign things and the thinking of cowards and lazybones." The Party committee of the shipyard and the Party committee of the shipbuilding company supported these revolutionary big-character posters, and they not only withdrew this erroneous notice, but more importantly, rectified this kind of erroneous thinking.

If it is said that the revolutionary big-character posters have vividly embodied the socialist activism radiated by the shipbuilding workers of Shanghai who have been tempered in the Great Proletarian Cultural Revolution, then perseverance in taking part in collective productive labor has reflected the socialist activism radiated by the broad masses of cadres of the shipbuilding system after their baptism in the Great Proletarian Cultural Revolution.

In the Hu-tung Shipyard, there is a cadres' "May 7" combat team which was set up by the Party committee of the shipyard for the sake of implementing Chairman Mao's "May 7" directive and the directive that "cadres should take part in collective productive labor," and it has been in existence for more than three years since its inception in 1971. The leading cadres at and above the unit and office level (apart from the old, the weak, the sick, and the disabled) all take part in labor at the average of 80 days per year. They not only persist in taking part in labor when work is busy, but also go to where the difficulties are greater. By battling together with the workers, they have not only created material wealth for the country, but also brought profound changes to their own spiritual outlook.

Some old cadres who were formerly electrical welders again took up the welding torch and returned to the slipway. The master craftsmen warmly said, "So the old welding torch is again in action, and our hearts are more closely linked together." A member of the Party committee of the shipyard constantly worked together with the workers until late at night when the production task was tense. An old master craftsman said, "We do not know which shift he worked in, and we also do not know when he began working or at what time he quit. But in all the three day and night shifts, we always saw him fighting shoulder to shoulder with the workers." This member of the Party committee not only played an active part in labor, but also paid attention to helping the backbone elements of shifts and team do their work well. Last September, a large passenger-cargo ship was scheduled for launching before October 1, and all other work had been completed except a certain test. However, the test which normally could be completed in five or six days dragged on for more than ten days without any sign of completion. Where did the key to the problem lie? He made a deep-going investigation in the course of labor, held heart-to-heart talks with the workers, and helped the backbone elements of the shifts and teams grasp vigorously class struggle. By strengthening revolutionary unity among the masses and bringing the enthusiasm of the masses into play, he snatched back the time that had been lost, and as a result, the task was completed in only three days, thus ensuring the launching of the large passenger-cargo ship according to schedule.

Examples of such perseverance by cadres in taking part in collective productive labor at the Hu-tung Shipyard can be seen everywhere in such units as the Chung-hua Shipyard, the Chiang-nan Shipyard, the Shanghai Shipyard, the Tung-hai Shipyard, the Ch'iu-hsin Shipyard, and the Kang-k'ou Machine Building Plant.

Recently, the Shanghai Municipal Shipbuilding Company organized large numbers of cadres led by the secretary of the Party committee to go to the basic level to labor together with the broad masses of workers and help them with their work. The workers said delightedly, "With the leadership setting the pace, we must step harder on the gas." This has boosted the revolution and production in these units and further developed the excellent situation.

The Fiery Years and the Sparkle of Youth

Like the waves of the Whangpoo River which push one another forward, each generation is stronger than the one before it. Nurtured by the sunshine and dew of the Party and in keeping with the tempo of the leap in the shipbuilding industry of Shanghai, a new generation of shipbuilding workers has matured and grown stronger in the Three Great Revolutionary Movements. At all slipways and in all workshops, everywhere could be seen groups of vigorous and active young shipbuilding workers of both sexes. "The young people are the most active and vital force in society. They are the most eager to learn and the least conservative in their thinking. This is especially so in the era of socialism."

At the Shanghai Shipyard, as we entered the forging workshop with its flaming furnaces and flying sparks, we were attracted by the lively scene of six young women working intensely by the side of a 500-kilogram electric forge. Look, how harmoniously they cooperated with one another in drawing material, operating the forge and tongs, and how proficiently they moved about. This was the famous women forging squad, the first generation of women shipbuilding workers. They used the steel tongs in their hands to smash the traditional concept that women could not be blacksmiths. When the women forging squad was first set up, the output amounted to only about 2 tons a month. At present, the monthly production target of 5 tons can be overfulfilled every month, and the highest monthly output reaches 11 tons. By humbly learning from the old master craftsmen and learning as they work, they have improved the dies for pressed bars and high head-flanges and trial-built successfully a unit of miniature machine for forging operations, thus reducing the intensity of labor and also raising work efficiency. Through the practice of struggle, some of the young women have gloriously joined the Party or the League.

In the shipbuilding installation workshop of the Chiang-nan Shipyard, there is a crane-operating squad consisting of young people whose average age is only nineteen. This is an assault force that dares to fight, charge, and break away from the old conventions of conservative rules. Once, the young people, under the leadership of two old master craftsmen, went aboard the freighter "Yüeh Yang" to take charge of the hoisting and installation of the propellers and ground shaft of this vessel. The chief engineer of the "Yüeh Yang" said in surprise, "In the past the hoisting and installation of so huge a part would take at least 15 to 16 men and half of them had to be old master craftsmen of the 5th and the 6th grade. Are you sure you can handle this?" "Certainly," the young people replied in a loud voice. They quickly took up their positions and started to dismantle and install things. They worked neatly and efficiently in an orderly manner without making a single mistake. When the battle was at its height, there was a sudden change in the weather, and it began to rain heavily. But they continued to work diligently in spite of the rain until the hoisting and installation assignment was victoriously completed. The chief engineer could not help but say in praise, "You truly are a fine second generation of the working class."

Yao Ping-yüan, a twenty-six-year-old member, is the chief welder of the Hu-tung Shipyard. When she first walked through the gate of the shipyard eight years ago, she was still a lass who knew nothing about shipbuilding. Under the care of the Party organization and with the help of the old workers, she has now become the deputy leader of a welding section with more than 300 workers. The welding section accepted an assignment which called for welding the hull of the "Hsü Chou," a 25,000-ton freighter, within a short time. This definitely was a battle for capturing a strong position and presented numerous difficulties. However, without demur, Yao Ping-yüan made her way to the slipway with heroic nonchalance. She came when the morning dew was still damp and left when the moon was high. She not only set the pace in taking part in labor and organizing production, but also found time to read and study seriously and pay attention to the progress of her class brothers and sisters. She used her own words and deeds to make a pledge, "I shall dedicate my youth to the slipway, and as long as there is life in me, the arc will never go out!" In the Hu-tung Shipyard, all workshops have their own youth combat shifts and teams with different names. These youth shifts and teams are trailblazers in class struggle and the two-line struggle, and they play the assault role in the revolution and production throughout the shipyard.

The "Fierce Tiger Squad" is the epitome of these advanced youth shifts and teams. They dedicate their red hearts to the socialist cause. Since July this year, for the sake of carrying out properly the movement to criticize Lin Piao and Confucius and fighting well the battle to make the shipbuilding industry stand on its own feet, they have put forward the battlecry that "if the ship is not launched we will not go home," and moved their beddings to the shipyard. In daytime, holding the welding set, they battle on the slipway. Back in the dormitory at night, they take up the works of Marx and Lenin or the writings of Chairman Mao, read and study seriously, make revolutionary mass criticism, and assiduously transform their world outlook. Not long ago, in the deep-going movement to study the history of the struggle between Confucianism and Legalism, they overcame the difficulty of low culture and lack of materials by writing short stories about their study of Legalist writings and criticism of Confucian books themselves, and turned out a total of 40 critical articles and lecture materials containing more than 70,000 words. They also gave lectures in the section which were welcomed by the old workers. With ideological consciousness raised, they show greater drive for production. At present, they are throwing themselves with high spirits into the battle for the construction of the 25,000-ton freighter "Hsü Chou."

The first generation of women forge operators in the new shipbuilding industry of China is growing up. The first generation of electrical welders in the shipbuilding industry is growing up! Thousands of revolutionary successors are growing up on the battlefront of the shipbuilding industry in Shanghai. They are wielding hammers, operating cranes, and holding welding torches in the battle to make the shipbuilding industry of China stand on its own feet. Where does their power come from? There is a very well-written song composed by an electrical welder: "The water of the river does not rise without a cause; without electricity the welding machine cannot sing. Holding the welding torch we are busily building ships; the electricity comes from the Communist Party."

At present, the shipbuilding workers of Shanghai, riding the east wind of the victorious return of the "Feng Ch'ing" and the "Feng Kuang," have whipped up another new upsurge. They are resolved to continue grasping firmly the struggle to criticize Lin Piao and Confucius, grasp vigorously the struggle between the two lines in the shipbuilding industry, build more and better ships for the revolution, and fight better the battle for making the shipbuilding industry stand on its own feet, strive to overfulfill in toto the production target for the whole year, and usher in the more glorious and formidable fighting tasks of 1975.

By Our Own Correspondent and Reporter

About the Editor

A graduate of Lafayette College, Stephen Andors received a Master's Degree and a Master's of Arts in Law and Diplomacy from the Fletcher School of Law and Diplomacy, a Certificate from the East Asian Institute at Columbia University and, in 1974, a Ph.D. in Political Science from Columbia.

Dr. Andors was formerly Editor of the Bulletin of Concerned Asian Scholars and is the author of Socialist Civilization and Revolutionary Industrialization: China 1949 to the Present (1977). He taught at the State University of New York, Oswego, from 1970 to 1975 and is currently a Research Associate at the East Asian Institute, Columbia University.

THE CHINA BOOK PROJECT Translation and Commentary

Each volume contains not only the complete text of an important Chinese book, but also an extended introduction by a Western scholar and frequently additional materials which illuminate the central text.

These translations offer insights into the complex world of contemporary China not only for those who do not read Chinese but also for scholars who do not have access to the originals. The series includes works published after the Cultural Revolution which display the radicalization and politicization of Chinese scholarship. In addition, the fact that most of the titles have been printed in editions astronomical by Western standards — hundreds of thousands, even millions, of copies — reflects their importance in China today.

The series will place primary emphasis on contemporary China as seen by Chinese scholars and by various writing groups responsible for recording the past and examining the present of this enormously complex and developing society.